W9-CMV-257

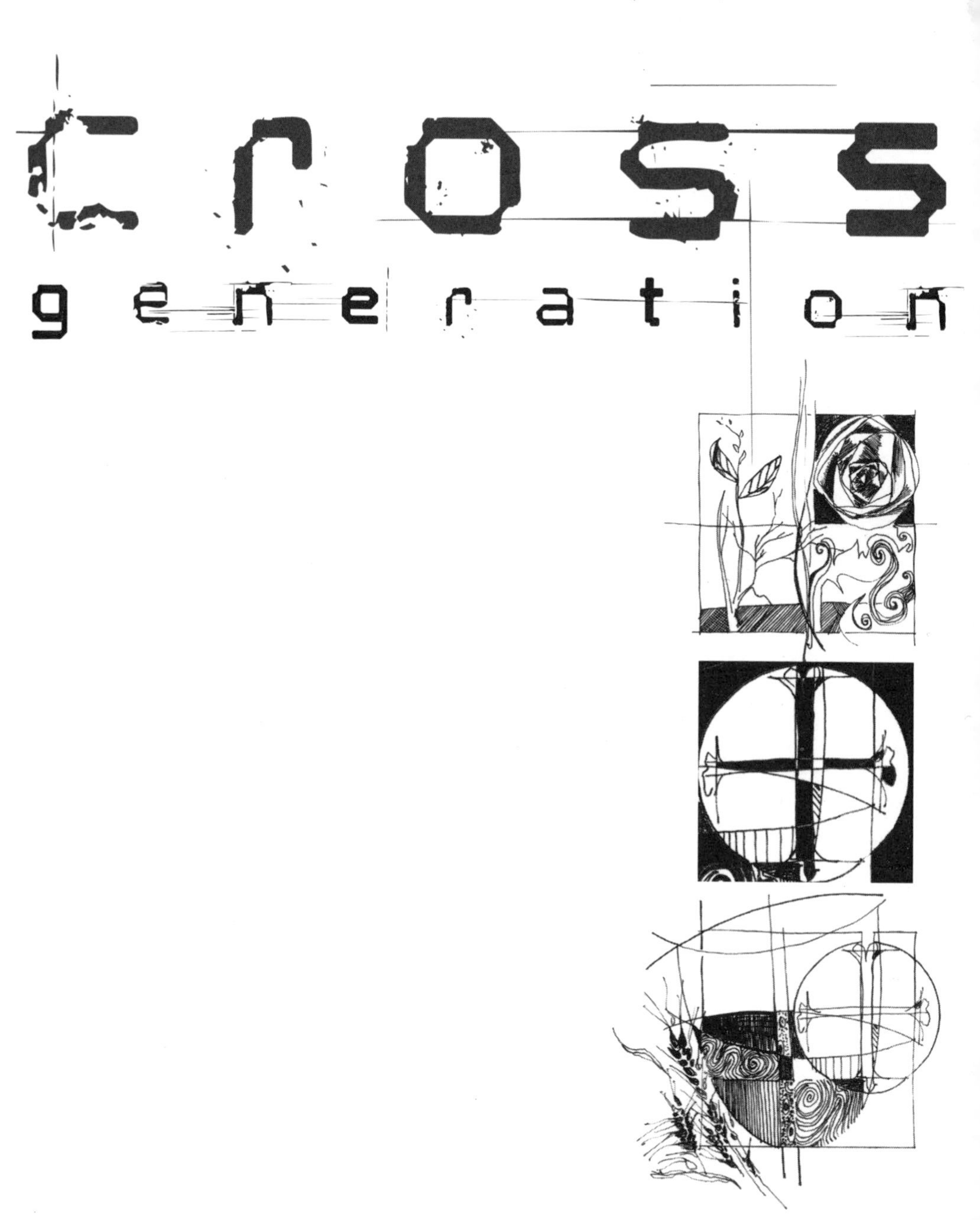
cross
generation

GIA Publications, Inc.
Chicago

GIA

G-7500

7404 S. Mason Ave., Chicago, IL 60638

Cover design, illustrations, and art direction by Andrew Schultz.

Book layout based upon *Worship—Third Edition* by Michael Tapia.

In accordance with c. 827 and n. 108 of *Sing to the Lord*, permission to publish has been granted by the Very Reverend John F. Canary, Vicar General of the Archdiocese of Chicago, on October 13, 2008. No legal responsibility is associated with this permission.

ISBN: 978-1-57999-748-9

1 2 3 4 5 6 7 8 9 10 11 12 13 14 15 16 17 18 19 20

PREFACE

For more than sixty years, the mission of GIA Publications, Inc. has been to publish quality music for the church, including recordings and printed editions across a wide spectrum of styles and genres. GIA's commitment to the song of the assembly has lead to the publication of hymnals and supplements, both soft and hardbound. The release of *Cross Generation* represents GIA's latest effort in this endeavor.

In the recent decade or so, contemporary music has continued to progress and develop a steady pattern of growth that began nearly half a century ago following the Second Vatican Council. New composers have appeared on the scene, new songs have found their way into mainstream worship, and the use of instrumental ensembles, including more extensive use of percussion, has flourished. As with all forms of music, the younger generation is often found at the forefront when new songs are experienced and developed in worship. At the same time, history has proven that "singing new songs to the Lord" is by no means the prerogative of just one age group or the privilege of the lovers of a particular musical style.

The heart of this songbook attempts to cross over the generations and bring together what the editors deemed the better contemporary selections currently in use in Catholic worship coupled with a sampling of time-honored selections that have enjoyed widespread use, some over past centuries. The editors carefully examined over 2,000 titles for possible inclusion and set out to create a collection that would contain music in a contemporary style intended to be sung primarily by a worshiping assembly. Every effort was made to consider titles from a broad range of individuals and publishers, those serving primarily the Roman Catholic Church as well as those who primarily serve other liturgical and evangelical sources. In addition, a broad range of new compositions is likewise included, a number of which are making their first appearance in this collection. While the musical style of the majority of the selections found in this edition might best be described as contemporary, this collection also includes samplings of chant, hymnody, Early American selections, world music, and folk tunes. This blending of musical styles coupled with the inclusion of time-honored texts—plus texts presented in various languages—links the modern church with its global communion and venerable musical past. However, even with the inclusion of these various selections, it would be prudent to mention that this relatively small collection is intended to be used as a supplemental resource.

Throughout this decade, innovative steps have been taken to broaden the catechetical experience of believers and seekers in every age bracket, often together in family and group situations. We hope the various short articles found in this songbook, which offer succinct insights and explanations about the tenets of the Catholic faith, will serve as a useful tool in the ongoing religious formation of the faithful, regardless of their age or past experience. Likewise, a number of quotes, edited by Michael A. Cymbala, are scattered throughout the book to offer additional inspiration.

The authors of the articles are identified by their initials, found at the end of each article: Tony E. Alonso (TA), Laurie Delgatto (LD), and Ronald F. Krisman (RK). Fr. Krisman also edited these elements. It is important to note that the articles are not always meant to identify sections of the book. While some do appear at the beginning of a section, as is the case with most of the liturgical seasons, others are placed before or after a song that has a particular connection to the essence of the information found in the article.

As this songbook goes to press, a new translation of the Roman Missal is in the process of attaining the required approval from the United States Conference of Catholic Bishops and the Vatican. At this time, it is not clear when the new translation will be promulgated and no specific date has been set for its implementation. As the Church waits for the new translation, the editors decided not to include any musical settings of the Order of Mass in this collection. Since numerous settings are well known by the faithful and the new translation will no doubt be learned in the future over a considerable period of time, the inclusion of known musical settings of the Order of Mass in a book primarily intended as a supplemental resource for newer hymns and songs seemed superfluous.

The editors would like to thank the following individuals whose expertise and creativity contributed significantly to this publication: Chris de Silva, who suggested the title for the hymnal; Laura Dankler, who was a member of the editorial committee during the first half of the editorial process; Jeffry Mickus, hymnal coordinator; Joshua Evanovich, editorial assistant; Clarence Reiels and Vicki Krstansky, proofreaders; Michael Boschert, permissions editor; Neil Borgstrom, index editor. Further acknowledgment is given to the following individuals who were asked to offer their opinions on the manuscript version of *Cross Generation*: Tony E. Alonso; Kate Cuddy; John Flaherty; Sr. Edith Prendergast, RSC; Paul Tate; and Tim Westerhaus.

Finally, the editors would like to pay tribute to GIA's publisher, Alexander Harris, and senior editor, Kelly Dobbs Mickus, as well as retired senior editor, Robert Batastini, who created the process for voting on the final contents of this songbook. The voting process Robert originated has been used to select the contents of numerous GIA hymnals and was originally developed for the publication of *Worship—Third Edition* in 1986.

That God may be glorified!

Ed Archer
Michael A. Cymbala (Chair)
Gary Daigle (Facilitator)
Julie Frazier
Paul Melley
Editors

CONTENTS

1 Advent
12 Christmas
17 Epiphany
18 Ash Wednesday
20 Lent
27 Palm Sunday
31 Holy Thursday
33 Good Friday
38 Easter
45 Pentecost
56 Trinity
58 Gospel Acclamations
62 Psalms
88 Canticle
89 Morning
92 Evening
93 Praise
115 Comfort / Healing
136 Light
141 Gathering
149 Discipleship
164 Faith
174 Petition
186 Conversion
195 Eternal Life
203 Blessed Virgin Mary
210 Social Concern
214 Peace
218 Church
220 Mission
232 Love
235 Trust
243 Lament
246 Jesus Christ
254 Hope
256 Providence
258 Thanksgiving
261 Christian Initiation of Adults
263 Eucharist
276 Anointing
277 Reconciliation
280 Marriage
281 Funeral

INDEXES

284 Acknowledgments
285 Scriptural Index
286 Liturgical Index
287 Topical Index
288 Index of Composers, Authors, and Sources
289 Index of First Lines and Common Titles

our liturgical year 1

ADVENT

The Church gives us the four weeks leading up to Christmas as a time to prepare us for Christ's arrival in our midst. The word advent comes from a Latin word that literally means "coming" or "arrival." The Scriptures proclaimed and the prayers prayed during Advent are filled with images of waiting and watching.

During Advent we hear the prophetic words of Isaiah, offering visions of the coming Savior. We hear the story of John the Baptist pointing the way to the imminent coming of Christ. And we hear the story of Mary, preparing the way for Jesus by accepting God's call to give birth to the Son of God. Two prominent Marian feasts within the season of Advent are the solemnity of the Immaculate Conception, recognizing Mary as having been born without original sin, and the feast of Our Lady of Guadalupe, celebrating Mary's appearance to St. Juan Diego.

With Mary, John the Baptist, and the prophets, Christians observe Advent as a time to prepare the way of the Lord, not just in history, but also in our daily lives. *LD*

One who sings well prays twice.

Ancient proverb

2 HALLELUJAH, HALLELU!

Refrain
Hal-le-lu-jah, Hal-le-lu! Re-joice, the Lord is near.
Gospel Accl: Hal-le-lu-jah, Hal-le-lu! Hal-le, hal-le-lu-jah!
Sing and be joy-ful! Ver-y soon the Sav-ior will ap-pear.
Hal-le-lu-jah, Hal-le-lu! Hal-le, hal-le-lu-jah!
Verses
Solo:
All:
1. Stay a-wake now, keep watch, and pray.
2. Out of the des-ert, hear him say,
3. "I have bap-tized to make you see,
4. Blest are you, Mar-y, full of grace.
Hal-le, hal-le-lu-jah!
Solo:
We do not know the hour or day.
"Make a straight path! Pre-pare God's way!"
there is one com-ing af-ter me!"
Soon we will see our Sav-ior's face.
All:
Hal-le, hal-le-lu-jah!
D.C.

Text: Michael Mahler, b.1981
Tune: Michael Mahler, b.1981

PREPARE! PREPARE! 3

Ostinato Refrain
Pre-pare! Pre-pare the way of the Lord.
Pre-pare! Pre-pare the way of the Lord, oh,
Pre-pare! Pre-pare the way of the Lord. The Lord our God is
To repeat
com - ing soon. Oh,
To verses
Last time
com - ing soon.
Verses
Cantor:
1. Pre - pare the way, the way of the Lord. Read-y your hearts.
2. Make straight the path, lev - el the hills, lift up the gates.
3. Jus - tice and peace, kind - ness and truth shall come to the earth.
4. Sing and re - joice! The Lord is near, I say re - joice!
5. A vir - gin will bear a son, Em - man - u - el: God with us!
3
To Ostinato Refrain
Oh, the Lord our God is com-ing soon!

Text: Stephen Pishner
Tune: Stephen Pishner

4 Awake to the Day

Refrain
A - wake to the day of the com-ing of the Lord. Sing
out! Re-joice in this land. Make straight the way for the
Last time to Coda
King-dom of God is at hand.
Verse 1
Cantor:
Choir:
1. Signs in the sun and the moon and the stars, We pre-pare for you,
Cantor:
Lord. Then all shall sing of the pow - er of God.
Choir:
All:
We pre-pare for you, Lord. As long as the sun shall re -
D.S.
main so the name of the Lord God will reign. A -
Verse 2
Cantor:
Choir:
2. Wrapped in the cloak of jus-tice from God, We pre-pare for you,

Cantor:
Lord. Gath-ered at the word of the Ho - ly One,
Choir:
We pre-pare for you, Lord.
All:
Ev-'ry moun-tain and hill be made low that the glo - ry of God we may know. A -
D.S.
Coda
hand. A - wake to the day of the com-ing of the Lord. Sing out! Re - joice in this land. Make straight the way for the King-dom of God is at hand. Make the way!
First time only

Text: Ed Bolduc, b.1969, and John Barker
Tune: Ed Bolduc, b.1969, and John Barker

5 Find Us Ready

Refrain

Find us ready-y, Lord, not stand-ing still.
Find us work-ing and lov-ing and do-ing your
will. Find us read-y, Lord, faith-ful in
love, build-ing the king-dom that's
here and a-bove, build-ing the
king-dom of mer-cy and love.
3

Verses

1. We must wait for the Lord for we know not the time.
   So here and today we gather and pray,
   discovering love in our midst.

2. We must make straight the path, God's love revealed.
   With sin cast aside, God's mercy alive,
   fear not for here is your God.

3. Lifting up those bowed down, we prepare for our God.
   Rejoice in the Lord, for hope has been born
   in hearts where our God finds a home.

Optional Coda
Brick by brick, stone by stone, find us
work - ing and lov - ing and do - ing your will. Find us
read-y, Lord, faith - ful in love, build - ing the
king - dom that's here and a - bove.
Last time

Text: Tom Booth, b.1961
Tune: Tom Booth, b.1961; acc. by Ed Bolduc, b.1969

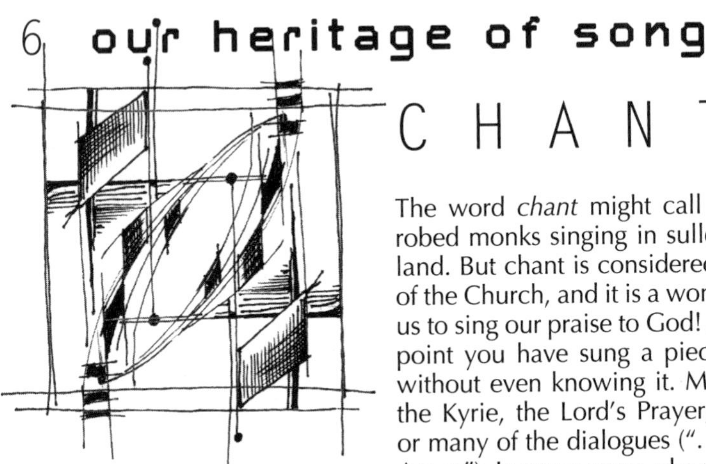

6 our heritage of song

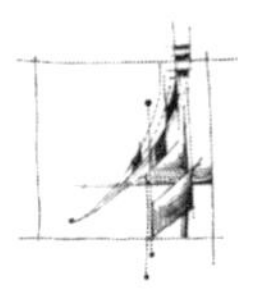

CHANT

The word *chant* might call to mind images of robed monks singing in sullen tones in a far-off land. But chant is considered the primary music of the Church, and it is a wonderful way for all of us to sing our praise to God! Most likely, at some point you have sung a piece of chant in Mass without even knowing it. Many churches chant the Kyrie, the Lord's Prayer, the Lamb of God, or many of the dialogues (". . . forever and ever. Amen"). In some ways, chant is like speaking set to music. While it is not metered, the words typically dictate the rhythm and phrasing of chant. This is one of the reasons chant is such a deep part of the Church's heritage of song: it allows the words of the prayers to guide the singing. Even as new types of music have been welcomed into the liturgy throughout the years, chant continues to hold a place of great honor in the Church. Chant is even found in modern compositions for the Church. The setting of "Creator of the Stars of Night" *(no. 8)* borrows the melody and text for its verses from the traditional chant "Creator alme siderum" *(no. 7)* and then adds an original refrain by its modern-day composer. *TA*

7 CREATOR ALME SIDERUM

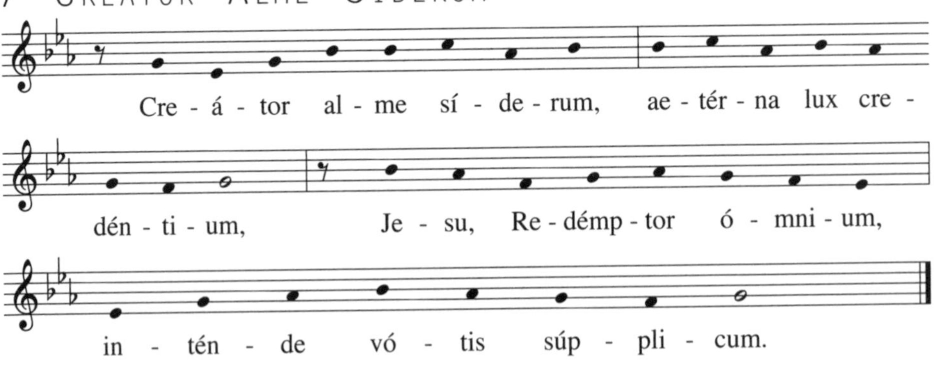
Cre - á - tor al - me sí - de - rum, ae - tér - na lux cre -
dén - ti - um, Je - su, Re - démp - tor ó - mni - um,
in - tén - de vó - tis súp - pli - cum.

Text: *Creator alme siderum,* Latin 9th. C.
Tune: CONDITOR ALME SIDERUM, LM; Mode IV

8 CREATOR OF THE STARS OF NIGHT

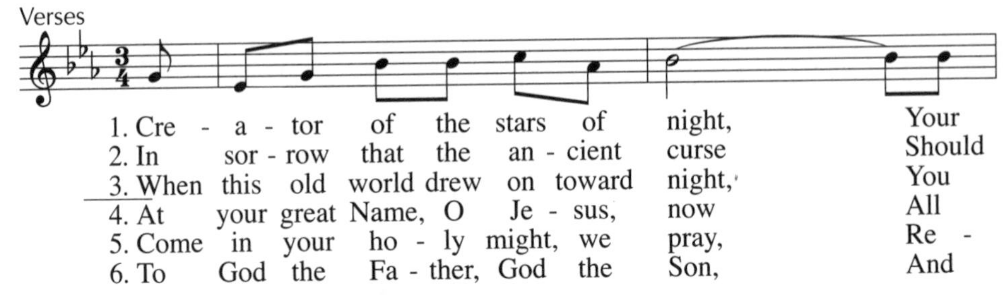
Verses
1. Cre - a - tor of the stars of night, Your
2. In sor - row that the an - cient curse Should
3. When this old world drew on toward night, You
4. At your great Name, O Je - sus, now All
5. Come in your ho - ly might, we pray, Re -
6. To God the Fa - ther, God the Son, And

peo - ple's ev - er - last - ing light, O
doom to death a u - ni - verse, You
came; but not in splen - dor bright, Not
knees must bend, all hearts must bow: All
deem us for e - ter - nal day; De -
God the Spir - it, Three in One, Praise,
Christ, Re - deem - er of us all, We
came, O Sav - ior, to set free Your
as a mon - arch, but the child Of
things on earth with one ac - cord, Like
fend us while we dwell be - low From
hon - or, might, and glo - ry be From
pray you hear us when we call.
own in glo - rious lib - er - ty.
Mar - y, blame - less moth - er mild.
those in heav'n, shall call you Lord.
all as - saults of our dread foe.
age to age e - ter - nal - ly.
To next verse*
To refrain
Refrain
Come, O Lord, and bring your light, O ra - diant
star, our hearts' de - light. O God - with - us, Em - man - u -
el, with your love, the dark dis - pel.
Last time

*Hymn may be sung without refrain.

Text: *Creator alme siderum*, Latin 9th. C.; tr. *The Hymnal 1982*, © 1985, The Church Pension Fund; refrain, Carol E. Browning, b.1956, © 2004, GIA Publications, Inc.
Tune: CONDITOR ALME SIDERUM, LM; Mode IV; acc. and refrain music by Carol E. Browning, b.1956, © 2004, GIA Publications, Inc.

9 hallmark songs of our faith

O COME, O COME, EMMANUEL

The hauntingly beautiful melody and profound words of "O Come, O Come, Emmanuel" *(no.10)* evoke the spirit of the Advent season like no other piece of music. The melody dates back to the fifteenth century but wasn't paired with the English text until the mid 1800s. Each verse is one of the O Antiphons, a series of prayers based on the many names given to the coming Savior found in the Hebrew Scriptures: Wisdom, Lord, Flower of Jesse, Key of David, Dawn, King, and Emmanuel. On each day leading up to Christmas, from December 17 until December 23 one of the O Antiphons is prayed as the anticipation builds for the birth of Jesus at Christmas. Consider making these prayers a part of your prayer time during Advent, meditating on each of the verses of this classic Advent hymn. *TA*

Music arises out of silence and returns to silence. God is revealed both in the beauty of song and in the power of silence.

Sing to the Lord: Music in Divine Worship

O Come, O Come, Emmanuel 10

1. O come, O come, Em - man - u - el, And ran-som cap - tive Is - ra - el, That mourns in lone - ly ex - ile here Un - til the Son of God ap - pear.
2. O come, O Wis - dom from on high, Who or - der all things might - i - ly; To us the path of knowl - edge show, And teach us in her ways to go.
3. O come, O come, great Lord of might, Who to your tribes on Si - nai's height In an - cient times once gave the law, In cloud, and maj - es - ty, and awe.
4. O come, O Rod of Jes - se's stem, From ev - 'ry foe de - liv - er them That trust your might - y pow'r to save, And give them vic - t'ry o'er the grave.
5. O come, O Key of Da - vid, come, And o - pen wide our heav'n - ly home; Make safe the way that leads on high, And close the path to mis - er - y.
Re - joice! Re - joice! Em - man - u - el Shall come to you, O Is - ra - el.

6. O come, O Dayspring from on high
And cheer us by your drawing nigh;
Disperse the gloomy clouds of night,
And death's dark shadow put to flight.

7. O come, Desire of nations, bind
In one the hearts of humankind;
O bid our sad divisions cease,
And be for us our King of Peace.

Text: *Veni, veni Emmanuel;* Latin 9th C.; tr. by John M. Neale, 1818–1866, alt.
Tune: VENI VENI EMMANUEL, LM with refrain; Mode I; adapt. by Gary Daigle, b.1957,

11 our liturgical year

CHRISTMAS

The waiting and watching of Advent comes to fulfillment at Christmas. During the Christmas season the Church invites us to reflect on the mystery of God becoming a human being and dwelling among his people: Jesus Christ. On Christmas Day (also known as the solemnity of the Nativity of the Lord), we celebrate Jesus' birth and all that it means in our lives. Christmas Day is a holy day second only to the Easter triduum during the liturgical year.

The Christmas season continues beyond Christmas Day to include the feast of the Holy Family (honoring Jesus, Mary, and Joseph), the solemnity of Mary, Mother of God (celebrating Mary's profound role as the mother of God), and the solemnity of the Epiphany of the Lord, (commemorating the revelation of Christ to all nations and peoples). The season ends with the feast of the Baptism of the Lord, when we recall Jesus' own baptism in the Jordan River. Christmas is a time to celebrate the fulfillment of God's promise in the gift of his beloved Son, Jesus. *LD*

12 Dream a Dream

Verses 1, 2
1. Dream a dream, a hope-ful dream, as chil-dren do on Christ-mas Eve, i - mag - in - ings, sur - pris-ing things to hold and to be-lieve. Dream a time, this Christ-mas time, when no one's hun-gry or a-fraid; that weap-ons go and har-vests
2. Dream a peace, our plan-et's peace, the green-ing of the earth at play, the ho - ly ground where life is found, where God has touched the clay. Dream a gift, the Christ-mas gift that chang-es ev - 'ry - thing we see: the shim-mer-ing of an - gel

grow, that friends are met and made.
wing, the Child, the Mys - ter -
Canon
(y.) Do - na no - bis pa - cem, pa - cem.
Do - na no - bis pa - cem.
Last time to Coda
Do - na no - bis pa - cem.
Do - na no - bis pa - cem.
Last time to Coda
Do - na no - bis pa - cem.
Do - na no - bis pa - cem.
Last time to Coda
Coda
Dream a gift, the Christ - mas gift that
chang-es ev - 'ry - thing we see: the shim-mer-ing of
an - gel wing, the Child, the Mys - ter - y.

Text: Shirley Erena Murray, b.1931, © 1998, Hope Publishing Company; *Dona Nobis Pacem*, traditional
Tune: Lori True, b.1961, © 2005, GIA Publications, Inc.; *Dona Nobis Pacem*, traditional

13 hallmark songs of our faith

SILENT NIGHT

Many of the most beautiful songs we sing at liturgy were originally inspired by very specific practical situations; "Silent Night" *(no. 14)* is no exception. At a small parish church in Austria in 1818, the organ broke down just before Christmas Eve Mass! To quickly adapt to the situation, the priest and organist wrote this simple song and sang it as a duet that Christmas evening with only guitar accompaniment. Over the years, it has been translated into many languages and has become one of the most widely sung hymns of the Christmas season inside and outside the walls of the church. *TA*

14 Silent Night / Noche de Paz

1. Si - lent night, ho - ly night, All is calm, all is bright Round yon Vir - gin Moth-er and Child, Ho - ly In - fant so ten - der and mild, Sleep in heav - en - ly peace, Sleep in heav - en - ly peace.
2. Si - lent night, ho - ly night, Shep-herds quake at the sight; Glo - ries stream from heav - en a - far, Heav'n - ly hosts sing al - le - lu - ia; Christ, the Sav - ior, is born! Christ, the Sav - ior, is born!
1. No - che de paz, no - che de a - mor. To - do duer - me en de - rre - dor, En - tre los as - tros que es - par - cen su luz, Be - lla a-nun - cian - do al ni - ñi - to Je - sús, Bri - lla la es - tre - lla de paz, Bri - lla la es - tre - lla de paz.
2. No - che de paz, no - che de a - mor. O - ye hu - mil - de el fiel pas - tor, Co - ros ce - les - tes que a - nun - cian sa - lud, Gra - cias y glo - rias en gran ple - ni - tud, Por nues - tro buen Re - den - tor, Por nues - tro buen Re - den - tor.

3. Silent night, holy night, Son of God, love's pure light
Radiant beams from thy holy face, With the dawn of redeeming grace,
Jesus, Lord, at thy birth, Jesus, Lord, at thy birth.

3. Noche de paz, noche de‿amor. Mira qué gran resplandor
Luce‿en el rostro del niño Jesús, En el pesebre, del mundo la luz,
Astro de‿eterno fulgor, Astro de‿eterno fulgor.

Text: *Stille Nacht, heilige Nacht;* Joseph Mohr, 1792–1848; English tr. by John F. Young, 1820–1885; Spanish tr. by Federico Fliedner, 1845–1901
Tune: STILLE NACHT, 66 89 66; Franz X. Gruber, 1787–1863

Night of Silence / Noche de Silencio 15

1. Cold are the peo-ple, win-ter of life, We trem - ble in
2. Voice in the dis - tance, call in the night, On wind you en -
1. Frí - a la gen-te, pue-blo sin luz. Ya tiem-bla‿en las
2. Des - de lo le - jos la voz ven - drá. El vien - to en -
shad - ows this cold end - less night. Fro - zen in the
fold us, you speak of the light. Gen - tle on the
som - bras, ya‿es - pe - ra‿a Je - sús. En la nie-ve‿es-
vuél - ve - nos y cal - ma - rá. Pues con e - sa
snow lie ros - es sleep-ing, Flow-ers that will ech - o
ear you whis-per, soft - ly, Ru - mors of a dawn so
tán dur-mien-tes ro - sas, Flo - res que a - nun - cian
voz nos ha - blas, sua - ve. Ha - blas de‿u-na Luz que
the sun - rise. Fire of hope is our on - ly
em - brac - ing. Breath-less love a - waits dark-ened
el al - ba. La‿es - pe - ran - za nos da ca -
nos a - ma. Nos es - pe - ra‿el A - mor de
warmth; Wea - ry, its flame will be dy - ing soon.
souls. Soon will we know of the morn - ing.
lor Y nos in - fla - ma el co - ra - zón.
Dios. Vie - ne la‿her - mo - sa ma - ña - na.

3. Spirit among us, shine like the star,
Your light that guides shepherds
and kings from afar.
Shimmer in the sky so empty, lonely,
Rising in the warmth of the Son's love.
Star unknowing of night and day,
Spirit, we wait for the loving Son.

3. Célica‿estrella, ¡qué resplandor!
A magos tú guías en su caminar.
En el cielo‿estás tan sola, fría:
Eres luz de Cristo,‿el Mesías.
Santa‿estrella, muestra tu‿Amor,
Porque‿esperamos al Salvador.

Text: Daniel Kantor, b.1960; tr. by Jeffrey Judge
Tune: Daniel Kantor, b.1960

16 Child of Mercy

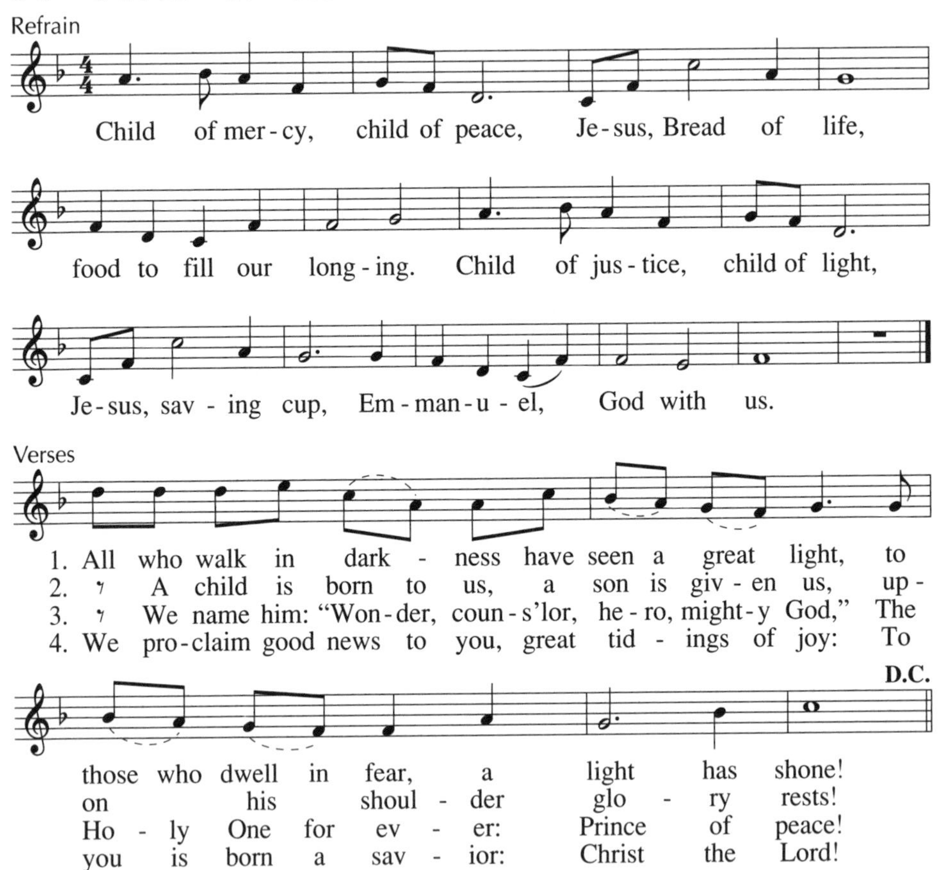
Refrain
Child of mer-cy, child of peace, Je-sus, Bread of life,
food to fill our long-ing. Child of jus-tice, child of light,
Je-sus, sav-ing cup, Em-man-u-el, God with us.
Verses
1. All who walk in dark-ness have seen a great light, to
2. A child is born to us, a son is giv-en us, up-
3. We name him: "Won-der, coun-s'lor, he-ro, might-y God," The
4. We pro-claim good news to you, great tid-ings of joy: To
D.C.
those who dwell in fear, a light has shone!
on his shoul-der glo-ry rests!
Ho-ly One for ev-er: Prince of peace!
you is born a sav-ior: Christ the Lord!

Text: Isaiah 9:1, 5; David Haas, b.1957
Tune: David Haas, b.1957

17 Rise Up in Splendor

Refrain
Rise up in splen-dor, rise up in splen-dor, rise up in splen-dor,
your light has come. Rise up in splen-dor, rise up in splen-dor,
rise up in splen-dor, your light has come.

Verses

D.C.
Rise up in splen-dor, your light has come.

1. Rise up in splendor, Jerusalem, your light has come.
   The glory of the Lord will shine upon you.
   See, darkness covers the earth. Thick clouds cover the people.

2. But upon you the Lord God shines and over you appears his glory. *Hey!**
   The nations shall walk by your light and kings in shining radiance, *yeah.*

3. Raise your eyes and look about you. They all gather and they come to you.
   Hey! Your sons come from afar, and your daughters in the arms of their nurses.
   And proclaiming the praises of the Lord.

4. Then you shall be radiant at what you see, your heart shall throb and overflow.
   For the riches of the sea shall be emptied out before you,
   and the wealth of nations shall be brought to you.
   Caravans of camels shall fill you, dromedaries from Midian and Ephah;
   all from Sheba shall come bearing gold, bearing frankincense,
   bearing myrrh, and proclaiming the praises of the Lord.

**Italicized text is not from the Bible.*

Alternate Verses for General Use

1. O heaven rejoicing, with ev'ry tongue on earth confess
   the lordship of Jesus, the Holy One of Righteousness.

2. O praise to the Father and glory to his only Son.
   Praise to the Spirit, the Holy God, the Three-in-One!

3. God calls us children in Jesus Christ, who sets us free.
   Come, let us worship; let all creation bend the knee!

4. Pray that the Spirit may fall on those who call God's name,
   strength for the weary and healing for the blind and lame.

5. O come to the water, all those who thirst for righteousness.
   Lay down your burdens, put on the robe of holiness!

6. Lord, save your people; from ev'ry sin deliver us.
   Send us your mercy; in you alone we place our trust!

7. One is the body, broken on the cross for sin.
   Merciful Savior, transform our hearts from deep within.

8. Look to the heavens and know that Christ will come again.
   Go make disciples and tell them of his love. Amen.

18 REMEMBER YOU ARE DUST / DEL POLVO ERES TÚ

Refrain / Estribillo
Turn a-way from sin and be faith - ful to the Gos-pel. Re - mem - ber you are dust, and to dust you will re - turn.
A-rre-pién - te-te y cre-e en el san - to e-van - ge - lio. Del pol - vo e - res tú, y al pol-vo has de vol - ver.
Verses / Estrofas
Cantor:
1.–4. Re - pent, the king-dom is at hand.
1.–4. El rei-no de Dios es-tá muy cer-ca.
All:
Re - pent, the king-dom is at hand.
El rei-no de Dios es-tá muy cer - ca.
*Cantor:
1. Rend your hearts, not your gar-ments.
2. Blow the trum - pet in Zi - on.
3. For - give one an - oth - er.
4. Now, the day of sal - va - tion.
1. Ras - ga hoy tu co - ra - zón.
2. En Sión to - ca la trom-pe - ta.
3. Per - do - na a tus her - ma - nos.
4. Dí - a de la sal - va - ción.
Now, the ac - cept - a - ble
Es a - ho - ra el tiem-po fa - vo -

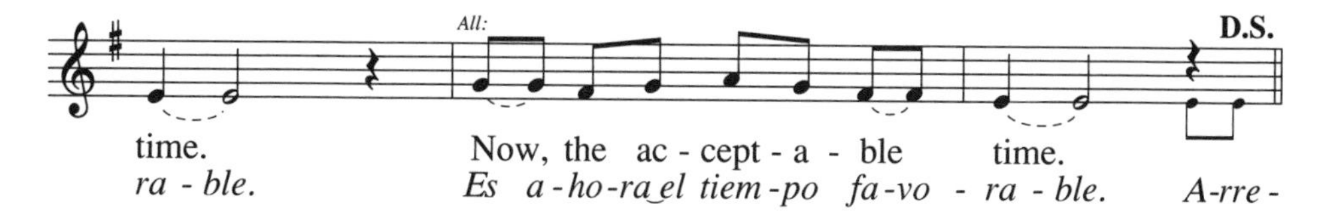
All:
D.S.
time. Now, the ac - cept - a - ble time.
ra - ble. Es a - ho - ra_el tiem - po fa - vo - ra - ble. A-rre -

*The following are verse tropes for the season of Lent:
Las siguentes son tropos adicionales para el uso durante la Cuaresma:

Seek the God of compassion…	*Busca_al Dios de compasión...*
Live in kindness and mercy…	*Sé amable, sé clemente...*
Trust in God and be faithful…	*En tu Redentor confía...*
Praise the God of salvation…	*A tu Salvador alaba...*
Let us bow down in worship…	*Rende culto_a tu Señor...*

our liturgical year 19

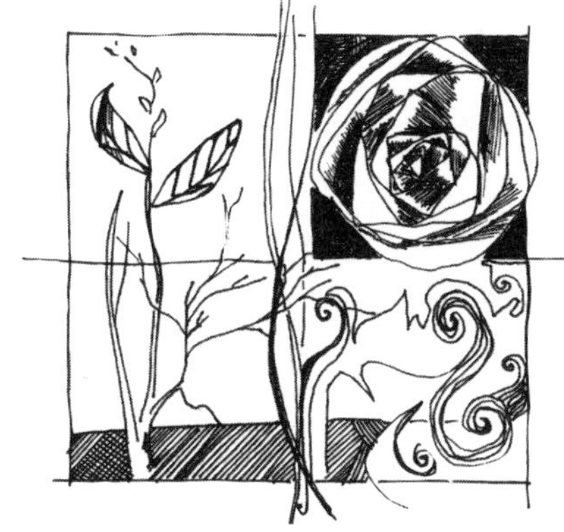

LENT

During the forty days of Lent, we recall the forty days Jesus spent in the wilderness fasting and praying. The biblical readings proclaimed during Lent remind us of God's boundless compassion and love as well as our call to conversion and repentance. The verses of the song "Be Forgiven" *(no. 20)* call to mind these profound gospel stories.

Lent begins on Ash Wednesday, when we are signed with ashes on our foreheads. The ashes are a sign of repentance, dating back to the Old Testament when King David shed his regal garb for sackcloth and ashes as a sign of repentance and mourning.

During Lent, we are encouraged to focus our energy on three disciplines: prayer, fasting, and almsgiving (sharing our gifts with the poor). Through these activities and our participation in the liturgies of Lent, we prepare ourselves to renew our baptismal promises to God at Easter. *LD*

Sacred silence also, as part of the celebration, is to be observed at the designated times.

General Instruction of the Roman Missal

20 Be Forgiven

Refrain
Be for-giv-en, be for-giv-en, be for-
giv-en of the sin that you hold on. Be for-giv-en,
be for-giv-en, Je-sus died and rose that you might
To verses
Last time
know his love, and be for-giv-en.
Verse 1
1. Je-sus told you he wants your peace, and Je-sus told
you he wants you healed. Je-sus lift-ed up the blind
man. He lift-ed up the dead. He lift-ed those who
mourn their own. He did just what he said, and Je-sus
rose for you, and he rose for me. He
D.S.
died and rose that we might know his peace and be for-

Verse 2
2. Je-sus walked the miles that it took to reach us. Je-sus touched
the lep-er that you should-n't touch. Je-sus
wept for Laz-a-rus. Don't you think he'll do the same for
you and me, when we are dead, and we are in our graves? And Je-sus
rose for you, and he rose for me. He
died and rose that we might know his peace and like the
Bridge
wom-an at the well, he looks in-to our eyes and tells us
ev-'ry-thing that we have ev-er done. And with a
love that's plain to see, he is call-ing you and me to
fol-low him that we might tru-ly be for-
D.S.

Text: Tom Booth, b.1961
Tune: Tom Booth, b.1961; acc. by Ed Bolduc, b.1969

21 GIVE ME JESUS

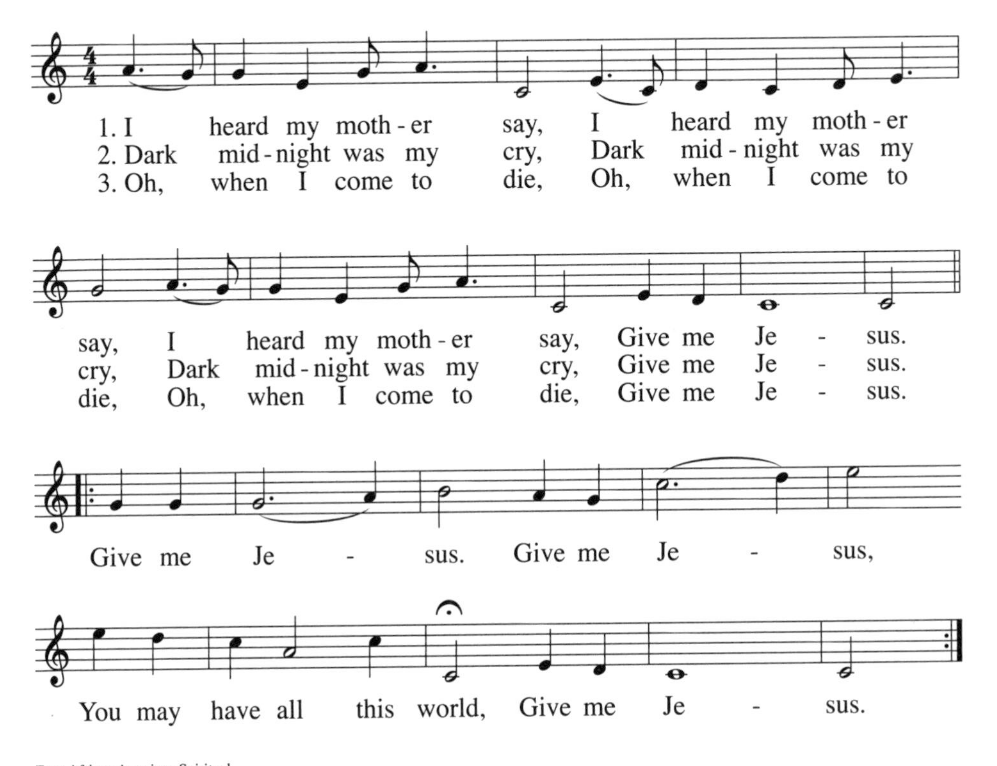
1. I heard my moth - er say, I heard my moth - er
2. Dark mid - night was my cry, Dark mid - night was my
3. Oh, when I come to die, Oh, when I come to
say, I heard my moth - er say, Give me Je - sus.
cry, Dark mid - night was my cry, Give me Je - sus.
die, Oh, when I come to die, Give me Je - sus.
Give me Je - sus. Give me Je - sus,
You may have all this world, Give me Je - sus.

Text: African American Spiritual
Tune: GIVE ME JESUS, 666 4 with refrain; African American Spiritual; arr. by Nolan Williams, Jr., b.1969, © 2000, GIA Publications, Inc.

22 LENTEN GOSPEL ACCLAMATION

Praise to you, Lord, Je - sus Christ, King of end - less
1.
2.
glo - ry.
glo - ry.

Text: ICEL, © 1969
Music: Ed Archer, © 2008, GIA Publications, Inc.

We Are Climbing Jacob's Ladder 23

Verses 1–3, 5
1. We are climb-ing Ja - cob's lad - der,
2. Ev - 'ry round goes high-er, high-er,
3. Sin - ner do you love your Je - sus,
5. If you love him why not serve him,
we are climb-ing Ja - cob's lad - der,
ev - 'ry round goes high-er, high-er,
sin - ner do you love your Je - sus,
if you love him why not serve him,
we are climb-ing Ja - cob's lad - der,
ev - 'ry round goes high-er, high-er,
sin - ner do you love your Je - sus,
if you love him why not serve him,
Sol - diers of the Cross.
Verse 4
4. Lord, let me walk close by your side;
I'll be your sheep, you'll be my guide. Lord, lift me up
and let me stand, and I will say at your com-mand:
D.C.

Text: African American spiritual
Tune: African American spiritual; arr. by Horace Clarence Boyer, b.1935, © 2003, GIA Publications, Inc.

24 Mercy, O God

Refrain
Mer-cy, O God, have mer-cy on us.
Send down your mer-cy to set us free.
Mer-cy, O God, have mer-cy on us.
Send down your mer-cy to set us free.
Verses
1. Gath - er the peo - ple, the chil - dren, the eld - ers;
2. Now is the hour, the day of sal - va - tion;
3. Long is the jour - ney and steep are the moun - tains,
4. Wash us a - new in your life - giv - ing wa - ter;
5. Once lost in dark-ness you did not for - sake us, but
6. Wake, O sleep - er, a - wake from your slum - ber;
come now and gath - er be - fore the Lord.
now is the time to re - turn to God.
come now and guide us, O gra - cious God.
come quench the thirst of our yearn - ing hearts.
called us your chil - dren and gave us light.
rise from the chains of the dark, cold tomb.

3
O - pen your hearts to com - pas - sion and mer - cy;
O - pen your lives to for - give - ness and mer - cy;
Show us your face, give us hope for the jour - ney;
Break through the si - lence, the fear and the long - ing; em -
O - pen our eyes, come re - move all our blind - ness.
Walk in the light of com - pas - sion and mer - cy;

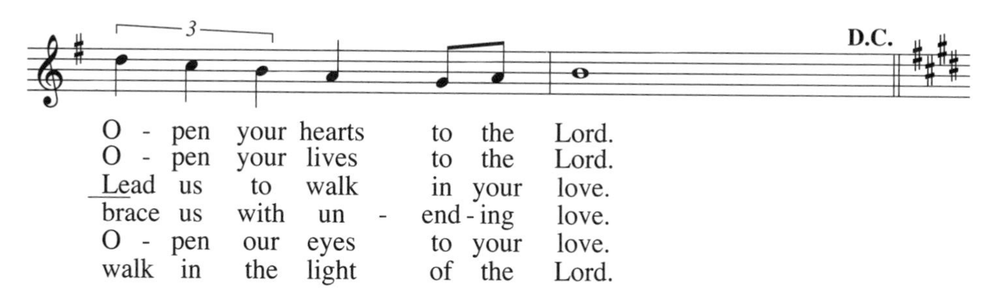
3
D.C.
O - pen your hearts to the Lord.
O - pen your lives to the Lord.
Lead us to walk in your love.
brace us with un - end - ing love.
O - pen our eyes to your love.
walk in the light of the Lord.

Text: Francis Patrick O'Brien, b.1958
Tune: Francis Patrick O'Brien, b.1958

25 Bring Us Home

1. Bring us home from our wan-d'ring the val - ley of death; come ran - som the peo - ple you filled with your breath. Bring us home from our ex - ile to love's warm em - brace; come gath - er your chil - dren who long for your face, come gath - er your chil - dren who long for your face. Bring us
2. Bring us home from the dark - ness and bathe us in light, though long we have stum - bled, and strayed from your sight. Bring us home to the cir - cle where love has no end, where out - cast and stran - ger are wel - comed as friend, where out - cast and stran - ger are wel - comed as friend. Bring us
3. Bring us home to the ban - quet, to bread and to wine, the fruit of the har - vest, the fruit of the vine. Bring us home to the ta - ble, to Love's sac - ri - fice, of blood and of bod - y, where grace will suf - fice, of blood and of bod - y, where grace will suf - fice. Bring us
4. Bring us home to the heav - ens where par - don and peace pass all un - der - stand - ing, where mourn - ing shall cease. Bring us home to the king - dom where Love sits en - throned, our hope and our prom - ise, our e - ter - nal home, our hope and our prom - ise, our e - ter - nal home. Bring us

home, bring us home, from val - leys of
home, bring us home, from dark - ness of
home, bring us home, to Love's sac - ri -
home, bring us home, to par - don and
death, bring us home! Bring us home,
night, bring us home! Bring us home,
fice, bring us home! Bring us home,
peace, bring us home! Bring us home,
bring us home, come fill us with
bring us home, come bathe us in
bring us home, where grace will suf -
bring us home, till mourn - ing shall
5
breath, bring us home!
light, bring us home!
fice, bring us home!
cease, bring us home!

Text: Deanna Light, b.1967 and Paul A. Tate, b.1968
Tune: Deanna Light, b.1967 and Paul A. Tate, b.1968

26 hallmark songs of our faith

JESUS, REMEMBER ME

This simple repetitive song is one of the most beloved songs of the Lenten season and the liturgies of the Easter triduum. The single line of text comes from the Passion according to Luke. Soon before his death, one of the criminals crucified next to Jesus said to him, "Jesus, remember me when you come into your kingdom." Jesus' love and compassion for the man is evident in his response: "Truly I tell you, today you will be with me in paradise" (Luke 23:42–43). This is God's promise for all of us: eternal life in paradise. As you sing this song, remember God's love and compassion for you.

The music comes from the Taizé community in France. For more information about this mantra-like song form (known as an ostinato) and its use in the Taizé community, see no. 28. "Jesus, Remember Me" *(no. 27)* is perhaps the most popular of the songs from the Taizé community. *TA*

27 Jesus, Remember Me / Jesús, Recuérdame

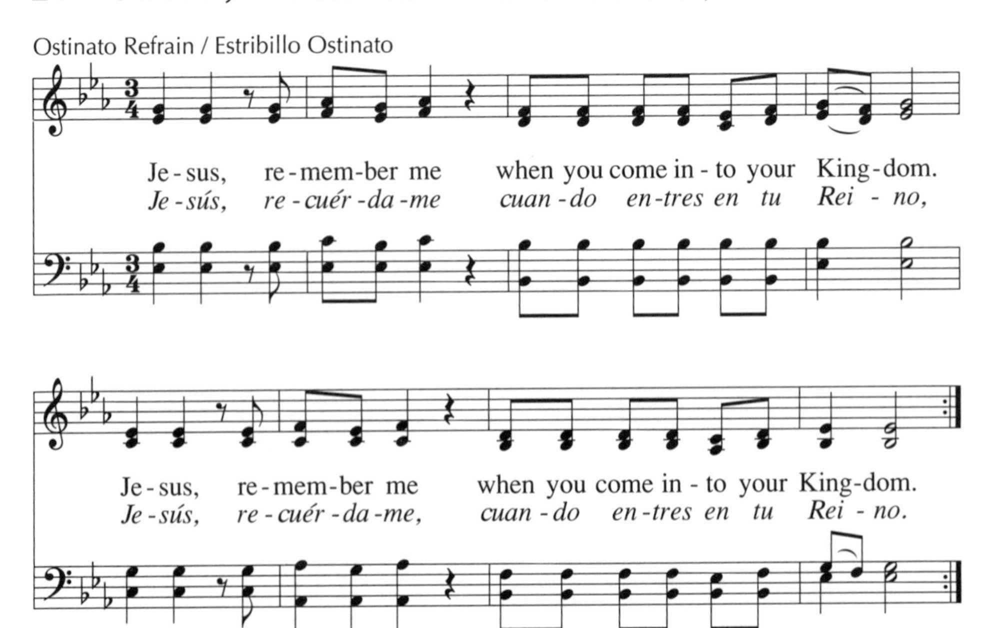
Ostinato Refrain / Estribillo Ostinato
Je-sus, re-mem-ber me when you come in-to your King-dom.
Je-sús, re-cuér-da-me cuan-do en-tres en tu Rei - no,
Je-sus, re-mem-ber me when you come in-to your King-dom.
Je-sús, re-cuér-da-me, cuan-do en-tres en tu Rei - no.

Text: Luke 23:42; Taizé Community, 1981; tr. by Ronald F. Krisman, b.1946
Tune: Jacques Berthier, 1923-1994

our heritage of song 28

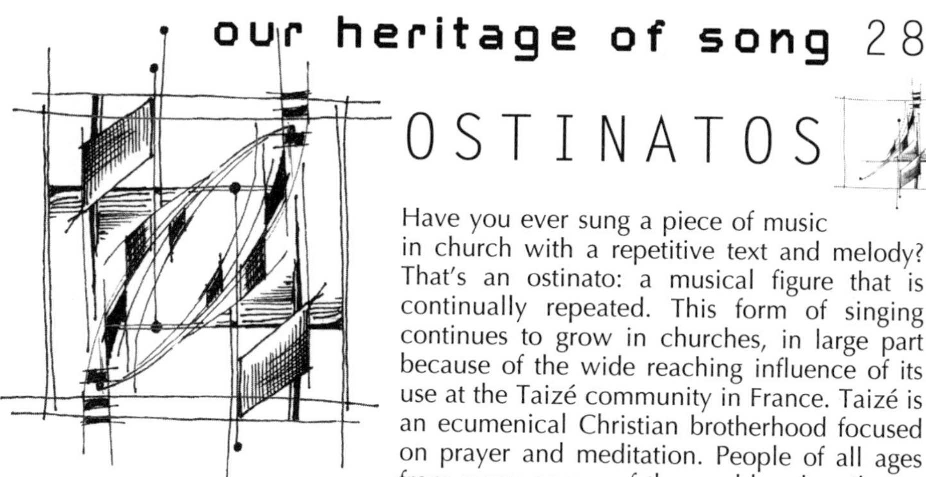

OSTINATOS

Have you ever sung a piece of music in church with a repetitive text and melody? That's an ostinato: a musical figure that is continually repeated. This form of singing continues to grow in churches, in large part because of the wide reaching influence of its use at the Taizé community in France. Taizé is an ecumenical Christian brotherhood focused on prayer and meditation. People of all ages from every corner of the world make pilgrimages to the Taizé community to pray with the brothers there. Because people of many cultures converge at Taizé so frequently, a repertoire of simple ostinatos has been composed over many years to help everyone to join in common prayer and song. In addition to their accessibility, these pieces continue to lead people into deeper prayer and contemplation. Some parishes celebrate Taizé prayer, which brings together many of these beautiful pieces. One of the most familiar songs to come out of the Taizé community is "Jesus, Remember Me" *(no. 27). TA*

AT YOUR NAME 29

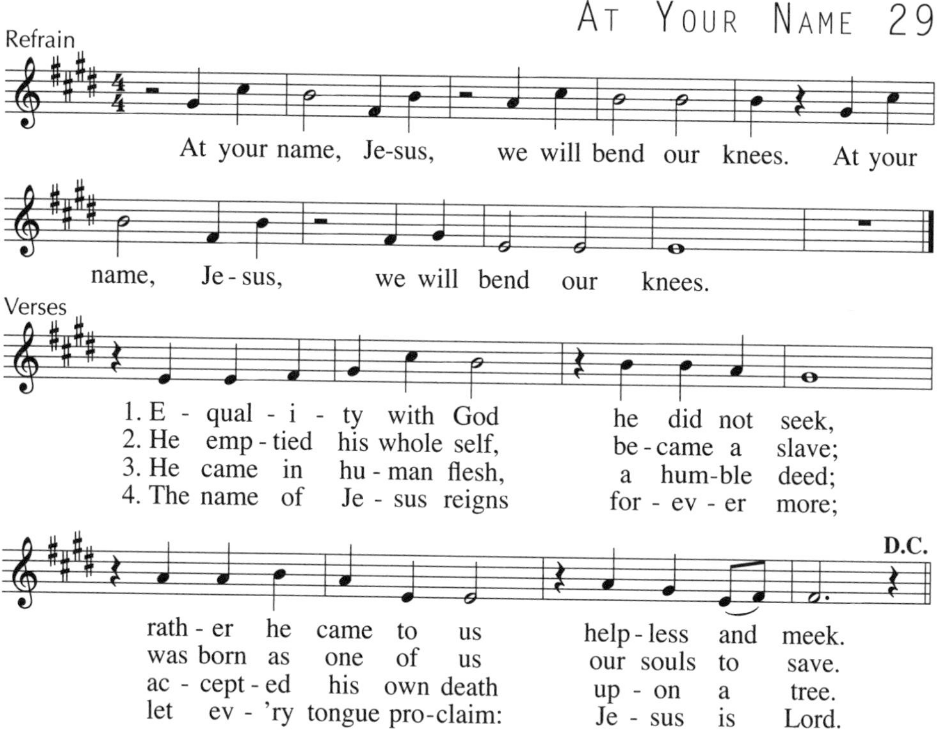
Refrain
At your name, Je-sus, we will bend our knees. At your name, Je - sus, we will bend our knees.
Verses
1. E - qual - i - ty with God he did not seek,
2. He emp - tied his whole self, be - came a slave;
3. He came in hu - man flesh, a hum-ble deed;
4. The name of Je - sus reigns for - ev - er more;
rath - er he came to us help - less and meek.
was born as one of us our souls to save.
ac - cept - ed his own death up - on a tree.
let ev - 'ry tongue pro-claim: Je - sus is Lord.
D.C.

Text: Based on Philippians 2:6–11; Shannon Cerneka, b.1975
Tune: Shannon Cerneka, b.1975

30 hallmark songs of our faith

UBI CARITAS

This chant is a cornerstone of the Church's musical heritage, dating back to the ninth century. The original Latin words (which mean "Where charity and love are, there God is found") remind us of the constant call to charity and service, which is at the heart of Christian living. The Sacramentary *(see no. 242)* calls for this song to be sung during the preparation of the gifts at the Holy Thursday liturgy during the offertory collection taken for the poor. It is often sung during the washing of the feet during the Holy Thursday liturgy and at other times throughout the year to remind us of our Christian responsibility to the least among us. *TA*

31 Where True Love and Charity Are Found / Ubi Caritas

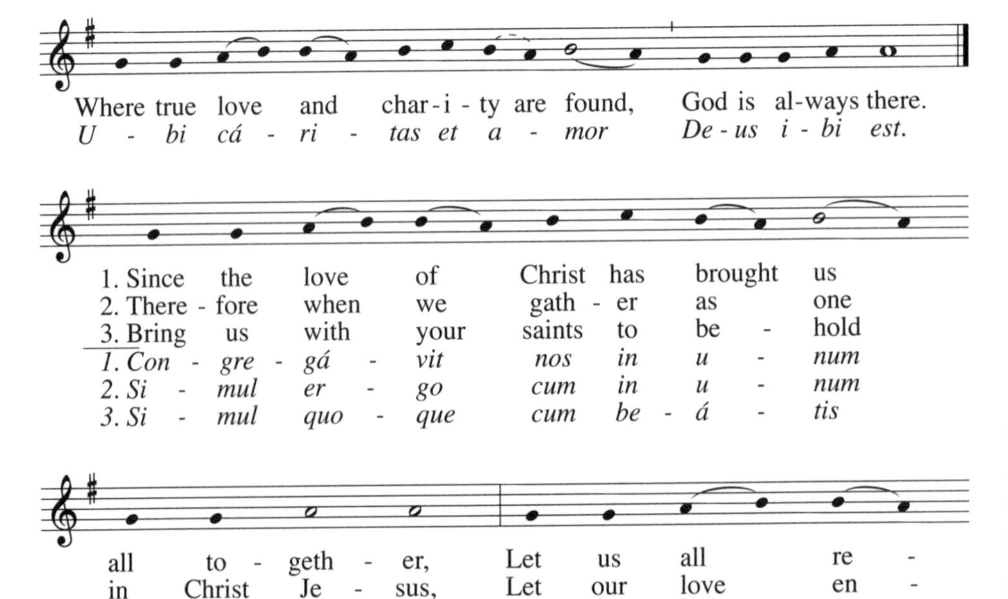
Where true love and char-i-ty are found, God is al-ways there.
U - bi cá - ri - tas et a - mor De - us i - bi est.
1. Since the love of Christ has brought us
2. There - fore when we gath - er as one
3. Bring us with your saints to be - hold
1. Con - gre - gá - vit nos in u - num
2. Si - mul er - go cum in u - num
3. Si - mul quo - que cum be - á - tis
all to - geth - er, Let us all re -
in Christ Je - sus, Let our love en -
your great beau - ty, There to see you,
Chri - sti a - mor. Ex - sul - té - mus
con - gre - gá - mur: Ne nos men - te
vi - de - á - mus. Glo - ri - án - ter

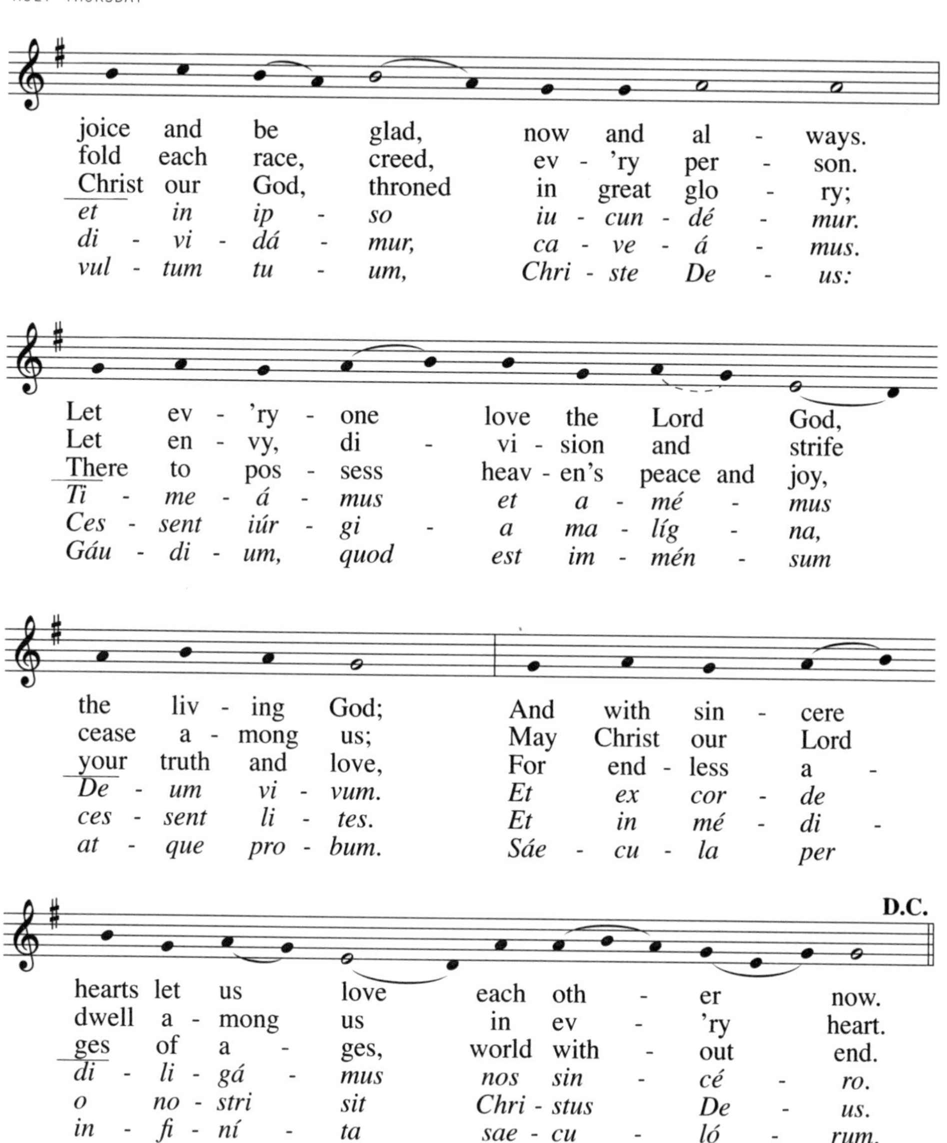
joice and be glad, now and al - ways.
fold each race, creed, ev - 'ry per - son.
Christ our God, throned in great glo - ry;
et in ip - so iu - cun - dé - mur.
di - vi - dá - mur, ca - ve - á - mus.
vul - tum tu - um, Chri - ste De - us:
Let ev - 'ry - one love the Lord God,
Let en - vy, di - vi - sion and strife
There to pos - sess heav - en's peace and joy,
Ti - me - á - mus et a - mé - mus
Ces - sent iúr - gi - a ma - líg - na,
Gáu - di - um, quod est im - mén - sum
the liv - ing God; And with sin - cere
cease a - mong us; May Christ our Lord
your truth and love, For end - less a -
De - um vi - vum. Et ex cor - de
ces - sent li - tes. Et in mé - di -
at - que pro - bum. Sáe - cu - la per
hearts let us love each oth - er now.
dwell a - mong us in ev - 'ry heart.
ges of a - ges, world with - out end.
di - li - gá - mus nos sin - cé - ro.
o no - stri sit Chri - stus De - us.
in - fi - ní - ta sae - cu - ló - rum.
D.C.

Text: Latin, 9th C.; tr. by Richard Proulx, b.1937, © 1975, 1986, GIA Publications, Inc.
Tune: UBI CARITAS, 12 12 12 12 with refrain; Mode VI; acc. by Richard Proulx, b.1937, © 1986, GIA Publications, Inc.

32 our liturgical year

EASTER TRIDUUM

The Easter triduum (pronounced TRIH-doo-um) is the three-day liturgical celebration of the last supper, suffering, death, and resurrection of Christ. These three days are at the heart of our identity as Catholics.

On Holy Thursday we remember the Last Supper. In this Mass, we wash feet as Jesus washed the feet of his disciples to remind us of our call to love, humility, and service. This liturgy concludes with a procession of the Eucharist to a chapel of reserve for adoration and prayer. Following the liturgy, the altar is stripped and the lights are extinguished in the worship space, symbolic of Jesus' betrayal in the Garden of Gethsemane.

The prayer of the Triduum continues with a liturgy on Good Friday when we remember Christ's passion and death. The Passion of Our Lord according to John is proclaimed, and we are given an opportunity to venerate the cross—with a reverent gesture, such as a bow, kiss, or touch. The liturgy concludes with a simple Communion service with the Eucharist reserved from Holy Thursday's liturgy. The liturgy begins and ends in silence to connect us with the liturgies that precede and follow it.

The Easter Vigil is celebrated on Saturday night after sundown. It begins with the kindling of the Easter fire, the blessing of the paschal candle, and several readings from the Old Testament, which tell of God's saving acts throughout history. At the Easter Vigil, we renew our baptismal promises and initiate new members through the sacraments of baptism, confirmation, and the Eucharist. The Easter Vigil marks the beginning of the fifty days of Easter. *LD*

33 Glory in the Cross

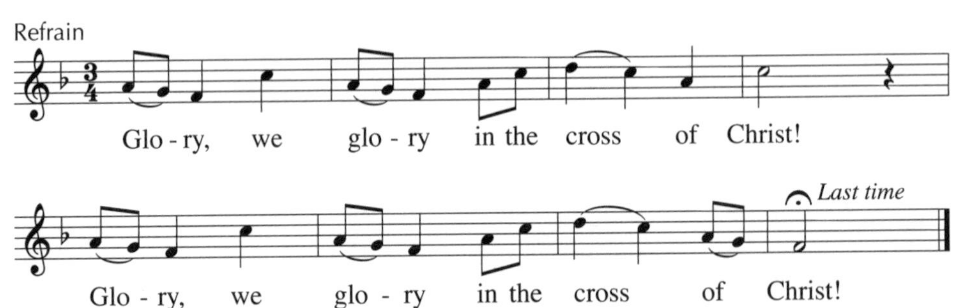
Refrain
Glo - ry, we glo - ry in the cross of Christ!
Last time
Glo - ry, we glo - ry in the cross of Christ!

Verses

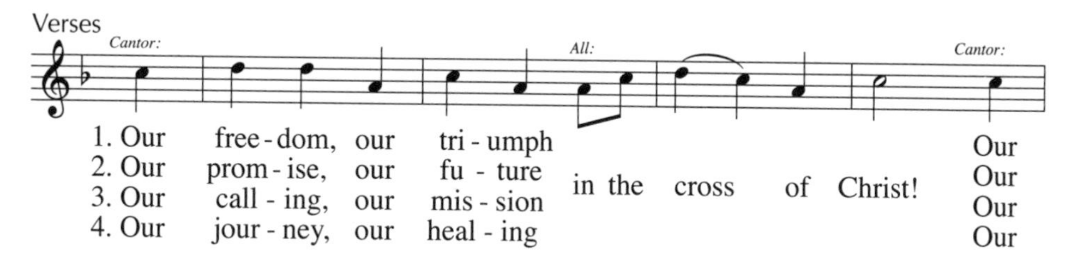
Cantor:
All:
Cantor:
1. Our free-dom, our tri-umph
2. Our prom-ise, our fu-ture
3. Our call-ing, our mis-sion
4. Our jour-ney, our heal-ing
in the cross of Christ!
Our
Our
Our
Our

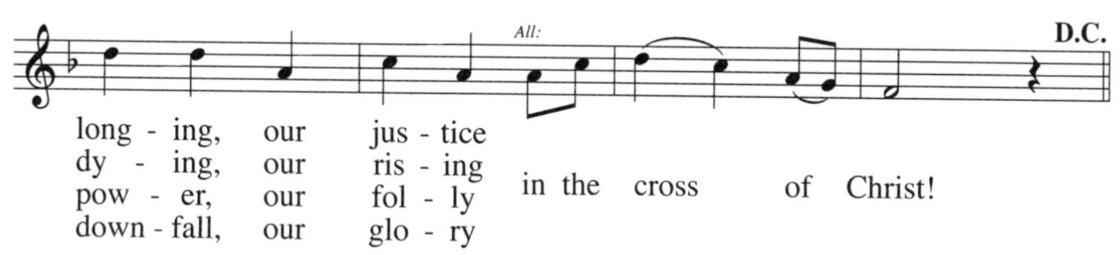
All:
D.C.
long-ing, our jus-tice
dy-ing, our ris-ing
pow-er, our fol-ly
down-fall, our glo-ry
in the cross of Christ!

Text: Galatians 6:14; Scott Soper, b.1961
Tune: Scott Soper, b.1961

Come and Gather 34

Refrain

Come and gath-er at the foot of the cross.

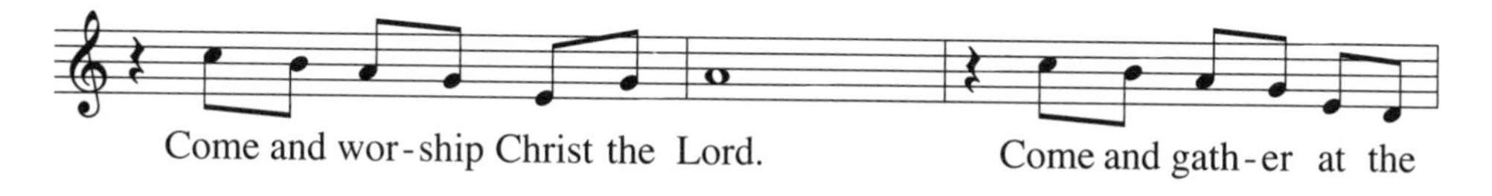
Come and wor-ship Christ the Lord.
Come and gath-er at the

foot of the cross.
O come, let us a-dore.

Verses

1. Can you feel the cold, damp air?
   Can you feel the sorrow and despair?
   Come and worship with your tears.
   He'll wash away your fears.

2. Can you see him crucified?
   On the cross our Lord Jesus died.
   Gave his life for you and me,
   he died on Calvary.

Bridge

If we all believe in Christ and accept him in our lives,
take up your cross and follow him and live again!

Text: John Angotti, b.1963
Tune: John Angotti, b.1963; arr. by Paul A. Tate, b.1968

35 I Give My Spirit

Refrain
Emp - ty, bro - ken, life - less, I give my
spir - it, Lord.
Verses
faster
1. In you, O Lord, I take ref - uge; let me
2. I am the scorn of all my en - e-mies, a
3. My fate lies sole - ly in your hands. My
4. Let your face shine on your ser - vant; come and
nev - er be put to shame. In your
hor - ror to all my friends. Like the
Fa - ther, de - liv - er me! O Lord, I
save me, O Lord of love. All who
jus - tice res - cue me. Re -
dead, I am for - got - ten; like a
say, "You are my God." I
wait for the Lord: Take
D.C.
deem me, O faith - ful God.
bro - ken and use - less ves - sel.
place all my trust in you.
cour - age, be strong, and hope!

Text: Based on Psalm 31; Shannon Cerneka, b.1975, and Orin Johnson, b.1973
Tune: Shannon Cerneka, b.1975, and Orin Johnson, b.1973

My Savior, My Friend 36

Verses
1. Je - sus, hang - ing on the cross, my heart would
2. Once I touched your wound-ed feet, my fin - gers
3. When I saw your wound-ed side, my heart reached
4. Je - sus, hung from bro - ken hands, O man of
share your pain, there in la - bor hang with
in the nail; there I saw the wine of
out to share; all your flesh was torn and
wound - ed heart, let me touch your wound - ed
you till all are born a - gain.
God cupped in the ho - ly grail.
wide, and all our pain was there.
feet and in your death be part.
Refrain
On the wood of the cross hung my Sav - ior, my friend.
Now I come, here I a - dore and give
praise to my Lord with - out end.
3

Text: Mark 15:34; Sr. Frances Teresa, OSC, ©
Tune: Chris de Silva, b.1967

EASTER

The fifty days of Easter are for celebration and rejoicing! During Easter, we celebrate Christ's resurrection and proclaim the mystery at the heart of our faith: *Dying he destroyed our death and rising he restored our life!* Easter's fifty days begin with the Easter Vigil, when we initiate new members into the Church and sing the great Alleluia, which we have kept silent throughout Lent.

Forty days after Easter we celebrate the Ascension of Jesus Christ into heaven and are reminded of Christ's promise to return again to bring his kingdom to completion. On the last day of Easter the Church celebrates Pentecost. On this day we recall the descent of the Holy Spirit upon the disciples fifty days after the resurrection. Because the Spirit gave them such great power to go out and share the good news and so many were baptized at the first Pentecost, it is often considered the "birthday" of the Church. The verses of the song "Easter Alleluia" *(no. 38)* contain images taken from the various gospels proclaimed during the Easter season. *LD*

The central image of Christianity is the cross,
calling to mind the passion, resurrection,
and Christ's final coming in glory.
Every work of Christian art or architecture
shares in this image and embraces the
ambiguities of suffering and death, healing
and resurrection, recognizing that
"by his wounds we are healed."

Built of Living Stones

Easter Alleluia 38

Refrain
Al-le-lu-ia, al - le - lu-ia, al-le-lu - ia!

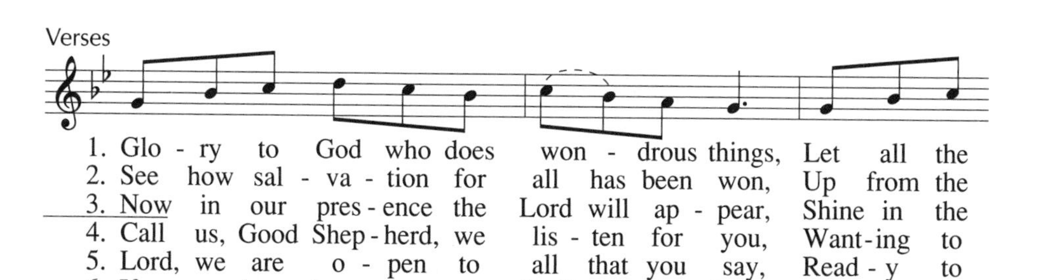
Verses
1. Glo - ry to God who does won - drous things, Let all the
2. See how sal - va - tion for all has been won, Up from the
3. Now in our pres - ence the Lord will ap - pear, Shine in the
4. Call us, Good Shep - herd, we lis - ten for you, Want-ing to
5. Lord, we are o - pen to all that you say, Read - y to
6. If we have love, then we dwell in the Lord, God will pro-

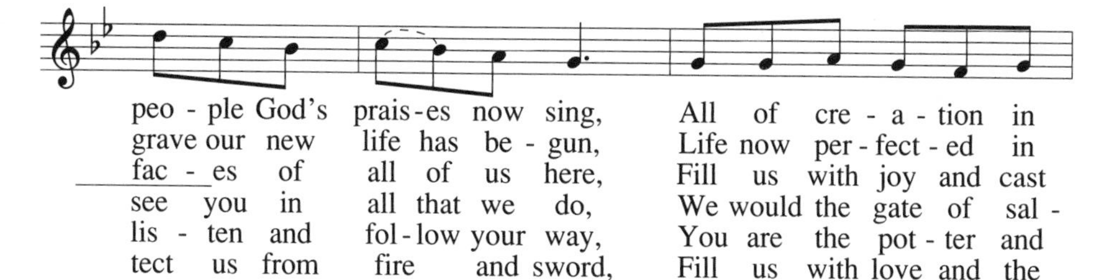
peo - ple God's prais-es now sing, All of cre - a - tion in
grave our new life has be - gun, Life now per - fect - ed in
fac - es of all of us here, Fill us with joy and cast
see you in all that we do, We would the gate of sal -
lis - ten and fol - low your way, You are the pot - ter and
tect us from fire and sword, Fill us with love and the

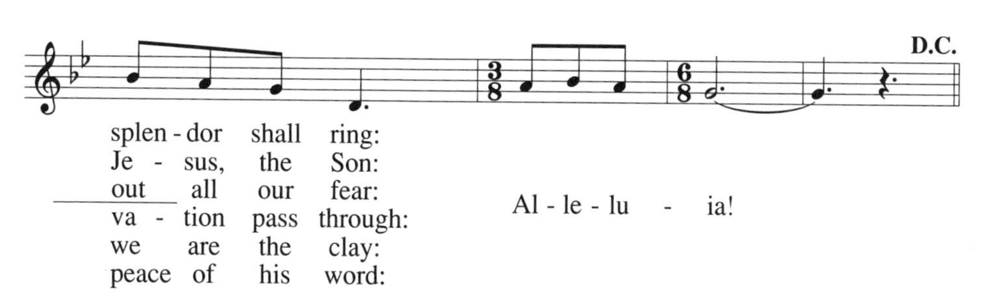
D.C.
splen - dor shall ring:
Je - sus, the Son:
out all our fear:
va - tion pass through:
we are the clay:
peace of his word:
Al - le - lu - ia!

Text: Marty Haugen, b.1950
Tune: O FILII ET FILIAE, 10 10 10 with alleluias; adapt. by Marty Haugen, b.1950

39 Come and See

Verse 1

1. We came there desp'rately, so hopeless and afraid,
 until we found the place where Jesus Christ was laid.
 Our sorrow and our fear were banished on that glorious day.
 The tomb was empty and the stone was rolled away!

Refrain

Come and see!
He is raised!
See what the Lord
He has washed
has done for you.
all our sins a - way.
Come be - lieve!
Lift your praise!
1.
Out of our death comes life a - new.
Je - sus has con -
2.
quered on this day.

Verse 2

2. Some stumble on the way in blindness and in sin.
 Some find the open door but fear to enter in.
 It doesn't matter how, or who, or when, or where, or why.
 All who believe and love shall never ever die! *Refrain*

Vamp: Christ is our Lord and King! O death, where is your sting?

Verse 3

3. Go out to all the world and shout the blessed news.
 Our lives have been made whole by Christ, the faith we choose.
 All chains are broken now, and those enslaved are all set free.
 All people lift your hearts and join the jubilee! *Refrain*

Text: Michael Mahler, b.1981
Tune: Michael Mahler, b.1981

O Sons and Daughters 40

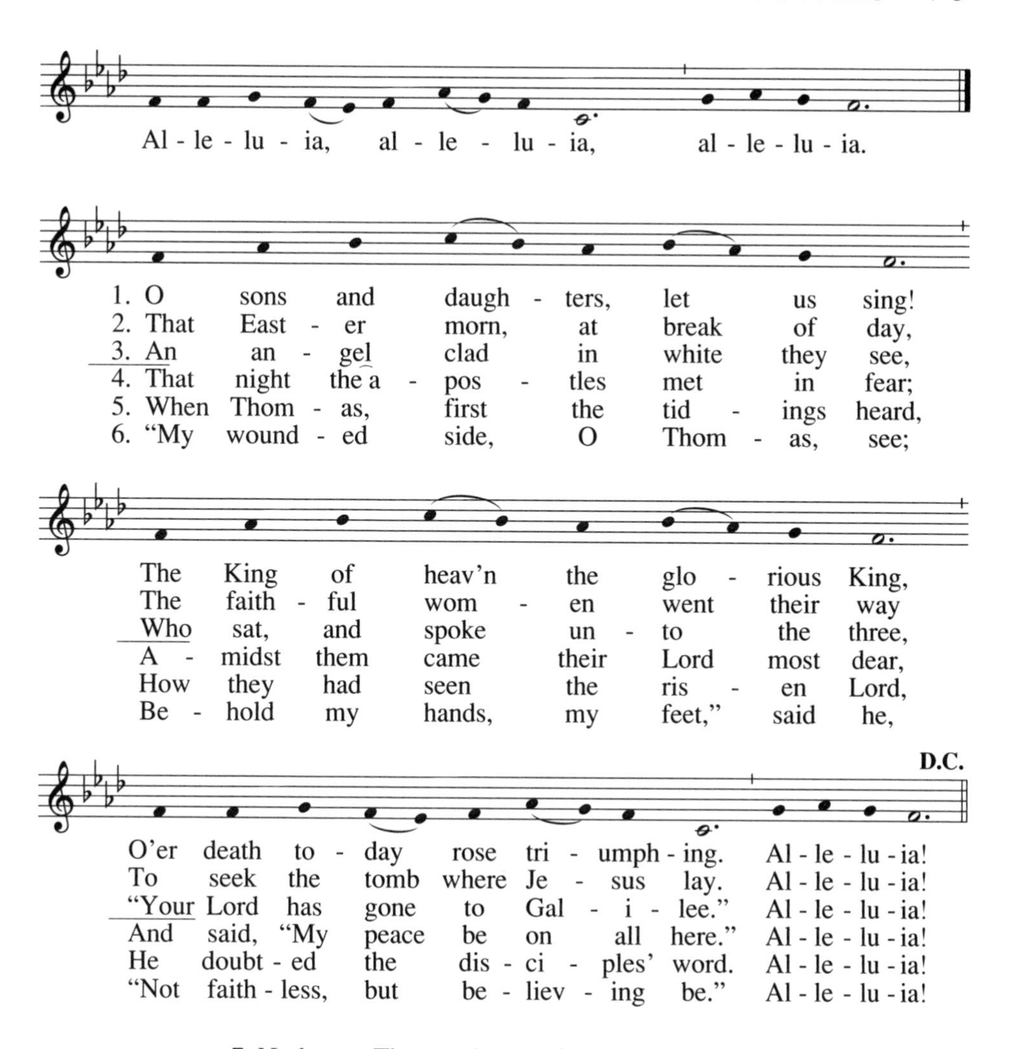
Al - le - lu - ia, al - le - lu - ia, al - le - lu - ia.
1. O sons and daugh - ters, let us sing!
2. That East - er morn, at break of day,
3. An an - gel clad in white they see,
4. That night the a - pos - tles met in fear;
5. When Thom - as, first the tid - ings heard,
6. "My wound - ed side, O Thom - as, see;
The King of heav'n the glo - rious King,
The faith - ful wom - en went their way
Who sat, and spoke un - to the three,
A - midst them came their Lord most dear,
How they had seen the ris - en Lord,
Be - hold my hands, my feet," said he,
D.C.
O'er death to - day rose tri - umph - ing. Al - le - lu - ia!
To seek the tomb where Je - sus lay. Al - le - lu - ia!
"Your Lord has gone to Gal - i - lee." Al - le - lu - ia!
And said, "My peace be on all here." Al - le - lu - ia!
He doubt - ed the dis - ci - ples' word. Al - le - lu - ia!
"Not faith - less, but be - liev - ing be." Al - le - lu - ia!

7. No longer Thomas then denied,
He saw the feet, the hands, the side;
"You are my Lord and God," he cried. Alleluia!

8. How blest are they who have not seen,
And yet whose faith has constant been,
For they eternal life shall win. Alleluia!

9. On this most holy day of days,
To God your hearts and voices raise,
In laud, and jubilee and praise. Alleluia!

Text: *O filii et filiae;* Jean Tisserand, d.1494; tr. by John M. Neale, 1818–1866, alt.
Tune: O FILII ET FILIAE, 888 with alleluias; Mode II; acc. by Richard Proulx, b.1937,

41 hallmark songs of our faith

JESUS CHRIST IS RISEN TODAY

It is difficult to imagine Easter Sunday Mass without the singing of this joyful hymn! Like many of the most popular hymns of the Church, it has evolved over time with people of many generations expanding it. The song was originally composed in Latin with only one verse (the first verse) in the fourteenth century. Many years later, it was translated into English and the second and third verses were added. The fourth verse was the final verse to be added in the mid 1700s. Hymns like "Jesus Christ Is Risen Today" *(no. 42)* connect us with many generations of faithful people who came before us. *TA*

42 Jesus Christ Is Risen Today / El Señor Resucitó

1. Je - sus Christ is ris'n to - day, Al - le - lu - ia!
2. Hymns of praise then let us sing, Al - le - lu - ia!
3. But the pains which he en - dured, Al - le - lu - ia!
4. Sing we to our God a - bove, Al - le - lu - ia!
1. El Se - ñor re - su - ci - tó, ¡A - le - lu - ya!
2. El que al pol - vo se hu-mi - lló, ¡A - le - lu - ya!
3. Cris - to, que la cruz su - frió, ¡A - le - lu - ya!
4. Cris - to, nues - tro Sal - va - dor, ¡A - le - lu - ya!

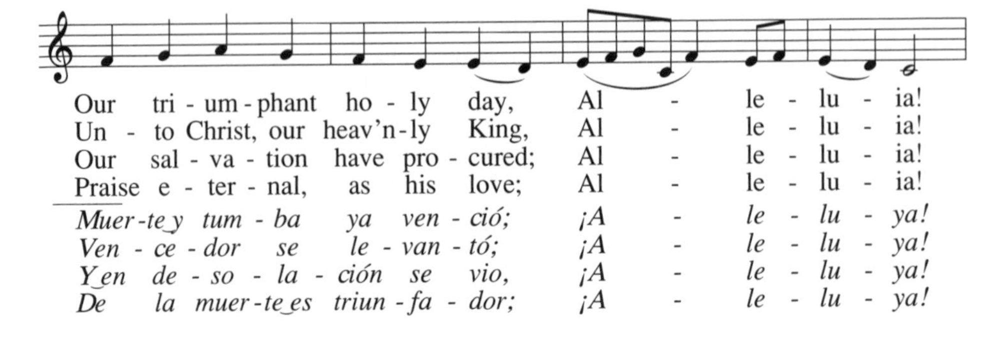
Our tri - um - phant ho - ly day, Al - le - lu - ia!
Un - to Christ, our heav'n - ly King, Al - le - lu - ia!
Our sal - va - tion have pro - cured; Al - le - lu - ia!
Praise e - ter - nal, as his love; Al - le - lu - ia!
Muer - te y tum - ba ya ven - ció; ¡A - le - lu - ya!
Ven - ce - dor se le - van - tó; ¡A - le - lu - ya!
Y en de - so - la - ción se vio, ¡A - le - lu - ya!
De la muer - te es triun - fa - dor; ¡A - le - lu - ya!

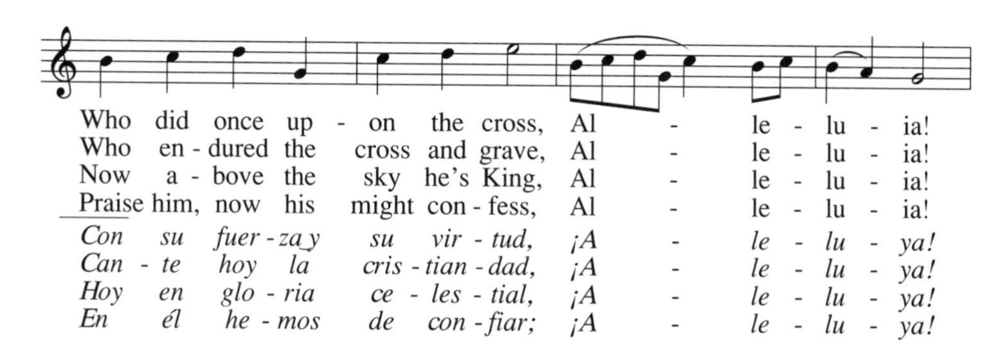
Who did once up - on the cross, Al - le - lu - ia!
Who en - dured the cross and grave, Al - le - lu - ia!
Now a - bove the sky he's King, Al - le - lu - ia!
Praise him, now his might con - fess, Al - le - lu - ia!
Con su fuer - za y su vir - tud, ¡A - le - lu - ya!
Can - te hoy la cris - tian - dad, ¡A - le - lu - ya!
Hoy en glo - ria ce - les - tial, ¡A - le - lu - ya!
En él he - mos de con - fiar; ¡A - le - lu - ya!

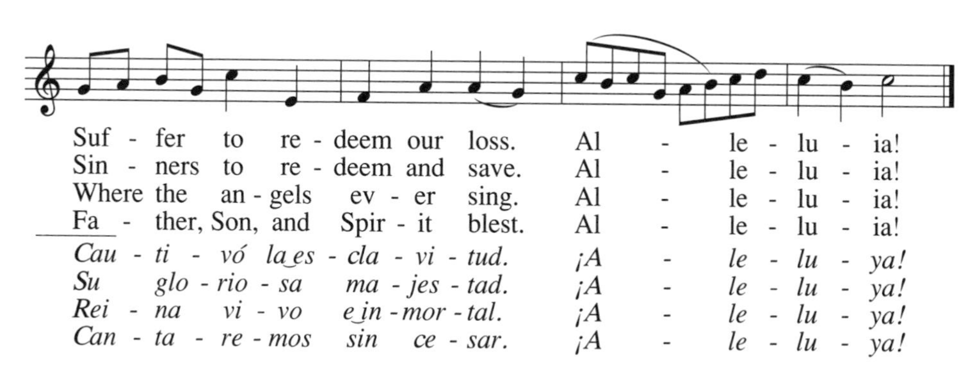
Suf - fer to re - deem our loss. Al - le - lu - ia!
Sin - ners to re - deem and save. Al - le - lu - ia!
Where the an - gels ev - er sing. Al - le - lu - ia!
Fa - ther, Son, and Spir - it blest. Al - le - lu - ia!
Cau - ti - vó la es - cla - vi - tud. ¡A - le - lu - ya!
Su glo - rio - sa ma - jes - tad. ¡A - le - lu - ya!
Rei - na vi - vo e in - mor - tal. ¡A - le - lu - ya!
Can - ta - re - mos sin ce - sar. ¡A - le - lu - ya!

Text: St. 1, *Surrexit Christus hodie*, Latin, 14th C.; para. in *Lyra Davidica*, 1708, alt.; st. 2, 3, *The Compleat Psalmodist*, c.1750, alt.; st. 4, Charles Wesley, 1707-1788, alt.; tr. by Juan Bautista Cabrera, 1837–1916, alt.
Tune: EASTER HYMN, 77 77 with alleluias; *Lyra Davidica*, 1708

As the day of Resurrection, Sunday is not only the remembrance of a past event: it is a celebration of the living presence of the Risen Lord in the midst of his own people.

Dies Domini

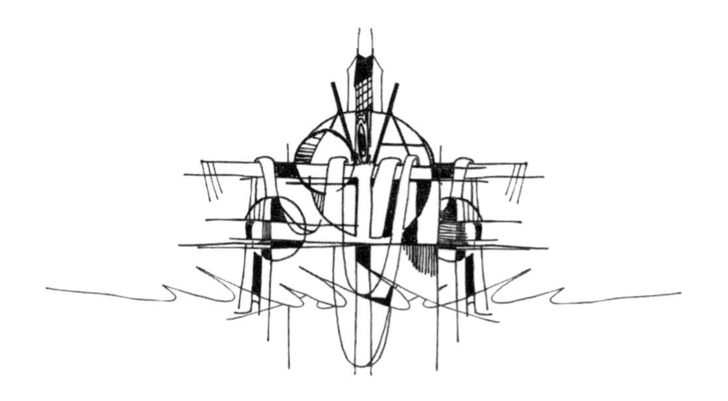

43 He Is Not Here

Verse 1 freely
Solo:
1. The an-gel spoke to the wom-en: "Do not be a-fraid,
If you are look-ing for Je-sus, He is ris-en from the dead!" Al-le -
In tempo ♩ = 80
lu - ia, Al-le-lu - ia, Al-le-lu -
ia, Al-le-lu - ia! He is not
All:
Refrain
(1., 2.) here; he is ris-en from the dead! He is not
(3.) lu - ia! Al - le -
Last time to Coda
here; he is ris-en from the dead! Al-le-lu-
lu - ia!
ia! Al-le-lu - ia! Al-le-lu -
ia! Al-le-lu - ia!
Verse 2
Solo:
2. "Go and tell the world Je-sus lives a-gain, In
Gal - i-lee he prom-is - es to meet you once a - gain!" Al-le -

lu - ia, Al - le - lu - ia, Al - le -
lu - ia, Al - le - lu - ia! 2. He is not
All:
D.S.
Verse 3
Solo:
3. "My peace be with you, You don't have to be a - fraid,
Go and tell the world I have ris - en from the grave!" Al - le -
lu - ia, Al - le - lu - ia, Al - le -
lu - ia, Al - le - lu - ia! 3. Al - le -
All:
D.S.
Coda
ris - en from the dead! Al - le - lu - ia! Al - le - lu -
Repeat 4 times
ia! Al - le - lu - ia! Al - le - lu -
Final Refrain
ia! He is not here; he is ris - en from the dead! He is not
omit last time
here; he is ris - en from the dead! He is not
4

Text: Based on Matthew 28:5–10; Derek Campbell, 1963–2004
Tune: Derek Campbell, 1963–2004

44 This Is the Day

Refrain
This is the day our God has made. This is the day, al - le - lu - ia! This is the day our God has made.
This is the day that our God has made for us!
Verses 1–4
1. Liv - ing wa - ter, you flow in us, giv - ing hope and e - ter - nal life; wash - ing all of our fears a - way; to nev - er be thirs - ty, nev - er be lone - ly a - gain.
2. O - pen arms, you have set us free, o - pen eyes, you have made us see; o - pen hearts so the blind be - lieve and nev - er see dark - ness, nev - er see hun - ger a - gain.
3. Glo - ry rolled the stone a - way, Ho - ly Spir - it, un - bind our way; and we trust in your word to - day; to nev - er know sick - ness, nev - er know death a - gain.
4. Dy - ing, your love has con - quered death, ris - ing, your grace has raised us up; we sing of your sal - va - tion that leads us to free - dom, leads us to glo - ry a - gain.
D.C.

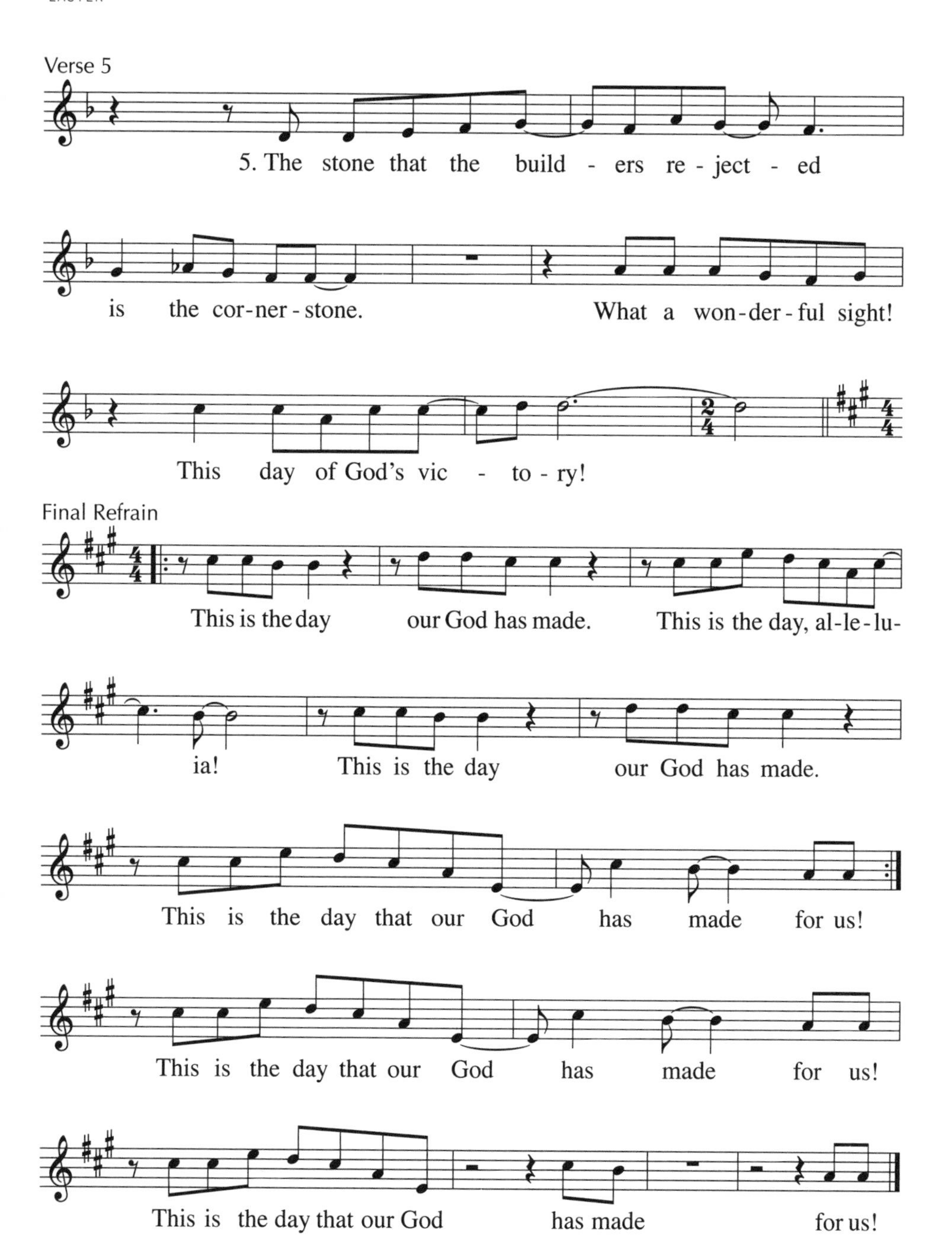
Verse 5
5. The stone that the build - ers re - ject - ed
is the cor-ner-stone.
What a won-der-ful sight!
This day of God's vic - to - ry!
Final Refrain
This is the day our God has made.
This is the day, al-le-lu-
ia!
This is the day our God has made.
This is the day that our God has made for us!
This is the day that our God has made for us!
This is the day that our God has made for us!

Text: Based on Psalm 118, John 4:14–15, 9:5, 11:25–26, 40–44; Chris de Silva, b.1967
Tune: Chris de Silva, b.1967

45 Let the River Flow

Verse
Let the poor man say, "I am rich in him." Let the
blind man say, "I can see a-gain." Let the
lost man say, "I am found in him." Oh,
dead man say, "I am born a-gain." Oh,
let the riv-er flow.
First time only:
Let the
Oh, let the riv-er flow.
Refrain
Let the riv-er flow. Let the riv-er flow.
Ho-ly Spir-it, come; move in pow-er. Let the
riv-er flow. Let the riv-er flow. Let the
riv-er flow. Let the riv-er flow.
1., 3.
7
D.C.
2.
D.S.

Text: Darrel Evans
Tune: Darrel Evans; arr. by Ed Bolduc, b.1969

SEND DOWN THE FIRE 46
Refrain
Send down the fire of your jus - tice,
Send down the rains of your love; Come,
send down the Spir - it, breathe life in your peo - ple, and
we shall be peo - ple of God.
Verses
1. Call us to be your com - pas - sion,
2. Call us to learn of your mer - cy,
3. Call us to an - swer op - pres - sion,
4. Call us to wit - ness your King - dom,
Teach us the song of your love; Give us
Teach us the way of your peace; Give us
Teach us the fire of your truth; Give us
Give us the pres - ence of Christ; May your
hearts that sing, Give us deeds that ring, Make us
hearts that feel, Give us hands that heal, Make us
right - eous souls, 'Til your jus - tice rolls, Make us
ho - ly light Keep us shin - ing bright, Ev - er
ring with the song of your love.
walk in the way of your peace.
burn with the fire of your truth.
shine with the pres - ence of Christ.
D.C.

Text: Marty Haugen, b.1950
Tune: Marty Haugen, b.1950

47 hallmark songs of our faith

COME, HOLY GHOST

The words of "Come, Holy Ghost" *(no. 48)* have been prayed through the ages to ask God's Spirit to come upon his people. The words are based on an ancient Latin text, "Veni, Creator Spiritus," dating back to the ninth century. Belgian Jesuit composer Louis Lambillotte wrote the lilting tune in the mid 1800s. This is the "hymn du jour" of the Church for any Masses celebrating the Holy Spirit, especially Pentecost, the sacrament of confirmation and Mass of the Holy Spirit (the Mass that traditionally marks the beginning of the academic year at a Catholic school). *TA*

48 COME, HOLY GHOST / EN NUESTRO SER MORA, CREADOR

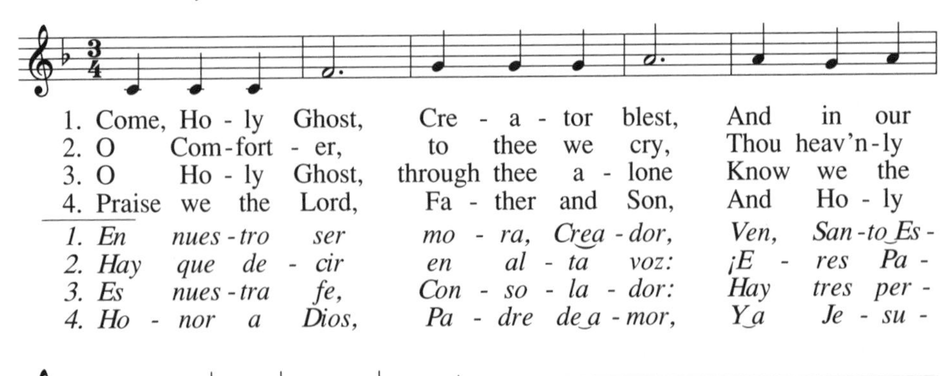
1. Come, Ho - ly Ghost, Cre - a - tor blest, And in our
2. O Com-fort - er, to thee we cry, Thou heav'n-ly
3. O Ho - ly Ghost, through thee a - lone Know we the
4. Praise we the Lord, Fa - ther and Son, And Ho - ly
1. En nues - tro ser mo - ra, Crea - dor, Ven, San - to Es -
2. Hay que de - cir en al - ta voz: ¡E - res Pa -
3. Es nues - tra fe, Con - so - la - dor: Hay tres per -
4. Ho - nor a Dios, Pa - dre de a - mor, Ya Je - su -

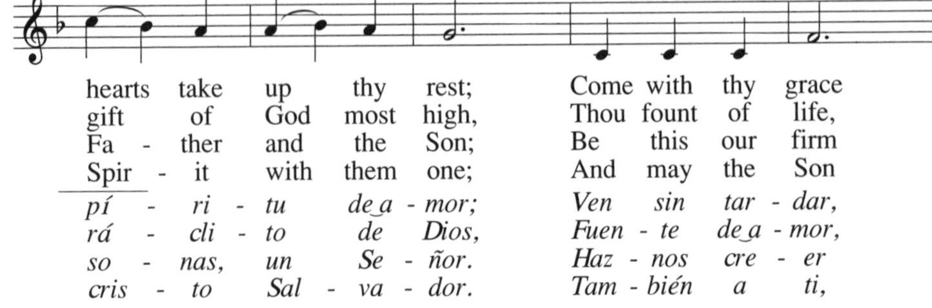
hearts take up thy rest; Come with thy grace
gift of God most high, Thou fount of life,
Fa - ther and the Son; Be this our firm
Spir - it with them one; And may the Son
pí - ri - tu de a - mor; Ven sin tar - dar,
rá - cli - to de Dios, Fuen - te de a - mor,
so - nas, un Se - ñor. Haz - nos cre - er
cris - to Sal - va - dor. Tam - bién a ti,

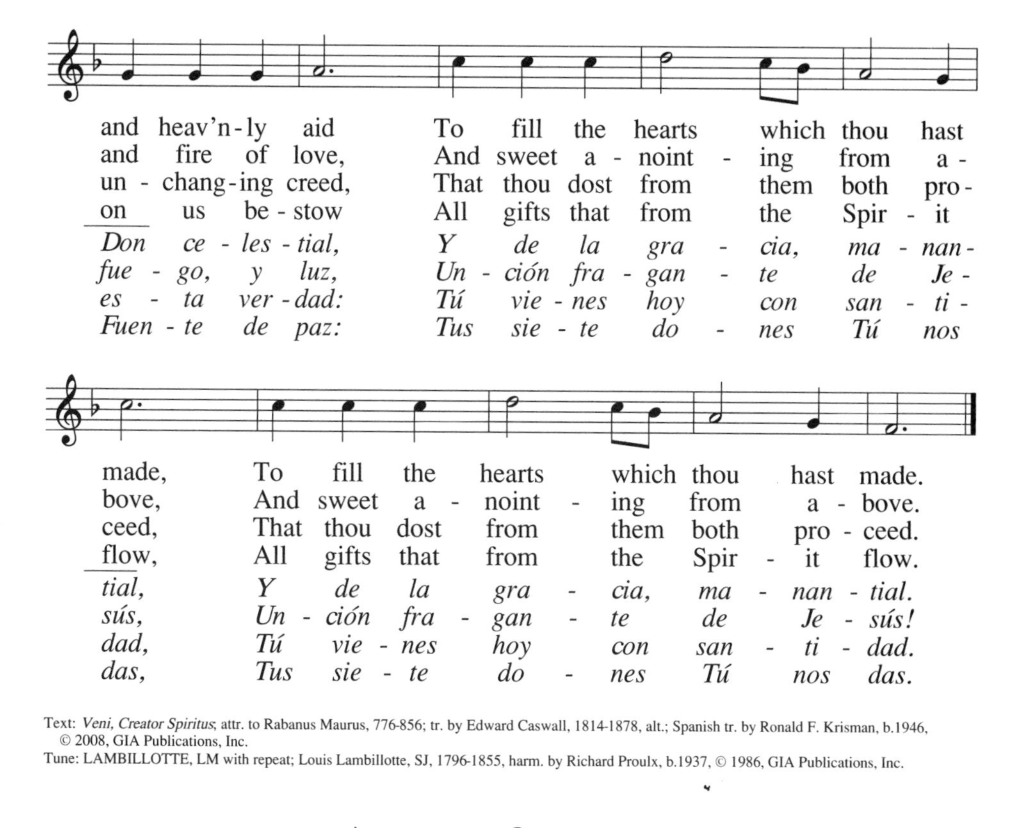
and heav'n-ly aid To fill the hearts which thou hast made, To fill the hearts which thou hast made.
and fire of love, And sweet a-noint-ing from a-bove, And sweet a-noint-ing from a-bove.
un-chang-ing creed, That thou dost from them both pro-ceed, That thou dost from them both pro-ceed.
on us be-stow All gifts that from the Spir-it flow, All gifts that from the Spir-it flow.
Don ce-les-tial, Y de la gra-cia, ma-nan-tial, Y de la gra-cia, ma-nan-tial.
fue-go, y luz, Un-ción fra-gan-te de Je-sús, Un-ción fra-gan-te de Je-sús!
es-ta ver-dad: Tú vie-nes hoy con san-ti-dad, Tú vie-nes hoy con san-ti-dad.
Fuen-te de paz: Tus sie-te do-nes Tú nos das, Tus sie-te do-nes Tú nos das.

Text: *Veni, Creator Spiritus*; attr. to Rabanus Maurus, 776-856; tr. by Edward Caswall, 1814-1878, alt.; Spanish tr. by Ronald F. Krisman, b.1946, © 2008, GIA Publications, Inc.
Tune: LAMBILLOTTE, LM with repeat; Louis Lambillotte, SJ, 1796-1855, harm. by Richard Proulx, b.1937, © 1986, GIA Publications, Inc.

Living Spirit, Holy Fire 49

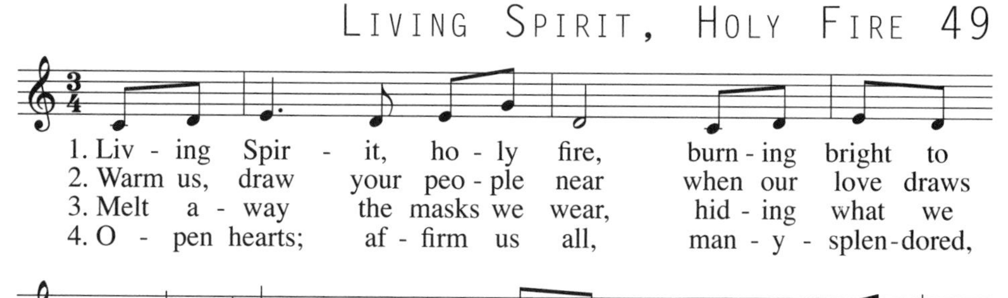
1. Liv-ing Spir-it, ho-ly fire, burn-ing bright to
2. Warm us, draw your peo-ple near when our love draws
3. Melt a-way the masks we wear, hid-ing what we
4. O-pen hearts; af-firm us all, man-y-splen-dored,

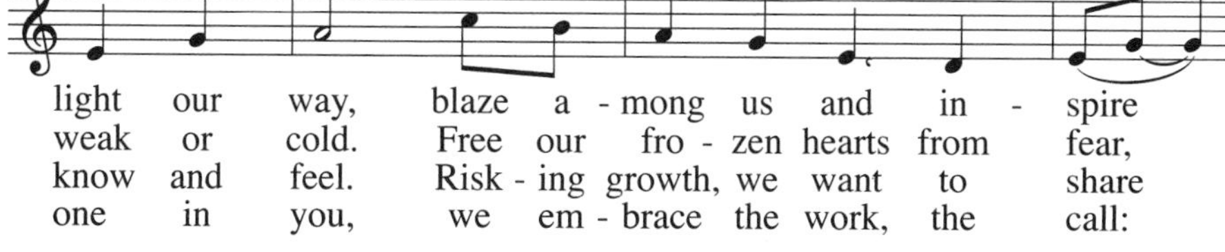
light our way, blaze a-mong us and in-spire
weak or cold. Free our fro-zen hearts from fear,
know and feel. Risk-ing growth, we want to share
one in you, we em-brace the work, the call:

lives that praise you day by day.
that each sto-ry may be told.
love in ac-tion, love that's real.
You are mak-ing all things new.

Text: Ruth Duck, b.1947, © 2005, GIA Publications, Inc.
Tune: Lori True, b.1961, © 2007, GIA Publications, Inc.

50 our heritage of song

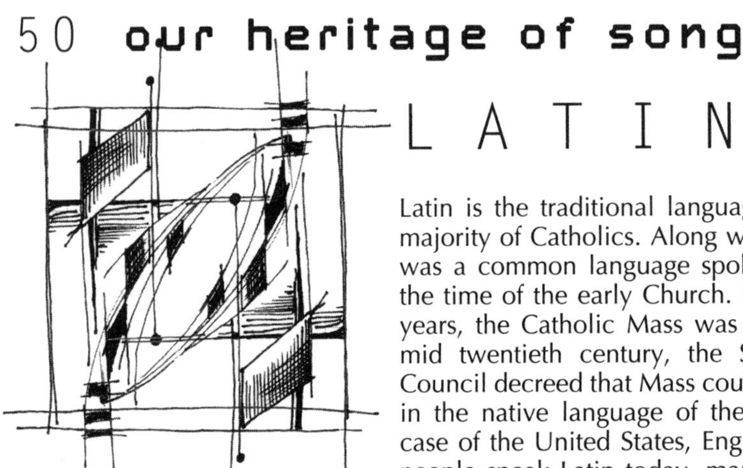

LATIN

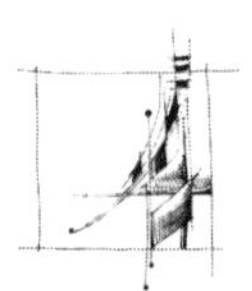

Latin is the traditional language for the great majority of Catholics. Along with Greek, Latin was a common language spoken in Rome in the time of the early Church. For hundreds of years, the Catholic Mass was in Latin. In the mid twentieth century, the Second Vatican Council decreed that Mass could be celebrated in the native language of the people (in the case of the United States, English). While few people speak Latin today, many of the words we sing at liturgy are translations of original Latin texts sung through the history of our Church. Many churches still sing some hymns or acclamations in Latin. The Lamb of God (Agnus Dei in Latin), among others, is still often chanted in Latin, connecting us with our long heritage. *TA*

51 Veni, Creator Spiritus

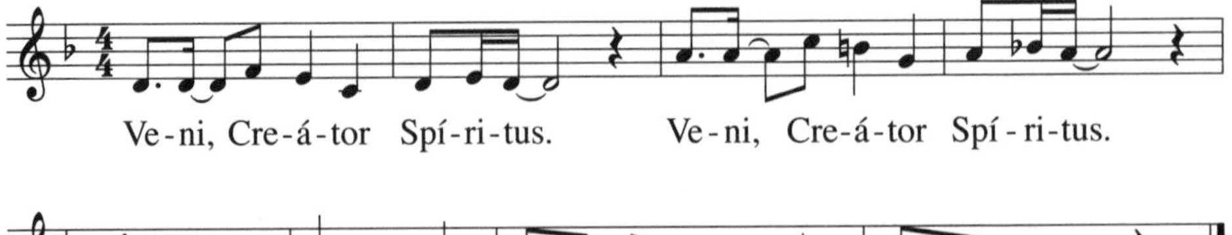
Ve-ni, Cre-á-tor Spí-ri-tus. Ve-ni, Cre-á-tor Spí-ri-tus.

Ve - ni, ve - ni, ve - ni Cre - á - tor Spí - ri - tus.

Text: *Veni, Creator Spiritus*
Tune: John Angotti, b.1963; arr. by Ed Bolduc, b.1969 and John Angotti, © 2004, World Library Publications

COME, HOLY SPIRIT 52

Refrain

Come, Ho - ly Spir-it, send down your fire. Come fill your peo-ple, re-

new and in-spire. We are your chil - dren who long to see your

face, con-firmed in one bap-tis-m, one hope, one Lord, one faith.

Verses

1. We shall not travel on this road alone.
   We need not fear the darkness,
   for you have sent your fire to light our way
   until we see you again.

2. Called to be merciful for the oppressed,
   called now to be Christ for the poor.
   Send down your Spirit, Lord; make us anew.
   Teach us to be your living sign.

3. Veni, Sancte Spiritus, send down your fire.
   Veni, Sancte Spiritus, come, Holy Spirit, come.
   Come, Holy Spirit, Veni, Sancte Spiritus, send down your fire.
   Veni, Sancte Spiritus, come, Holy Spirit, come.

Text: John Angotti, b.1963
Tune: John Angotti, b.1963; arr. by Ed Bolduc, b.1969

53 All Who Are Led by the Spirit

Refrain
All who are led by the Spir-it of Je-sus,
Last time: We who are led by the Spir-it of Je-sus,
all those who walk in the foot-steps of Christ,
we who will walk in the foot-steps of Christ,
all those who fol-low where Love may lead them are the
we who will fol-low where Love may lead us are the
Last time
sons and the daugh-ters, the chil-dren of God.
sons and the daugh-ters, the chil-dren of God.
3
Verses
1. The Spir-it of God is no spir-it of slav-'ry;
2. The Spir-it of God bids us cry, "Ab-ba, Fa-ther";
3. The Spir-it of God gives us pa-tience in suf-f'ring;
4. The Spir-it of God groans with all of cre-a-tion;
the Spir-it of God
drives all fear from our hearts;
makes a home in our hearts;
in-ter-cedes for our needs;
bless-es dreams from the past;
the
Spir-it of God
shat-ters all that would bind us.
helps our spir-its bear wit-ness.
is our prom-ise of glo-ry:
sets a vi-sion be-fore us:
The

D.C.
Spir-it of God makes us chil-dren of God.

Text: Based on Romans 8; Michael Joncas, b.1951
Tune: Michael Joncas, b.1951

SPIRIT OF GOD 54

Refrain
Spir - it of God, who dwells in me, O - pen my
eyes that I may see. Come fill my heart
and make me whole. Spir - it of God, I am yours.
Verses
1. This is the Spir-it of the liv-ing God,
2. Come, Ho - ly Spir-it, and set me free
Who hears your ev - 'ry sin-gle prayer. O
To do the best I can. O
this is the Spir - it of the liv - ing God,
come, Ho - ly Spir - it, and set me free
Who is al - ways right there.
To be all that I am.
D.C.

Text: James E. Moore, Jr., b.1951
Tune: James E. Moore, Jr., b.1951

55 Breath of Life

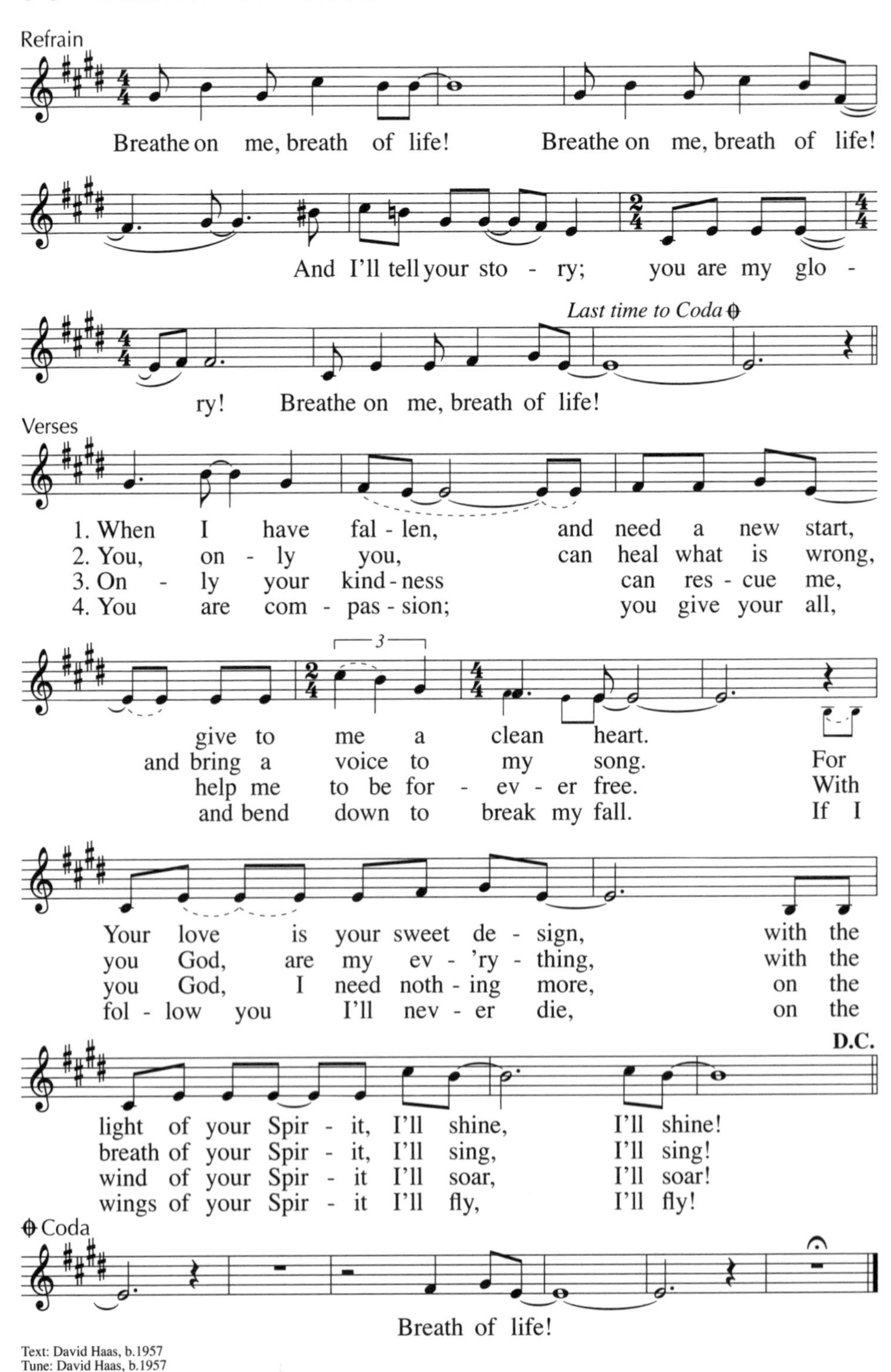
Refrain
Breathe on me, breath of life! Breathe on me, breath of life!
And I'll tell your sto - ry; you are my glo -
ry! Breathe on me, breath of life!
Last time to Coda
Verses
1. When I have fal - len, and need a new start, give to me a clean heart.
2. You, on - ly you, can heal what is wrong, and bring a voice to my song. For
3. On - ly your kind - ness can res - cue me, help me to be for - ev - er free. With
4. You are com - pas - sion; you give your all, and bend down to break my fall. If I
Your love is your sweet de - sign, with the light of your Spir - it, I'll shine, I'll shine!
you God, are my ev - 'ry - thing, with the breath of your Spir - it, I'll sing, I'll sing!
you God, I need noth - ing more, on the wind of your Spir - it I'll soar, I'll soar!
fol - low you I'll nev - er die, on the wings of your Spir - it I'll fly, I'll fly!
D.C.
Coda
Breath of life!

Text: David Haas, b.1957
Tune: David Haas, b.1957

To Know Darkness 56

1. God, our Fa - ther, we long to see you as you are. If we
2. O Christ Je - sus, we long to see you face to face. If we
3. Ho - ly Spir-it, we long to see you in our lives. If we
seek you in the heav-ens, in stars, in the sky, you are
seek you in each per - son, in each hu - man heart, you are
seek you in our be - ing, in each liv - ing soul, you are
there. Lights of our own cre - a - tion may
there. Lights of our own cre - a - tion may
there. Lights of our own cre - a - tion may
keep us from know - ing your pres - ence a - bove. God our
keep us from know - ing your pres - ence be - low. O Christ
keep us from know - ing your pres - ence with - in. Ho - ly
Fa - ther, help us to know dark - ness so that
Je - sus, help us to know dark - ness so that
Spir - it, help us to know dark - ness so that
1. D.C. 2., 3. 3
we may see your light.
we may see your light.
we may see your light.

Text: Orin Johnson, b.1973
Tune: Orin Johnson, b.1973

57 Let There Be Light

Refrain
Ho - ly and bless - ed Three, glo - ri - ous Trin - i - ty:
Wis - dom, Love, and Might! Let there be light! Let there be light!
Verses 1, 2
1. You, whose al - might - y word cha - os and dark - ness heard.
2. Hope for all you bring, on your re - deem - ing wing.
Let there be light! Vic - tor of sin and death,
Let there be light! Dawn out of sin - ful night,
D.C.
giv - er of ho - ly breath. Let there be light!
mak - ing the dark - ness bright. Let there be light!
Verse 3
3. Spir - it of truth and love, life - giv - ing Ho - ly Dove.
Let there be light! Bring - er of ho - ly fire,
aim of our heart's de - sire. Let there be light!
Final Refrain
Solo, last time:
Ho - ly and bless - ed Three, glo - ri - ous Trin - i -

ty: Wis - dom, Love, and Might! Let there be light! Let there be
light! Oh, let there be light!

Text: John Marriott, 1780–1825; adapt. by Paul Melley
Tune: Paul Melley

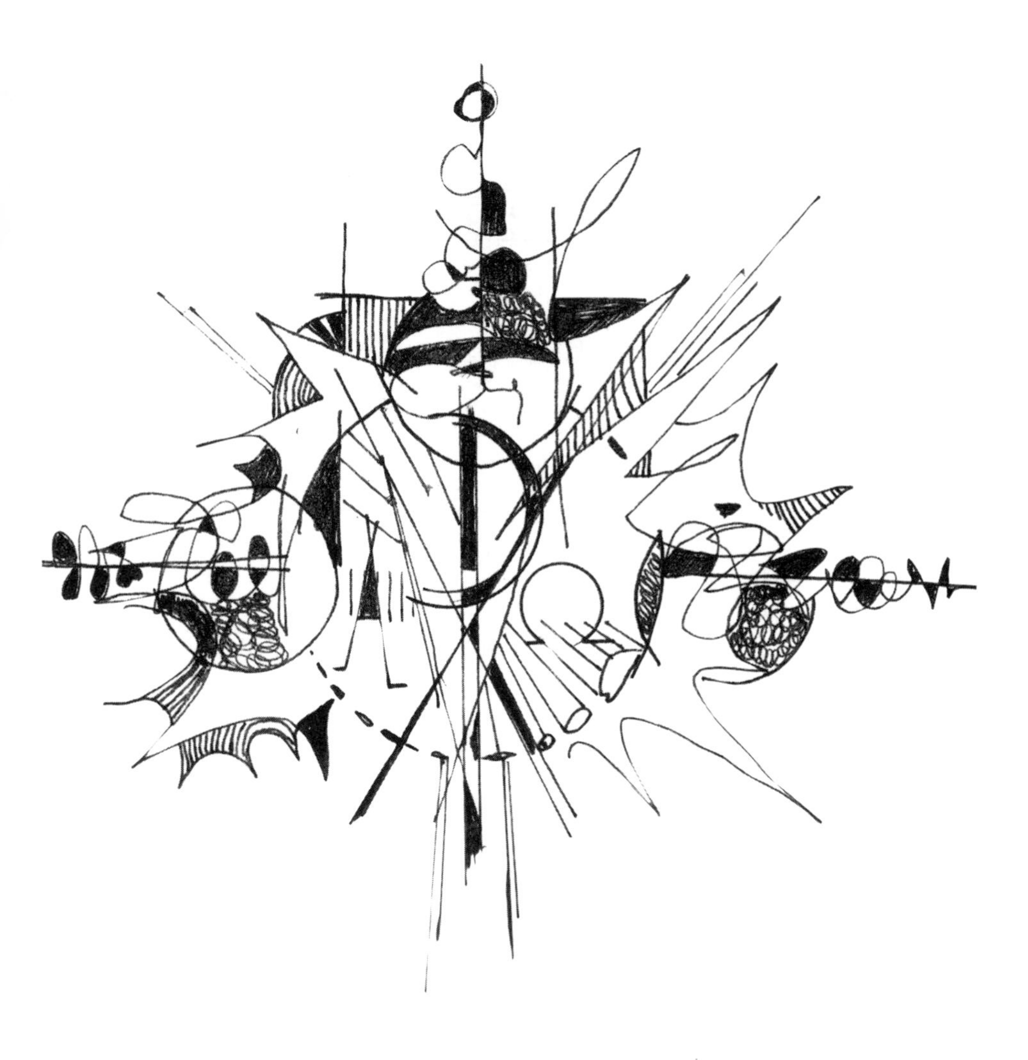

58 Alleluia! Give the Glory

Refrain
Al - le - lu - ia! Al - le - lu - ia! Al - le -
lu - ia! Give the glo - ry and the
1.
hon - or to the Lord!
2.
glo - ry and the hon - or to the Lord!

Text: Matthew 18:20, John 15:5; adapt. by Ken Canedo and Bob Hurd
Music: Ken Canedo; choral arr. by Craig S. Kingsbury; acc. by Dominic MacAller

59 Gospel Acclamation

Refrain
Al - le - lu - ia, al - le - lu - ia, al - le - lu - ia!

Text: English trans. of verses for Ordinary Time, Easter, and Pentecost from the *Lectionary for Mass*, © 1968, 1981, 1997, ICEL
Music: Stephen Pishner, © 2002, GIA Publications, Inc.

Alleluia: Song of the Spirit 60

Refrain
Cantor:
Al - le - lu - ia,
Assembly:
al - le - lu - ia,
Cantor:
al - le - lu - ia,
Assembly:
al - le - lu - ia,
Cantor:
al - le - lu - ia, al - le - lu - ia,
Assembly:
al - le - lu - ia, al - le - lu - ia.
Verse Responses
I, II
Al - le - lu - ia,
III
al - le - lu - ia, al - le - lu - ia.
D.C.

Text: Tony E. Alonso
Music: Based on LAMBILLOTTE, Louis Lambillotte, SJ, 1796–1855; adapt. by Tony E. Alonso

The Christian should be an Alleluia from head to foot.

Augustine of Hippo

61 our heritage of song

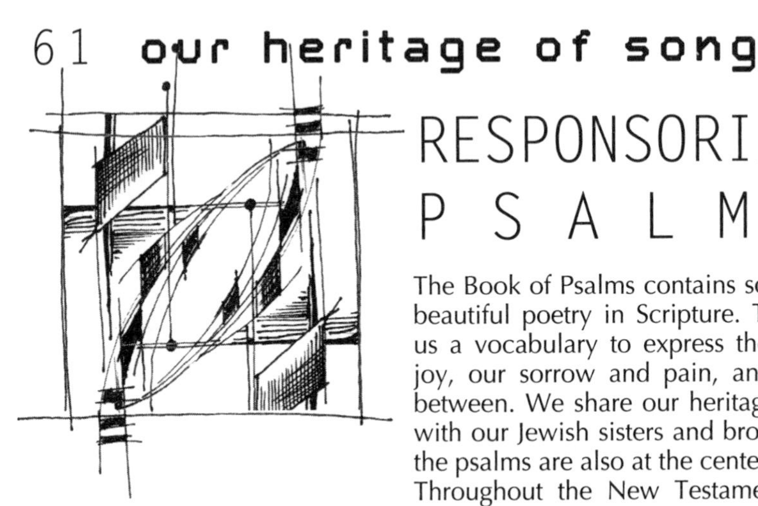

RESPONSORIAL PSALM

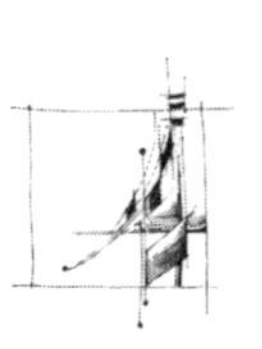

The Book of Psalms contains some of the most beautiful poetry in Scripture. The psalms give us a vocabulary to express the depths of our joy, our sorrow and pain, and everything in between. We share our heritage of the psalms with our Jewish sisters and brothers, for whom the psalms are also at the center of their liturgy. Throughout the New Testament, we witness Jesus praying the psalms as part of his own prayer life.

Following the first reading at Mass, we join in the singing of a psalm. Most commonly, the assembly sings a refrain and a cantor sings the verses. This psalm is strongly connected to the liturgical season and the Scriptures of the Mass. When we go to pray on our own throughout the week, we don't need to invent new prayers all the time! The psalms are prayers we can carry with us, giving us a way to converse with God. Consider making the psalm you sing at Mass a part of your prayer life during the week. *TA*

62 Psalm 18: I Love You, Lord, My Strength

Refrain

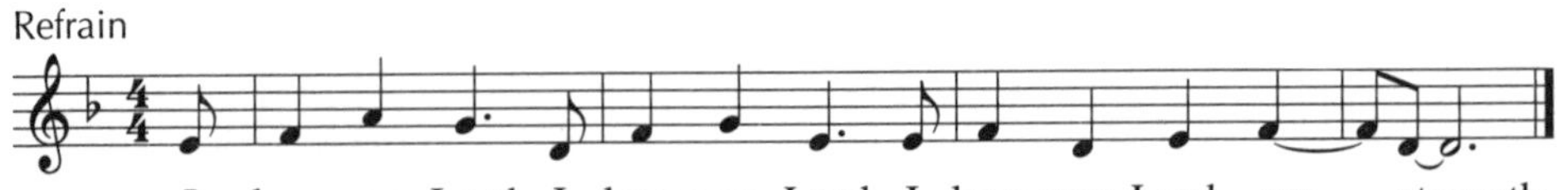
I love you, Lord, I love you, Lord, I love you, Lord, my strength.

Verses

1. I love you, O Lord, my strength,
   O Lord, my rock, my fortress, my deliverer.

2. My God, my rock of refuge,
   my shield, the horn of my salvation, my stronghold!
   Praised be the Lord, I exclaim,
   and I am safe from my enemies.

3. The Lord lives and blessed be my rock!
   Extolled be God, my Savior.
   You who gave great vict'ries to your king
   and showed kindness to your anointed.

our greatest gift, the Eucharist 63

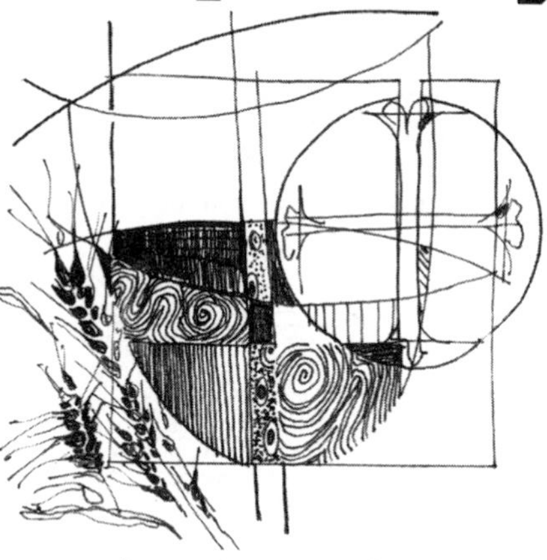

WORD

After the introductory rites have gathered us as a community, we are ready to hear God's Word. During the Liturgy of the Word, we hear the first reading (usually from the Old Testament), the second reading (from the New Testament), and the gospel (from one of the four evangelists). There are moments of silence following each of the first two readings to allow for reflection. Between the first two readings, we join in the singing of a psalm. Before the gospel, we sing an acclamation (Alleluia, except in Lent). The first reading, psalm, and gospel are always bound together by common images and emphases.

After we have listened attentively to the Scriptures and prayed the psalm, the homilist (usually the presider) weaves together the Scriptures with the life of the world and the community to make them come alive and summon us to deeper Christian living. The Liturgy of the Word continues with the Creed (Profession of Faith) and concludes with the general intercessions. In the general intercessions we pray for the needs of the Church, the world, and the community (including members who are ill or who are deceased). The sharing of Scripture in the Liturgy of the Word, along with what we are about to do in the Liturgy of the Eucharist, is at the heart of our celebration. *TA*

Psalm 19: Lord, You Have the Words 64

Refrain

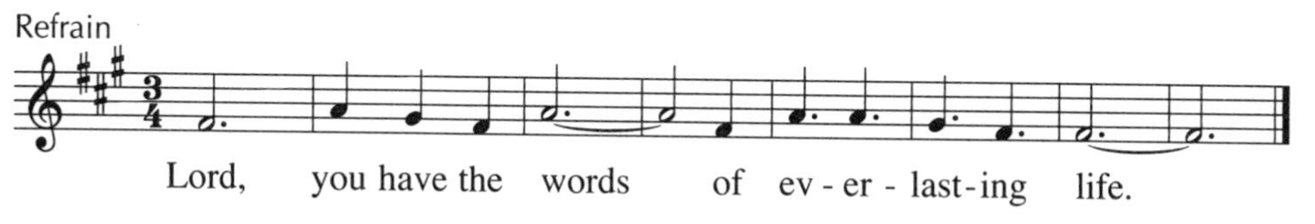
Lord, you have the words of ev - er - last-ing life.

Verses

1. The law of the Lord is perfect, refreshing the soul;
   the decree of the Lord is trustworthy, giving wisdom to the simple.

2. The precepts of the Lord are right, rejoicing the heart;
   the command of the Lord is clear, enlight'ning the eye.

3. The fear of the Lord is pure, enduring forever;
   the ordinances of the Lord are true, all of them just.

4. They are more precious than gold, than a heap of purest gold;
   sweeter also than syrup or honey from the comb.

65 Psalm 25: I Lift My Soul to You

Refrain
I lift my soul to you, O Lord. To you I lift my hands, I lift my heart, my soul. I lift my soul to you, O Lord. To you I lift my hands, I lift my heart, my soul.

Verses

1. Lord, make me know your ways, keep me on your path.
   Walk with me in your truth and teach me.
   You save my life, you are my song.

2. Your ways are good and just.
   You find the lost, you lead the humble to righteousness.
   You help the poor to find the way.

3. You hold true to your promise,
   your friendship is with those who keep your covenant.
   Let us humbly walk in your name.
   Forgive the past and wash away our guilt.

Text: Psalm 25; Lori True
Music: Lori True; acc. by Paul A. Tate

Psalm 25: To You, O Lord, I Lift My Soul 66

Refrain
To you, O Lord, I lift my soul.
Last time to Coda
Last time*
To you, O Lord, I lift my soul.
Coda (optional)
I lift my soul! I lift my soul! I lift my soul, lift my soul.
I lift my soul to you, to you O
1.
Lord, I lift my soul.
2.
Lord, I lift my soul, To you, O Lord, I lift my soul.

Verses

1. Your ways, O Lord, make known to me; teach me your paths,
   guide me in your truth and teach me, for you are God my Savior,
   and for you I wait all the day.

2. Good and upright is the Lord; thus he shows sinners the way.
   He guides the humble to justice, and teaches the humble his way.

3. All the paths of the Lord are kindness and constancy
   toward those who keep his covenant and his decrees.
   The friendship of the Lord is with those who fear him,
   and his covenant, for their instruction.

If not using optional Coda

67 Psalm 25: To You, O God, I Lift Up My Soul

Refrain

To you, O God, I lift up my soul; lift up my

spir-it to my Lord. To you I lift up my soul.

Verses

1. Make me to know your ways, O God;
   teach me your paths, guide me.
   You are my savior.

2. Good and upright our gracious God,
   showing the way,
   guiding the humble to justice.

3. Steadfast and kind your ways, O God;
   all who revere your covenant know your friendship.

Text: Based on Psalm 25:1, 4–5, 8–9, 10, 14; Bob Hurd
Music: Bob Hurd; acc. by Dominic MacAller

68 Psalm 33: The Earth Is Full of the Goodness

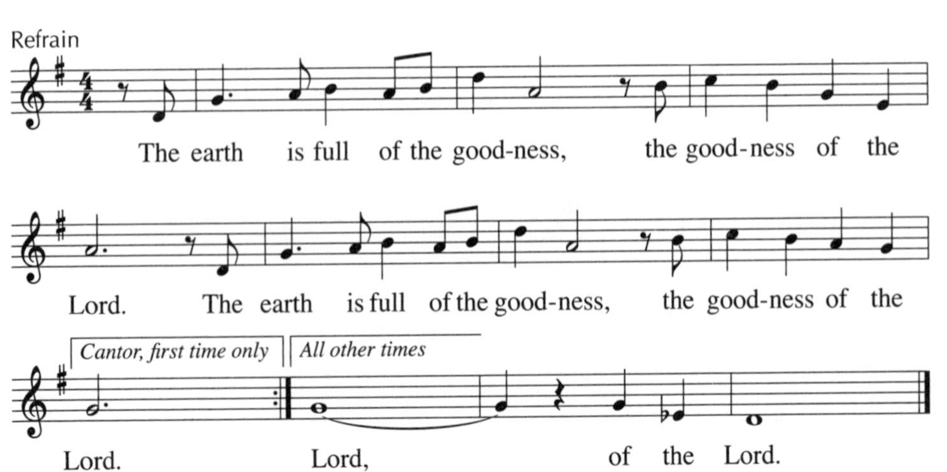
Refrain
The earth is full of the good-ness, the good-ness of the
Lord. The earth is full of the good-ness, the good-ness of the
Cantor, first time only
All other times
Lord. Lord, of the Lord.

Verses

1. Blessed the nation whose God is the LORD,
   the people he has chosen for his own inheritance.
   But see, the eyes of the LORD are upon those who fear him,
   upon those who hope for his kindness.

2. Our soul waits for the LORD, who is our help and our shield,
   For in him our hearts rejoice; in his holy name we trust.

3. May your kindness, O LORD, be upon us
   who have put our hope in you.

PSALM 34: I WILL BLESS THE LORD AT ALL TIMES 69

Refrain

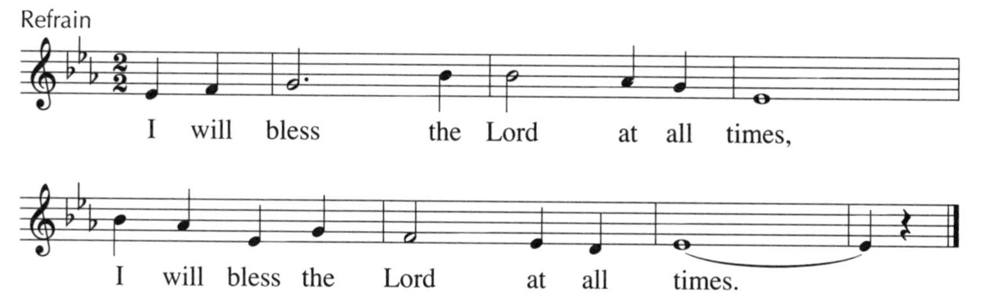
I will bless the Lord at all times,
I will bless the Lord at all times.

Verses

1. I will bless the LORD at all times;
   his praise shall be ever in my mouth.
   Let my soul glory in the LORD;
   the lowly will hear me and be glad.

2. Glorify the LORD with me,
   let us together extol his name.
   I sought the LORD, and he answered me
   and delivered me from all my fears.

3. Look to him that you may be radiant with joy,
   and your faces may not blush with shame.
   When the poor one called out, the LORD heard,
   and from all his distress he saved him.

70 Psalm 40: Here I Am

Refrain

Here I am, here I am, I come to do your will.
Here I am, here I am, I come to do your will.

Verses

1. I waited for God, who bent down to hear me.
   God put a new song in my mouth,
   a hymn of praise!

2. You did not seek offerings or sacrifice.
   You opened my eyes to see, my ears to hear.
   Yes, I will come to do your will!

3. I proclaim your greatness, Lord, to all those around me.
   My lips are not sealed, never holding back the story.
   You know this is true, I come to do your will!

Text: Psalm 40:2, 4, 7, 10; Tony E. Alonso
Music: Tony E. Alonso

71 Psalm 47: God Mounts His Throne

Refrain

Ascension: God mounts his throne to shouts of joy:
Common: God mounts his throne to shouts of joy,
a blare of trum - pets for the Lord.
to shouts, to shouts of joy.
3

Verses

1. All you peoples, clap your hands,
   shout to God, shout to God with cries of gladness.
   For the Lord the Most High, the awesome,
   is the great king over all the earth.

2. God mounts his throne amid shouts of joy;
the LORD, amid trumpet blasts.
Sing praise to God, to God, sing praise;
sing praise to our king, sing praise.

3. For king of all the earth is God;
sing hymns of praise.
God reigns over all the nations,
God sits upon his holy throne.

Psalm 63: My Soul Is Thirsting 72

Refrains
I My soul is thirst - ing for you, O Lord, thirst - ing for you, my God. My soul is thirst - ing for you, O Lord, thirst - ing for you, my God, thirst - ing for you, my God.
II As morn - ing breaks I look to you; be my strength this day. As morn - ing breaks I look to you; be my strength this day, be my strength this day.

Verses

1. O God, you are my God, and I will always praise you.
In the shadow of your wings I cling to you and you hold me high.

2. Through the day you walk with me; all the night your love surrounds me.
To the glory of your name I lift my hands, I sing your praise.

3. I will never be afraid, for I will not be abandoned.
Even when the road grows long and weary your love will rescue me.

73 PSALM 72: EVERY NATION ON EARTH

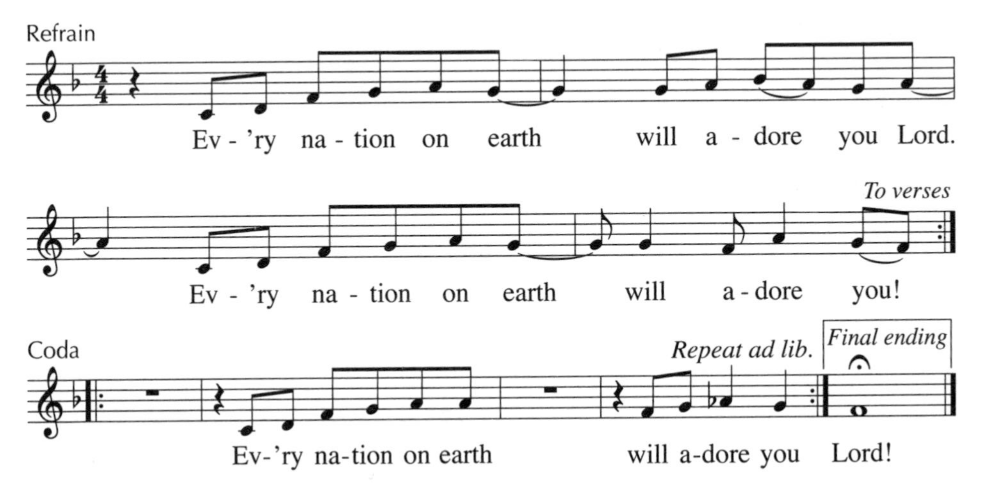
Refrain
Ev - 'ry na - tion on earth will a - dore you Lord.
To verses
Ev - 'ry na - tion on earth will a - dore you!
Coda
Repeat ad lib.
Final ending
Ev-'ry na-tion on earth will a-dore you Lord!

Verses

1. O God, give your judgment to the king and to his son
   that they govern with grace, and bring justice to the poor.
   May the mountains and hills bring forth justice and peace.
   May the king defend the poor and save their children!

2. You will rescue the poor when they cry out for help.
   You pity the weak and save them all from death.
   The lives of the pris'ners are precious in your sight.
   They will pray for you always and bless you all the day!

3. Like the sun and the moon, you endure from age to age,
   your mercy descending like raindrops on the earth.
   Justice shall flourish abundant all our days,
   and peace overflow 'til the moon falls from the sky.

4. Blessed be the Lord, the God of Israel,
   for only with God can all of this be done.
   Ever blessed be our God's fantastic name.
   May the glory of the Lord fill the earth. Amen!

Text: Psalm 72:1–7, 12–15, 17–19; Michael Mahler
Music: Michael Mahler

Psalm 85: Lord, Show Us Your Mercy and Love 74

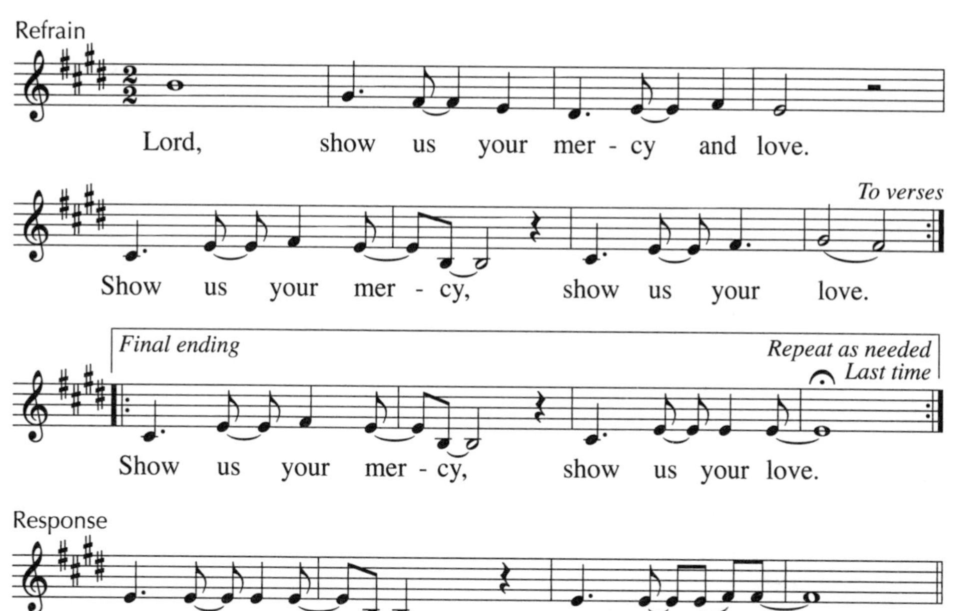
Refrain
Lord, show us your mer - cy and love.
To verses
Show us your mer - cy, show us your love.
Final ending
Repeat as needed
Last time
Show us your mer - cy, show us your love.
Response
Show us your mer - cy. show us your love.

Verses

1. I will hear what you proclaim: words of peace for all. *Response*
   You are always near to those who seek salvation. *Response*

2. How your glory fills the earth, flowing through our land! *Response*
   Kindness and truth shall meet, peace and justice kiss. *Response*

3. Fountains of truth shall spring up fresh from the earth. *Response*
   Justice shall smile upon the earth from up in heaven. *Response*

4. You provide ev'rything we need.
   Oh, you provide a land that gives us food.
   Holy God let justice walk before you,
   and peace will light the way.

75 Psalm 85: Let Us See Your Kindness

Refrain
Lord, let us see your kind - ness,
Final ending
and grant us your sal - va - tion.

Verses

1. I will hear what God proclaims;
   the Lord— for he proclaims peace.
   Near indeed is his salvation to those who fear him,
   glory dwelling in our land.

2. Kindness and truth shall meet;
   justice and peace shall kiss.
   Truth shall spring out of the earth,
   and justice shall look down from heaven.

3. The Lord himself will give his benefits;
   our land shall yield its increase.
   Justice shall walk before him,
   and prepare the way of his steps.

...reason and faith go hand in hand, and the concept of a holy war is...against the nature of God.

Benedict XVI

Psalm 96: Sing a Song to the Lord 76

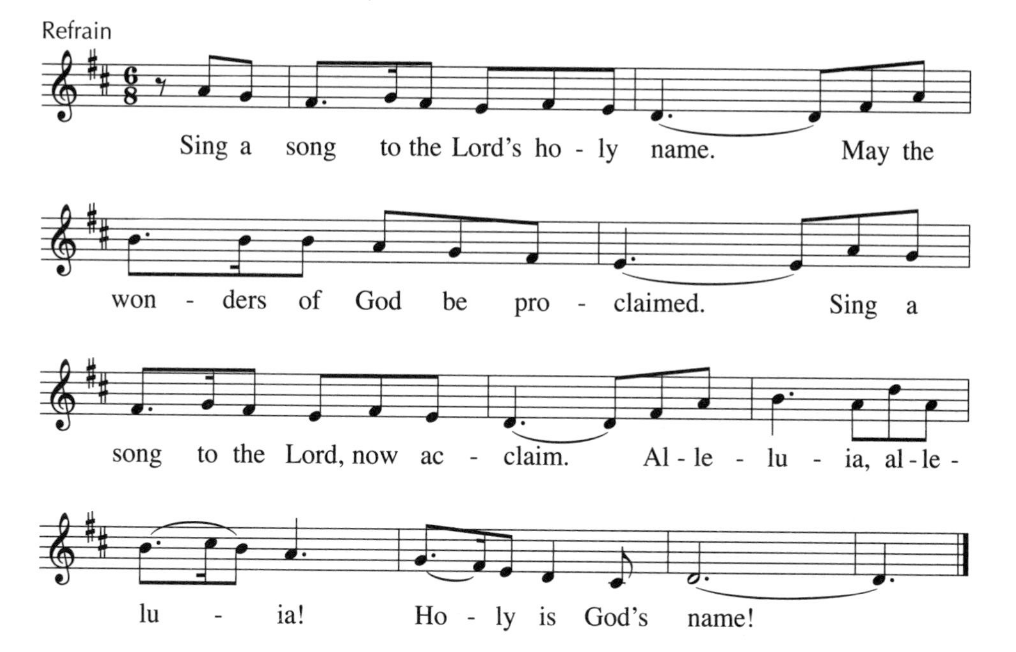
Refrain
Sing a song to the Lord's ho - ly name. May the
won - ders of God be pro - claimed. Sing a
song to the Lord, now ac - claim. Al - le - lu - ia, al - le -
lu - ia! Ho - ly is God's name!

Verses

1. Give the Lord, you families of people, give the Lord glory and power.
   Give the Lord a heart that is grateful. Let us tell of the glory of God.

2. Tell the world our God rules with justice. Tell the world its praises to sing.
   Tell the world God's people know fairness. Let our voices proclaim God is King.

3. Day by day we count on God's blessings. Day by day we seek for God's strength.
   Day by day may love be our lesson. May our wonder of God have no end.

Text: Psalm 96; Liam Lawton
Music: Liam Lawton; arr. by John McCann

77 Psalm 96: Proclaim God's Marvelous Deeds

Antiphon

Pro - claim God's mar-vel-ous deeds. Pro - claim God's mar-vel-ous deeds.

Oh! Pro - claim God's mar-vel-ous deeds to all the na - tions.

Verses

1. Sing a new song to the Lord!
   Ev'ryone on this earth, sing praises to the Lord,
   sing and praise his name.
   Ev'rybody singing!

2. Announce his salvation day after day.
   Tell his glory among the nations,
   among all people his wondrous deeds.
   Ev'rybody singing!

3. Say among the nations the Lord is King.
   He has made the world firm, not to be moved.
   He governs the people, the people with equity.
   Ev'rybody singing!

Text: Psalm 96:1–3, 10; Kenneth W. Louis
Music: Kenneth W. Louis

78 our sacraments and rites

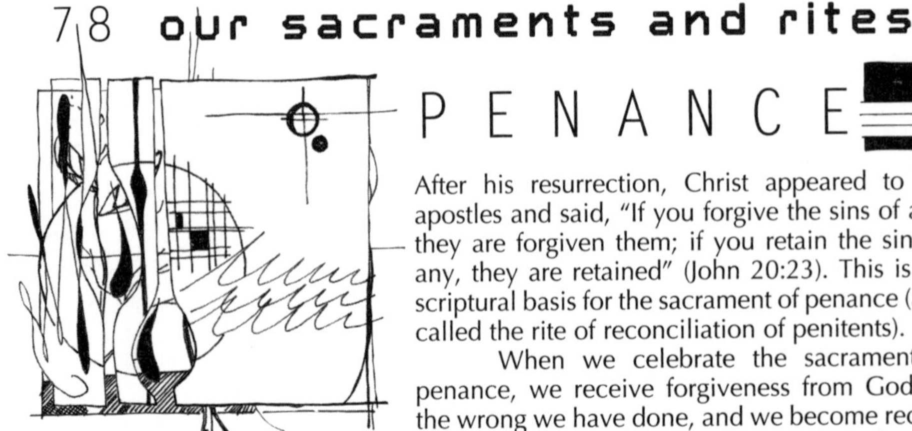

PENANCE

After his resurrection, Christ appeared to the apostles and said, "If you forgive the sins of any, they are forgiven them; if you retain the sins of any, they are retained" (John 20:23). This is the scriptural basis for the sacrament of penance (also called the rite of reconciliation of penitents).

When we celebrate the sacrament of penance, we receive forgiveness from God for the wrong we have done, and we become reconciled with God and those who have been hurt by our sins. The sacrament provides us with the grace that is needed to help us change our lives.

The sacrament includes several actions: *contrition* (or repentance), in which we express our sorrow for sin and our desire to change our lives; *confession*, in which we vocalize our sins to a priest (who represents God); *reparation*, in which we consider what is needed to make amends for our sin and what will help us prevent further sin; and *absolution*, the pronouncement by the priest of God's forgiveness. *LD*

Psalm 103: Bless the Lord, My Soul 79

Refrain
Bless the Lord, my soul, all my be - ing, bless his name.

Verses

1. Do not forget the gifts of the Lord
   who pardons you from your sins.
   Surrounding you with compassion and love,
   filling your days with goodness. Oh! Oh!

2. The Lord brings justice to all the oppressed,
   the Lord does righteous deeds.
   Merciful and gracious is God,
   ever abounding in kindness. Oh! Oh!

3. The Lord, indeed, knows how we are formed,
   knows that we are dust.
   And though we are dust, God's love never ends,
   is faithful from age to age. Oh! Oh!

4. All dwellings of the living God,
   all who do God's will,
   all creation, bless the Lord.
   Bless the Lord, my soul! Oh! Oh!

Text: Based on Psalm 103: Shannon Cerneka and Orin Johnson
Music: Shannon Cerneka and Orin Johnson

80 Psalm 118: This Is the Day

Refrain
This is the day that the Lord has made. Let us re-joice
and be glad. This is the day that the Lord has
Last time to Coda
To verses
made. Let us re-joice and be glad.
Coda
glad. Let us re-joice and be glad.

Verses

1. Give thanks to the Lord, for he is good,
   for his mercy endures forever.
   Let the house of Israel say,
   "His mercy endures forever."

2. "The right hand of the Lord has struck with power;
   the right hand of the Lord is exalted.
   I shall not die, but live,
   and declare the works of the Lord.

3. The stone which the builders rejected
   has become the cornerstone.
   By the Lord has this been done;
   it is wonderful in our eyes.

Psalm 121: Our Help Is from the Lord 81

Refrain
Our help is from the Lord, who made heav - en and who made earth. Our help is from the Lord,
Last time to Coda
who made heav - en and earth.
To verses
Coda
Our help is from the Lord. Our help is from the Lord.

Verses

1. I lift up my eyes toward the mountains;
   whence shall help come to me?
   My help is from the Lord,
   who made heaven and earth.

2. May he not suffer your foot to slip;
   may he slumber not who guards you:
   indeed he neither slumbers nor sleeps,
   the guardian of Israel.

3. The Lord is your guardian; the Lord is your shade;
   he is beside you at your right hand.
   The sun shall not harm you by day,
   nor the moon by night.

4. The Lord will guard you from all evil;
   he will guard your life.
   The Lord will guard your coming and your going,
   both now and forever.

82 Psalm 122: Let Us Go Rejoicing

Refrain
Let us go re - joic-ing, let us go to the
house of the Lord. Let us go re -
joic - ing, let us go to the house of the Lord.

Verses

1. I rejoiced because they said to me,
   "We will go up to the house of the Lord."
   And now we have set foot within your gates,
   O Jerusalem.

2. Jerusalem, built as a city, a city with unity.
   To it, to it the tribes go up,
   the tribes, the tribes of the Lord.

3. As it was decreed for Israel,
   to give thanks, give thanks to the Lord.
   For here are the thrones of justice,
   the thrones of David's house.

4. For the peace of Jerusalem, pray!
   May peace be within your walls.
   May those who love you find prosperity,
   May peace be within your walls.

5. Because of my fam'ly and friends I will say,
   "May peace be with you!"
   Because of the house of the Lord, our God,
   I will pray, will pray for your good.

Psalm 130: With the Lord There Is Mercy 83

Refrain

With the Lord there is mer-cy and full-ness of re-demp-tion.

Verses

1. Out of the depths I cry to you, O Lord;
   Lord, hear my voice!
   Let your ears be attentive
   to my voice in supplication.

2. If you, O Lord, mark iniquities,
   Lord, who can stand?
   But with you is forgiveness,
   that you may be revered.

3. I trust in the Lord;
   my soul trusts in his word.
   More than sentinels wait for the dawn,
   let Israel wait for the Lord.

4. For with the Lord is kindness
   and with him is plenteous redemption;
   and he will redeem Israel
   from all their iniquities.

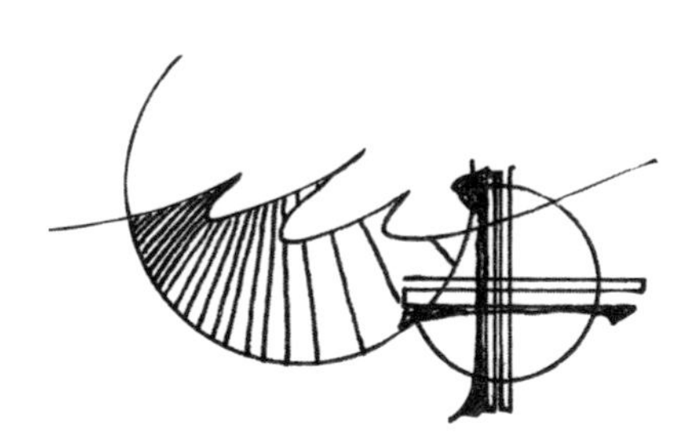

84 Psalm 130: Out of the Depths

Refrain

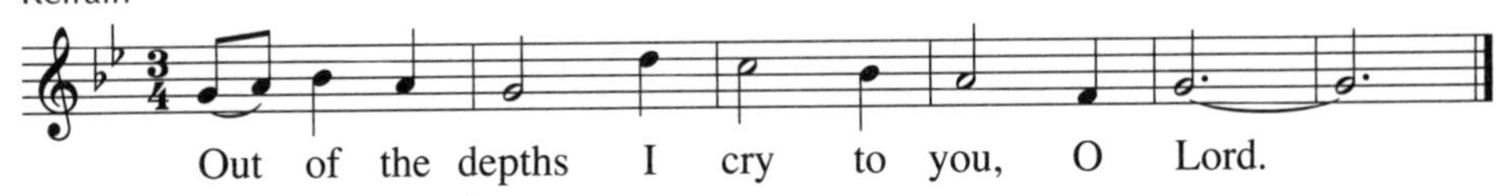
Out of the depths I cry to you, O Lord.

Verses

1. Out of the depths I cry to you;
   Lord, hear my voice!
   Let your ears be attentive
   to my prayer for help.

2. If you, O Lord,
   should mark our guilt,
   Lord, who could stand?
   But with you there is mercy,
   that you may be revered.

3. I put my trust in God, the Lord,
   trusting his word.
   My soul waits for the Lord
   more than sentinels wait for the dawn.

4. More than sentinels wait for the dawn,
   Israel waits for God.
   For with God there is kindness,
   and with God, plenteous redemption.

Text: Psalm 130; Paul Melley
Music: Paul Melley

85 Psalm 138: Lord, I Thank You

Refrain

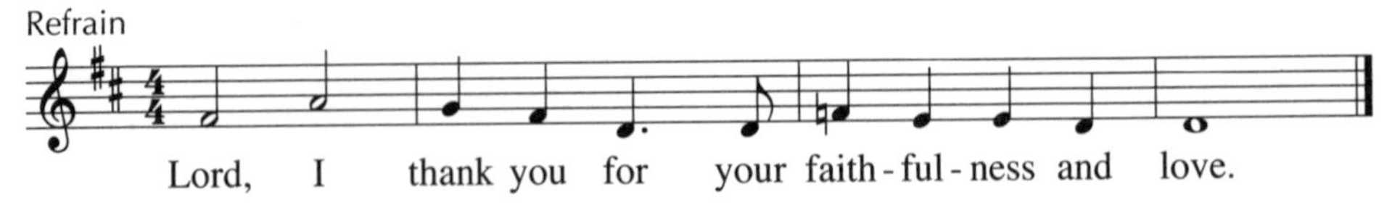
Lord, I thank you for your faith-ful-ness and love.

Verses

1. I will give thanks to you, O Lord, with all my heart,
   for you have heard the words of my mouth;
   in the presence of the angels I will sing your praise;
   I will worship at your holy temple.

2. I will give thanks to your name,
   because of your kindness and your truth.
   When I called, you answered me;
   you built up strength within me.

3. All the kings of the earth shall give thanks to you, O LORD,
 when they hear the words of your mouth;
 And they shall sing of the ways of the LORD:
 "Great is the glory of the LORD."

Text: Psalm 138:1–2, 2–3, 4–5; *New American Bible*, © 1970, Confraternity of Christian Doctrine; refrain by Shannon Cerneka, © 2008, GIA Publications, Inc.
Music: Shannon Cerneka, © 2008, GIA Publications, Inc.

PSALM 139: BEFORE I WAS BORN 86

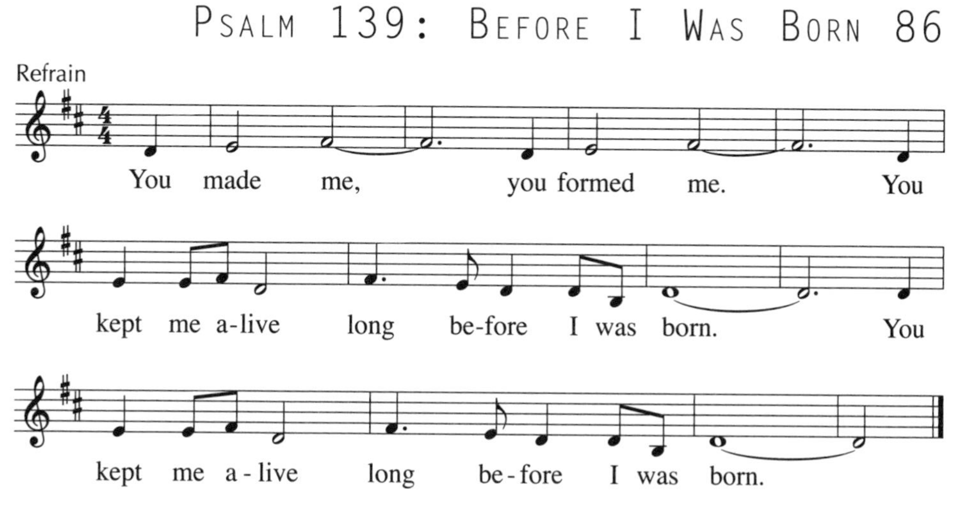
Refrain
You made me, you formed me. You
kept me a-live long be-fore I was born. You
kept me a - live long be - fore I was born.

Verses

1. You have sought me out, and found me; you know where I sit or stand.
 You know the depths of my heart, whenever I move or rest,
 you find me wherever I am. You find me wherever I am.

2. Before the word comes from my mouth, you know what I want to say.
 You come close to me, you lay your hand upon me.
 All of this is too much for me. All of this is too much for me.

3. How can I ever hide from you? Where can I run from you?
 Above and below—you are there. To the dawn or to the sea—you are there.
 Your hand will guide my way. Your hand will guide my way.

4. You have created ev'ry inch of me, you have knit me to my mother's womb.
 You have record of all my days, long before they ever began.
 How amazing your thoughts, O God. How amazing your thoughts, O God.

Text: Psalm 139:1–10, 13, 16b–17; David Haas
Music: David Haas

87 Psalm 141: Like Burning Incense, O Lord

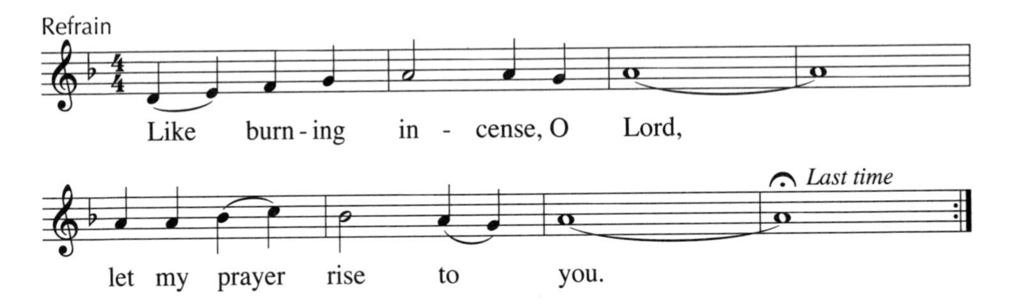
Refrain
Like burn - ing in - cense, O Lord,
Last time
let my prayer rise to you.

Verses

1. I call out to you, come quickly to my aid.
   My song cries out to you, O listen to me now.
   I raise my hands in off'ring to you.

2. Let me speak your truth; watch over all I say.
   Keep my thoughts on you; let goodness rule my heart.
   Keep me far from those who do harm.

3. Never let me dine with those who seek to harm.
   Keep your holy ones always at my side.
   Plant your wisdom deep in my soul.

4. I look to you for help; I seek your loving eyes.
   Guard my life for you; spare me from all wrong.
   Keep all evil far from my heart.

5. Glory be to God and to God's only Son,
   glory to the Spirit, three in one,
   now and forever. Amen.

Text: Psalm 141; Lori True
Music: Lori True; keyboard arr. by Marshall Keating

Exodus 15: Let Us Sing to the Lord 88

Refrain

Let us sing to the Lord songs of free-dom and sal - va - tion. Let us

Last time
sing to the Lord for our God will lead us home.

Verses

1. God is our strength. God is our might. We will sing praises day and night.
   Drowning our foes deep in the sea, Lord, your right hand has set us free!

2. Who is like you, holy and great? Only your love can conquer hate.
   We have been saved! Let us proclaim! Lord, we will praise your holy name!

3. Pharoah's army lost in the sea. God has won the victory.
   Pharoah's army lost in the sea. God has won the victory!

Text: Exodus 15; adapt. by Michael Mahler
Music: Michael Mahler

Whatever did not fit in with my plan
did lie within the plan of God.

Edith Stein

89 Morning Has Broken

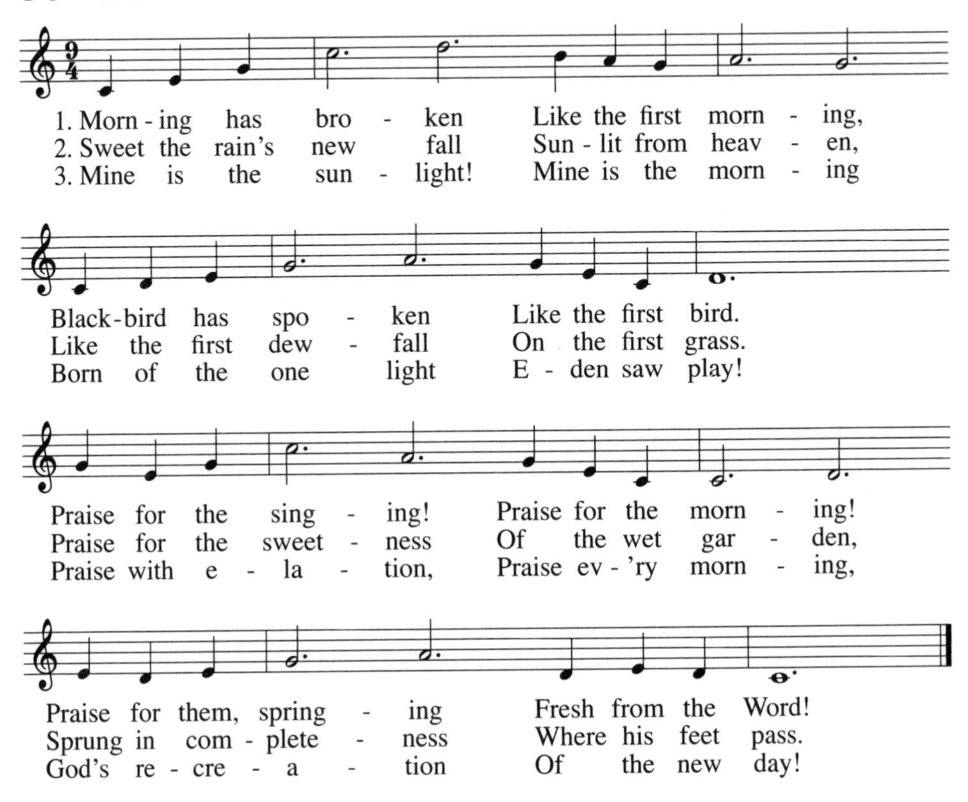
1. Morn - ing has bro - ken Like the first morn - ing,
2. Sweet the rain's new fall Sun - lit from heav - en,
3. Mine is the sun - light! Mine is the morn - ing
Black-bird has spo - ken Like the first bird.
Like the first dew - fall On the first grass.
Born of the one light E - den saw play!
Praise for the sing - ing! Praise for the morn - ing!
Praise for the sweet - ness Of the wet gar - den,
Praise with e - la - tion, Praise ev - 'ry morn - ing,
Praise for them, spring - ing Fresh from the Word!
Sprung in com - plete - ness Where his feet pass.
God's re - cre - a - tion Of the new day!

Text: Eleanor Farjeon, 1881–1965, *The Children's Bells,* © David Higham Assoc. Ltd.
Tune: BUNESSAN, 5 5 5 4 D; Gaelic; arr. by Paul A. Tate, b.1968, © 2008, GIA Publications, Inc.

90 Fresh as the Morning

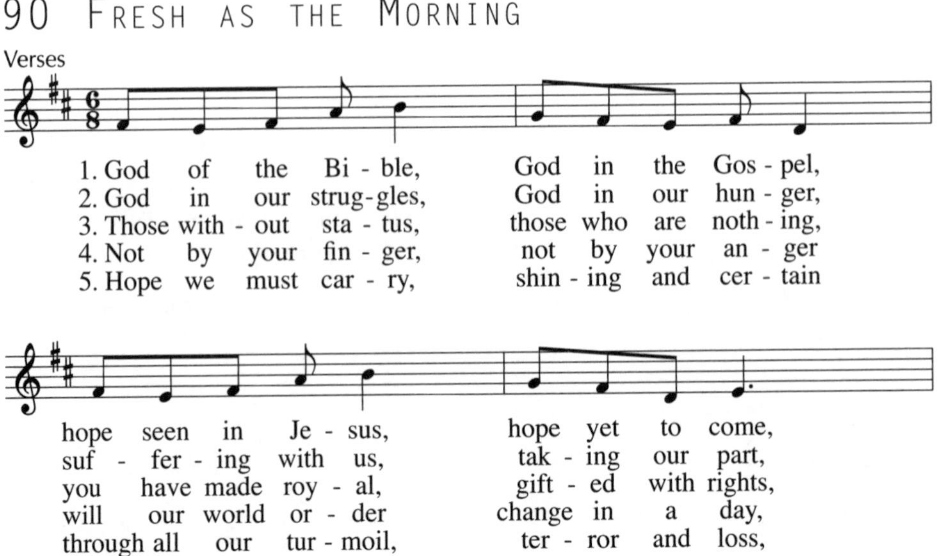
Verses
1. God of the Bi - ble, God in the Gos - pel,
2. God in our strug-gles, God in our hun - ger,
3. Those with - out sta - tus, those who are noth - ing,
4. Not by your fin - ger, not by your an - ger
5. Hope we must car - ry, shin - ing and cer - tain
hope seen in Je - sus, hope yet to come,
suf - fer - ing with us, tak - ing our part,
you have made roy - al, gift - ed with rights,
will our world or - der change in a day,
through all our tur - moil, ter - ror and loss,

MORNING
you are our cen - ter, day - light or dark - ness,
still you em - pow'r us, moth - er - ing Spir - it,
cho - sen as part - ners, mid - wives of jus - tice,
but by your peo - ple, fear - less and faith - ful,
bond - ing us glad - ly one to the oth - er,
free - dom or pris - on, you are our home.
feed - ing, sus - tain - ing, from your own heart.
birth - ing new sys - tems, light - ing new lights.
small pa - per lan - terns, light - ing the way.
till our world chang - es fac - ing the Cross.
Refrain
Fresh as the morn - ing, sure as the sun - rise,
God al - ways faith - ful, you do not change.
Fresh as the morn - ing, sure as the sun - rise,
God al - ways faith - ful, you do not change.
3

Text: Shirley Erena Murray, b.1931, © 1996, Hope Publishing Co.
Tune: Tony E. Alonso, b.1980, © 2001, GIA Publications, Inc.

91 We Arise

Verses
1. We a - rise for Christ is ris - en. We who
2. Lord, we know your way is kind - ness and your
3. May we use this day we're giv - en to live
4. In the morn - ing's crys - tal fresh - ness may we
5. Sav - ing God, for all your bless - ings, may our
slept have been re - stored. Now we
love is un - sur - passed. It was
out the truth we've seen. Where your
see with God's own grace the re -
prais - es nev - er cease 'til the
choose to come to - geth - er giv - ing
by your stead - fast mer - cy that last
chil - dren are di - vid - ed let us
flect - ed light of Je - sus shin - ing
dawn of each new morn - ing brings a
thanks to Christ our Lord.
night was not our last.
build a bridge be - tween. We are
clear in ev - 'ry face.
day of hope and peace.
Refrain
ris - en with the morn - ing, ris - en for the form - ing of a
par - a - dise, ris - en with the sun - light,

ris - en with the one light in our o - pen eyes.

We a - rise!

1.–4.
D.C.
5.
Repeat as desired
We a - rise!

Text: Michael Mahler, b.1981
Tune: Michael Mahler, b.1981

LET EVENING FALL 92

1. Let eve - ning fall gen - tly a - round us,
2. Let eve - ning fall gen - tly with - in us,
3. Let eve - ning fall gen - tly up - on us.
Christ's love sur - rounds us, warmth through the night.
now sa - cred si - lence brings us to you.
Sun - light has fad - ed, day's work is done.
Love laid be - fore us, hopes and dreams too,
Put to rest cha - os, cry - ing, and pain,
Now you pro - tect us, held in your sight
prayer now up - holds us, clos - er to you.
gen - tly sus - tain us, speak - ing our name.
in ho - ly dark - ness till morn - ing's light.
3

Text: Tony E. Alonso, b.1980
Tune: Tony E. Alonso, b.1980

93 Glory to God Most High

Refrain
Glo - ry! Glo - ry to God! Glo - ry
in the high - est! Glo - ry! Glo - ry to God!
1.–5.
To verses
Repeat 1st and last time
Last time
molto rit.
3
Glo-ry to God Most High!
Glo-ry to God Most High!
Verse 1
1. O God, Ho - ly One, al - might-y God and Fa -
ther, we wor-ship you, we give
you thanks, we praise you for your glo - ry!
D.C.
Verse 2
2. O Lord, Je - sus Christ, Ho-ly One, Re - deem -er,
Lord God, Lamb of God, you take a - way the sin of the world.
D.C.
Verse 3
3. You a - lone are the Ho - ly One, you a - lone are the Lord,

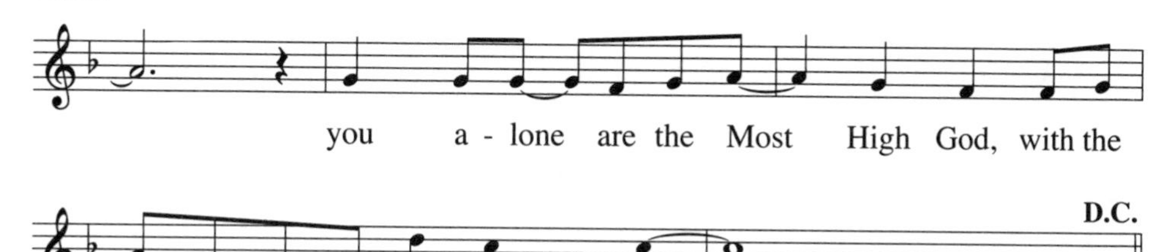
you a - lone are the Most High God, with the
Spir - it in the glo - ry of God!
D.C.

Music: Jesse Manibusan, b.1958; acc. by Ken Canedo, b.1953, © 1993, 1999, Jesse Manibusan. Published by OCP.

I Will Lift Up Your Name 94

Refrain
I will lift up your name: praise to my king and God,
for you are ho - ly. Oh, I will lift up your name:
praise to my king and my God on high!
Verses
1. I will give you glo - ry, Lord;
2. Al - ways faith - ful, kind and gen - tle,
3. Ev - 'ry crea - ture, great and small,
I will bless your name for - ev - er.
slow to an - ger, filled with love.
tells the glo - ry of your name,
I will praise you day af - ter day.
Oh, how great is the Lord of all!
and pro - claims to all your might - y ways.
D.C.

Text: Based on Psalm 145:1–2, 8–11; Steve Angrisano, b.1965
Tune: Steve Angrisano, b.1965 and Thomas N. Tomaszek, b.1950; acc. by Rick Modlin, b.1966

95 Canticle of the Turning

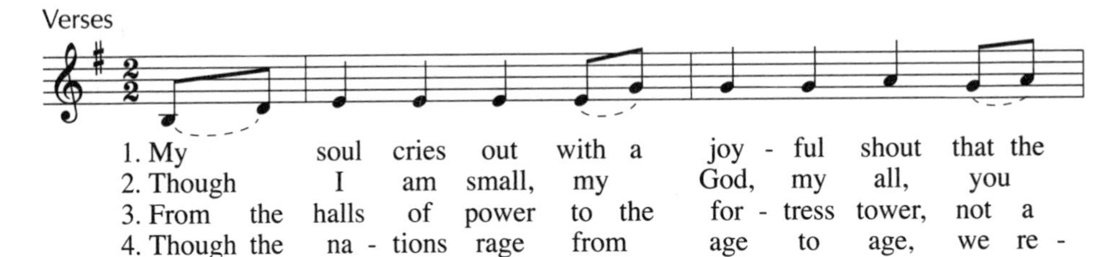
Verses
1. My soul cries out with a joy - ful shout that the
2. Though I am small, my God, my all, you
3. From the halls of power to the for - tress tower, not a
4. Though the na - tions rage from age to age, we re -

God of my heart is great, And my spir - it sings of the
work great things in me, And your mer - cy will last from the
stone will be left on stone. Let the king be - ware for your
mem - ber who holds us fast: God's mer - cy must de -

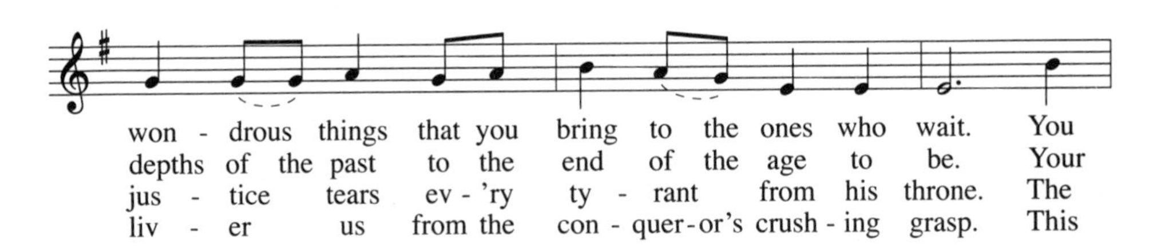
won - drous things that you bring to the ones who wait. You
depths of the past to the end of the age to be. Your
jus - tice tears ev - 'ry ty - rant from his throne. The
liv - er us from the con - quer-or's crush - ing grasp. This

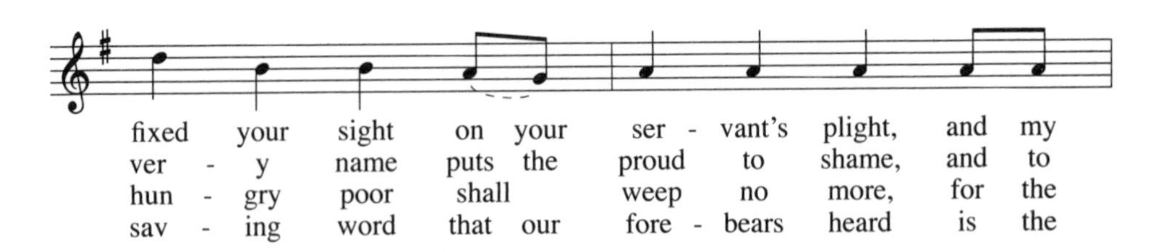
fixed your sight on your ser - vant's plight, and my
ver - y name puts the proud to shame, and to
hun - gry poor shall weep no more, for the
sav - ing word that our fore - bears heard is the

weak - ness you did not spurn, So from east to west shall my
those who would for you yearn, You will show your might, put the
food they can nev - er earn; There are ta - bles spread, ev - 'ry
prom - ise which holds us bound, 'Til the spear and rod can be

name be blest. Could the world be a - bout to turn?
strong to flight, for the world is a - bout to turn.
mouth be fed, for the world is a - bout to turn.
crushed by God, who is turn - ing the world a - round.
Refrain
My heart shall sing of the day you bring. Let the
fires of your jus - tice burn. Wipe a - way all tears, for the

dawn draws near, and the world is a - bout to turn!

Text: Luke 1:46-58; Rory Cooney, b.1952
Tune: STAR OF THE COUNTY DOWN; Irish traditional; arr. by Rory Cooney, b.1952

The aim and final end of all music should be none other than the glory of God and the refreshment of the soul.

Johann Sebastian Bach

96 Lord, I Lift Your Name on High

1.
2., 3.
1.
3 D.C.
2.
Lord, I lift your name on high. Lord, I love to sing your prais - es. I'm so glad you're in my life. I'm so glad you came to save us. save us.
You came from heav - en to earth to show the way. From the earth to the cross, my debt to pay. From the cross to the grave, from the grave to the sky; Lord, I lift your name on high.
high. Lord, I lift your name on high. Lord, I lift your name on high. Lord, I lift your name on high.

Text: Rick Founds, b.1954
Tune: Rick Founds, b.1954; arr. by Ed Bolduc, b.1969

Shout to the North 97

Verses
1. Men of faith, rise up and sing of the great and glo - rious King, you are strong when you feel weak in your bro - ken - ness com - plete.
2. (Rise up,) wom - en of the truth, stand and sing to bro - ken hearts, who can know the heal - ing pow'r of our awe - some King of love.
3. (Rise up,) Church with bro - ken wings, fill this place with songs a - gain of our God who reigns on high, by his grace a - gain we'll fly.
Refrain
Shout to the North and the South, sing to the East and the West; Je - sus is Sav-ior to all, Lord of heav-en and earth.
1., 3., 5.
We will
2.
earth.
D.S.
2. Rise up,
4.
earth.
To bridge
Last time
earth.
Bridge
We've been through fire, we've been through rain, we've been re-fined by the pow'r of his name; We've fall - en deep-er in love with you, you've burned the truth on our lips.
D.S.
3. Rise up,

Text: Martin Smith
Tune: Martin Smith; acc. by Ed Bolduc, b.1969

98 Let Us Worship the Lord

Refrain
Let us wor-ship the Lord, our light and sal-va-tion,
rock and foun-da-tion, faith-ful and true! Let us wor-ship the Lord, whose
mer-cy and kind-ness free us from blind-ness and make all things new!
Let us wor-ship the Lord!
Verses
1. Dwell not on days of the past.
2. Hear now the voice from a-bove,
3. Look at the stars in the sky,
4. O-pen our eyes to your grace,
See, the Lord makes all things new.
giv-er of won-ders and signs,
so your de-scen-dants shall be.
o-pen our ears to your truth.
Riv-ers will flow in the des-ert, all
"I AM for all gen-er-a-tions." All
Daugh-ters and sons of the Fa-ther, your
Lead us with love and com-pas-sion. All
D.C.
crea-tures will cry out in praise!
peo-ples will cry out in praise!
chil-dren will cry out in praise!
na-tions will cry out in praise!

Text: Paul L. Berrell, b.1980 and Paul A. Tate, b.1968
Tune: Paul L. Berrell, b.1980 and Paul A. Tate, b.1968

How Excellent Is Thy Name 99

Refrain
I will sing prais - es un - to the Fa - ther
for he's wor - thy to be praised. I will sing praises un - to the Fa - ther for he's wor -
To verses 1, 3
thy to be praised.
To verses 2, 4
thy to be praised.
Verses 1, 3
1., 3. Lord how ex - cel - lent is thy name
in all the earth. I will sing prais -
D.S.
Verses 2, 4
2., 4. Let ev - 'ry-thing that has breath, that has breath,
praise the Lord. O Lord, how ex -
cel - lent is thy name in all the earth,
how ex - cel - lent is thy ho - ly name!
D.C.

Text: John W. Higdon
Tune: John W. Higdon; arr. by Joseph Joubert, b.1958

100 Cry the Gospel

Verses 1, 2

1. You are the light of the world, you are the light of the world. Shine for all to see, so in the Father they'll believe. You are the light of the world.
2. You are the salt of the earth, you are the salt of the earth, bringing mercy and peace to ev'ry person that you meet. You are the salt of the earth.

Refrain

Leader: Say not that you are too young. *All:* "We are holy we are strong!" *Leader:* With purity and love and faith, *All:* "Proclaiming Christ today!" be holy. The Lord be glorified! Be holy, cry the gospel with your life! Standing at the gateway of our faith, on the rock of Peter and the saints, with the Holy Spirit showing us the way to be

ho - ly, and cry the gos-pel, cry the gos-pel with your life!
Last time to Coda
Oh!
Oh!
Verse 3
3. Lord, we come to do your will. Yes, Lord, we come to do your
will. Not on - ly in our words, but in our
liv - ing it is heard: Lord, we come to do your will.
D.S.
Coda
Oh!
Oh!
Oh!
4

Text: Tom Booth, b.1961
Tune: Tom Booth, b.1961, acc. by Ed Bolduc, b.1969

...the singing of the faithful gathered for the celebration of Holy Mass, no less than the prayers, the readings and the homily, express in an authentic way the message of the Liturgy while fostering a sense of common faith and communion in charity.

Liturgiam authenticam

101 All Generations Will Praise Your Name

Refrain
I will pro-claim your great-ness, my God, I will pro - claim
your good - ness, my King, great deeds you have done,
all gen-er - a - tions will praise your name, all gen-er - a -
To repeat refrain and verse 1
To verses 2, 3 and Last time
tions will praise your name.
Verses
1. I will speak of your glo - ry, I will
2. With my eyes full of hope, Lord, I will
3. You are just, you are faith - ful, you are
tell of your maj - es - ty and sing of your kind-
look to your gra - cious - ness. You o - pen your hand
near when I call your name. Lord, hear and an -
D.C.
ness and com - pas - sion.
to fill my hun - ger.
swer those who love you.

Text: Based on Psalm 145; Chris de Silva, b.1967
Tune: Chris de Silva, b.1967

I Will Sing a Song of Love 102
Refrain
I will sing a song of love to the one who first loved me,
and I'll sing it as a child of God who is
named and known and free. For the love of God is good,
it is broad and deep and long, and a - bove all else that
mat - ters God is wor - thy of my song.
Verses
1. And I will not sing a - lone But with
2. And I'll sing with ev - 'ry soul, Ev - 'ry
3. And I'll sing for what is right And a -
4. As I bring to God my joy, So I'll
5. While my life on earth still runs, May my
earth and sky and sea, For cre - a - tion
lan - guage, ev - 'ry race, Which pro - claims this
gainst all that is wrong, Be - cause God is
bring to God my pain, For there is no
song to God be giv'n, Till through grace I
D.C.
raised its voice well in ad - vance of me.
world is good for God has blessed this place.
nev - er neu - tral who in - spires my song.
hurt which God re - quires me to re - tain.
join the har - mo - ny of all in heav'n.

Text: John L. Bell, b.1949
Tune: NAMED AND KNOWN, 7 7 13 with refrain; John L. Bell, b.1949

103 Thanks and Praise

Verse 1

Cantor:

1. Praise you, Lord, for your good-ness. Praise you, Lord, for your grace.

Praise you, Lord, for your mer - cy

in ev - 'ry time and place. Trust you, Lord, in the strug-

gle; it's just a mat-ter of faith. Help me, Lord, if I stum-

ble. In my weak-ness you will be my strength.

Refrain

All:

Lift your voic-es to the sky! Raise your hands and lift them high!

Sing your praise and shout, "Al - might - y!" All you

peo - ple of the land, know that God is in com-mand.

2nd time to Bridge

Sing your praise and shout, "Al - might - y!"

Verse 2

2. Praise you, Lord, for your good - ness. Praise you, Lord, for your grace.

Praise you, Lord, for your mer - cy in
ev - 'ry time and place. Trust you, Lord, in the strug - gle;
it's just a mat - ter of faith. Help me, Lord, if I stum-
ble. In my weak-ness you will be my strength. Lift your
D.S.
Bridge
Right to give him thanks and praise! Right to lift up Je - sus' name!
Right to say, "I do be - lieve he is our Sav - ior."
Interlude
7
Final Refrain
Lift your voic-es to the sky! Raise your hands
and lift them high! Sing your praise and shout, "Al - might-y!"
All you peo-ple of the land, know that God is in com-mand.
1.
2.
Sing your praise and shout, "Al - might-y!" Lift your y!"

Text: John Angotti, b.1963 and Ed Bolduc, b.1969
Tune: John Angotti, b.1963 and Ed Bolduc, b.1969

104 Make a Joyful Noise

Verses
1. Come with me and I will show you all that you can be. Pray with me and I will give you peace e - ter - nal - ly.
2. Live the ho - ly Word of God with o - pen heart and mind; all the good-ness, peace and love in Je - sus you will find.
Cantor:
1., 2. Bless-ed are you, hap-py are you, bless-ed are you,
Response:
1. the poor in spir - it, who weep and mourn, who are hum -
Response:
2. who are mer - ci-ful, the pure in heart, who work for peace,

ho - ly are you,
ble,
who do God's will,
God's per - se - cu - ted,
All:
for great in - deed is your re - ward in heav - en.
Refrain
Make a joy - ful noise un - to the Lord. For
great is your re - ward in heav - en and on earth.
Make a joy - ful noise un - to the Lord. For
ev - 'ry day's a new be - gin - ning in God's eyes. True
Last time to Coda
hap - pi - ness lies in the heart of all who an - swer to God's call.
5 D.C.
Coda
Hap - pi - ness lies in your heart,
hap - pi - ness lies in your heart.

Text: Based on Matthew 5:3–12; Chris de Silva, b.1967
Tune: Chris de Silva, b.1967

105 Blessed Be Your Name

Verses
1. Bless - ed be your name in the land that is plen - ti - ful, where your streams of a - bun- dance flow, bless - ed be your name.
Bless - ed be your name when I'm found in the des - ert place, though I walk through the wil - der - ness, bless - ed be your name.
2. Bless - ed be your name when the sun's shin - ing down on me, when the world's all as it should be, bless - ed be your name.
Bless - ed be your name on the road marked with suf - fer - ing, though there's pain in the of - fer - ing, bless - ed be your name.
Ev-'ry bless-ing you pour out I'll turn back to praise.
When the dark - ness clos - es in, Lord, still I will say,
Refrain
"Bless-ed be the name of the Lord! Bless-ed be your name!
Bless-ed be the name of the Lord!
Bless-ed be your glo - ri - ous name!"
1.
D.C.

2., 4.
3.
To bridge
Last time
"Bless-ed be the
You
Bridge
give and take a - way! You give and take a -
way! My heart will choose to say, "Lord,
1.
2.
To refrain
bless-ed be your name!" You name!"

Text: Based on Job 1:20–22; Habakkuk 3:17–18; Matt and Beth Redman
Tune: Matt and Beth Redman; arr. by Ed Bolduc, b.1969

The Church knew what the psalmist knew:
Music praises God. Music is well or better
able to praise him than the building of the
church and all its decoration;
it is the Church's greatest ornament.

Igor Stravinsky

106 Halle, Halle, Halle

1. Gathering Song

Hal - le, hal - le, hal - le - lu - jah! Hal - le, hal - le, hal-

le - lu - jah! Hal - le, hal - le, hal - le -

lu - jah, hal - le - lu - jah! Hal - le - lu - jah!

Optional Acclamation during Blessing of Water

Hal - le - lu - jah! Hal - le - lu - jah!

2. Sprinkling Rite

Verses

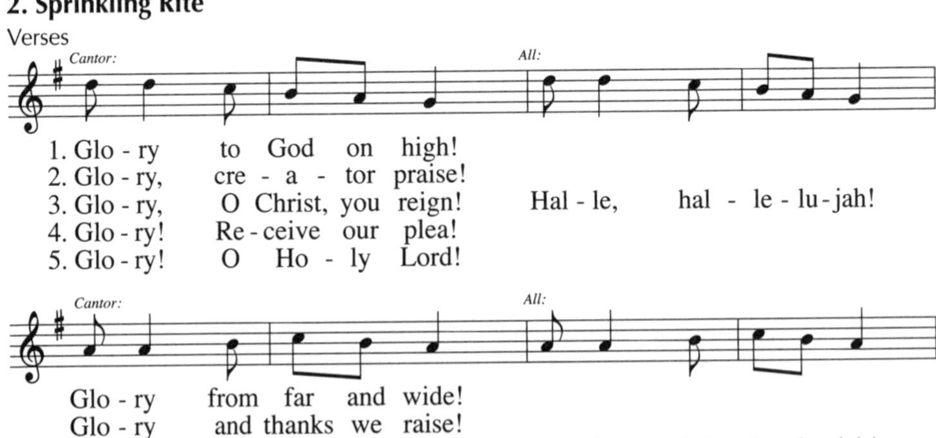
Cantor:
All:
1. Glo - ry to God on high!
2. Glo - ry, cre - a - tor praise!
3. Glo - ry, O Christ, you reign!
4. Glo - ry! Re - ceive our plea!
5. Glo - ry! O Ho - ly Lord!
Hal - le, hal - le - lu - jah!
Cantor:
All:
Glo - ry from far and wide!
Glo - ry and thanks we raise!
Glo - ry, O Lamb, once slain!
Glo - ry to Christ now be!
Glo - ry! O Christ, a - dored!
Hal - le, hal - le - lu - jah!

Cantor:
All:
Glo - ry and peace on earth a - bide!
Glo - ry and bless - ing all our days!
Glo - ry, O Lord, let loss be gain!
Glo - ry! The world from sin set free!
Glo - ry! O Spir - it, now out - poured!
Hal - le -

D.C.
lu - jah, hal - le - lu - jah!

Text: Trad. Caribbean; sprinkling rite verses by Gabe Huck, b.1941; adapt. by Tony E. Alonso, b.1980,
Tune: Refrain, trad. Caribbean; arr. by John L. Bell, b.1949, sprinkling rite verses and adapt. by Tony E. Alonso, b.1980,

SING TO THE GLORY OF GOD 107

Refrain
Sing to the glo-ry of God. Sing to your glo-ry with-in.
Sing with all of your heart.
Sing and be made whole.
To verses
Final ending
Sing.
Verses
1. Look in - to the eyes of a child.
2. God is right here a - mong us,
Tell me, what do you see?
here as you and as me.
See the light shin - ing in them, re -
Let us love one an - oth - er, and
mind - ing us of who we can be.
set each oth - er free.
D.C.

Text: James E. Moore, Jr., b.1951
Tune: James E. Moore, Jr., b.1951

108 FOREVER

Verses

1. Give thanks to the Lord our God and King; his love en - dures for - ev - er. For he is good, he is a - bove all things; his love en - dures for - ev - er.
2. With a might - y hand and out - stretched arm; his love en - dures for - ev - er. For the life that's been re - born; his love en - dures for - ev - er. Sing
3. From the ris - ing to the set - ting sun his love en - dures for - ev - er. And by the grace of God we will car - ry on; his love en - dures for - ev - er.

praise, sing

1. praise.

2., 3. praise, sing praise, sing praise!

Refrain

For - ev - er God is faith - ful, for - ev - er God is strong, for - ev - er God is with us, for - ev -

1. er. *To verse 3*

2. er, and ev - er. For - ev - **D.S.**

Last time

er and ev - er. For - ev - er!

Text: Chris Tomlin, b.1972
Tune: Chris Tomlin, b.1972; acc. by Ed Bolduc, b.1969

Shout to the Lord 109

Verse
My Je-sus, my Sav-ior; Lord, there is none like you.
All of my days I want to praise the won-ders of your
might - y love. My com-fort, my shel-ter,
tow-er of ref - uge and strength; let ev - 'ry breath,
all that I am, nev-er cease to wor - ship you.
Refrain
Shout to the Lord, all the earth; let us sing pow-er and maj-es-ty, praise
to the king. Moun-tains bow down and the seas will roar at the
sound of your name. I sing for joy at the work
of your hands. For-ev-er I'll love you, for-ev - er I'll stand.
Noth-ing com-pares to the prom-ise I have in you.
3 D.C.
Final ending

Text: Darlene Zschech, b.1965
Tune: Darlene Zschech, b.1965; arr. by Ed Bolduc, b.1969

110 We Praise You

Verses
Cantor:
All: We praise you,
1. For your sun that bright-ens the day:
2. For the glo - ry of all cre - a - tion:
3. For your love that greets the morn-ing: praise you,
4. For the treas - ure of joy and laugh-ter:
5. For your Word, your Ho - ly Wis - dom:
Lord!
Cantor:
All: We
For your moon that guides the night:
For all crea - tures great and small:
Lord! For your faith - ful - ness through night: We
For the mys - t'ry of sor - row and tears:
For the bread, the work of our hands:
praise you, Lord!
Cantor:
For your source of light
For the seas, the hills
praise you, Lord! For your voice that sings
For the gift of love
For the wine, the cup
All: We praise you, Lord!
and breath:
and val - leys:
in all of us: praise you, Lord!
and heal - ing:
of bless - ing,
Cantor:
All: We praise you,
For your song of death to life:
For the moun - tains strong and tall:
For your call to love and serve: We praise you,
For the awe - some pow'r of prayer:
For us all, your sa - cred pres - ence,

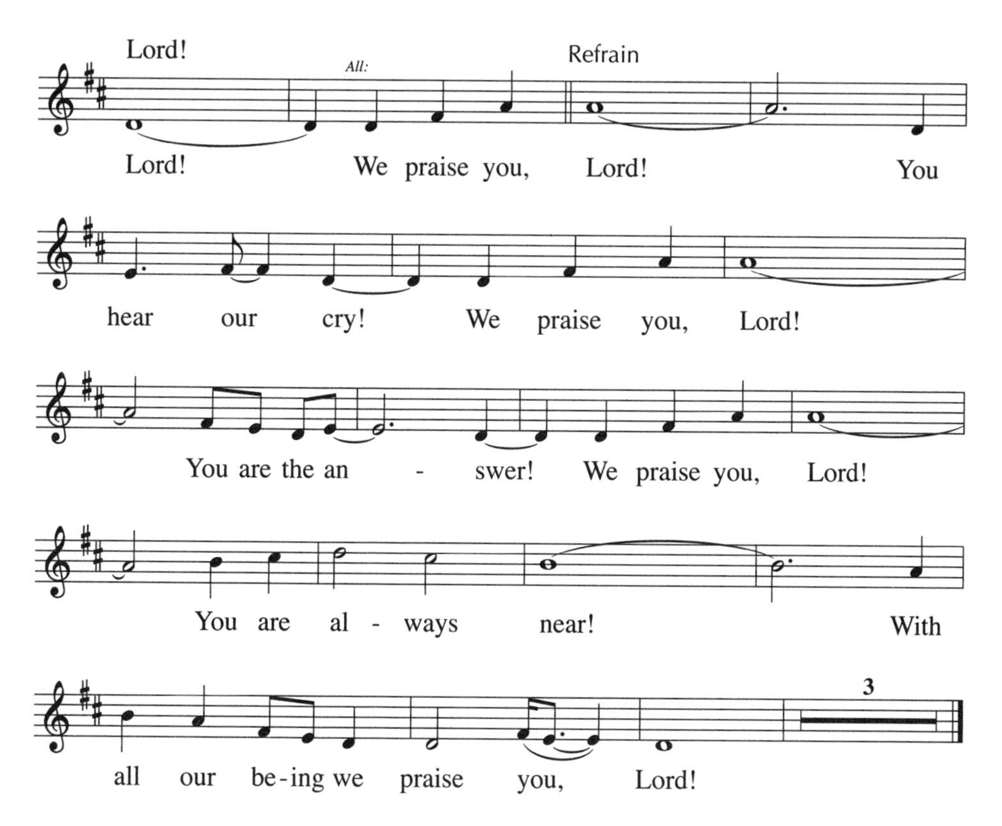
Lord!
All:
Refrain
Lord! We praise you, Lord! You
hear our cry! We praise you, Lord!
You are the an - swer! We praise you, Lord!
You are al - ways near! With
all our be-ing we praise you, Lord!
3

Text: David Haas, b.1957
Tune: David Haas, b.1957

111 God of Wonders

Verses
1. Lord of all cre-a - tion, of wa-ter, earth and sky, the heav-ens are your tab-er-na - cle. Glo - ry to the Lord on high!
2. Ear - ly in the morn - ing I will cel - e - brate the light. When I stum-ble in the dark - ness, I will call your name by night.
Refrain
God of won-ders be-yond our gal - ax - y, you are ho - ly, ho - ly, The u - ni - verse de-clares your maj-es - ty. You are ho - ly, ho - ly,
Precious Lord, re-veal your heart to me. Fa-ther, hold me, hold me,
Lord of heav-en and earth, Lord of heav-en and earth.
First time D.C.
Last time
Bridge
Hal-le - lu - jah, Hal-le - lu - jah,

Hal-le - lu - jah,

Interlude
D.S.

Text: Steve Hindalong and Marc Byrd
Tune: Steve Hindalong and Marc Byrd; arr. by Rick Modlin, b.1966

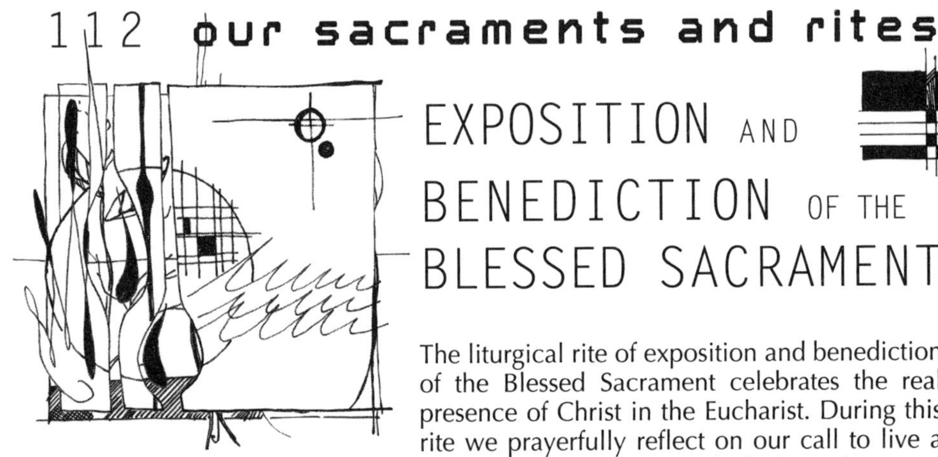

112 our sacraments and rites

EXPOSITION AND BENEDICTION OF THE BLESSED SACRAMENT

The liturgical rite of exposition and benediction of the Blessed Sacrament celebrates the real presence of Christ in the Eucharist. During this rite we prayerfully reflect on our call to live a more faithful Christian life, while deepening our devotion to the holy Eucharist.

The service is made up of four parts: exposition, adoration, benediction, and reposition. During exposition, the Eucharist is placed in a monstrance (a special vessel) and set on the altar. Adoration includes prayers, Scripture readings, the singing of hymns and psalms, periods of silence, and the recitation of the Divine Praises (a naming of the blessings of God). The benediction takes place when the celebrant, wearing a special veil (called a humeral veil), blesses those present by lifting the monstrance above his head and tracing the sign of the cross. Finally, during reposition, the Blessed Sacrament is removed from the monstrance and placed back in the tabernacle. "Holy God, We Praise Thy Name" *(no. 113)* is the hymn that is often sung at the conclusion of this rite. *LD*

HOLY GOD, WE PRAISE THY NAME 113

1. Ho - ly God, we praise thy name;
2. Hark! the loud ce - les - tial hymn
3. Lo! the ap - os - tol - ic train
4. Ho - ly Fa - ther, Ho - ly Son,
Lord of all, we bow be - fore thee!
An - gel choirs a - bove are rais - ing;
Join, the sa - cred name to hal - low;
Ho - ly Spir - it, Three we name thee;
All on earth thy scep - ter claim,
Cher - u - bim and Ser - a - phim,
Proph - ets swell the loud re - frain,
While in es - sence on - ly One,
All in heav'n a - bove a - dore thee;
In un - ceas - ing cho - rus prais - ing,
And the white - robed mar - tyrs fol - low;
Un - di - vid - ed God we claim thee;
In - fi - nite thy vast do - main,
Fill the heav'ns with sweet ac - cord:
And from morn to set of sun,
And a - dor - ing bend the knee,
Repeat ad lib.
Ev - er - last - ing is thy reign.
"Ho - ly, ho - ly, ho - ly Lord!"
Through the Church the song goes on.
While we own the mys - ter - y.

Text: *Grosser Gott, wir loben dich;* ascr. to Ignaz Franz, 1719–1790; tr. by Clarence Walworth, 1820–1900
Tune: GROSSER GOTT, 7 8 7 8 77; *Katholisches Gesangbuch*, Vienna, c.1774

114 MIGHTY KING

Verses
Cantor:
1. You are the spir-it bring-ing us light, ig-nit-ing the fire of faith in our lives.
2. You are the voice an-cient and new, speak-ing with cour-age, pro-claim-ing truth.
All:
You are the Lord; you are a might-y king!
You are the Lord; you are a might-y king!
Cantor:
You are the riv-er wash-ing us clean, giv-ing us life, set-ting us free.
You are the sav-ior, God be-come man. Love be-came real when you stretched out your hands.
All:
You are the Lord; you are a might-y king!
You are the Lord; you are a might-y king!
Refrain
We shout with joy; you're the rock of our sal-va-tion. Let our hearts all your prais-es

sing.
We lift our voice to the one
who made the earth, the sky, the sea. You are a
3
might - y king!
1.
To verse 2
2.
D.S.
3.
3
4
king!
king!

Text: Steve Angrisano, b.1965
Tune: Steve Angrisano, b.1965; acc. by Ken Canedo, b.1953

115 WITH YOU BY MY SIDE

Verses
Cantor:
1. When I'm feel - ing all a - lone, and I'm far a - way from home, God, I need you to hear me.
2. When I feel all sick in - side, with no safe place to hide, God, I need you to lis - ten.
3. And as I go through my life, I will keep you in my sight to walk with me and be my strength.
When my friends all turn a - way, then I ache to hear you say that you are with me through it all.
When it seems I can't go on, then I long to hear the song re - mind - ing me you are my friend.
God, I know your plan for me: to help all those in need. To you a - lone I give my life!
Refrain
All:
You are the light, you're the song that I'm sing - ing; whom should I fear when you are with me? For you are my God, and with you there is noth - ing I can't do, with you by my side.

Text: David Haas, b.1957
Tune: David Haas, b.1957; choral arr. by David Haas and Kate Cuddy, b.1953

HOW CAN I KEEP FROM SINGING? 116

1. My life flows on in end-less song. A -
2. Through all the tu - mult and the strife I
3. What though my joys and com-fort die? The
4. The peace of Christ makes fresh my heart, A
bove earth's lam - en - ta - tion I hear the clear though
hear that mu - sic ring - ing. It finds an ech - o
Lord my sav - ior liv - eth. What though the dark - ness
foun - tain ev - er spring-ing! All things are mine since
far - off hymn That hails a new cre - a - tion.
in my soul; How can I keep from sing-ing?
gath - er round? Songs in the night he giv-eth.
I am his! How can I keep from sing-ing?
No storm can shake my in-most calm While to that Rock I'm
cling - ing. Since Christ is Lord of heav-en and earth,
How can I keep from sing - ing?

Text: Robert Lowry, 1826–1899
Tune: HOW CAN I KEEP FROM SINGING, 8 7 8 7 with refrain; Robert Lowry, 1826–1899; harm. by Robert J. Batastini, b.1942,

117 Rain Down

Refrain
Rain down, rain down, rain down your love on your peo - ple. Rain down, rain down, rain down your love, God of life.
Verses
1. Faith - ful and true is the word of our God.
2. We who re - vere and find hope in our God
3. God of cre - a - tion, we long for your truth;
All of God's works are so wor - thy of trust.
live in the kind - ness and joy of God's wing.
you are the wa - ter of life that we thirst.
God's mer - cy falls on the just and the right;
God will pro - tect us from dark - ness and death;
Grant that your love and your peace touch our hearts,
full of God's love is the earth.
God will not leave us to starve.
all of our hope lies in you.
D.C.

Text: Based on Psalm 33; Jaime Cortez, b.1963
Tune: Jaime Cortez, b.1963; acc. by Craig S. Kingsbury, b.1952

Be with Me, Lord 118
Refrain
Be with me, Lord. Be with me, my Lord. When I'm in trou-ble and I don't know where to go, be with me, Lord.
Verse 1
1. When I'm blind, when I can-not see, when all life's trou-ble sweeps o-ver me.
When I'm in dark-ness and all I see is me,
be with me, Lord.
D.C.
Verse 2
2. When I re-fuse to hear your word, when I hear your voice and do not fol-low,
when I'm in trou-ble and I don't know where to go,
be with me, Lord.
D.C.

Text: Refrain, traditional; verses, Tom Booth, b.1961
Tune: Refrain, traditional; verses and arr. by Tom Booth, b.1961; acc. by Ed Bolduc, b.1969

119 May the Road Rise to Meet You

Refrain
May the road rise to meet you. May the wind be at your back. May the sun shine warm up-on your face,
May the rain fall soft-ly on your fields, And un-til we meet a-gain, may you
Last time
keep safe in the gen-tle, lov-ing arms of God.
Verses
1.–6. For ev-'ry thing there is a sea-son; a time for
meet-ing, a time to say good-bye.
lis-t'ning, a time to speak the truth.
laugh-ter, a time for tears and pain.
search-ing, a time for calm and peace.
lov-ing, a time for let-ting go.
liv-ing, a time for go-ing home.
In all things
God is near, al-ways guid-ing your way.
D.C.

Text: Traditional Irish Blessing; verses based on Ecclesiastes 3:2–8; adapt. by Lori True, b.1961
Tune: Lori True, b.1961

Breathe 120

Verses
1. This is the air I breathe. This is the air I breathe. Your ho - ly pres - ence liv - ing in me.
2. This is my dai - ly bread. This is my dai- ly bread. Your ver - y word spo - ken to me.
1.
2.
Refrain
And I, I'm des-p'rate for you.
And I, I'm lost with-out you.
1. D.C.
2.
I'm lost with-out you.
Repeat ad lib.
I'm lost with-out you.
This is the air I breathe.
This is the air I breathe.

Text: Marie Barnett
Tune: Marie Barnett; arr. by Rick Modlin, b.1966

121 our liturgical year

ORDINARY TIME

Ordinary Time encompasses the part of the liturgical year that does not fall within the seasons of Advent, Christmas, Lent, or Easter. Ordinary Time, meaning "ordered," or "numbered," time, is celebrated from the Monday following the Baptism of the Lord to Ash Wednesday, and from the Monday after Pentecost to the First Sunday of Advent.

Ordinary Time is anything but ordinary! It celebrates the mystery of Christ in all its fullness. During these weeks we are invited to meditate on the life, miracles, and teachings of Christ. The Sundays of Ordinary Time also help us to understand more fully how to live out our faith in our daily lives. Many important feast days and solemnities occur in Ordinary Time, including the Most Holy Trinity, the Most Holy Body and Blood of Christ, the Assumption of the Blessed Virgin Mary, All Saints, and All Souls. *LD*

122 In Every Age

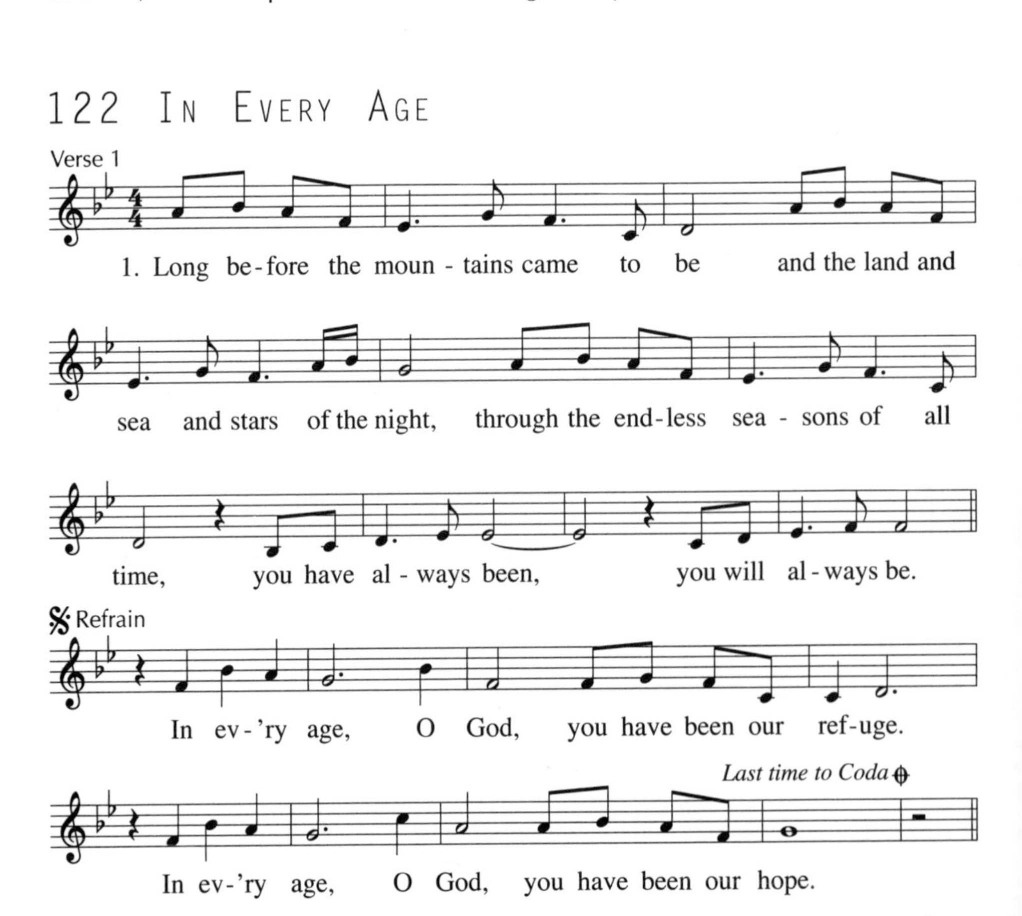
Verse 1
1. Long be-fore the moun - tains came to be and the land and
sea and stars of the night, through the end-less sea - sons of all
time, you have al - ways been, you will al - ways be.
Refrain
In ev-'ry age, O God, you have been our ref-uge.
Last time to Coda
In ev-'ry age, O God, you have been our hope.

Verses 2, 3
2. Des - ti - ny is cast, and at your si - lent word we re - turn to dust and scat - ter to the wind. A thou - sand years are like a sin - gle mo - ment gone, as the light that fades, at the end of day.
3. Teach us to make use of the time we have. Teach us to be pa - tient e - ven as we wait. Teach us to em - brace our ev - 'ry joy and pain. To sleep peace - ful - ly, and to rise up strong.
D.S.
Coda
In ev - 'ry age, O God, you have been our ref - uge. In ev - 'ry age, O God, you have been our hope, you have been our ref - uge, you have been our hope.

Text: Based on Psalm 90:1–4, 12, Janèt Sullivan Whitaker, b.1958
Tune: Janèt Sullivan Whitaker, b.1958

123 Come, Lord Jesus

Refrain
Come, Lord Je - sus, come. Come and fill my heart
with your life. Hold me close, Lord, hold
Last time to Coda
Repeat first time only
me tight, and come, Lord Je - sus, come.
Verse 1
1. Where there's de - spair in life, Lord, let me
be your voice of hope. Where there's in - ju - ry, Lord,
D.C.
let me be your voice of peace.
Verse 2
2. Where there is sad - ness let me be your
com - fort and your joy. When there's fear in our hearts
D.C.
let me be a sign of faith.

Coda
Hold me close, Lord, hold me tight.
4
Come, Lord Je - sus, come.

Text: Steve Angrisano, b.1965 and Tom Tomaszek, b.1950
Tune: Steve Angrisano, b.1965 and Tom Tomaszek, b.1950; acc. by Rick Modlin, b.1966

AMAZING GRACE 124

1. A - maz - ing grace! how sweet the sound, That saved a wretch like me! I once was lost, but now am found, Was blind, but now I see.
2. 'Twas grace that taught my heart to fear, And grace my fears re - lieved; How pre - cious did that grace ap - pear The hour I first be - lieved!
3. The Lord has prom - ised good to me, His word my hope se - cures; He will my shield and por - tion be As long as life en - dures.
4. Through man - y dan - gers, toils, and snares, I have al - read - y come; 'Tis grace has brought me safe thus far, And grace will lead me home.
5. When we've been there ten thou - sand years, Bright shin - ing as the sun, We've no less days to sing God's praise Than when we'd first be - gun.

Text: St. 1–4, John Newton, 1725–1807; st. 5, attr. to John Rees, fl.1859
Tune: NEW BRITAIN, CM; *Virginia Harmony,* 1831; arr. by Paul A. Tate, b.1968, © 2008, GIA Publications, Inc.

125 Here I Am

Refrain
Here I am, stand-ing right be-side you. Here I
am; do not be a-fraid. Here I am, wait-ing like a
lov-er. I am here; here I am.
1.–3.
To verses
Last time
am. I am here; here I am.
3
Verse 1
1. Do not fear when the tempt-er calls you. Do not
fear e-ven though you fall. Do not fear, I have con-quered
e-vil. Do not fear; nev-er be a-fraid.
D.S.
Verse 2
2. I am here in the face of ev-'ry child. I am
here in ev-'ry warm em-brace. I am here with ten-der-ness and
mer-cy. Here I am; I am here.
D.S.

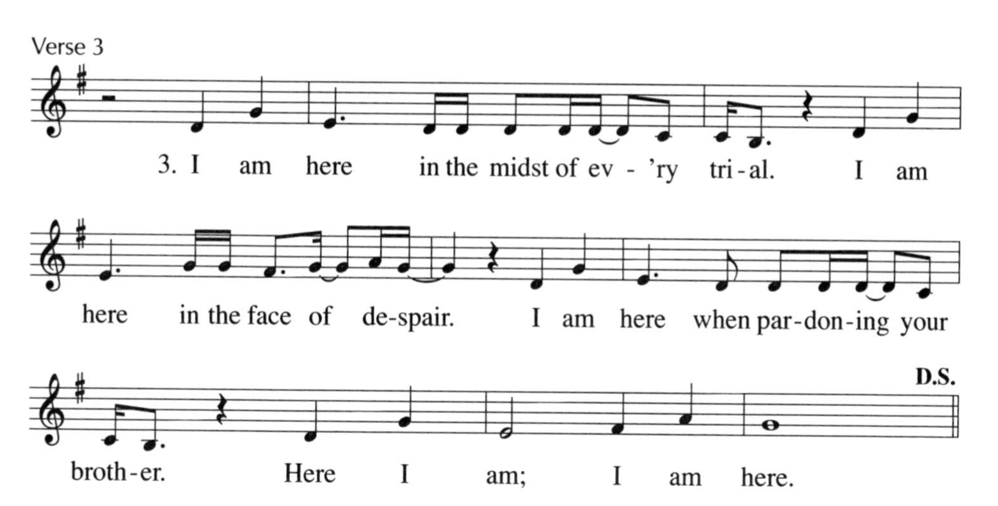
Verse 3
3. I am here in the midst of ev - 'ry tri - al. I am
here in the face of de-spair. I am here when par-don-ing your
broth - er. Here I am; I am here.
D.S.

Text: Tom Booth, b.1961
Tune: Tom Booth, b.1961; acc. by Ed Bolduc, b.1969

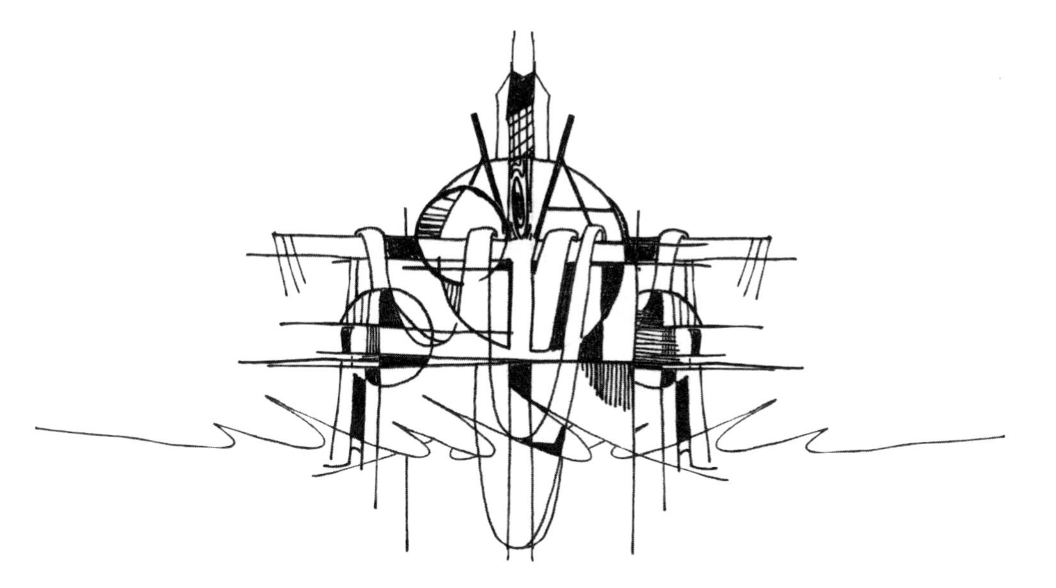

126 No More Fear

Verses
1. No more fear, though you stum-ble in the dark-ness, no more fear, though you stum-ble in the dark-ness, no more fear, though you stum-ble in the dark-ness,
2. No more fear, though your flesh is bruised and bro-ken, no more fear, though your flesh is bruised and bro-ken, no more fear, though your flesh is bruised and bro-ken,
3. No more fear, though your en-e-mies sur-round you, no more fear, though your en-e-mies sur-round you, no more fear, though your en-e-mies sur-round you,
4. No more fear, though your mind can-not re-mem-ber, no more fear, though your mind can-not re-mem-ber, no more fear, though your mind can-not re-mem-ber,
5. No more fear, though the shad-ows close up-on you, no more fear, though the shad-ows close up-on you, no more fear, though the shad-ows close up-on you,
6. No more fear, though they burn a cross be-fore you, no more fear, though they burn a cross be-fore you, no more fear, though they burn a cross be-fore you,
Refrain
all you see be-fore you lost and fad-ing, and the lov-ing God who con-quered death is wait-ing

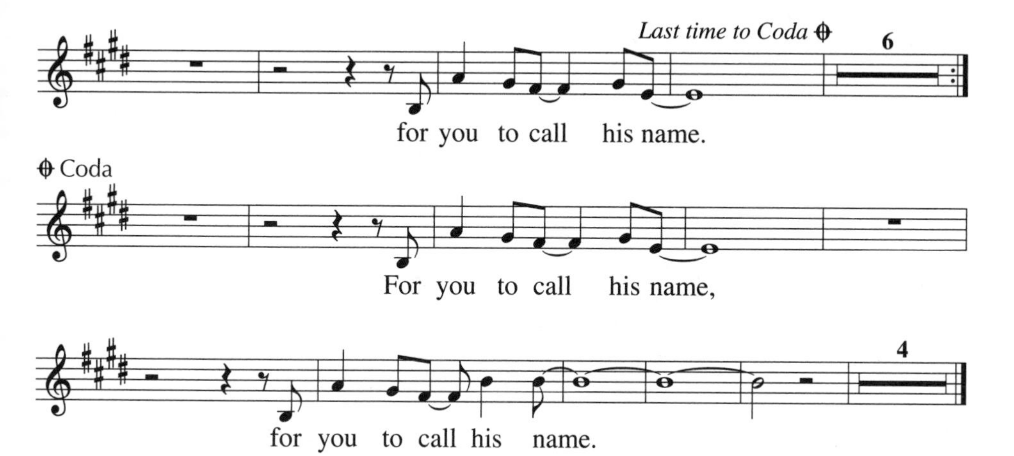
Last time to Coda
6
for you to call his name.
Coda
For you to call his name,
4
for you to call his name.

Text: Aaron Thompson, b.1967
Tune: Aaron Thompson, b.1967; acc. by Ed Bolduc, b.1969

Is anyone among you suffering? He should pray. Is anyone in good spirits? He should sing praise.

James 5:13

127 You Are My King (Amazing Love)

Verse
I'm for-giv-en be-cause you were for-sak-en.
I'm ac-cept-ed; you were con-demned.
I'm a-live and well, your Spir-it is with-in me be-
cause you died and rose a-gain.
1.
2., 3.
Refrain
A-maz-ing love, how can it be
that you, my King, would die for me?
A-maz-ing love, I know it's true;
and it's my joy to hon-or you in all I
do, I hon-or you.
1.
To verse

2.
To bridge
Last time
you.
you.
Bridge
You are my King. You are my King. Je-sus,
you are my King. You are my King.
D.S.

Text: Billy James Foote
Tune: Billy James Foote; arr. by Ed Bolduc, b.1969

128 You Are Mine / Contigo Estoy

Verses / Estrofas

1. I will come to you in the si - lence,
2. I am hope for all who are hope - less,
3. I am strength for all the de - spair - ing,
4. am the Word that leads all to free - dom, I
1. Te_ha - bla - ré_en la paz del si - len - cio,
2. es - pe - ran - za de quien an - he - la, la
3. Soy la for - ta - le - za del dé - bil;
4. Soy pa - la - bra li - be - ra - do - ra, la

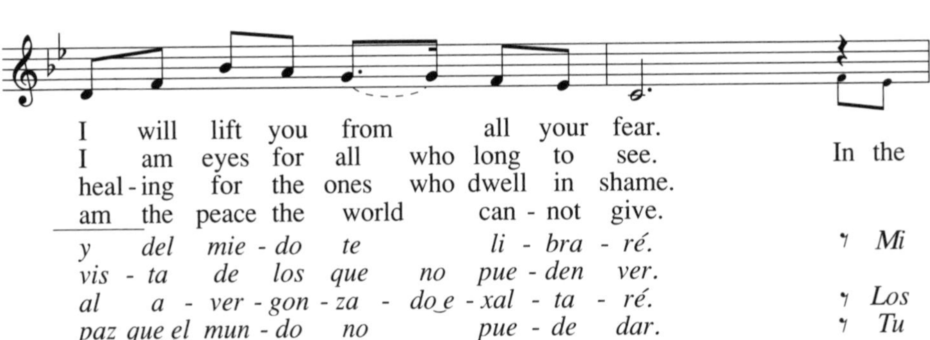
I will lift you from all your fear.
I am eyes for all who long to see. In the
heal - ing for the ones who dwell in shame.
am the peace the world can - not give.
y del mie - do te li - bra - ré. Mi
vis - ta de los que no pue - den ver.
al a - ver - gon - za - do_e - xal - ta - ré. Los
paz que_el mun - do no pue - de dar. Tu

You will hear my voice, I claim you as my choice, be
shad - ows of the night, I will be your light,
All the blind will see, the lame will all run free, and
I will call your name, em - brac - ing all your pain. Stand
voz es - cu - cha - rás, y mí - o tú se - rás.
Con in - ten - si - dad bri - lla - ré_en la_os - cu - ri - dad.
cie - gos ve - rán, los li - sia - dos co - rre - rán. Mi
nom - bre lla - ma - ré; tu llan - to to - ma - ré. Le -

still and know I am here. (To verse 2)
come and rest in me. (To refrain)
all will know my name. (To refrain)
up, now walk, and live! (To refrain)
Jun - to a ti es - ta - ré. (A la Estrofa 2) 2. Soy
Tu des - can - so quie - ro ser. (Al Estribillo)
nom - bre re - ve - la - ré. (Al Estribillo)
ván - ta - te a ca - mi - nar. (Al Estribillo)

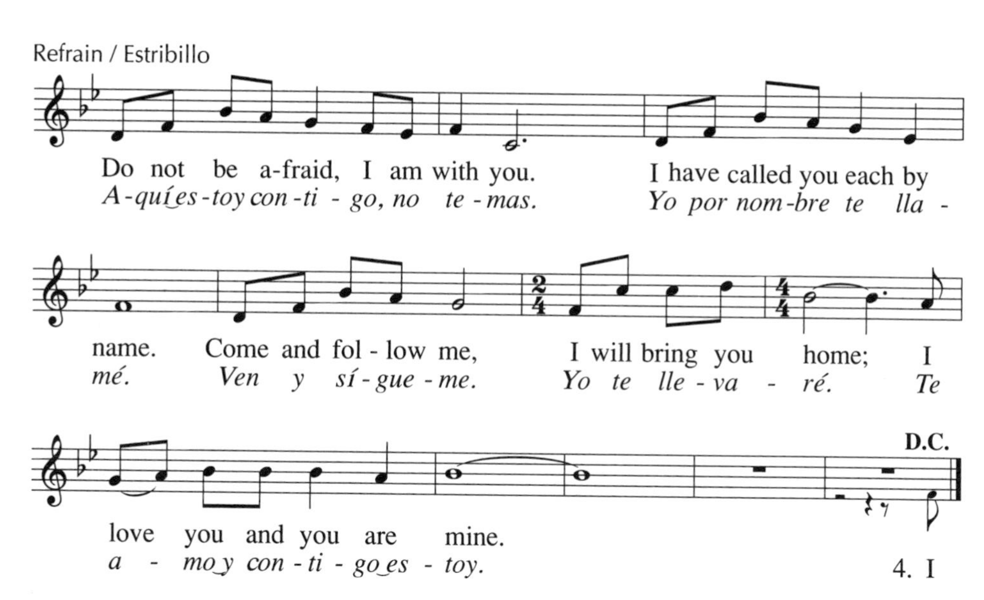
Refrain / Estribillo
Do not be a-fraid, I am with you. I have called you each by name. Come and fol - low me, I will bring you home; I love you and you are mine.
A-quí es-toy con-ti - go, no te - mas. Yo por nom-bre te lla - mé. Ven y sí - gue - me. Yo te lle - va - ré. Te a - mo y con - ti - go es - toy.
D.C.
4. I

Text: David Haas, b.1957; tr. by Santiago Fernández, b.1971
Tune: David Haas, b.1957

May the Grace of God Be with You / 129
Ki Ri Su To No

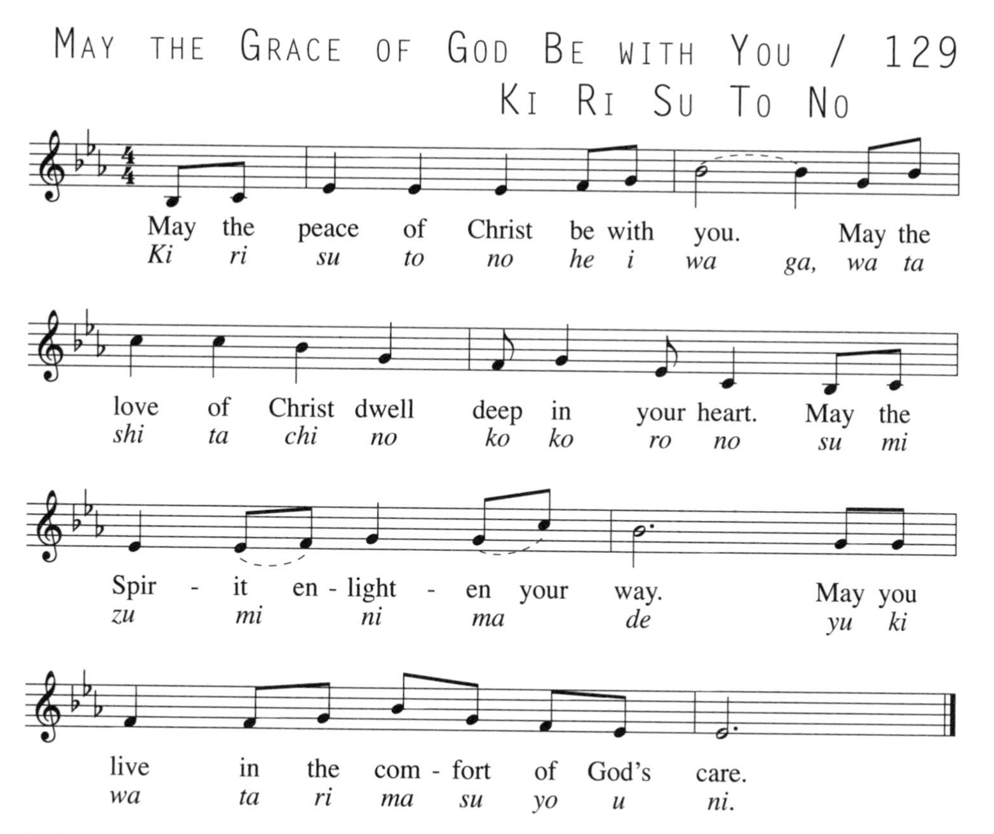
May the peace of Christ be with you. May the love of Christ dwell deep in your heart. May the Spir - it en - light - en your way. May you live in the com - fort of God's care.
Ki ri su to no he i wa ga, wa ta shi ta chi no ko ko ro no su mi zu mi ni ma de yu ki wa ta ri ma su yo u ni.

Text: Japanese blessing; additional text by Lori True, b.1961, © 2008, GIA Publications, Inc.
Tune: Japanese folk melody

130 Live in the Light

Refrain
Let your love be a light for our days, and a
fire to keep us warm in the night.
Let your love be a guide on our way. May we
learn to al - ways live in the light.
Last time
Verses 1, 2
Cantor:
1. When I'm a - lone or when I lose my way.
2. When I'm a - fraid of do - ing what is right,
Yours is the hand I can hold on
when there is no one who will help
to.
me.
When I was fall - en you
When I am sti - fled by
lift - ed me up. I was weak Lord, and you
fear and re - gret, your com - pas - sion and strength

D.C.
pulled me through!
set me free!
Verse 3
Cantor:
3. God of all cre - a - tion,
God be - yond all time and all space,
God, look down with mer - cy and
D.C.
keep me al - ways in your em - brace.

Text: Michael Mahler, b.1981
Tune: Michael Mahler, b.1981

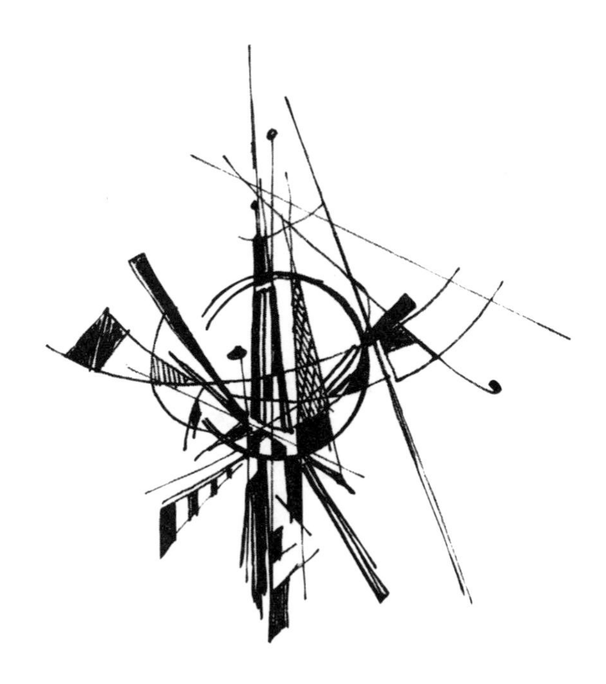

131 The Clouds' Veil

Refrain
E-ven though the rain hides the stars, e-ven though the mist swirls the hills,
e-ven when the dark clouds veil the sky, God is by my side.
E-ven when the sun shall fall in sleep, e-ven when at dawn the sky shall weep,
e-ven in the night when storms shall rise, God is by my side. God is by my side.
Verses
1. Bright the stars at night that mir-ror heav-en's way to you. Bright the stars in
2. Deep the feast of life where saints shall gath-er in deep peace. Deep in heav-en's
3. Blest are they who sing the fel-low-ship of saints in light. Blest is heav-en's

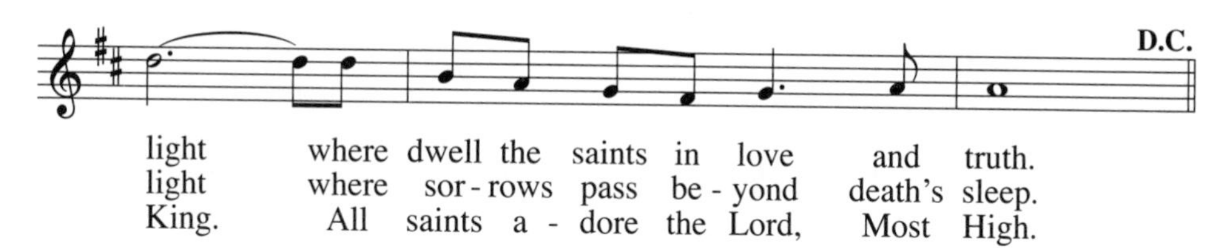
D.C.
light where dwell the saints in love and truth.
light where sor - rows pass be - yond death's sleep.
King. All saints a - dore the Lord, Most High.

Text: Liam Lawton, b.1959
Tune: Liam Lawton, b.1959; arr. by John McCann, b.1961

BE STILL 132

Refrain
Be still, be still and know that I am God. Be
still, be still and lis - ten with your heart. Be
still, be still and o - pen up your mind. Be
still and know that I am God.
1.–3.
To verses
4.
God.
Verses
1. Why do you wor - ry and why do you fret?
2. I am with you in all of your trials.
3. Think of me al - ways in things that are true.
D.C.
Have I ev - er failed you yet?
Trust me al - ways, I'll be your guide.
Feel me with you, what - ev - er you do.

Text: Based on Psalm 46; James E. Moore, Jr., b.1951
Tune: James E. Moore, Jr., b.1951

133 Be with Me

Verses 1–3
1. Be with me when I am in trou-ble.
(2. Walk be -) side me when I am in trou-ble.
(3. Give me) com-fort when I am in trou-ble.
Be with me when I am a - fraid. Be
Walk be - side me when I am a - fraid. Walk be-
Give me com-fort when I am a - fraid. Give me
with me when I am a - lone. Be
side me when I am a - lone. Walk be -
com-fort when I am a - lone. Give me
with me, Lord, I pray.
side me, Lord, I pray.
com-fort, Lord, I pray.
1., 2.
2. Walk be -
3. Give me
3.
Verse 4
4. Raise me high-er when I am in trou-ble. Raise me
high-er when I am a - fraid. Raise me high-er when I
am a - lone. Raise me high-er, Lord, I pray.
I pray. I pray.

Optional extra verses

After verse 1: Stand beside me...
After verse 3: Make me stronger...

Text: Matt Wessel, b.1981
Tune: Matt Wessel, b.1981

You Are Good to Me 134
Refrain
God, you are good to me, your love will guide me home. God, you are good to me, your love will guide me home.
Verses 1, 2
1. Waters may gather on either side, but you will show the way, clearing a path which sets me free from all that brings me harm.
2. Storm-clouds may gather and waves collide, but you will keep me warm, sheltered from winds that tear me down, safe within your arms.
D.C.
Verse 3
3. Come, sing your praise, all you people. Oh, cherish the life you have. Open your hearts to the reign of God that the seed of faith may thrive.
D.C.

Text: Ian Callanan
Tune: Ian Callanan; arr. by Gary Daigle, b.1957

135 Quietly, Peacefully

Refrain
Qui - et-ly, peace - ful-ly let me rest in you.
Qui - et-ly, peace - ful-ly lead me back to you.
Verses
1. In my weak - ness I have strayed, drift - ing far from you. In your good - ness stead - y me, light my path to you.
2. Breathe your law deep in me, plant it in my soul. Let your jus - tice be my song, kind - ness be my goal.
3. Save me from my self - ish ways, keep me from my pride. By your grace, bring me home, safe - ly by your side.
4. Lov - ing wis - dom, you a - lone know all I can be. You, the hope my spir - it seeks, come and set me free.
5. Hap - py is the heart that's free, choos-ing life with you. Break the chains that bind my soul, let me walk with you.
6. In the night I call to you; can you hear me cry? Sad and fear - ful, still I plead: do not pass me by.
7. Heal - ing grace, take my pain, guard me night and day. Show - er me with your love, wash my tears a - way.
D.C.

CHRIST, BE OUR LIGHT 136

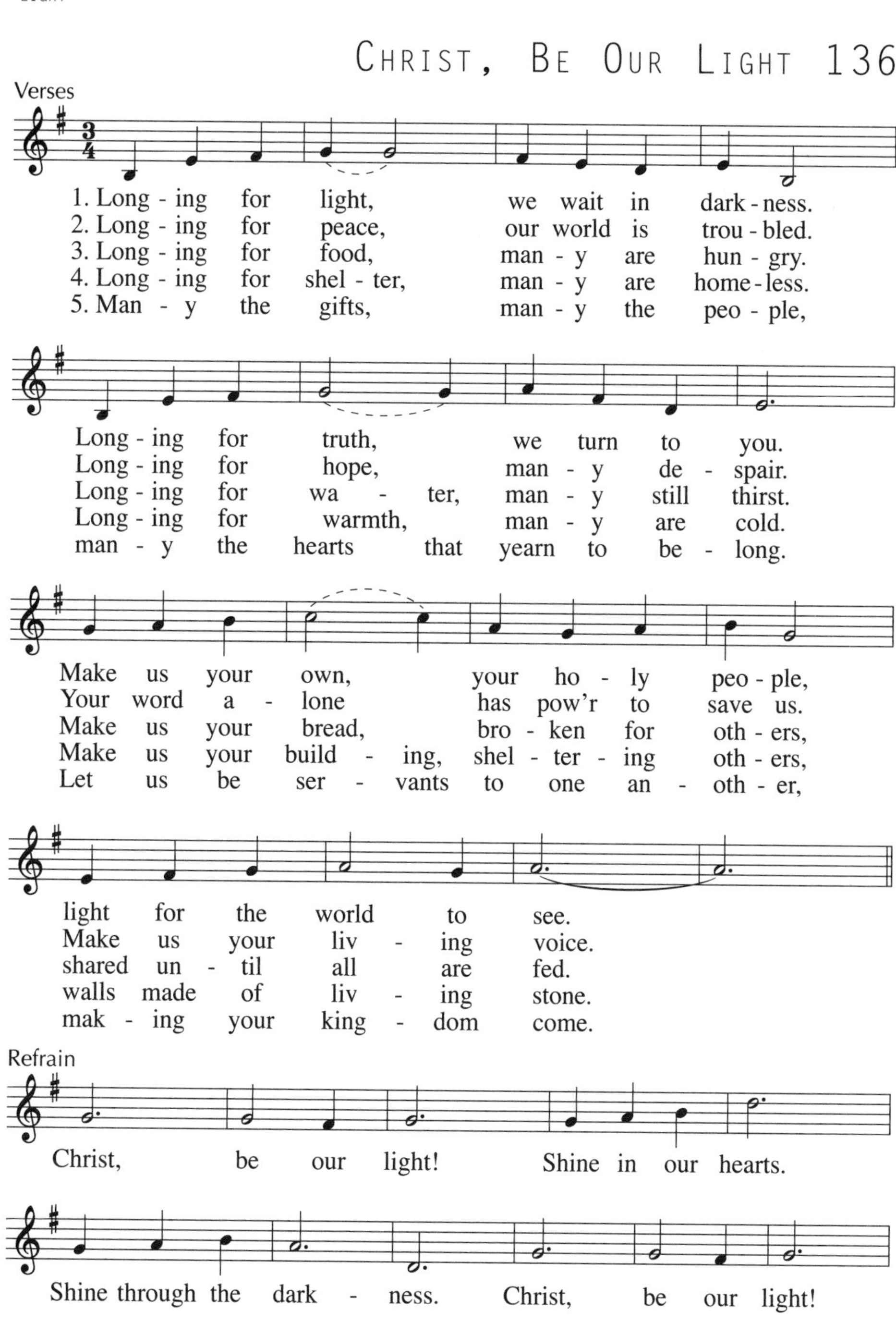
Verses
1. Long - ing for light, we wait in dark - ness.
2. Long - ing for peace, our world is trou - bled.
3. Long - ing for food, man - y are hun - gry.
4. Long - ing for shel - ter, man - y are home - less.
5. Man - y the gifts, man - y the peo - ple,
Long - ing for truth, we turn to you.
Long - ing for hope, man - y de - spair.
Long - ing for wa - ter, man - y still thirst.
Long - ing for warmth, man - y are cold.
man - y the hearts that yearn to be - long.
Make us your own, your ho - ly peo - ple,
Your word a - lone has pow'r to save us.
Make us your bread, bro - ken for oth - ers,
Make us your build - ing, shel - ter - ing oth - ers,
Let us be ser - vants to one an - oth - er,
light for the world to see.
Make us your liv - ing voice.
shared un - til all are fed.
walls made of liv - ing stone.
mak - ing your king - dom come.
Refrain
Christ, be our light! Shine in our hearts.
Shine through the dark - ness. Christ, be our light!
Shine in your church gath-ered to - day.

Text: Bernadette Farrell, b.1957
Tune: Bernadette Farrell, b.1957

137 Go Light Your World

Verse 1
1. There is a can-dle in ev-'ry soul; some bright-ly burn-ing,
some dark and cold. There is a Spir-it who brings a
fire, ig-nites a can-dle and makes his home.
Refrain
So, car-ry your can-dle, run to the dark-ness, seek out the
1. hope-less, con-fused and torn.
2. lone-ly, the tired and worn.
Hold out your
Last time to Coda
can-dle for all to see it. Take your can-dle and go light your
world. Take your can-dle and go light your world.
Verse 2
2. Frus-trat-ed broth-er, see how he's tried to light his own
can-dle some oth-er way. See now your sis-ter,

LIGHT
D.S.
she's been robbed and lied to, still holds a can-dle with-out a flame.
Coda
can-dle and go light your world.
Verse 3
3. We are a
fam - 'ly whose hearts are blaz-ing, so let's raise our can-dles
and light up the sky, pray-ing to our Fa-ther, in the name of
Je - sus: make us a bea-con in dark-est time. So, car-ry your
Final Refrain
can-dle, run to the dark-ness, seek out the
1. help-less, de-ceived and poor.
2. hope-less, con-fused and torn.
Hold out your can - dle for all to see it. Take your
1.
can - dle and go light your world. Car - ry your
2.
can - dle and go light your world. Take your
can - dle and go light your world.
Text: Chris Rice
Tune: Chris Rice
© 1993, BMG Songs, Inc. (ASCAP)

138 We Are Marching

We are march - ing* in the light of God, we are
1.
march-ing in the light of God.
2.
march - ing in the light of God,
march-ing in the light of, the
march - ing in the light of God,
we are march - ing,
light of God, we are march-ing, march-ing, we are
Oo we are
march-ing, march-ing, we are march-ing in the light of God.

*Alternate text: dancing, singing, praying

Text: South African
Tune: South African

SHINE, JESUS, SHINE 139

Verses
1. Lord, the light of your love is shin - ing, in the midst of the
2. Lord, I come to your awe - some pres - ence, from the shad-ows in-
3. As we gaze on your king - ly bright-ness, so our fac - es dis-
dark - ness, shin - ing. Je - sus, Light of the world, shine up - on us.
to your ra - diance. By the blood I may en - ter your bright-ness.
play your like - ness, ev - er chang-ing from glo - ry to glo - ry.
Set us free by the truth you now bring us.
Search me, try me, con-sume all my dark-ness. Shine on
Mir - rored here, may our lives tell your sto - ry.
me, shine on me.
Refrain
Shine, Je - sus, shine; fill this land with the Fa-ther's glo - ry.
Blaze, Spir - it, blaze; set our hearts on fire.
Flow riv - er, flow; flood the na - tions with grace and mer - cy.
Send forth your Word, Lord, and let there be light.
1.–3.
To verses
4.
D.S.
light.
Last time
light.

Text: Graham Kendrick, b.1950
Tune: Graham Kendrick, b.1950; arr. by Rick Modlin, b.1966

140 Shine on Us

Verses
1. We, though man - y, are one bod - y. We, though man - y, are
2. With this cup of life we share in, we will drink of your
3. As we break the bread of Je - sus, suf-f'ring, sor-row, and
4. When we tend the sad and lone-ly, when we care for the
5. As we see your bod - y bro-ken, as we wit-ness your
6. In our res - ur - rec - tion liv-ing, al - le - lu - ia be -
one in you. As one blood and as one bod - y,
death, O Lord. We will taste your res - ur - rec - tion
pain are changed, In your sac - ri - fice once giv - en,
poor and weak, Christ is pres - ent in those mo - ments,
blood poured out, We are one with ev - 'ry suf - f'ring,
comes the song. Al - le - lu - ia, al - le - lu - ia,
we are liv - ing sign. We are one in the
till you come a - gain. Pre - cious blood that was
all is sanc - ti - fied. Let us eat at this
giv - ing light for all. In the home-less and
pain and a - go - ny. We are one in all
sing it loud and strong! Roll the stone a - way
light of God, as we live the feast. Be
shed for us, we par - take as one. Re -
king-dom meal; let us drink with joy. We
starv - ing ones, those in thirst and pain, there
ris - ing, too, res - ur - rec - tion joy. New
from your tombs, Je - sus lives a - gain! The
sac - ri - fice, be bro - ken bread, be
new the light of faith so bright. In -
live as one for all the world. As
Christ is found for all a - round to
life is ours like spring - time flowers, trans -
Christ is raised, our God be praised, re -

LIGHT

Christ to all those we meet.
flame our hearts with your hope.
Church we sing and re - joice!
build the king - dom of God.
formed from death to new life.
joice, sing al - le - lu - ia!
Refrain
Shine on us, ho - ly light, ev - er blest, ev - er bright.
Warm our hearts with your rays, through the mist, in the haze.
Guide our time on this earth, out of death to re - birth.
Shine on us, shine on us, shine on us.

Text: Rob Glover, b.1950
Tune: Rob Glover, b.1950

141 Come, Now Is the Time to Worship

1. Come, now is the time to wor - ship.
2. Come, just as you are to wor - ship.

Last time to Coda

Come, now is the time to give your heart.
Come, just as you are be-fore your God.

Come.
One day ev - 'ry tongue will con - fess

you are God.
One day ev-'ry knee will bow.

Still the great - est treas - ure re - mains for those who glad -

D.C.
ly choose you now.

Coda
Come.
Come.
Come,

just as you are.
Come.

Text: Brian Doerksen
Tune: Brian Doerksen; arr. by Ed Bolduc, b.1969

WHAT IS THIS PLACE 142

1. What is this place where we are meet - ing?
2. Words from a - far, stars that are fall - ing,
3. And we ac - cept bread at his ta - ble,
On - ly a house, the earth its floor,
Sparks that are sown in us like seed.
Bro - ken and shared, a liv - ing sign.
Walls and a roof shel - ter - ing peo - ple,
Names for our God, dreams, signs and won - ders
Here in this world, dy - ing and liv - ing,
Win - dows for light, an o - pen door.
Sent from the past are all we need.
We are each oth - er's bread and wine.
Yet it be - comes a bod - y that lives When
We in this place re - mem - ber and speak A -
This is the place where we can re - ceive What
we are gath - ered here, And know our God is near.
gain what we have heard: God's free re - deem - ing word.
we need to in - crease: Our jus - tice and God's peace.
1. D.C.
2.
3 D.C.
3.

Text: *Zomaar een dak boven wat hoofen*; Huub Oosterhuis, b.1933; trans. by David Smith, b.1933, © 1967, Gooi en Sticht, bv., Baarn, The Netherlands. Exclusive English language agent: OCP.
Tune: Gary Daigle, b.1957, © 2008, GIA Publications, Inc.

143 Here I Am to Worship

Verses

1. Light of the world, you stepped down in - to dark - ness,
2. King of all days, oh so high - ly ex - alt - ed,

o - pened my eyes, let me see. Beau - ty that made this
glo - rious in heav - en a - bove. Hum - bly you came to the

heart a - dore you, hope of a life spent with you.
earth you cre - at - ed, all for love's sake be - came poor.

Refrain

Here I am to wor - ship, here I am to bow down, here I am to

say that you're my God. You're al-to-geth-er love - ly, al - to-geth-er

wor - thy, al - to-geth-er won - der - ful to me.

1., 3. *Last time* **D.C.**

2. Bridge

And I'll nev - er know how much it cost to see

my sin up-on that cross. I'll nev - er know how much

it cost to see my sin up-on that cross. I'll nev-

er know how much it cost to see my sin up-on

that cross. I'll nev - er know how much it cost to see
my sin up-on that cross.
D.S.
Here I am to

Text: Tim Hughes
Tune: Tim Hughes

Gather Your People 144

Refrain
Gath-er your peo-ple, O Lord. Gath-er your peo-ple, O
Lord. One bread, one bod-y, one spir-it of
love. Gath-er your peo-ple, O Lord.
Verses
1. Draw us forth to the ta - ble of life:
2. We are parts of the bod - y of Christ,
3. No more harm on the moun - tain of God;
4. Wash us, Lord, in the wa - ters of life;
broth - ers and sis - ters, each of us called to
need - ing each oth - er, each of the gifts the
swords in - to plow-shares. Free us, O Lord, from
wa - ters of mer - cy, wa - ters of hope that
walk in your light.
Spir - it pro - vides.
hard - ness of heart.
flow from your side.
D.C.

Text: 1 Corinthians 12, Isaiah 2:3–4, 11:9; Bob Hurd, b.1950
Tune: Bob Hurd. b.1950; choral arr. by Craig S. Kingsbury, b.1952; acc. by Dominic MacAller, b.1959

145 All Are Welcome

1. Let us build a house where love can dwell And
2. Let us build a house where proph - ets speak, And
3. Let us build a house where love is found In
4. Let us build a house where hands will reach Be -
5. Let us build a house where all are named, Their
all can safe - ly live, A place where saints and
words are strong and true, Where all God's chil - dren
wa - ter, wine and wheat: A ban - quet hall on
yond the wood and stone To heal and strength - en,
songs and vi - sions heard And loved and treas - ured,
chil - dren tell How hearts learn to for -
dare to seek To dream God's reign a -
ho - ly ground, Where peace and jus - tice
serve and teach, And live the Word they've
taught and claimed As words with - in the
give. Built of hopes and dreams and vi - sions, Rock of
new. Here the cross shall stand as wit - ness And as
meet. Here the love of God, through Je - sus, Is re -
known. Here the out - cast and the stran - ger Bear the
Word. Built of tears and cries and laugh - ter, Prayers of
faith and vault of grace; Here the
sym - bol of God's grace; Here as
vealed in time and space; As we
im - age of God's face; Let us
faith and songs of grace, Let this

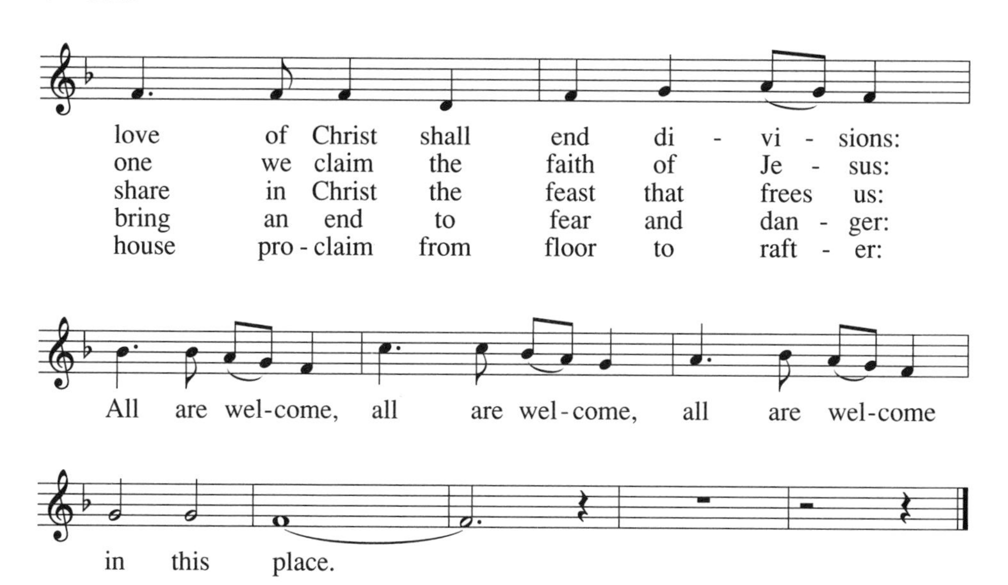
love of Christ shall end di - vi - sions:
one we claim the faith of Je - sus:
share in Christ the feast that frees us:
bring an end to fear and dan - ger:
house pro - claim from floor to raft - er:
All are wel-come, all are wel-come, all are wel-come
in this place.

Text: Marty Haugen, b.1950
Tune: TWO OAKS, 9 6 8 6 8 7 10 with refrain; Marty Haugen, b.1950

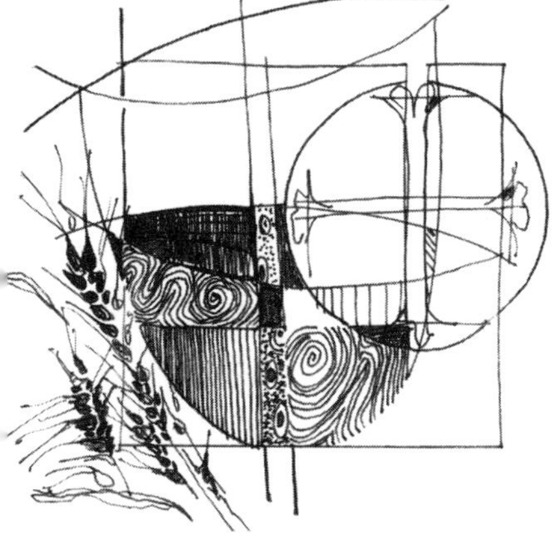

GATHERING

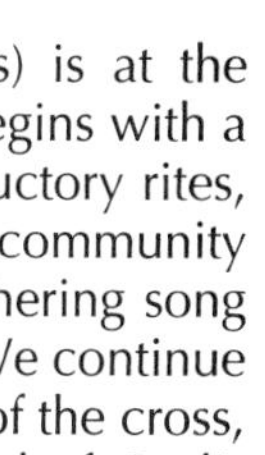

The celebration of Eucharist (Mass) is at the heart of our prayer life. The Mass begins with a series of elements called the introductory rites, which help us to gather as a united community of faith. We begin by singing a gathering song to unify our hearts and our minds. We continue by marking ourselves with the sign of the cross, a reminder of our own baptism and of God's promise of eternal life. We call to mind our sins and praise God for his mercy in the penitential rite (usually the Kyrie), we sing a hymn of praise (the Gloria), and the opening prayer is spoken by the priest and affirmed with our amen. While there are slight variations to these elements depending on the liturgical season, they always serve the same purpose: to gather us as one people and to prepare us to listen to God's word in the Liturgy of the Word, which flows out of the introductory rites. *TA*

147 Come All You People / Uyai Mose

Verses 1–3

1. Sky and earth, moon and star:
2. Tree and flow - er, leaf and vine: come and praise your Mak - er.
3. Ev - 'ry wom - an, child and man:

Des-ert, mead - ow, sea and shore:
Liv - ing things that crawl and climb: come and praise your Mak - er.
Ev - 'ry na - tion, ev - 'ry land:

Moun-tain - top and o - cean-floor:
Plants and crea - tures, hu - man - kind: come and praise your Mak - er.
Ev - 'ry cul - ture, creed and clan:

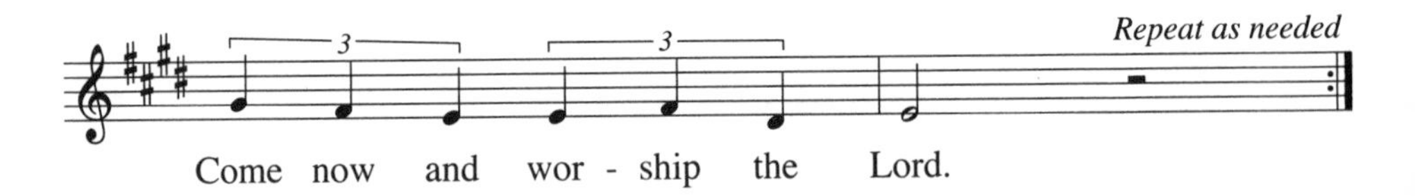

Repeat as needed

Come now and wor - ship the Lord.

Refrain

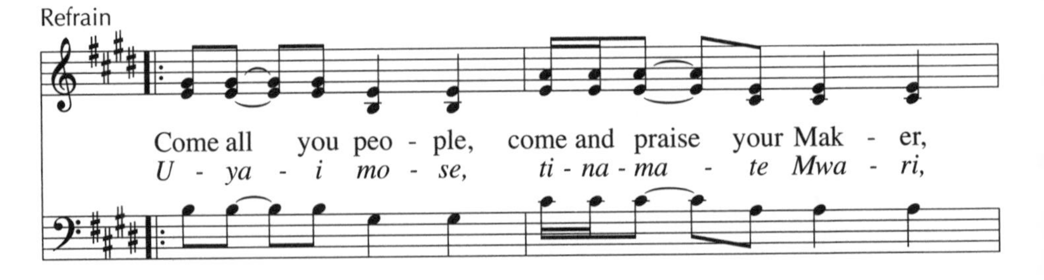

Come all you peo - ple, come and praise your Mak - er,
U - ya - i mo - se, ti - na - ma - te Mwa - ri,

Verses 4–7

4. Fire, wind, snow and rain:
   Blizzard, earthquake, hurricane:
   Thunderclouds and lightening:

5. Citizens and immigrants:
   Laborers and management:
   Lobbyists and government:

6. Friend and stranger, host and guest:
   Refugee and resident:
   Native, alien and homeless:

7. Young and old, rich and poor:
   Weak and strong, broken, cured:
   Lonely, loved, afraid, secure:

Come all you peo - ple, come and praise your Mak - er,
U - ya - i mo - se, ti - na - ma - te Mwa - ri,
Come all you peo - ple, come and praise your Mak - er,
U - ya - i mo - se, ti - na - ma - te Mwa - ri,
Repeat refrain as needed
Come now and wor - ship the Lord.
U - ya - i mo - se zvi - no.
Come now and wor - ship the Lord.
U - ya - i mo - se zvi - no.
Come now and wor - ship the Lord.
U - ya - i mo - se zvi - no.

Text: Alexander Gondo, b.1936; additional text by Gary Daigle, b.1957,
Tune: Alexander Gondo, b.1936; adapt. by Gary Daigle, b.1957, from an arr. by John L. Bell, b.1949,

148 Now Is the Time

Refrain
Come to us, you who say, "I will not for-get you."
Be with us, you who say, "Do not be a-fraid."
Take hold of us, our hearts, our minds, our whole be - ing.
Make us your own, now is the time.
Verses 1, 2
Cantor:
All:
1. Spir-it of love, crush the pain of ha - tred.
2. Spir-it of peace, si - lence tongues of an - ger.
Cantor:
All:
Spir - it of hope, stand be - fore our eyes.
Spir - it of life, break the chains of death.
Cantor:
All:
Spir - it of light, dance with - in our dark - ness.
Spir - it of joy, o - ver-come our sad - ness.
D.C.
Make us your own, now is the time.
Make us your own, now is the time.

Verse 3
Cantor:
3. Spir - it of faith,
All:
rise a - bove our doubt - ing.
Cantor:
Spir - it of truth,
All:
save us from our lies.
Cantor:
Spir - it of God,
All:
walk a - mong your peo - ple. Make us your own, now is the time.
Final refrain
Come to us, you who say, "I will not for - get you."
Be with us, you who say, "Do not be a - fraid."
Take hold of us, our hearts, our minds, our whole be - ing.
Make us your own, now is the time.

Text: Tom Kendzia, b.1954
Tune: Tom Kendzia, b.1954

149 The Summons / El Llamado

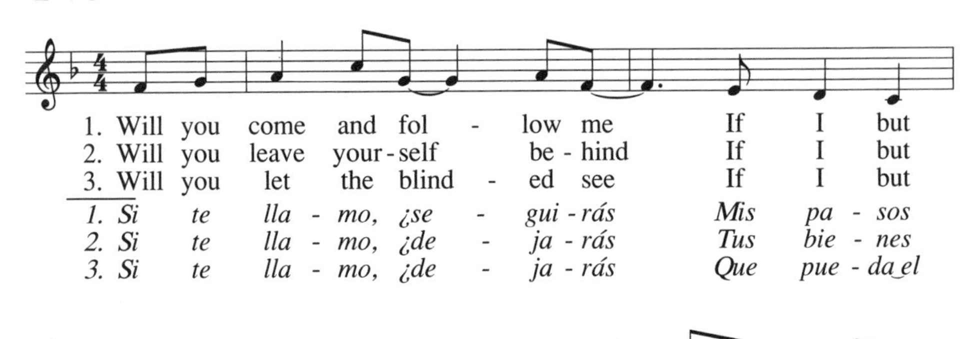
1. Will you come and fol - low me If I but
2. Will you leave your - self be - hind If I but
3. Will you let the blind - ed see If I but
1. Si te lla - mo, ¿se - gui - rás Mis pa - sos
2. Si te lla - mo, ¿de - ja - rás Tus bie - nes
3. Si te lla - mo, ¿de - ja - rás Que pue - da el

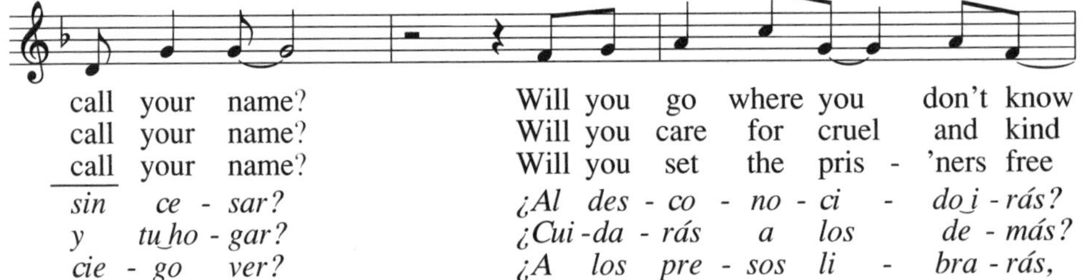
call your name? Will you go where you don't know
call your name? Will you care for cruel and kind
call your name? Will you set the pris - 'ners free
sin ce - sar? ¿Al des - co - no - ci - do i - rás?
y tu ho - gar? ¿Cui - da - rás a los de - más?
cie - go ver? ¿A los pre - sos li - bra - rás,

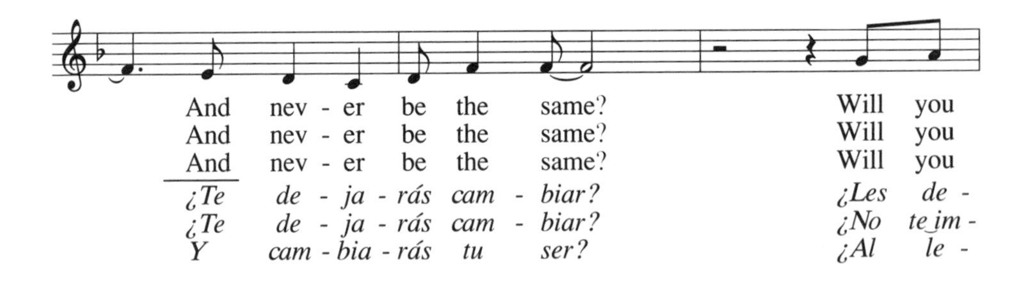
And nev - er be the same? Will you
And nev - er be the same? Will you
And nev - er be the same? Will you
¿Te de - ja - rás cam - biar? ¿Les de -
¿Te de - ja - rás cam - biar? ¿No te im -
Y cam - bia - rás tu ser? ¿Al le -

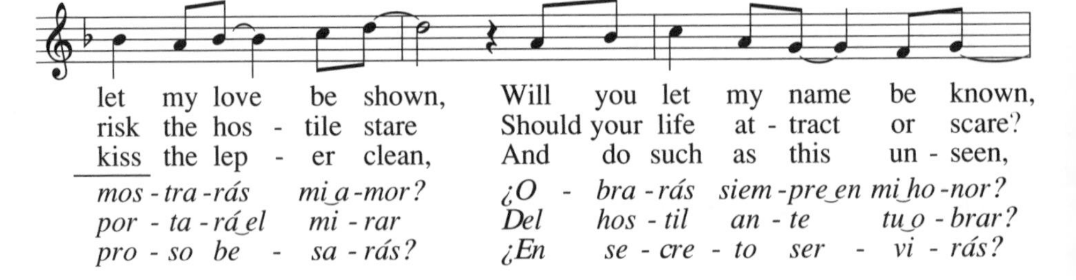
let my love be shown, Will you let my name be known,
risk the hos - tile stare Should your life at - tract or scare?
kiss the lep - er clean, And do such as this un - seen,
mos - tra - rás mi a - mor? ¿O - bra - rás siem - pre en mi ho - nor?
por - ta - rá el mi - rar Del hos - til an - te tu o - brar?
pro - so be - sa - rás? ¿En se - cre - to ser - vi - rás?

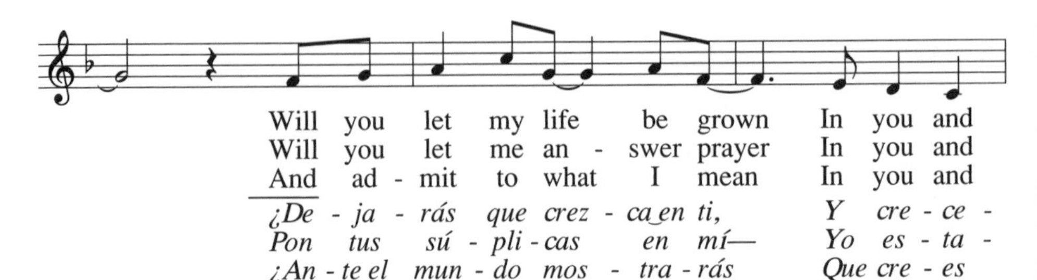
Will you let my life be grown In you and
Will you let me an - swer prayer In you and
And ad - mit to what I mean In you and
¿De - ja - rás que crez - ca en ti, Y cre - ce -
Pon tus sú - pli - cas en mí— Yo es - ta -
¿An - te el mun - do mos - tra - rás Que cre - es

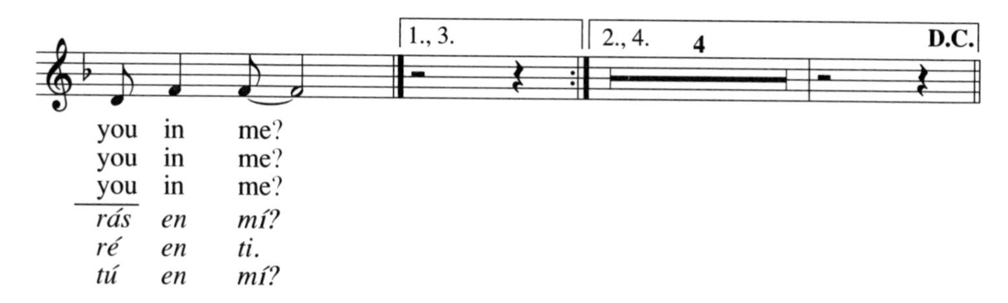
1., 3.
2., 4.
4
D.C.
you in me?
you in me?
you in me?
rás en mí?
ré en ti.
tú en mí?

4. Will you love the 'you' you hide
If I but call your name?
Will you quell the fear inside
And never be the same?
Will you use the faith you've found
To reshape the world around,
Through my sight and touch and sound
In you and you in me?

5. Lord, your summons echoes true
When you but call my name.
Let me turn and follow you
And never be the same.
In your company I'll go
Where your love and footsteps show.
Thus I'll move and live and grow
In you and you in me.

4. Si te llamo, ¿amarás
Tu verdadero ser?
¿Tu temor rechazarás?—
Podrás en mí vencer.
¿Traerás a mi creación
Nueva vida, paz, perdón?
¿Vivirás como viví
Y vivo yo en ti?

5. Tú me llamas, seguiré
Tus pasos, mi Señor.
Y cambiado estaré,
Seguro en tu‿amor.*
Junto‿a ti caminaré,
Donde vayas, yo iré.
Por tu fuerza viviré
En ti, y tú en mí.

**Segura*

150 Go Make a Difference

Refrain
Go make a dif - f'rence. We can make a dif - f'rence.
Go make a dif - f'rence in the world.
Go make a dif - f'rence. We can make a dif - f'rence.
To verses
To repeat refrain
Go make a dif - f'rence in the world.
Verses 1, 2
1. We are the salt of the earth, called to let the peo - ple
2. We are the hands of Christ reach-ing out to those in
see the love of God in you and me.
need, the face of God for all to see.
We are the light of the world, not to be hid - den but be
We are the spir - it of hope; we are the voice of
D.C.
seen. Go make a dif - f'rence in the world.
peace. Go make a dif - f'rence in the world.

Verse 3
3. So let your love shine on, let it shine for all to see.
Go make a dif - f'rence in the world. And the
spir - it of Christ will be with us as we go.
Go make a dif-f'rence in the world.
D.C.

Text: Matthew 5:13–16; Steve Angrisano, b.1965, and Tom Tomaszek, b.1950
Tune: Steve Angrisano, b.1965, and Tom Tomaszek, b.1950; acc. by Rick Modlin, b.1966

Those who are placed over others should glory in such an office only as much as they would were they assigned the task of washing feet.

Benedict the African

151 Sometimes by Step

Verses
1. Some-times the night is beau - ti - ful. Some-times the sky
2. Some-times I think of A - bra-ham, how one star he saw
was so far a-way. Some-times it seems to be so close
had been lit for him. He was a stran - ger in this land.
you could touch it but your heart would break.
And I am that, no less than he,
Some-times the morn - ing came too soon. Some-times the day
and on the road to right-eous - ness. Some-times the climb
could be so hard. There was so much work left to do,
can be so steep I may fal - ter in my steps,
but so much you'd al - read - y done.
and nev - er be - yond your reach.
Refrain
O God, you are my God, and I will ev-er praise
you. O God, you are my God, and I will ev-er praise
you. And I will seek you in the morn - ing and I will

learn to walk in your ways. And step by step you'll lead me,
and I will fol-low you all of my days.
1.
D.C.
2.
days. And I will
fol-low you all of my days. And I will fol-low you all of my
days. And step by step you'll lead me, and I will
Repeat ad lib.
fol-low you all of my days. And I will

Text: Richard Mullins, 1955–1997, and Beaker
Tune: Richard Mullins, 1955–1997, and Beaker

152 Get It Together

Refrain
Got-ta get it, got-ta get it, got-ta get it, got-ta
get it, got-ta get it to-geth-er, and share the
Gos-pel of Je-sus. Got-ta get it, got-ta
get it, got-ta get it, got-ta get it, got-ta get it to-geth-
er, and share the light of the world.
Last time to Coda
Verses 1, 2
1. Come on, get up! Let's get go-ing. Can't you feel your faith is grow-ing? Don't just keep it locked in-side you. Who
2. Bear-ing wit-ness is more than preach-ing. You'll need to find more ways of teach-ing. Live your life out in the light. Know

D.C.
knows what God can do through you?
that Je - sus will be your guide.
Verse 3
3. Love your neigh-bor. Love God too.
Je - sus said that's what we've got to
do. Re-spect an - oth - er's dig - ni - ty.
D.C.
Work for jus-tice and pray for peace.
Coda
And share the light of the world,
and share the light of the world.

Text: Shannon Cerneka, b.1975
Tune: Shannon Cerneka, b.1975; choral arr. by Orin Johnson, b.1973, and Gary Daigle, b.1957

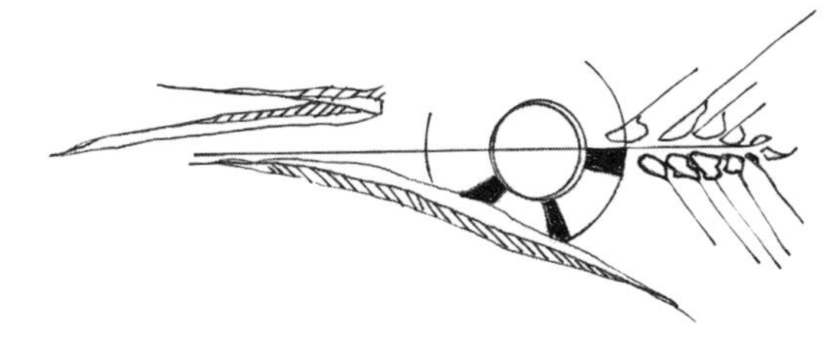

153 I Will Choose Christ

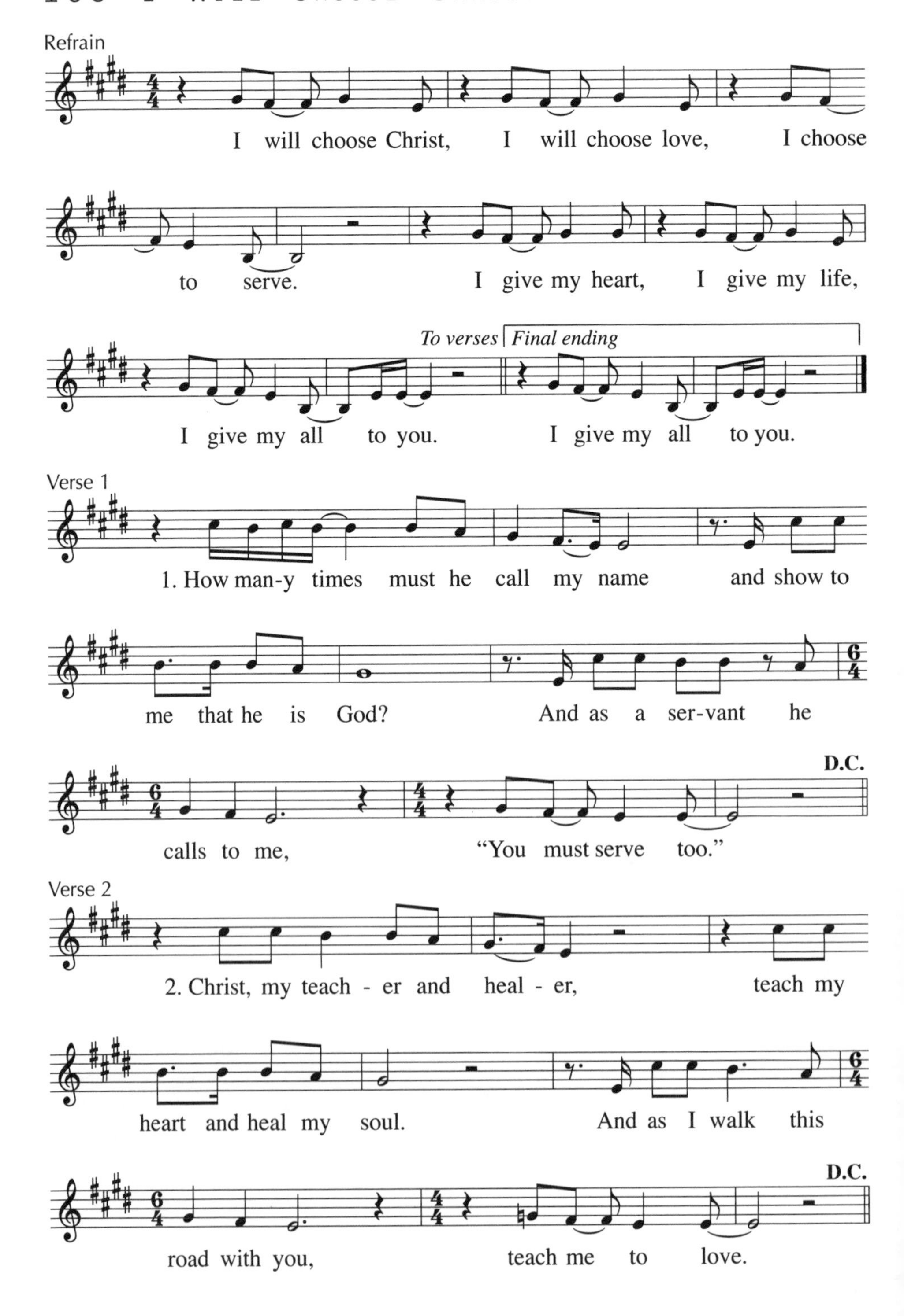
Refrain
I will choose Christ, I will choose love, I choose to serve.
I give my heart, I give my life,
I give my all to you.
To verses
Final ending
I give my all to you.
Verse 1
1. How man-y times must he call my name and show to me that he is God?
And as a ser-vant he calls to me, "You must serve too."
D.C.
Verse 2
2. Christ, my teach - er and heal - er, teach my heart and heal my soul.
And as I walk this road with you, teach me to love.
D.C.

Verse 3
3. As I look up - on your cross, so too must I
die with you. And with the death of my
own de - sires, I'll rise with you.
D.C.

Text: Tom Booth, b.1961
Tune: Tom Booth, b.1961; acc. by Ed Bolduc, b.1969

Holiness Is Faithfulness 154

Refrain
Ho - li - ness is faith-ful - ness. Ho - li - ness is joy. I
am not bound to lone - li - ness when I fol-low Christ, my Lord.

Verses

1. I am looking for my Lord.
I am looking for my way.
Must I sacrifice my glory?
Will I die in living shame?

Take your cross and follow me.
Follow my steps and you will see.
Give it up and you'll be free.
Do not fear death; you'll rise in me.

2. I have lost my strength; I've fallen.
My mother, Mary, whispers,
I am so afraid.
Will you bear with me my burden?

Rise up, Son, to your feet.
In my heart you'll always be with me.
Here comes Simon of Cyrene.
Jesus, behind you I will carry.

3. She gazes in my eyes.
I have fallen once again,
Daughters of Jerusalem,
Father, catch me in your arms.

Veronica kneels at his feet.
And she wipes the face that bleeds.
Do not weep for me!
For I am strong when I am weak.

4. You know that I love you.
I lay down my life for my friends.
They have pierced my hands and feet.
On a tree between two thieves.

No greater love than this.
Jesus' body now is stripped.
Crucified the heavenly king
Jesus redeemed the world from sin.

Text: Danielle Rose, b.1980
Tune: Danielle Rose, b.1980

155 WITH ONE VOICE

Verses
1. Take the Word and go out to ev - 'ry land:
2. Take the Word to our neigh - bor - hoods and streets:
3. Take the Word to the peo - ple in de - spair:
4. Take the Word to the na - tions ev - 'ry - where:
shine the light of Christ for all to see! May the
shine the light of Christ for all to see! May we
shine the light of Christ for all to see! May our
shine the light of Christ for all to see! May the
lives of those we touch sing praise to God a - bove.
all set out to live in peace and har - mo - ny.
ac - tions and our deeds bring com - fort to their needs.
wit - ness of our lives trans - form the world a - new.
Let us sing, we'll sing:
They will see and sing:
And they'll know and sing:
And we'll shine, we'll shine.
Refrain*
With one voice we'll pass the Word a - long;
with one voice, bring jus - tice to the world.
And with all the an - gels we'll

Last time through Refrain, sing unaccompanied for the first 6 bars, with handclaps on beat 3.

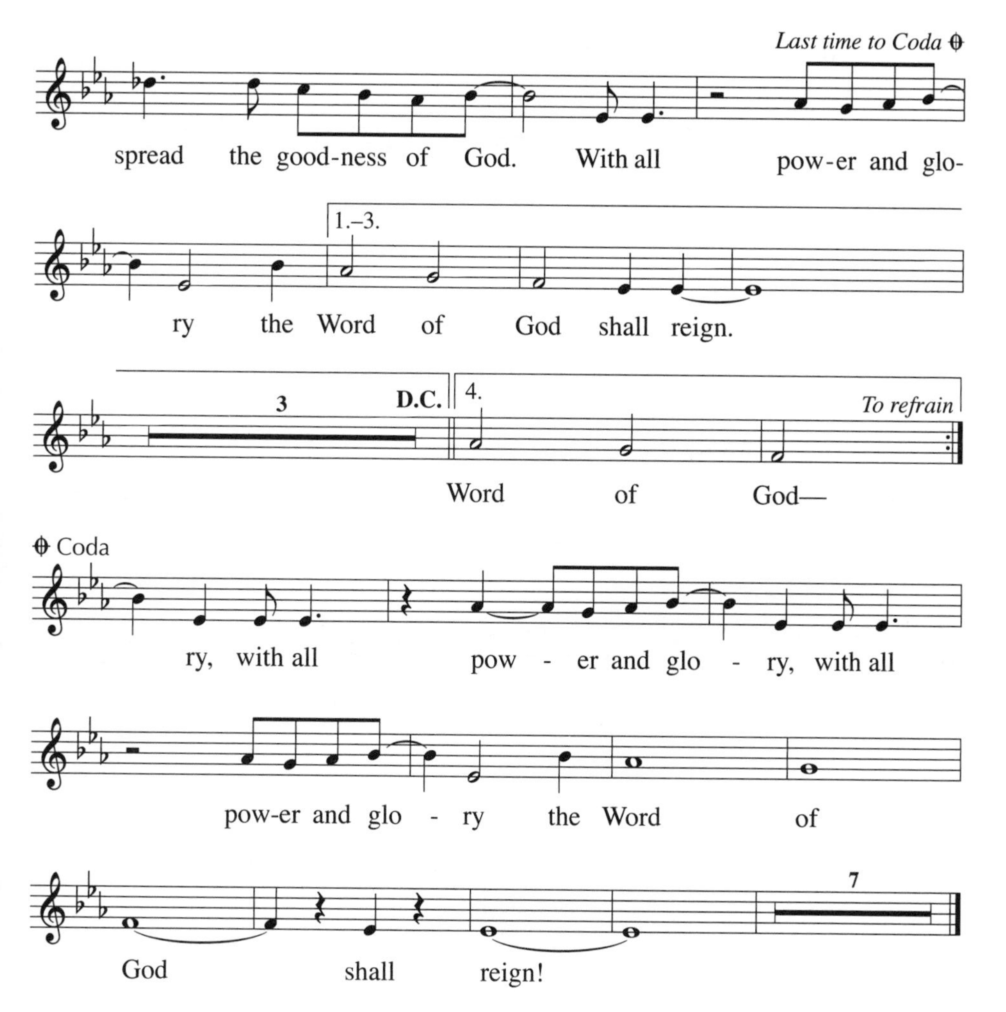
Last time to Coda
spread the good-ness of God. With all pow-er and glory the Word of God shall reign.
1.–3.
3
D.C.
4.
To refrain
Word of God—
Coda
ry, with all pow - er and glo - ry, with all
pow-er and glo - ry the Word of
God shall reign!
7

Text: Ricky Manalo, b.1965
Tune: Ricky Manalo, b.1965

156 Go Out in the World

Refrain
Go out in the world, got-ta go out in the world.
Go out in the world, tell ev-'ry-one the Good News!
Go out in the world, got-ta go out in the world,
go out in the world, tell ev-'ry-one the Good, Good News!
1.
2., 3.
Good, Good News!
Verses
Cantor:
1. Go and make dis-ci-ples of all the na-tions.
2. See, the Lord is faith-ful to all his peo-ple.
All:
Go out in the world, tell ev-'ry-one the Good News!
Cantor:
Go and make dis-ci-ples of all his peo-ple.
See, the Lord is faith-ful! He loves his peo-ple.
All:
Go out in the world, tell ev-'ry-one the

1.
To refrain
2.
Good, Good News!
Good, Good News!
Final Refrain
Go out in the world, got-ta go out in the world.
Go out in the world, tell ev-'ry-one the Good News! Go out
in the world, got-ta go out in the world, go out in the world,
Repeat as desired
Last time
tell ev-'ry-one the Good, Good News!
Good, Good News!

Text: Ed Bolduc. b.1969
Tune: Ed Bolduc, b.1969

You don't have to love the song I sing,
but you have to love me when I sing it.

Attributed to Joseph Gelineau, SJ

157 our sacraments and rites

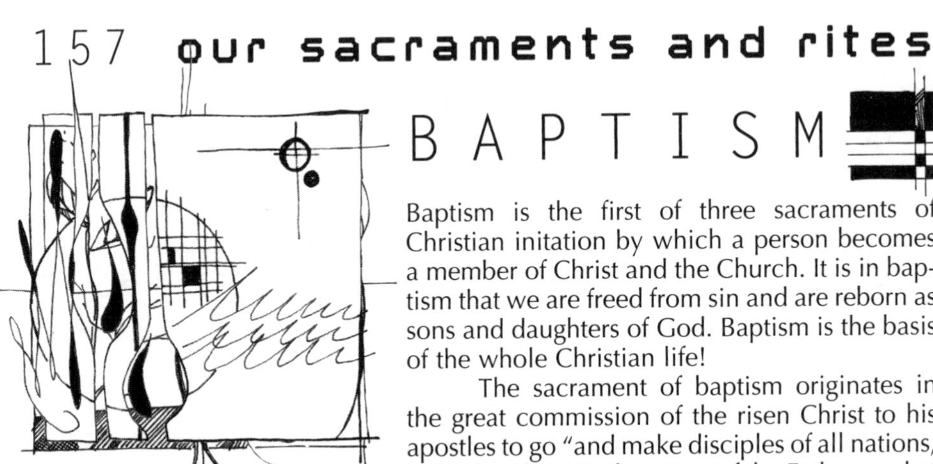

BAPTISM

Baptism is the first of three sacraments of Christian initation by which a person becomes a member of Christ and the Church. It is in baptism that we are freed from sin and are reborn as sons and daughters of God. Baptism is the basis of the whole Christian life!

The sacrament of baptism originates in the great commission of the risen Christ to his apostles to go "and make disciples of all nations, baptizing them in the name of the Father, and of the Son, and of the Holy Spirit" (Matthew 28:19). The Church teaches that baptism is necessary for salvation and is required before one may have access to the other sacraments.

The essential rite (action) of the sacrament is celebrated either by a triple immersion of the candidate in baptismal water or a triple pouring of water over the candidate's forehead, while the baptismal formula is pronounced by the minister. The rite signifies and actually brings about death to sin and entry into new life, the life of the triune God. *LD/RK*

158 I Send You Out

Verse 1
Cantor:
1. I bap-tize you in the name of the Fa-ther. I bap-tize
you in the name of the Son. I bap-tize you
with the Ho-ly Spir-it. Go out and spread Good News!
All:
Refrain
I send you out on a mis-sion of love. I send you out

on a mis-sion of love. I send you out
on a mis-sion of love, and know that I am with
you al-ways un-til the end of the world.
Verse 2
Cantor:
2. Well, it's time for us to be-come peo-ple with spirit. It's time for us to be-come peo-ple of love. It's time for
us to know that Je-sus Christ is ris-en, for-
gives our sins, and brings us new life!
All:
D.S.
I send you out

Text: John Angotti, b.1963
Tune: John Angotti, b.1963; arr. by Paul A. Tate, b.1968

159 Give the Lord Your Heart

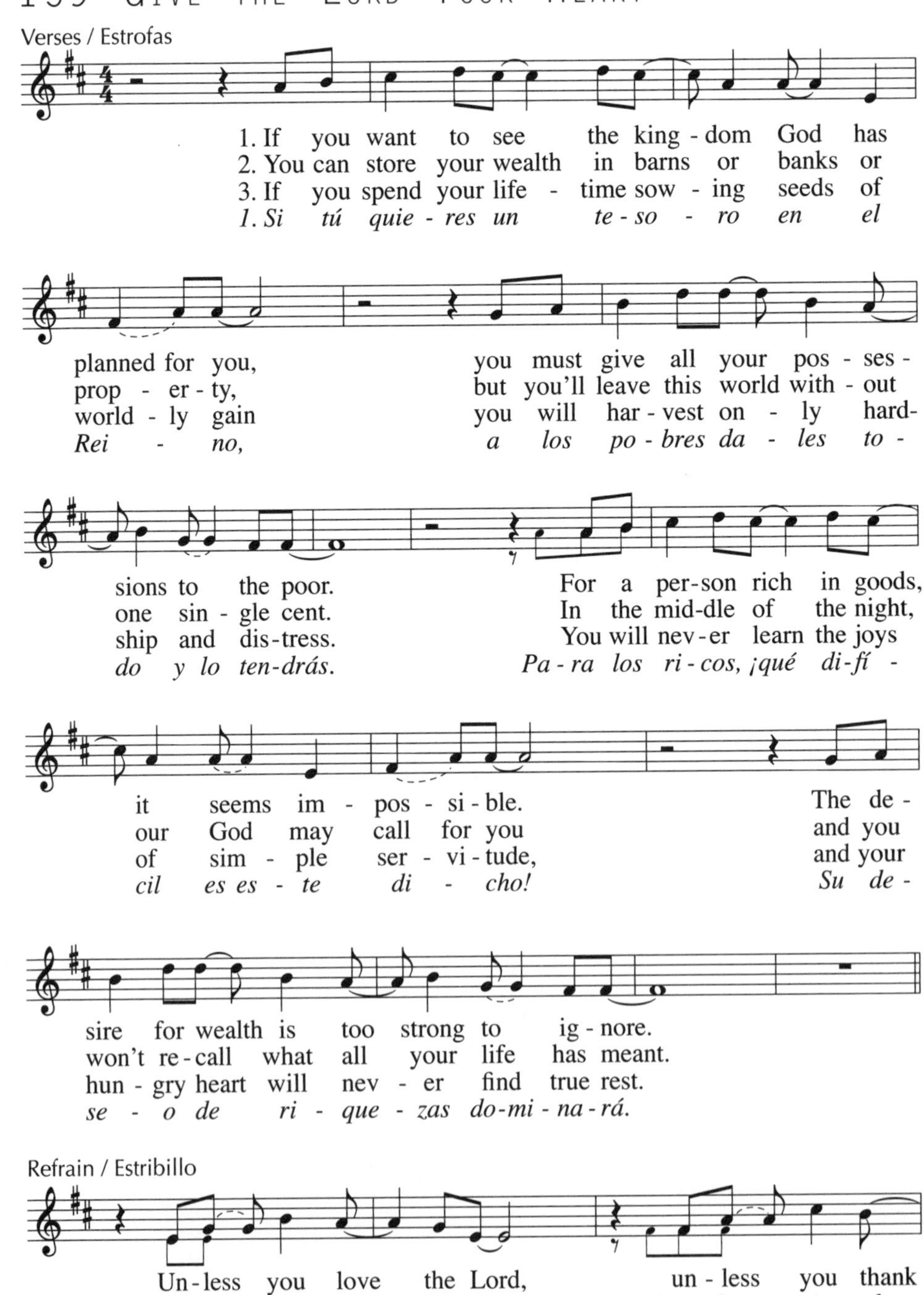
Verses / Estrofas
1. If you want to see the king - dom God has planned for you, you must give all your pos - ses - sions to the poor. For a per-son rich in goods, it seems im - pos - si - ble. The de - sire for wealth is too strong to ig - nore.
2. You can store your wealth in barns or banks or prop - er - ty, but you'll leave this world with - out one sin - gle cent. In the mid-dle of the night, our God may call for you and you won't re - call what all your life has meant.
3. If you spend your life - time sow - ing seeds of world - ly gain you will har - vest on - ly hard-ship and dis-tress. You will nev - er learn the joys of sim - ple ser - vi - tude, and your hun - gry heart will nev - er find true rest.
1. Si tú quie - res un te - so - ro en el Rei - no, a los po - bres da - les to - do y lo ten-drás. Pa - ra los ri - cos, ¡qué di-fí - cil es es - te di - cho! Su de - se - o de ri - que - zas do-mi - na - rá.
Refrain / Estribillo
Un-less you love the Lord, un - less you thank
Si no a-mas al Se - ñor, si no das gra-cias al

the Lord, un - less you give the Lord your heart.
Se - ñor, si no le das tu co - ra - zón.
Un - less you love the Lord,
Si no a-mas al Se - ñor,
un - less you thank the Lord,
si no das gra - cias al Se - ñor,
un - less you give the Lord your heart.
si no le das tu co - ra - zón.

Text: Based on Luke 12:16-21, Matthew 19:21-23; Michael Mahler, b.1981
Tune: Michael Mahler, b.1981

160 I AM FOR YOU
1. There is a moun-tain, there is a sea.
2. There was a wom-an small as a star,
3. There was a man who walked in the storm,
4. We are a-noint-ed, ser-vants of God;
5. There is a world that waits in the womb;
There is a wind with-in all breath-ing,
Full of the pa-tient dreams of her na-tion,
Caught in be-tween the waves and the light-ning,
We have been born a-gain of Spir-it.
There is a hope un-born God is bear-ing,
There is an arm to break ev-'ry chain,
Wel-com-ing in an an-gel of God,
Shar-ing his bread with those cast a-side,
We are the word God speaks to the world,
Though the powers of death prowl the night,
There is a fire in all things liv-ing.
Wel-com-ing in God's bold in-vi-ta-tion.
Heal-ing by touch the lost and the dy-ing.
Free-dom and light to all who will hear it.
There is a day our God is pre-par-ing.
There is a voice that speaks from the flame:
"Let it be done," she sang, "un-to me.
Send-ing us forth, he says to his friends:
So let us be the word of the Lord:
Sing 'round the fire to wak-en the dawn:
"I am for you, I am for you, I am for you is my name."
I am for you, I am for you, I am for you: let it be."
"I am for you, I am for you, I am for you to the end."
I am for you, I am for you, I am for you ev-er-more.
I am for you, I am for you, I am for you: We are one.

Text: Rory Cooney, b.1952
Tune: Rory Cooney, b.1952

our sacraments and rites 161

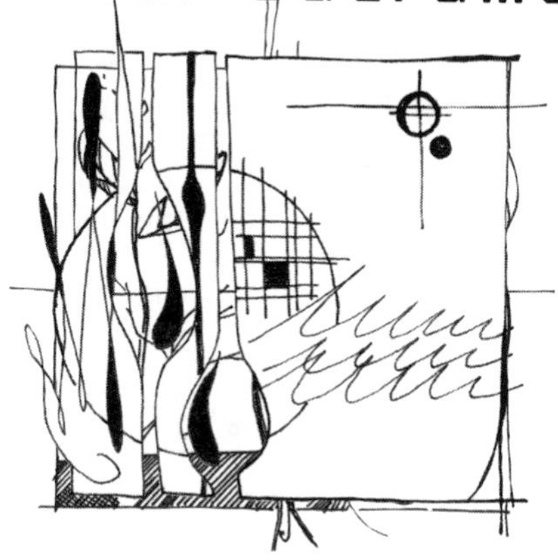

ANOINTING OF THE SICK

At some point in life each of us may be in need of the special help of God's grace that is received in the sacrament of anointing of the sick. The sacrament strengthens us when we are struggling with a serious illness and unites us more fully with Christ's Passion, so that our sufferings can take on a new meaning.

The anointing of the sick has its roots in St. James' epistle: "Are there any sick among you? Then let them send for the priests and let the priests pray over them, anointing them with oil" (James 5:14).

The sacrament can be received by anyone whose health is seriously impaired by sickness or old age. This includes those who are physically, emotionally, or mentally ill. Some Catholics are under the impression that they can only receive the sacrament on their deathbed, but this is not true.

The rite consists of the laying on of hands and the anointing of the hands and forehead with holy oil. Through these actions (administered by a priest) God is asked to provide us with both physical and spiritual healing. *LD*

TAKE, O TAKE ME AS I AM 162

Ostinato Refrain
Take, O take me as I am; sum - mon out what I shall
be; set your seal up-on my heart and live in me.

Text: John L. Bell, b.1949
Tune: John L. Bell, b.1949

163 Come and Follow Me / Ven y Sígueme

Verses / Estrofas
1. Come, be my light, be my voice to the na - tions. Be my hands, be my heart for the world.
2. Go, take your gift to the poor and the lone- ly. As you love, so will I live in you.
1. Ven, sé mi luz, sé mi voz en el mun- do. Sé mis ma - nos y mi pro - pio co - ra-zón.
2. Ve, da mi luz a los po - bres y a - le - ja - dos. Cuan-do a - mas, vi - vi - ré en tu ser.
Would you go where I go? Where I lead, will you fol - low? Would you leave ev-'ry - thing for my sake?
Will you feed, feed my lambs? Share your hope with the hope - less? Bring new sight to the blind in my name?
¿I - rás tú don - de voy? ¿Se - gui - rás cuan - do guí - o? ¿De - ja - rás lo que tie - nes, si es por mí?
¿Cui - da - rás a los mí - os? ¿Po - drás dar la es - pe - ran - za? ¿En mi nom - bre a los cie - gos sa - na - rás?
By the pow - er of the Spir- it, ev - 'ry - one with ears to hear it will em-
With a tow - el and a ba - sin, t'ward the king - dom we will has - ten, through the
Al Es - pí - ri - tu voy a dar - te. Si tú quie - res es - cu - char - me, cuan - do
Con to - a - lla y con la - va - bo, ca - mi - ne - mos ha - cia el rei - no, por las

brace the call to love with-in their heart.
nar - row gate that leads to Cal - va - ry.
lla - mo a ser - vir, te a-yu - da - rá.
sen - das que nos lle - van a la cruz.
Refrain / Estribillo
If an - y - one would come and fol - low me, my dis -
Si quie - res tú ve - nir a don - de voy y te -
ci - ple you would be. Leave the past be - hind, seek and you will
ner la paz que doy, De - ja to-do a-trás, tú en-con-tra -
find all you're called to be. If an - y - one would
rás lo que has de ha - cer. Si quie-res tú se -
come and fol - low me, know the truth will make you free.
guir - me con a - fán, mis pa - la - bras te guia - rán.
Give and you re - ceive. Trust me and be -
Da, re - ci - bi - rás. En mí cre - e -
lieve. Come and fol-low me.
rás. Ven y sí - gue - me.
1., 3.
3
Final ending
2.
7
me.
me.
With a tow - el and a ba -
Con to - a - lla y con la-va -

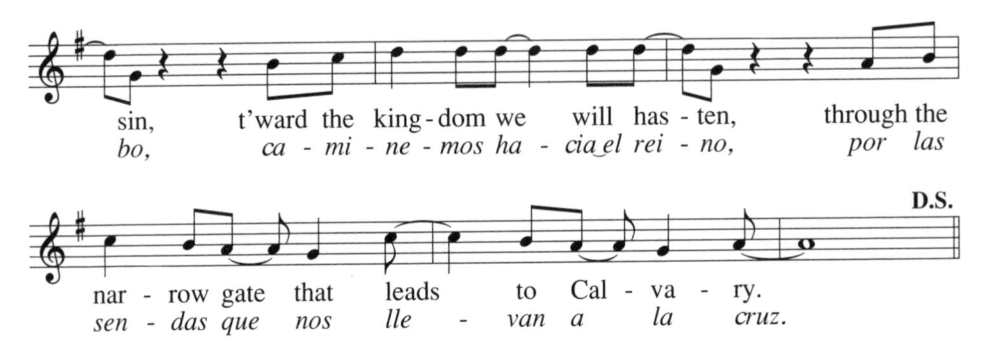
sin, t'ward the king - dom we will has - ten, through the
bo, ca - mi - ne - mos ha - cia el rei - no, por las
D.S.
nar - row gate that leads to Cal - va - ry.
sen - das que nos lle - van a la cruz.

Text: Tom Franzak, b.1954; tr. by Ronald F. Krisman, b.1946
Tune: Tom Franzak, b.1954; acc. by Gerard Chiusano, b.1953

164 I Could Sing of Your Love Forever

Verse
O-ver the moun-tains and the sea your riv-er runs with love for me,

and I will o - pen up my heart and let the Heal-er set me free.

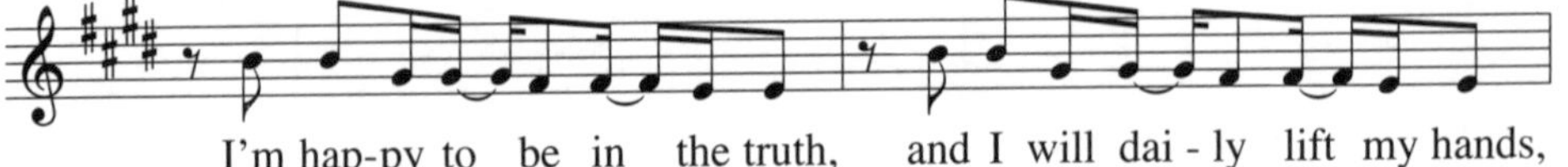
I'm hap-py to be in the truth, and I will dai - ly lift my hands,

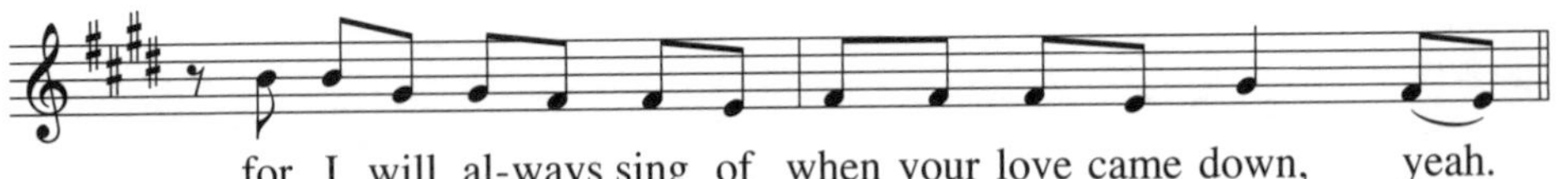
for I will al-ways sing of when your love came down, yeah.

Refrain
I could sing of your love for - ev - er. I could
sing of your love for - ev - er. I could sing of your love
for - ev - er. I could sing of your love
1. To bridge
for - ev - er.
2. D.S.
for - ev - er.
Last time
for - ev - er.
Bridge
Oh, I feel like danc - ing; it's fool-ish-ness I
know. But when the world has seen the light, they will dance
with joy like we're danc - ing now.
4 D.S.

Text: Martin Smith
Tune: Martin Smith; arr. by Ed Bolduc, b.1969

165 You Are the Way

Refrain
You are the Way, you are the Truth, you are the Life, my sal - va - tion. You are the Way, you are the Truth,
To verses
Final ending
you are the Life, the gate - way to my soul.
Verses 1, 2
1. We come to - geth - er now, we cel - e - brate and shout,
2. In a world that's mov - ing fast, we seek what will not last.
for you have shown the way.
We miss the nar - row road. But
We lift our voic - es high, we sing, we dance, we cry:
when we look in - side our-selves, we find that no one else
D.C.
"You are the on - ly way!"
but you can make us whole.
Verse 3
3. If we ask you we will re - ceive.
If we seek you then we shall find.

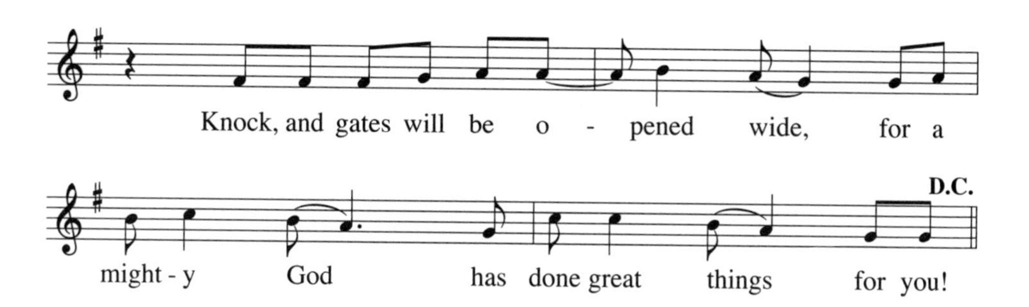
Knock, and gates will be o - pened wide, for a
might - y God has done great things for you!
D.C.

Apart from the cross, there is no other ladder by which we may get to heaven.

Rosa of Lima

166 How Beautiful

Verses 1–3
1. How beau - ti - ful the hands that served the wine and the bread and the sons of the earth. How beau - ti - ful the feet that walked the long dust - y roads and the hill to the cross.
2. How beau - ti - ful the heart that bled, that took all my sin and bore it in - stead. How beau - ti - ful the ten - der eyes that choose to for - give and nev - er de - spise. How
3. How beau - ti - ful the ra - diant bride who waits for her groom with his light in her eyes, How beau - ti - ful when hum - ble hearts give the fruit of pure lives so that oth - ers may live.
beau - ti - ful, how beau - ti - ful, how beau - ti - ful is the
Last time to Coda
1.
2.
Bod - y of Christ.
Christ.
Bridge
And as he laid down his life, we of - fer

this sac - ri-fice that we will live just as he
died: will-ing to pay the price,
molto rit.
D.C.
will-ing to pay the price.
Coda
Verse 4
rit.
a tempo
Christ. 4. How beau - ti-ful the
feet that bring the sound of good news and the
love of the King. How beau - ti - ful the
hands that serve the wine and the bread and the
sons of the earth. How beau - ti - ful,
how beau - ti - ful, how beau - ti-
molto rit.
a tempo
6
ful is the Bod-y of Christ.

Text: Twila Paris, b.1958
Tune: Twila Paris, b.1958

167 The Face of God

Verses

1. I be-lieve in my Lord Je - sus,
2. I be-lieve that there's a mer - cy

Son of God and Son of man, who
flow - ing from the hand of God, my God, to

died and rose for the sake of all. He is the Lamb. Oh,
wash me clean from the stain of sin. His love goes on. Oh,

I be - lieve that there's a Spir - it, a
I be - lieve that we are peo - ple

gift to ev - 'ry child of God. So as we stum-ble to
born to live a life for God. And if we fol - low the

make our way, it leads us on. Oh. Oh.
shep - herd's way, then life goes on. Oh. Oh.

Refrain

And I be-lieve in God, God of love

and God of mer - cy. I be-lieve that I have seen

the face of God in the land of the liv-ing.

3

Text: Ed Bolduc, b.1969
Tune: Ed Bolduc, b.1969

Every Move I Make 168

Ev-'ry move I make I make in you. You make me move, Je-sus.

Ev - 'ry breath I take I breathe in you.

Ev-'ry step I take I take in you. You are my way, Je-sus.

Ev-'ry breath I take I breathe in you. Waves of mer-cy,

waves of grace. Ev - 'ry-where I look I see your face.

Your love has cap-tured me. O my God, this love,

how can it be? Na na na na na na na, na na na na na na na.

D.C.
Final ending

Na na na na na na na, na na na na na na na.

Text: David Ruis
Tune: David Ruis, acc. by Ed Bolduc, b.1969

169 Trading My Sorrows

Refrain
I'm trad-ing my sor-rows, I'm trad-ing my shame;
I'm trad-ing my sick-ness, I'm trad-ing my pain;
I'm lay-ing them down for the joy of the Lord.
I'm lay-ing them down for the joy of the Lord.
1.
2.
We say
yes, Lord, yes, Lord, yes, yes, Lord, yes, Lord, yes, Lord,
yes, yes, Lord, yes, Lord, yes, Lord, yes, yes, Lord. A-men.
To verses 1, 2
To verse 3
Last time
1., 2. I am pressed
3. La
Verses 1, 2
but not crushed, per-se-cut-ed, not a-ban-doned,
struck down but not de-stroyed. I am blessed
be-yond the curse, for his prom-ise will en-dure, that his

joy is gon-na be my strength.
Though the sor - row may
last for the night, his joy comes with the morn-ing.
D.C.
Verse 3
la la la la la la la la la la la
la la la la la la la la la la la la la la la la la
la la la la la la.
First time only:
D.C.
La

Text: Darrell Evans
Tune: Darrell Evans

170 YOUR GRACE IS ENOUGH

Verses
1. Great is your faith - ful - ness, O God of Ja-cob;
2. Great is your love and jus - tice, God of Ja-cob;
you wres - tle with the sin - ner's rest - less heart.
you use the weak to lead the strong.
You lead me by still wa - ters in - to mer - cy
You lead us in the song of heav - en's vic - t'ry,
where noth - ing can keep us a - part.
and all your peo - ple sing a - long.
So re -
mem - ber your peo - ple, re - mem - ber your chil - dren, re -
mem - ber your prom - ise, O God.
Refrain
For your grace is e-nough, yeah, your grace is e-nough,
yeah, your grace is e-nough, yeah, your grace
Last time to Coda
1.
is e-nough for me.

D.C.
2.
6
for me.
So re - mem - ber your peo - ple, re - mem - ber your
chil - dren, re - mem - ber your prom - ise, O God.
Coda
8
For your for me.

Text: Matt Maher
Tune: Matt Maher, acc. by Ed Bolduc, b.1969

171 Deny Yourself

Refrain
De-ny your - self. Take up your cross.
De-spite the pain, de - spite the cost.
Leave all be - hind, and fol - low me.
To verse 3 and Coda
To verses 1, 2
De-ny your - self, be free.
Verse 1
1. For what will it prof - it to gain the world and lose your life?
Those who would save their life will lose it.
What can you give in re-turn for your life?
For those who would lose their life,
D.S.
lose their life, will find it. De-ny your - self.
Verse 2
2. Come, take up your cross and dai - ly fol - low me,

and you will have rich re-ward in heav - en.
Those who have left their home and fam - 'ly for my sake
in - her - it one hun - dred fold,
in-her-it e - ter - nal life. De - ny your - self.
D.S.
Verse 3
3
3. Lord, you re - veal the depth of
your life and your love in your ev - er-last-ing cov-
e-nant. Strength-en this faith we share, fill our world
with your love, and bring all of us to grace,
to the grace you prom-ise. De-ny your - self.
6
D.S.
Coda

Text: Mark 8:34–38; Paul Melley, b.1973
Tune: Paul Melley, b.1973

172 God Is Good

Refrain
Cantor: God is good
Assembly: all the time!
Cantor: All the time
Assembly: God is good!
Cantor: God is good
Assembly: all the time!
Cantor: All the time
Assembly: God is good!
Cantor: All the time
Assembly: God is good!
Cantor: God is good
Assembly: all the time!
Last time to Coda
Cantor: All the time
Assembly: God is good!
1.
Cantor: God is good
2.
good!
Verses
1. Bless you, O God, for your good - ness, mer - cy
2. Praise you, O God, for your jus - tice, for your
3. Re - joic - ing, O God, in your pres - ence, for ev - 'ry -
4. We of - fer, O Lord, all our liv - ing, we
flows from you in end - less ways; your
jus - tice is the truth you bring; the
where your grace a - bounds, cre -
mar - vel in your lov - ing ways. Re -
good - ness giv - ing birth to cre - a - tion, and all cre -
pow - er - ful are hum - bled and si - lenced while the
a - tion shouts a might - y wit - ness; in a
ceive from us a sim - ple song, Lord, in

Cantor:
D.S.
a - tion cries a thank-ful praise!
low - ly and the poor now sing.
gen - tle whis - per you are found.
grat - i - tude and hum - ble praise.
God is good
Coda
Assembly:
Cantor:
time! God is good! All the
Assembly:
time! God is good!

Text: Jesse Manibusan, b.1958
Tune: Jesse Manibusan, b.1958; acc. by Mary Howarth

No one in the world can change truth.

Maximilian Kolbe

173 our sacraments and rites

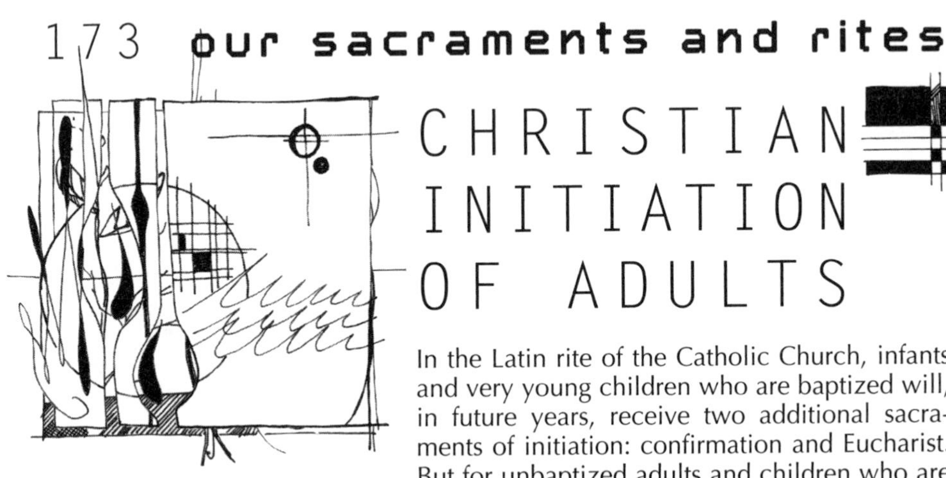

CHRISTIAN INITIATION OF ADULTS

In the Latin rite of the Catholic Church, infants and very young children who are baptized will, in future years, receive two additional sacraments of initiation: confirmation and Eucharist. But for unbaptized adults and children who are old enough to be catechized, their initiation into the Christian life is done in stages, culminating in the reception of baptism, confirmation, and Eucharist in one liturgical celebration.

Once one of these persons has made sufficient inquiry about the Christian life and has expressed the desire for baptism, he or she is received into the Church as a catechumen, a person who is being formed in the Christian life. After a suitable period of prayer, study of the Scriptures and church teachings, and participation in the life of the Church—one year or longer—if the catechumen is judged to be ready for sacramental initiation, he or she is chosen, or "elected," usually by the bishop on the First Sunday of Lent. The six weeks of Lent serve as a time of intense final preparation for the "elect," who will celebrate the sacraments of Christian initiation at the Easter Vigil. *RK*

174 Open My Eyes

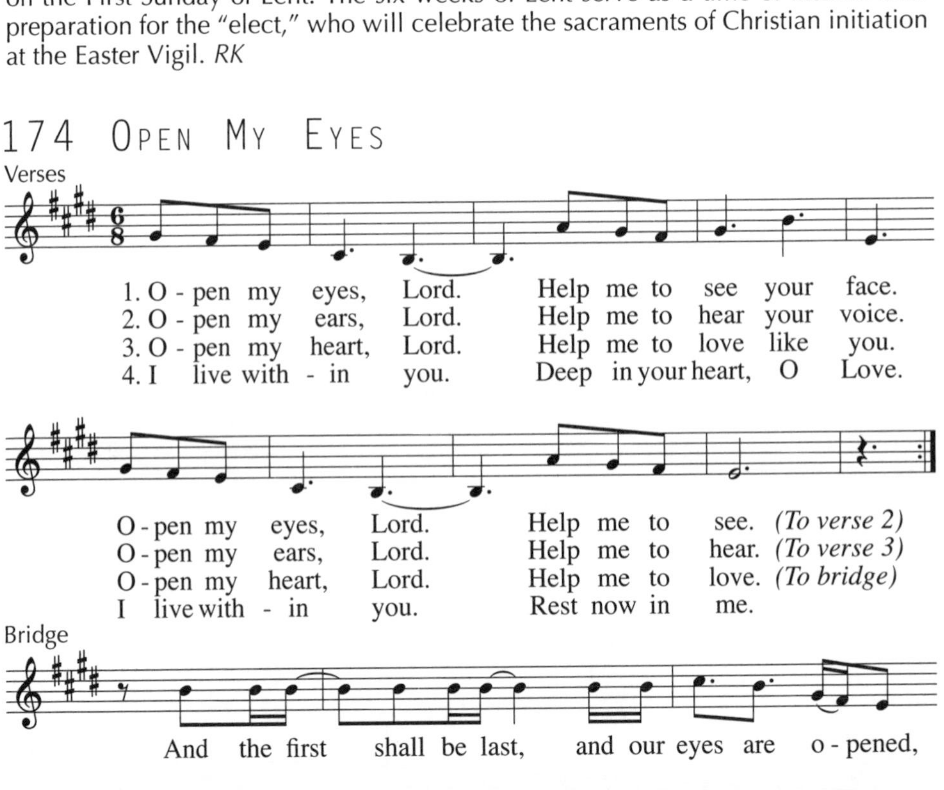
Verses
1. O - pen my eyes, Lord. Help me to see your face.
2. O - pen my ears, Lord. Help me to hear your voice.
3. O - pen my heart, Lord. Help me to love like you.
4. I live with - in you. Deep in your heart, O Love.
O - pen my eyes, Lord. Help me to see. (To verse 2)
O - pen my ears, Lord. Help me to hear. (To verse 3)
O - pen my heart, Lord. Help me to love. (To bridge)
I live with - in you. Rest now in me.
Bridge
And the first shall be last, and our eyes are o - pened,

and we'll hear like nev-er be - fore. And we'll speak in new ways,
and we'll see God's face in plac-es we've nev-er known.
D.C.
Refrain
Hold us, Je - sus, help us, Je - sus, heal us, Je-sus, we pray.

Text: Based on Mark 8:22–25; Jesse Manibusan, b.1958
Tune: Jesse Manibusan, b.1958; acc. by Ed Bolduc, b.1969, choral arr. by Ken Canedo, b.1953

HOLD US, JESUS 175

Hold us, Je - sus, help us, Je - sus, heal us, Je-sus, we pray.

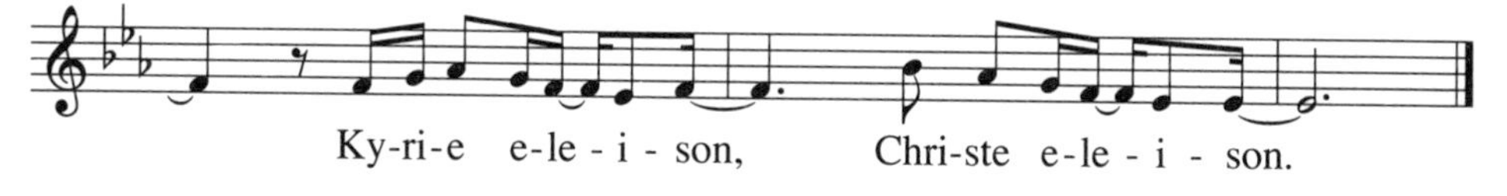
Ky-ri-e e-le - i - son, Chri-ste e-le - i - son.

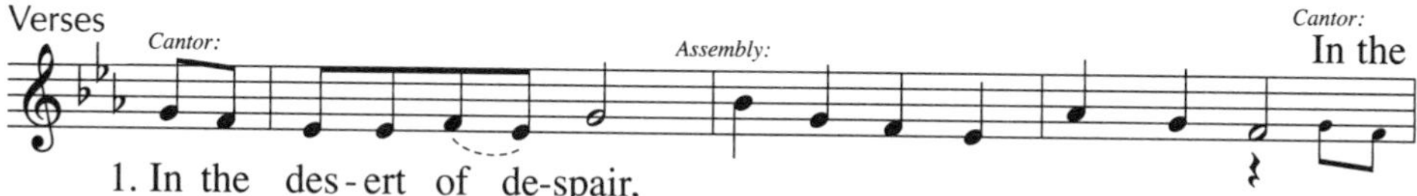
Verses
Cantor:
Assembly:
Cantor:
In the
1. In the des-ert of de-spair,
2. In the des-ert of pain,
3. In the des-ert of sin,
be with us, Lord, quench our thirst.

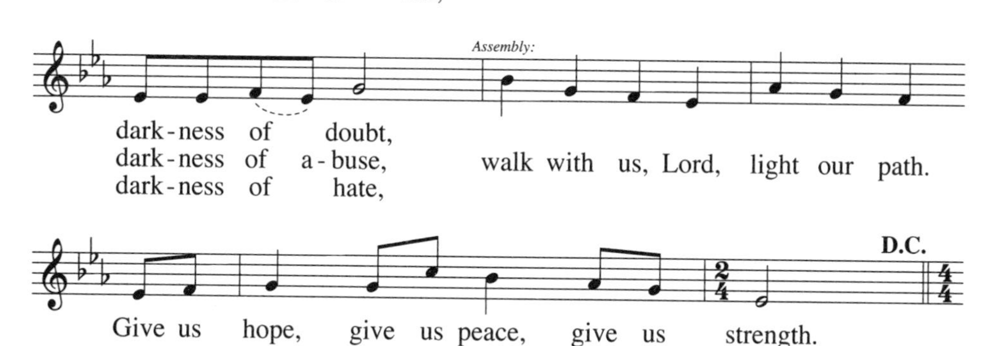
Assembly:
dark-ness of doubt,
dark-ness of a-buse,
dark-ness of hate,
walk with us, Lord, light our path.
D.C.
Give us hope, give us peace, give us strength.

Text: Chris de Silva, b.1967
Tune: Chris de Silva, b.1967

176 The Lord Is My Light and My Salvation

Refrain

The Lord is my light and my sal - va - tion; whom shall I fear?

The Lord is my life, my life's ref - uge; of

whom should I be a-fraid?

1. The Lord is my light

2.–4. *To verses*

Verse 1

1. Hear, O Lord, the sound of my call; be gra-cious

and an-swer me. For you, O Lord, my heart

is long-ing. With all my heart your face I seek.

D.C.

Verse 2

2. Your pres - ence, O Lord, I seek; do not hide

your face from me. Do not in an - ger turn a -

way your ser-vant. You are my help; do not for - sake me.

D.C.

Verse 3
3. I be - lieve I shall see the good-ness of the Lord in the
land of the liv - ing. Be strong; let your heart take cour-age.
Wait for the Lord, wait for the Lord.
Final Refrain
The Lord is my light and my sal - va - tion; whom shall I fear?
The Lord is my life, my life's ref-
uge; of whom should I be a - fraid?

Text: Psalm 27:1, 7–8, 8–9, 13–14; Jesse Manibusan, b.1958
Tune: Jesse Manibusan, b.1958; acc. by Gus Pappelis

177 Open the Eyes of My Heart

Refrain

O - pen the eyes of my heart, Lord,

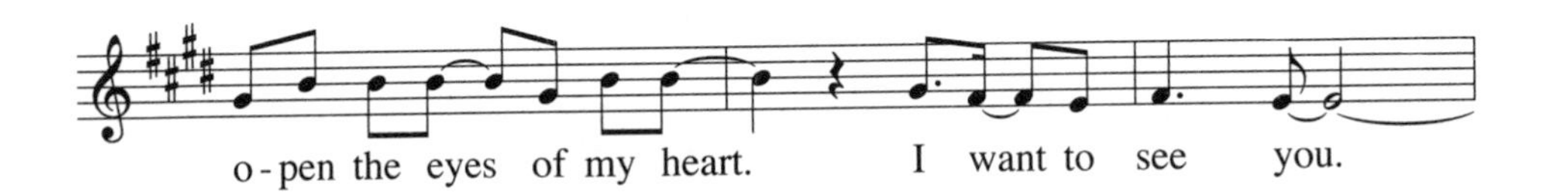
o - pen the eyes of my heart. I want to see you.

1.
2.
I want to see you. To see you

Verse

high and lift - ed up, shin - ing in the light of your glo-

ry. Pour out your pow'r and love as we sing

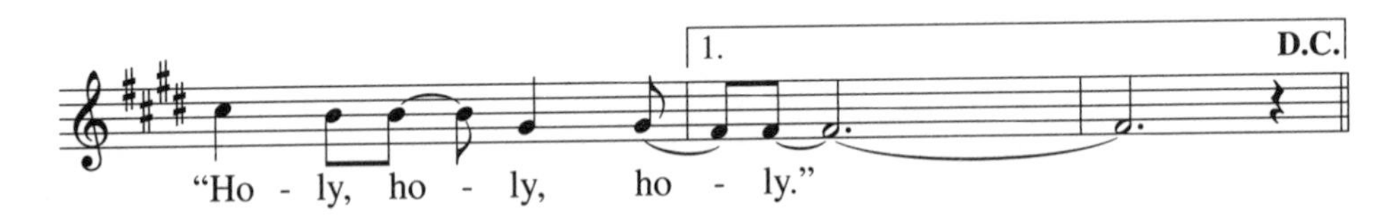
1.
D.C.
"Ho - ly, ho - ly, ho - ly."

2.
To final refrain
ly." To see you ly."

Final Refrain

*Melody 1
1. Ho - ly, ho - ly, ho - ly,
*Melody 2
2. O - pen the eyes of my heart, Lord.

ho - ly, ho - ly, ho - ly, ho - ly, ho - ly, ho-
O-pen the eyes of my heart I want to see you.

ly, I want to see you.
I want to see you.

*May be sung separately or together, as desired.

Text: Paul Baloche, b.1962
Tune: Paul Baloche, b.1962; acc. by Ed Bolduc, b.1969

178 Litany of the Saints

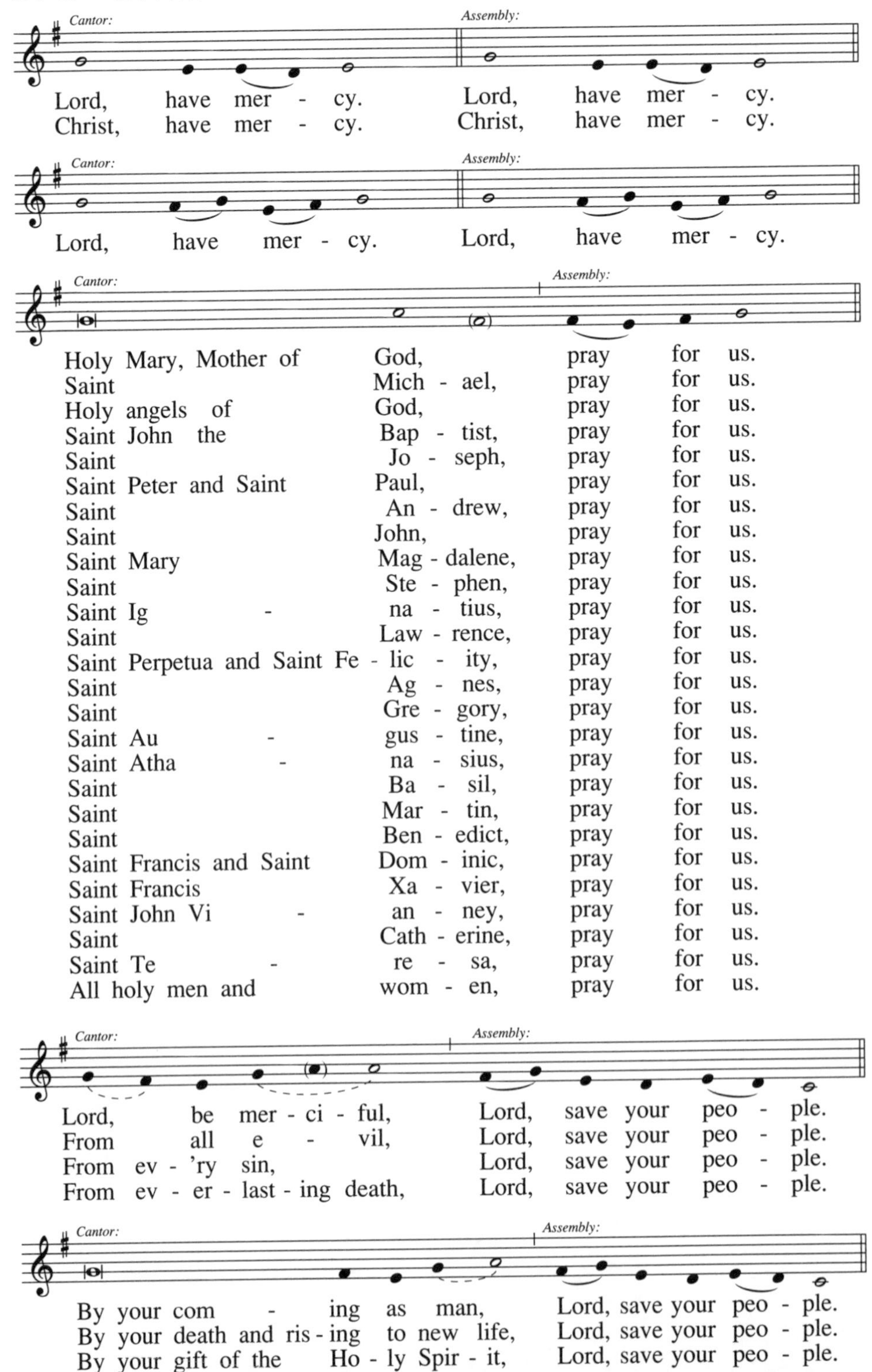
Cantor:
Assembly:
Lord, have mer - cy. Lord, have mer - cy.
Christ, have mer - cy. Christ, have mer - cy.
Cantor:
Assembly:
Lord, have mer - cy. Lord, have mer - cy.
Cantor:
Assembly:
Holy Mary, Mother of God, pray for us.
Saint Mich - ael, pray for us.
Holy angels of God, pray for us.
Saint John the Bap - tist, pray for us.
Saint Jo - seph, pray for us.
Saint Peter and Saint Paul, pray for us.
Saint An - drew, pray for us.
Saint John, pray for us.
Saint Mary Mag - dalene, pray for us.
Saint Ste - phen, pray for us.
Saint Ig - na - tius, pray for us.
Saint Law - rence, pray for us.
Saint Perpetua and Saint Fe - lic - ity, pray for us.
Saint Ag - nes, pray for us.
Saint Gre - gory, pray for us.
Saint Au - gus - tine, pray for us.
Saint Atha - na - sius, pray for us.
Saint Ba - sil, pray for us.
Saint Mar - tin, pray for us.
Saint Ben - edict, pray for us.
Saint Francis and Saint Dom - inic, pray for us.
Saint Francis Xa - vier, pray for us.
Saint John Vi - an - ney, pray for us.
Saint Cath - erine, pray for us.
Saint Te - re - sa, pray for us.
All holy men and wom - en, pray for us.
Cantor:
Assembly:
Lord, be mer - ci - ful, Lord, save your peo - ple.
From all e - vil, Lord, save your peo - ple.
From ev - 'ry sin, Lord, save your peo - ple.
From ev - er - last - ing death, Lord, save your peo - ple.
Cantor:
Assembly:
By your com - ing as man, Lord, save your peo - ple.
By your death and ris - ing to new life, Lord, save your peo - ple.
By your gift of the Ho - ly Spir - it, Lord, save your peo - ple.

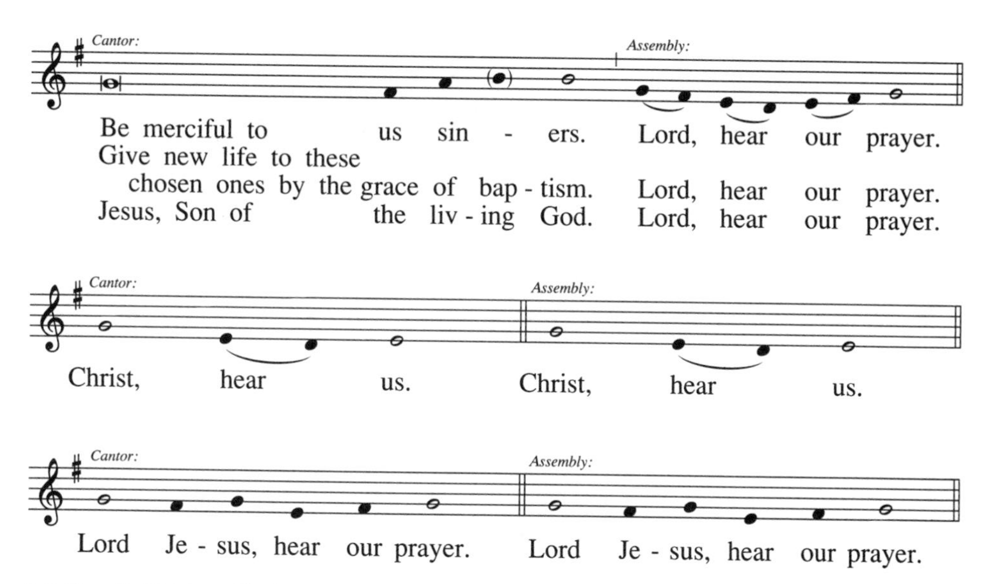
Cantor:
Assembly:
Be merciful to us sin - ers. Lord, hear our prayer.
Give new life to these chosen ones by the grace of bap - tism. Lord, hear our prayer.
Jesus, Son of the liv - ing God. Lord, hear our prayer.
Cantor:
Assembly:
Christ, hear us. Christ, hear us.
Cantor:
Assembly:
Lord Je - sus, hear our prayer. Lord Je - sus, hear our prayer.

Text: *Litany of the Saints, Roman Missal*
Music: *Litany of the Saints, Roman Missal*

our heritage of song 179

ACCLAMATIONS AND LITANIES

There are many different ways we sing our prayer and praise to God during liturgy. In addition to hymns, songs, and responsorial psalms, there are acclamations and litanies. Acclamations are short statements of praise or expressions of faith. Examples include the gospel acclamation ("Alleluia" except during the season of Lent) and the acclamations sung during the eucharistic prayer (Holy, memorial acclamation, and Amen).

A litany is a repetitive form of prayer in which a cantor or presider sings a petition and the assembly responds each time with the same or slightly altered response. The most well known litany of the Church is probably the Litany of the Saints, *(no. 178)* in which the cantor invokes the names of various saints and all respond, "Pray for us." In the Mass, the Kyrie and Lamb of God are examples of litanies.

Litanies and acclamations are meant to be sung and are composed in a variety of styles to reflect the many seasons and cultures of the Church. *TA*

180 MAKE US WORTHY

Refrain
Lord, make us wor-thy. Make us wor-thy to see your face.
Fill us with your word, O Lord, and heal us with your grace.
Verses
1. O - pen up your ten - der arms
2. Of - fer all your praise to God
3. You are strength when we are weak.
4. Fash - ion plough - shares from our swords.
5. Lord, you sent your heal - ing word
for your lost ones have come home.
who has blessed us with great love.
You are warmth when we are cold.
Rip the ha - tred from our minds.
to re - deem us from our sins.
Let the sprin - kling of your joy - ful tears
Should we stum - ble on our way, O Lord,
You are light for those in dark - ness.
Help us choose your paths of jus - tice.
You have made us fit to walk with you
wash us clean a - gain.
you will lead us home.
You are hope for all.
Bless us all with peace.
down the path of life.
D.C.

Text: Michael Mahler, b.1981
Tune: Michael Mahler, b.1981

STOP BY, LORD 181

Refrain
Stop by, Lord, stop by. Stop by, Lord, stop by. Some-bod-y needs
To optional Coda
Last time
one touch from you, Lord, oh, stop by, Lord, stop by.
Verses
Solo:
1. I need thee, oh, I need thee. I
2. I need thee, oh, I need thee. I
need thee, Je - sus, I need thee.
need thee, Je - sus, I need thee.
Some-bod - y needs one touch from you, Lord, oh,
I've got prob - lems that I can't solve, oh,
D.C.
stop by, Lord, stop by.
stop by, Lord, stop by.
Coda (optional)
stop, oh, stop, oh, stop, oh, stop, oh,
stop by, oh, stop by, oh, stop by, oh, stop by, oh,
D.S.
stop by now, oh, stop by now, oh, stop by now, oh, stop by now.

Text: Doris Wesley Bettis, b.1954
Tune: Doris Wesley Bettis, b.1954

182 Lord's Prayer

Cantor:
All:
Our Fa - ther, Our Fa - ther, who art in
heav - en, hal-low-ed be thy name;
thy king-dom come; thy
will be done on earth as it is in heav - en.
Give us this day our dai - ly bread; and for -
give us our tres - pass - es as we for -
give those who tres - pass a - gainst us;
and lead us not in-to temp-ta - tion,
but de - liv - er us from e - vil.

Priest: Deliver us, Lord...the coming of our Savior, Jesus Christ.

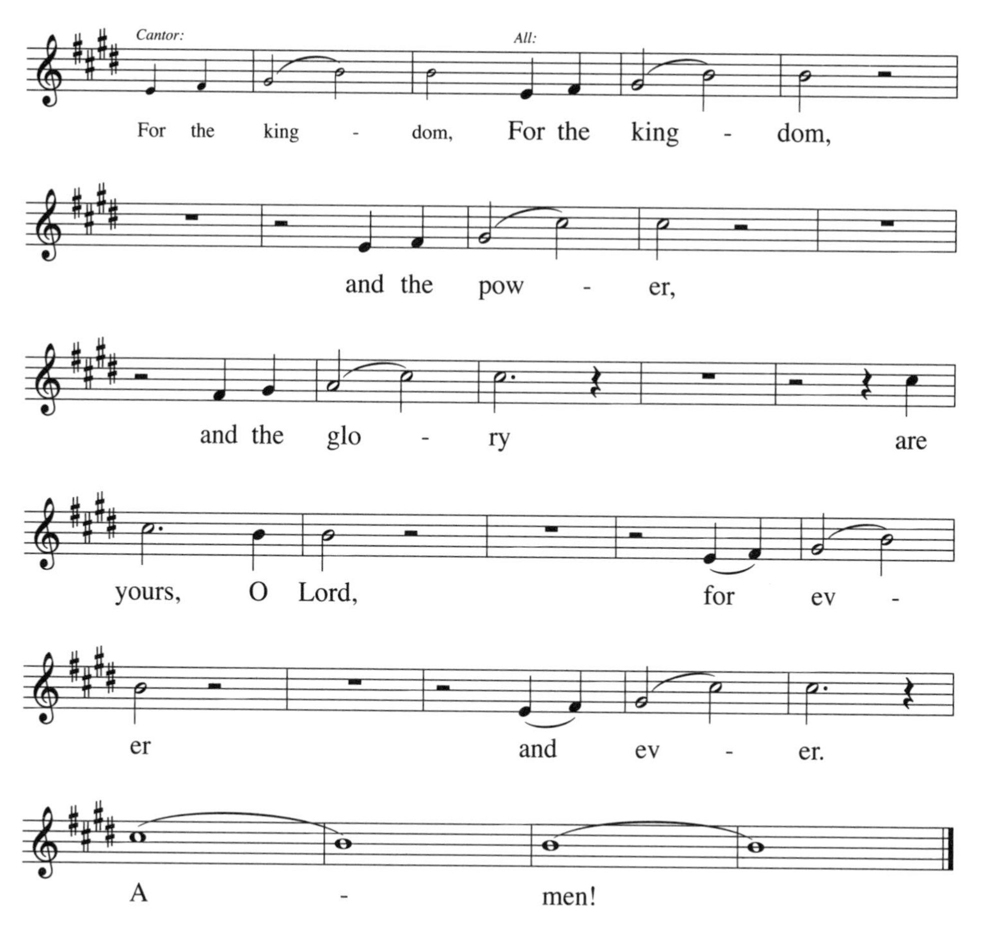
Cantor:
All:
For the king - dom, For the king - dom,
and the pow - er,
and the glo - ry are
yours, O Lord, for ev -
er and ev - er.
A - men!

Music: Jerome V. Andrews, © 1978, F.E.L. Publications, Ltd., assigned 1991 to The Lorenz Corp.; arr. by Daniel Houze, © 2008, GIA Publications, Inc.

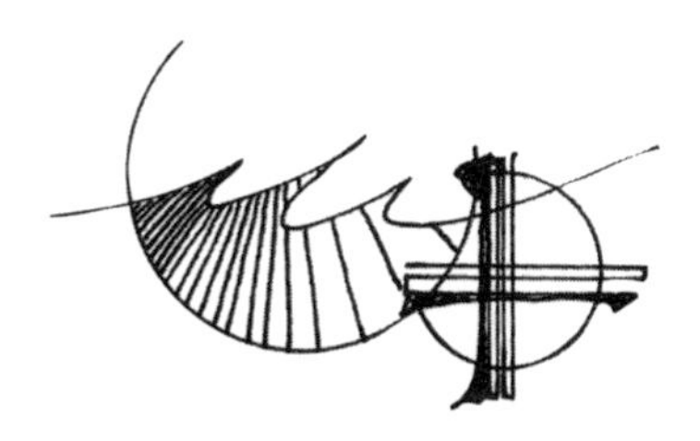

183 For All Time

Verse 1
1. Search-ing for you, I get lost, out in the night,
I feel I'm in dark-ness, can - not find the light.
Help me see that you're the way, the truth, the life.
3
Verse 2
2. In this world a - round me
I feel Sa - tan's grip: Greed and pride have sent your
peo-ple on a pow-er trip. Je-sus, come to me, re -
mind me how to serve. Je - sus,
Refrain
I need you to reach in - to my arms and
step in - to my feet for all time. Je - sus,
I need you to get in - side my head and

Repeat last time only
To verses 3, 4
3
Final ending
7
move in - to my heart for all time.
Verse 3
3. Ev-'ry mo - ment is a choice in front of me.
Some-times I can't tell just where you're lead - ing me.
Let me know where you want me at to - day.
Yeah, to - day.
D.S.
Je - sus,
Verse 4
4. Gift-ed peo - ple— I know quite a few—
they can't see all gifts be - gin in you.
Tell me, Lord, what I should do
to help them see.
D.S.
Je - sus,

Text: Shannon Cerneka, b.1975, and Orin Johnson, b.1973
Tune: Shannon Cerneka, b.1975, and Orin Johnson, b.1973

184 THE GOD OF SECOND CHANCES

1. Come now, O God of sec - ond chanc - es;
2. Come now, O God, re - lease our de - mons;
3. Come now, O God, and still our an - ger;
4. Come now, O God, shake our re - sent - ment;
5. Come now, O God, and grant com - pas - sion;
6. Come now, O God of sec - ond chanc - es;
O - pen our lives to heal.
O - pen our eyes to see
O - pen our minds to peace.
O - pen our way to choose
O - pen our hearts to love.
May we for - give our - selves,
Re - move our hate, and melt our rage.
The shame with - in, our guilt and pain.
Em - brace our fear, and hold us close.
The way of love o - ver re - venge.
May we let go of all our hurt.
May we be - come your liv - ing sign:
Save us from our - selves.
Mend us; make us whole.
Calm the storm with - in.
Show us a new way.
Help us to move on.
Chil - dren of God's love.
1., 2.
3.–6.
4

Text: David Haas, b.1957
Tune: NEW BEGINNING, 9 6 8 5; David Haas, b.1957

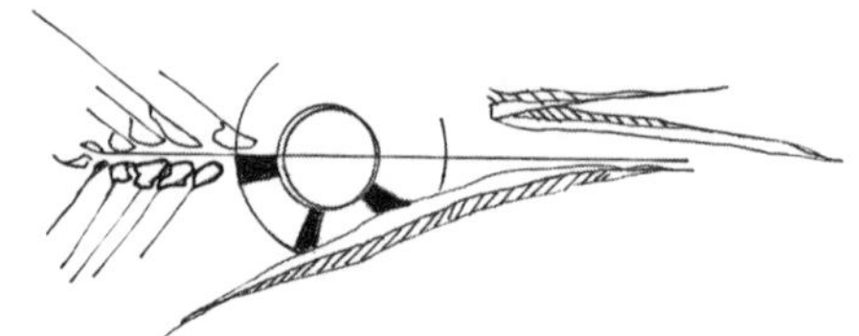

LORD, HEAR MY PRAYER / ÓYENOS, SEÑOR 185

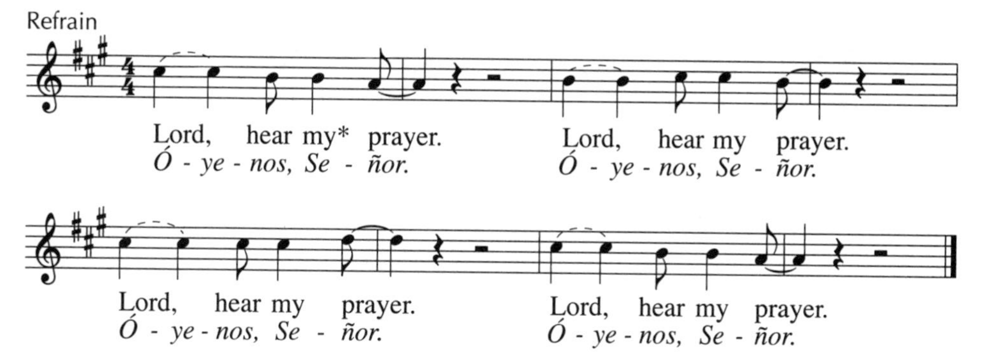
Refrain
Lord, hear my* prayer. Lord, hear my prayer.
Ó - ye - nos, Se - ñor. Ó - ye - nos, Se - ñor.
Lord, hear my prayer. Lord, hear my prayer.
Ó - ye - nos, Se - ñor. Ó - ye - nos, Se - ñor.

Verses

1. Feed all the hungry. Heal all the sick. Take all the pain away.
   Help us live this life the way you intended us to live.
   Lord, hear my prayer.

2. No more war, no more rage, no more prejudice and hate.
   Help us live this life the way you intended us to live.
   O Lord, hear my prayer.

3. Hope for the children, peace across the land, ev'rybody workin' hand in hand.
   Help us live this life the way you intended us to live.
   O Lord, hear my prayer.

1. Por los que sufren, por los enfermos,
que nuestra compasión sea un reflejo de tu misericordia.
Óyenos, Señor.

2. Que no haya guerras. Que no haya odio.
Que no haya discriminación. Que seamos un reflejo de tu misericordia.
Óyenos, Señor.

3. Que las naciones tengan la esperanza;
Que trabajemos en unión. Que seamos un reflejo de tu misericordia.
Óyenos, Señor.

*"Our" may be substituted for "my" throughout.

Text: Jim Gibson, b.1952; tr. by Jaime Cortez, b.1963
Tune: Jim Gibson, b.1952; vocal arr. and acc. by Carol Browning, b.1956

186 Now

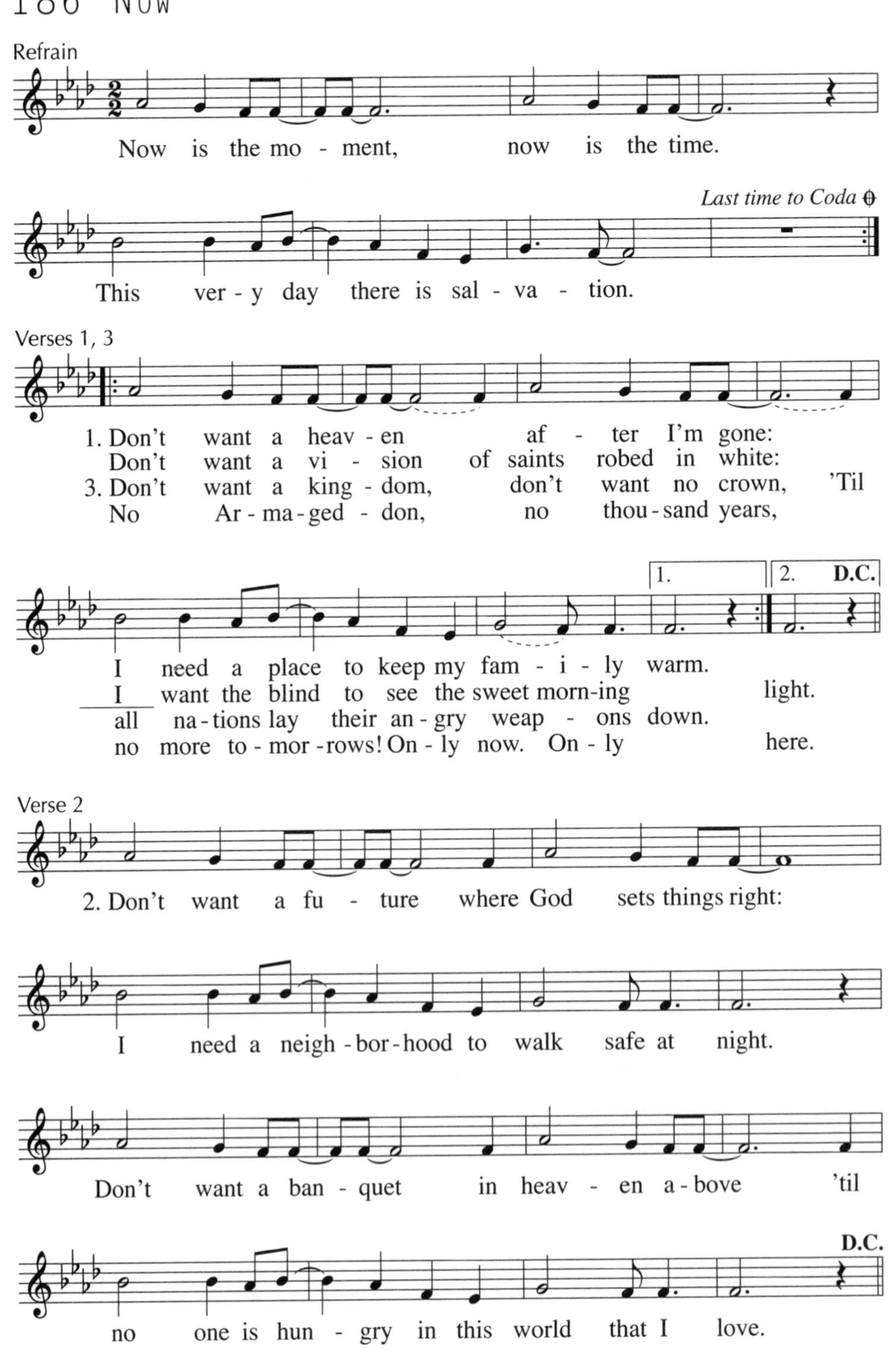
Refrain
Now is the mo - ment, now is the time.
Last time to Coda
This ver - y day there is sal - va - tion.
Verses 1, 3
1. Don't want a heav - en af - ter I'm gone:
Don't want a vi - sion of saints robed in white:
3. Don't want a king - dom, don't want no crown, 'Til
No Ar - ma - ged - don, no thou - sand years,
1.
2. D.C.
I need a place to keep my fam - i - ly warm.
I want the blind to see the sweet morn - ing light.
all na - tions lay their an - gry weap - ons down.
no more to - mor - rows! On - ly now. On - ly here.
Verse 2
2. Don't want a fu - ture where God sets things right:
I need a neigh - bor - hood to walk safe at night.
Don't want a ban - quet in heav - en a - bove 'til
D.C.
no one is hun - gry in this world that I love.

Coda
This very - y day there is sal - va - tion.

This ver - y day there is sal - va - tion.

Text: Rory Cooney, b.1952
Tune: Rory Cooney, b.1952; adapt. and arr. by Gary Daigle, b.1957

187 Strength for the Journey

Refrain
I will be, I will be, I will be
strength for the jour - ney. I will be, I will be,
I will be strength for the jour - ney.
Verses
1. There is a road meant for you to trav - el.
2. There is a cross meant for you to car - ry.
3. How man-y times have you doubt-ed my word?
Nar - row and steep is the shep-herd's way, and
There is a cross meant for you a - lone, and
How man - y times must I call your name? And
as you say, "Yes," let - ting me guide you,
as you bow down in hum-ble sur - ren - der,
as you say, "Yes," let - ting me love you,
D.C.
I will be strength for the jour - ney.

Text: Michael John Poirier, b.1960
Tune: Michael John Poirier, b.1960; arr. by Ed Bolduc, b.1969

SHELTER YOUR NAME 188
Refrain
You are all I am not. Oh, you are all that I am.
Break down these walls. Take all my bro-ken-ness. Re-
1., 4.
build me to shel-ter your name.
2., 3.
build me to shel-ter your name.
To verses
Last time
build me to shel - ter your name.
Verse 1
Cantor:
1. Help me for-give my-self. Help me to lift the cross I've laid up-on my soul.
Help me to look at my-self through your eyes, to see all I am,
and still be sat-is-fied. Help me for - give my - self.
D.C.
Verse 2
Cantor:
2. With-in my se-crets, Je - sus, there you re-side. And I need you to
rec-on - cile, to re-new all that's in - side. For if I want to love you, then
with your love, Je-sus, I must love my-self hum - bly, too.
D.C.

Text: Danielle Rose, b.1980
Tune: Danielle Rose, b.1980

189 River of Life

Refrain
Riv - er of life, come and wash
a - way my sin. Riv - er of life,
fill my thirst - y soul with - in. Riv-er of life,
Last time to Coda
3
re - new me once a - gain.
Verse 1
1. There is a riv - er run - ning wild that I can't cross o -
ver. The wa-ter is deep and the waves are
high and the wind is blow - ing. I don't know where
it goes, which way the cur - rent flows;
D.C.
I'm just dy - ing to jump in.

Verse 2
2. Gen-tle waves sweep me a - way, and I can't fight
it. They bring me to a ho - ly place
where the sun is shin - ing. I'm pour-ing o -
ver all the white - caps and wa - ter - falls
and drown-ing in an o - cean of your love.
D.C.
Coda
There is a place where warm springs flood my empty heart; a sanc - tu - ar - y
where on - ly God can car - ry all my broken - ness a - way.
D.C.

Text: Joshua Blakesley, b.1976
Tune: Joshua Blakesley, b.1976; acc. by David Brinker

190 Purify My Heart

Verses
1. Pu - ri - fy my heart, let me be as gold
2. Pu - ri - fy my heart, cleanse me from with - in
and pre - cious sil - ver. Pu - ri - fy my heart
and make me ho - ly. Pu - ri - fy my heart
let me be as gold, pure gold.
cleanse me from my sin, deep with - in.
Refrain
Re - fin - er's fire, my heart's one de - sire is to
be ho - ly, set a - part for you, Lord. I choose to
be ho - ly set a - part for you, my mas - ter,
ready - y to do your will.
1., 3.
6
D.C.
2.
D.S.

Text: Brian Doerksen
Tune: Brian Doerksen

191 One Lord

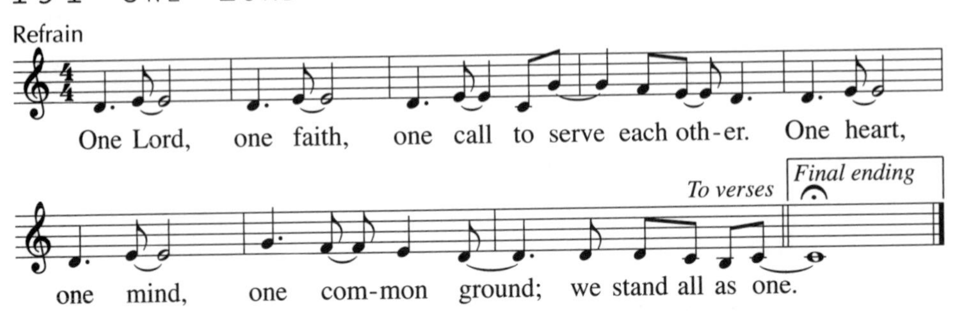
Refrain
One Lord, one faith, one call to serve each oth - er. One heart,
one mind, one com - mon ground; we stand all as one.
To verses
Final ending

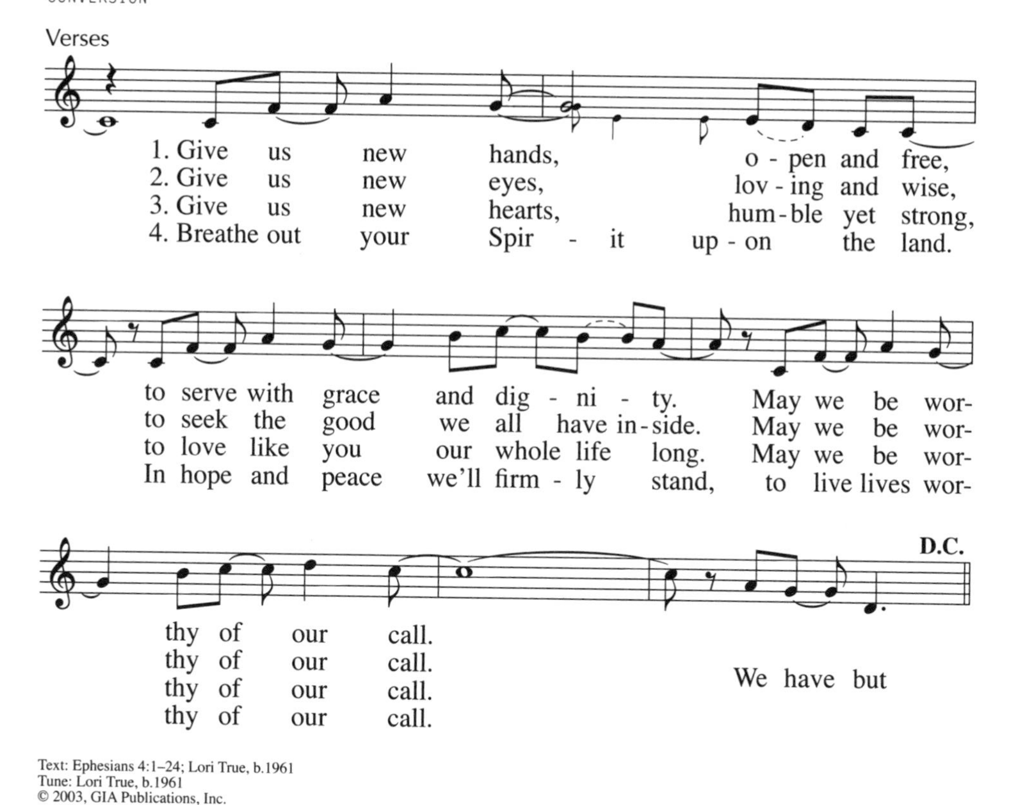
Verses
1. Give us new hands, o - pen and free, to serve with grace and dig - ni - ty. May we be wor- thy of our call.
2. Give us new eyes, lov - ing and wise, to seek the good we all have in - side. May we be wor- thy of our call.
3. Give us new hearts, hum - ble yet strong, to love like you our whole life long. May we be wor- thy of our call.
4. Breathe out your Spir - it up - on the land. In hope and peace we'll firm - ly stand, to live lives wor- thy of our call.
We have but
D.C.

Text: Ephesians 4:1–24; Lori True, b.1961
Tune: Lori True, b.1961

our sacraments and rites 192

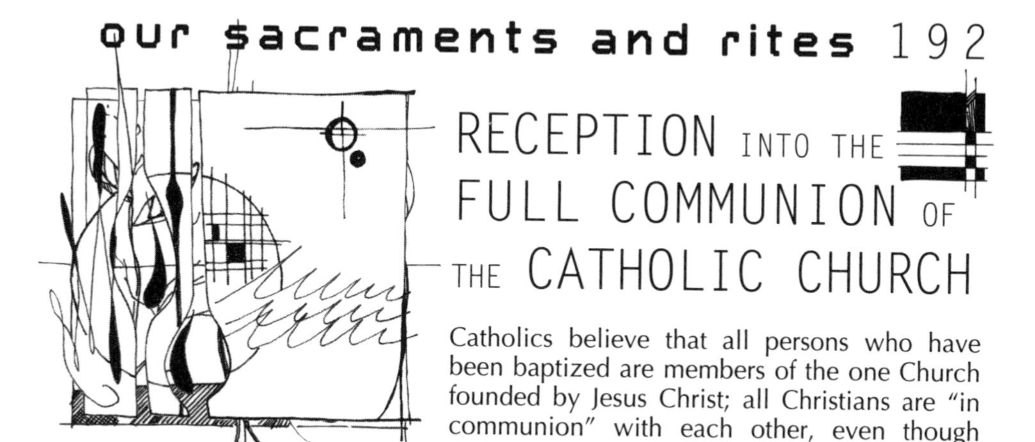

RECEPTION INTO THE FULL COMMUNION OF THE CATHOLIC CHURCH

Catholics believe that all persons who have been baptized are members of the one Church founded by Jesus Christ; all Christians are "in communion" with each other, even though their communion in faith and love may not be complete. The Catholic Church does not rebaptize persons who have already been validly baptized. When a person baptized in a Church or community other than the Catholic Church wishes to become Catholic, after suitable instruction they are received into the *full communion* of the Catholic Church through a profession of faith, the celebration of confirmation, and their reception of the holy Eucharist. This reception may take place at any time during the church year. *RK*

193 Way, Truth, and Life

Verses 1, 2
Solo:
1. Make us a way worth walk-ing, pil-grim peo-ple in mo-tion, A road that leads to wis-dom, call-ing each to the jour-ney. Oh, make us a path to peace, that the whole world might sing to-geth-er.
2. Make us a truth worth seek-ing, peo-ple full of com-pas-sion, Who live the word we're speak-ing, liv-ing Christ in our bod-ies. Oh, give us in-teg-ri-ty, so our deeds shine with gos-pel glo-ry.
Refrain
All:
You are the way, you are the truth, God of all life, send your wis-dom a-mong us. Show us the way, teach us the truth, Give us your life, fill the earth with your Spir-it.
1.
3
2.
Solo:
it. Right be-fore us we see death and life, Come and make us your Christ, Oh, help us all choose

Verse 3
All:
life! 3. Make us a life worth liv - ing, full of
vi - sion and cour - age, A peo-ple kind and giv - ing,
bound for free - dom and jus - tice. Oh, make us your
3
church at last, one with you, one in Christ our Sav - ior.
Final Refrain
You are the way, you are the truth, God of all life,
send your wis - dom a-mong us. Show us the way,
teach us the truth, Give us your life, fill the
1. Repeat as needed
2.
earth with your Spir - it. earth with your Spir - it.

Text: Rory Cooney, b.1952
Tune: Gary Daigle, b.1957

194 Turn My Heart, O God

Refrain

Turn my heart, O God. Turn my heart, O God. Take my pain and bro - ken - ness; shape my life for you. Come and

To verses | *To repeat refrain and last time*

turn my heart, O God.

Verses

turn my heart, O God.

Cantor:

1. From all that leads to death, to seek the way of life:
2. From bit - ter - ness and hate, to ten - der-ness and care:
3. O let your Spir - it come and cleanse my in - most heart:
4. O bring me home to you, Most Ho - ly, Bless - ed One:

Assembly:

Come and turn my heart, O

From
From
Give
And

Assembly:
God.
Come and
all that leads to sin,
to ho - li - ness and grace:
self - ish - ness and greed,
to gen-'rous car - ing love:
back to me the joy
of walk - ing in your way:
let my spir - it rest
with - in your lov - ing heart:
turn my heart, O God.
From all de - spair and grief, to
From all de - ceit and lies, to
O fill me with your grace that
For you a - lone can raise my
Assembly:
D.C.
Come and turn my heart, O God.
D.C.
hope of life re - newed:
faith - ful - ness and truth:
I might sing your praise:
wea - ry soul to life:
Text: Marty Haugen, b.1950
Tune: Marty Haugen, b.1950
© 2002, GIA Publications, Inc.

195 On That Holy Mountain

Verses
Cantor:
1. The wolf is the guest of the lamb,
2. The poor shall re - ceive from the rich,
3. Jus - tice shall flow'r for all time,
All:
Cantor:
on that ho - ly moun - tain. And the calf and the lion shall lie
on that ho - ly moun - tain. And the sick and the lame shall be
on that ho - ly moun - tain. As long as the sun still can
All:
Cantor:
down, on that ho - ly moun - tain. To - geth - er they shall
healed, on that ho - ly moun - tain. The wick - ed shall be
shine, on that ho - ly moun - tain. Peace till the
All:
rest with the child, on that ho - ly moun-
slain by God's breath, on that ho - ly moun-
moon be no more, on that ho - ly moun-
tain, on that ho - ly moun - tain,
tain, on that ho - ly moun - tain,
tain, on that ho - ly moun - tain,
on that ho - ly moun - tain of the Lord.
on that ho - ly moun - tain of the Lord.
on that ho - ly moun - tain of the Lord.

Refrain
No harm or ruin on that holy mountain.
That sacred day shall be filled with knowl-edge.
There shall be peace, led by all the chil-dren,
on that ho-ly moun-tain, on that ho-ly moun-tain, on that ho-ly moun-tain of the Lord.
Last time to Coda
D.C.
Coda
Ho-ly and peace-ful the day of the moun-tain.

Text: Joe Mattingly, b.1957
Tune: Joe Mattingly, b.1957

196 Better Is One Day

Verse 1
1. How love - ly is your dwell - ing place,
O Lord Al - might - y. For my soul longs and
e - ven faints for you.
2. For
(3. One)
Verses 2, 3
here my heart is sat - is - fied, with-in your pres - ence.
thing I ask and I would seek; to see your beau - ty,
I sing be - neath the shad - ow of your wings.
to find you in the place your glo - ry dwells.
Refrain
Bet-ter is one day in your courts, bet-ter is
one day in your house, bet-ter is one day in your courts than thou - sands
else - where. Bet-ter is one day in your courts, bet-ter is
Last time to Coda
one day in your house, bet-ter is one day in your courts than thou-sands

1.
D.S.
else-where, than thou-sands else-where.
3. One
2.
To bridge
3.
else - where.
else-where.
Bet-ter is
Bridge
My heart and flesh cry out for you, the liv - ing God;
I've tast - ed and I've seen, come once a - gain to me;
1.
2.
your Spir-it's wa-ter for my soul.
I will draw near to you,
To refrain
I will draw near to you, to you.
Coda
else-where, than thou - sands else - where.
than thou - sands else-where.

Text: Based on Psalm 84:2–4, 7, 11; Matt Redman
Tune: Matt Redman; arr. by Matt Maher; acc. by Ed Bolduc, b.1969

197 LEAD ME HOME

Verse 1

1. Thank you for the cross, thank you for your love, the per-fect sac-ri-fice of praise to God a-bove. Thank you for the gift, thank you for the price of los-ing ev-'ry-thing to gain e-ter-nal life. Thank you. Thank you. Thank you. 2. Thank you for your

Verses 2, 3

2. joy, thank you for the pain of long - ing for peace in my suf-fer-ing Thank you for my hun-ger, for my pov-er-ty, that I would fall in - to the arms of mer - cy.

3. bro-ken, I praise you when I'm lost, that it would keep me hon-est, in need of you a-lone. I praise you for the past, for the mess of sin, that I would nev - er want to turn from you a - gain.

Ev - 'ry road leads back to you, ev-'ry jour-ney lies in you, so

Refrain

Lead me home, my lov - er, Sav - ior. Lead me home, my Mas-

1.
ter, Re-deem-er. Lead me home and I will rest in you.
D.S.
2.
3. I praise you when I'm will rest in you.
Lead me home, Lord. Lead me home,
Lord. Lead me home, Lord.
Ev-'ry road leads back to you, ev-'ry jour-ney lies in you, so
Final Refrain
Lead me home, my lov - er, Sav - ior. Lead me home, my Mas-
1.
ter, Re-deem-er. Lead me home and I will rest in you.
2.
will rest in you. Lead me home and I
will rest in you. Lead me home and I will rest in you.
I will rest in you.

Text: Matt Maher
Tune: Matt Maher; acc. by Ed Bolduc, b.1969

198 On That Day

Refrain
On that day, on that hal - le - lu - ia day, on that
day, on that hal - le - lu - ia day there'll be
Last time to Coda
sing-in', there'll be shout - in', and joy flows like a foun - tain on that
day.
1. We'll
2. Twelve
3. No
Verses
see the ho - ly cit - y there; the
gates to the king - dom we shall see; all
need of the sun or moon to shine; the
new Je - ru - sa - lem. No more
na - tions will walk as one. Lift - ing our
glo - ry of God is there. Dark - ness to
sor - row, no more cry - in'.
voic - es, claim - ing our choic - es.
light, God's face in our sight.

D.S.
No more death, no more pain. On that
Glo - ry and hon - or shall be on that
Joy from God's love we will share on that
Coda
day, on that day!

Text: Kate Cuddy, b.1953
Tune: Kate Cuddy, b.1953; arr. by Kate Cuddy and Gary Daigle, b.1957

I Am Sure I Shall See 199

Ostinato Refrain
I am sure I shall see the good-ness of the Lord in the
land of the liv - ing. Yes, I shall see the
good-ness of our God, hold firm, trust in the Lord.
Last time
Last time

Text: The Taizé Community
Tune: The Taizé Community

200 Sign Me Up

Refrain
Solo:
All:
Sign me up, Sign me up for the Chris - tian ju - bi - lee,
Solo:
All:
Write my name, Write my name on the roll.
Solo:
All:
For, I've been changed, I've been changed since the
Lord has lift - ed me, I want to be
1.
2.
read - y when Je - sus comes.
Verse 1
1. When Je - sus comes, oh, the trum - pet will sound
loud, When my Sav - ior comes, all the
saints in Christ shall rise, Oh, I'm glad I've been
changed since he lift - ed me, I
D.C.
want to be read - y when Je - sus comes.

Verse 2
2. You know not the day nor the hour he shall ap - pear, But we know in our hearts that he's com-ing back a - gain, My heart is fixed and my mind's made up. I want to be read-y when Je-sus comes.
D.C.

Text: Kevin Yancy and Jerome Metcalfe
Tune: Kevin Yancy and Jerome Metcalfe; harm. by Kenneth Morris, 1917–1988

201 Yours Is the Kingdom

Verses
Cantor:
1. Bless - ed are you, the hum - ble in spir - it.
2. You who hun - ger and thirst for jus - tice,
3. Bless - ed are you, the pure and whole - heart - ed.
4. When they per - se - cute you as Chris - tians,
All:
Yours is the king - dom.
Cantor:
You who mourn will find con - so - la - tion.
Right - eous - ness will fill and sus - tain you.
You who work for peace are God's chil - dren.
Like the proph - ets who came be - fore you,
All:
Yours is the king - dom.
Cantor:
Bless - ed are you, the meek and the low - ly.
You, the mer - ci - ful, shall have mer - cy.
Bless - ed are you, the blame - less who suf - fer.
Then re - joice, for yours is God's boun - ty!
All:
Yours is the king - dom.
Cantor:
Come and re - ceive
All:
the king - dom of God.
1.
D.C.
2.–4.
The

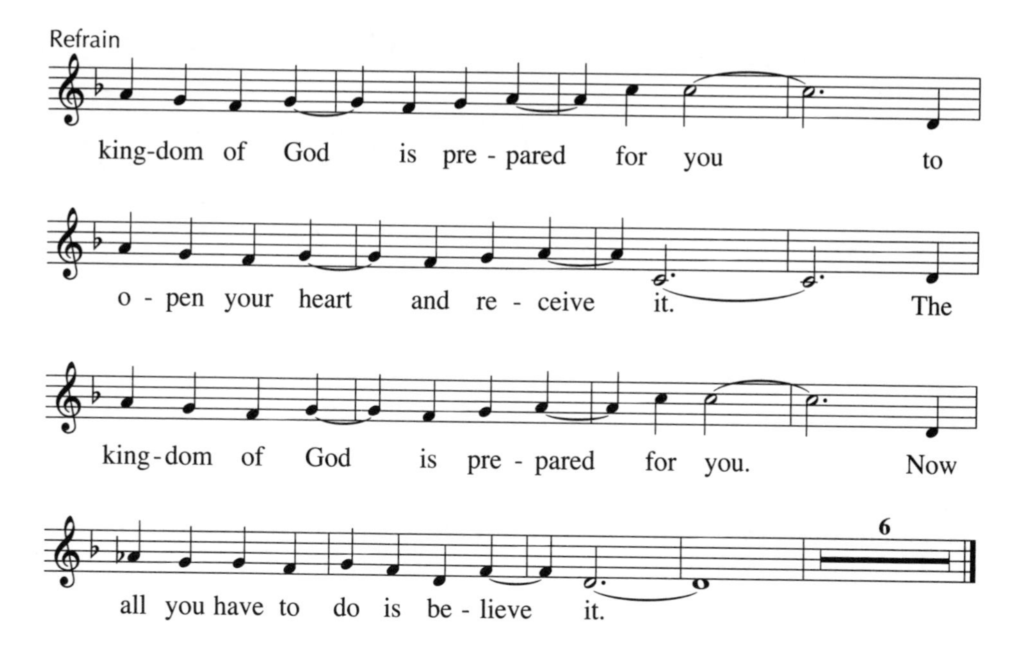
Refrain
king-dom of God is pre - pared for you to
o - pen your heart and re - ceive it. The
king-dom of God is pre - pared for you. Now
all you have to do is be - lieve it.
6

Text: Matthew 5:3–12; Michael Mahler, b.1981
Tune: Michael Mahler, b.1981

202 hallmark songs of our faith

AVE MARIA

The Ave Maria (Hail Mary in English) is the most familiar prayer of the Church directed to the Blessed Mother. It has been set to music in countless ways in each generation. Each musical setting of this text makes the prayer come alive in different ways; the profound beauty of this chant is no exception. This setting weaves together a traditional chant tune dating back to the tenth century and a new melody added by contemporary composer Dan Kantor. The chant has been one of the cornerstones of the Catholic Church. This weaving together of two melodies simultaneously is called a quodlibet. It is a wonderful way to weave together old and new! *TA*

203 Ave Maria

A - ve Ma - rí - a, grá - ti - a ple - na, Dó - mi - nus te - cum,
be - ne - dí - cta tu in mu - li - é - ri - bus,
et be - ne - dí - ctus fru - ctus ven - tris tu - i, Je - sus.
San - cta Ma - rí - a, Ma - ter De - i, o - ra pro no - bis
pec - ca - tó - ri - bus, nunc et in ho - ra mor - tis no - strae. A - men.

Text: Luke 1:29; Latin, 13th C.
Music: Chant Mode I

204 Ave Maria

Verses

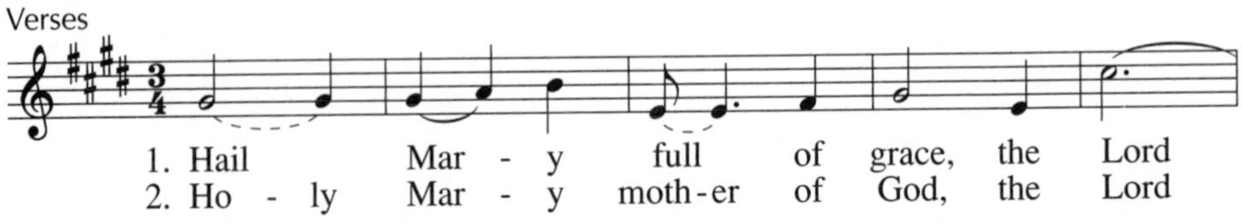
1. Hail Mar - y full of grace, the Lord
2. Ho - ly Mar - y moth - er of God, the Lord

is with you. Bless-ed are you a - mong all
is with you. Pray for us sin - ners, pray for us
wom-en, Blest is the fruit of your womb.
sin - ners, Now and at the hour of our death.
Refrain
Je - sus, formed in your faith, A - ve Ma - ri - a al - le -
lu - ia. Je - sus, born in your love,
A - ve Ma - ri - a al - le - lu - ia.
7

Text: Hail Mary; additional text by Dan Kantor, b.1960
Tune: Dan Kantor, b.1960; arr. by Rob Glover, b.1950

our liturgical year 205

HOLY DAYS OF OBLIGATION

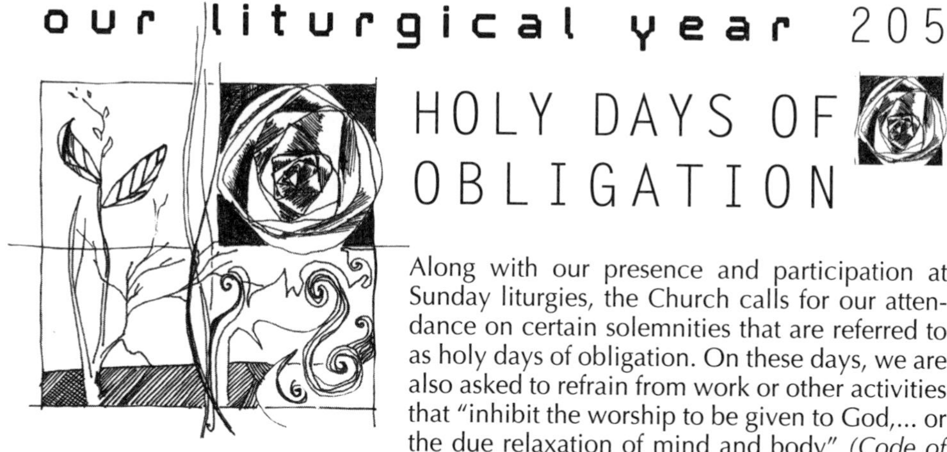

Along with our presence and participation at Sunday liturgies, the Church calls for our attendance on certain solemnities that are referred to as holy days of obligation. On these days, we are also asked to refrain from work or other activities that "inhibit the worship to be given to God,... or the due relaxation of mind and body" *(Code of Canon Law, 1247)*. Celebrating these feast days honoring our Lord, Mary, and the saints is a part of our commitment to our Catholic faith. These important feast days (known as solemnities) include:

the solemnity of the Blessed Virgin Mary, Mother of God
the solemnity of the Ascension
the solemnity of the Assumption of the Blessed Virgin Mary
the solemnity of All Saints
the solemnity of the Immaculate Conception
the solemnity of the Nativity of Our Lord Jesus Christ *LD*

206 Among All

Refrain
A-mong all, you are blessed, and full of grace and ho-liness. A-mong all, you said yes to do God's will with o - pen-ness. O La-dy, full of grace, Mar-y, Moth-er of God, be with us, pray for us.
Last time to Coda
Solo or section:
1. You
2. You
3. You
Verses
teach us to o-bey the liv-ing word of God. You show us how to lis-ten to his voice that calls us each by name.
teach us how to serve God's king-dom here on earth. You bring to birth a wil-ling-ness to share our lives with joy and love.
teach us how to pray with hum-ble-ness of heart. You guide us to be in-stru-ments of peace and hope for all the world.
D.C.
Coda
Solo:
Litany of Petitions
That we may love like Christ,
peace in ev - 'ry land,
we may spread God's word,
us.*
All:
Mar-y,

*Sing on repeat.

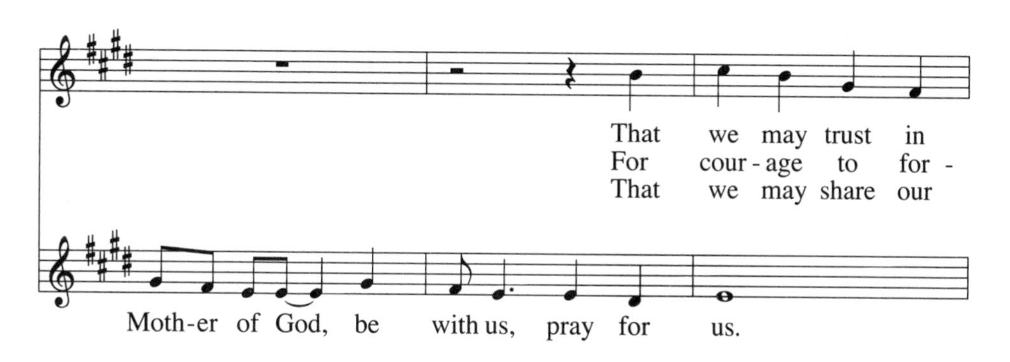
That we may trust in
For cour - age to for -
That we may share our
Moth-er of God, be with us, pray for us.

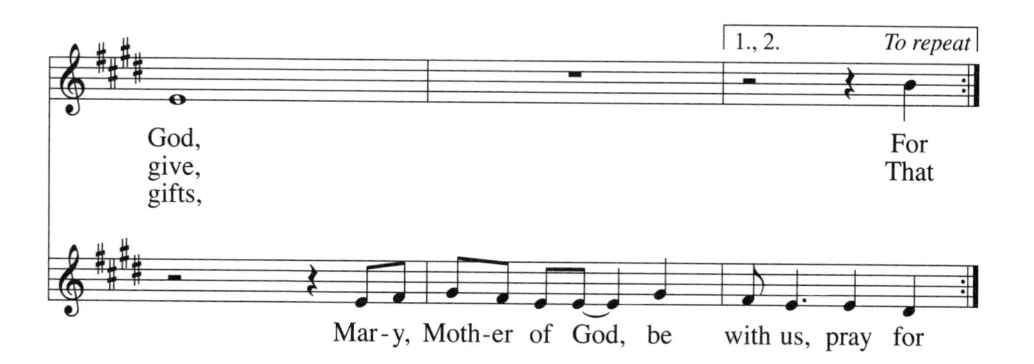
1., 2.
To repeat
God,
give,
gifts,
For
That
Mar-y, Moth-er of God, be with us, pray for

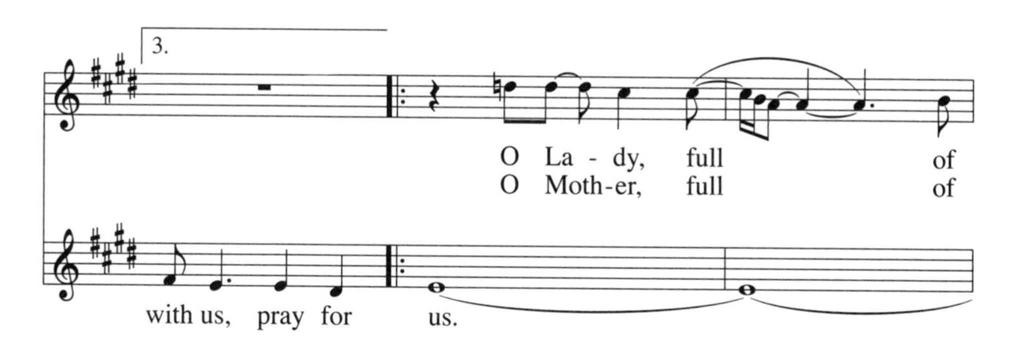
3.
O La - dy, full of
O Moth-er, full of
with us, pray for us.

Repeat as needed
Last time
grace, pray for us.
love, pray for us.
Pray for

Text: Chris de Silva, b.1967
Tune: Chris de Silva, b.1967

207 our liturgical year

SOLEMNITIES AND FEASTS

Solemnities and feast days commemorate important events in the life of Jesus Christ, as well as the witness of the saints, especially Mary, the Mother of God. These days include (in chronological order throughout the year):

The Blessed Virgin Mary, the Mother of God
The Baptism of the Lord
The Presentation of the Lord
St. Joseph, Husband of the Blessed Virgin Mary
The Annunciation of the Lord
Easter Sunday: The Resurrection of the Lord
The Ascension of the Lord
Pentecost Sunday
The Most Holy Trinity
The Most Holy Body and Blood of Christ
The Most Sacred Heart of Jesus
The Nativity of Saint John the Baptist
Saints Peter and Saint Paul
The Transfiguration of the Lord
The Assumption of the Blessed Virgin Mary
The Exaltation of the Holy Cross
All Saints
The Commemoration of All of the Faithful Departed (All Souls)
The Dedication of the Lateran Basilica in Rome
Our Lord Jesus Christ the King
The Immaculate Conception of the Blessed Virgin Mary
The Nativity of the Lord (Christmas) *LD/RK*

208 Holy Is Your Name

Verse 1
1. My soul is filled with joy as I sing to God my savior:
you have looked upon your servant, you have visited your people.

Refrain

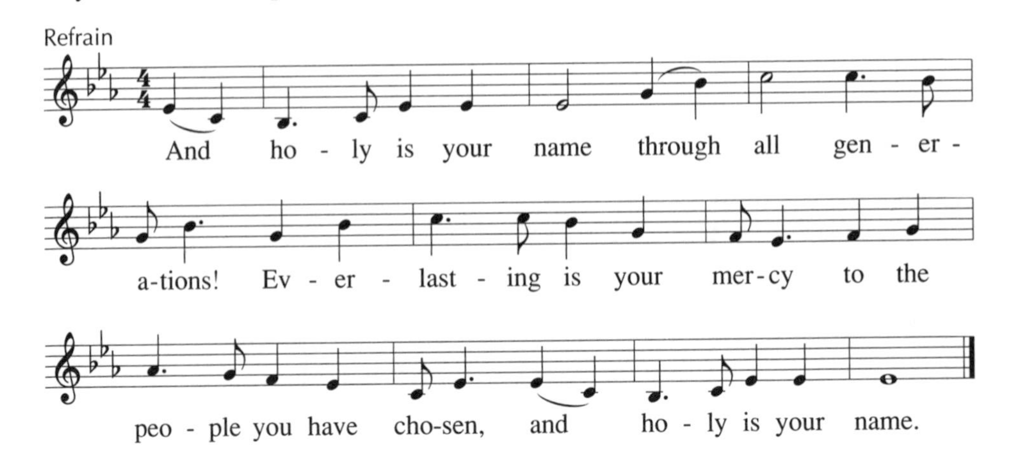
And ho - ly is your name through all gen - er -
a-tions! Ev - er - last - ing is your mer-cy to the
peo - ple you have cho-sen, and ho - ly is your name.

Verses 2–5

2. I am lowly as a child, but I know from this day forward
   that my name will be remembered, for all will call me blessed.

3. I proclaim the pow'r of God, you do marvels for your servants;
   though you scatter the proud hearted, and destroy the might of princes.

4. To the hungry you give food, send the rich away empty.
   In your mercy you are mindful of the people you have chosen.

5. In your love you now fulfill what you promised to your people.
   I will praise you Lord, my savior, everlasting is your mercy.

Text: Luke 1:46-55, David Haas, b.1957
Tune: WILD MOUNTAIN THYME, Irregular; Irish traditional; arr. by David Haas, b.1957

209 Litany of Mary / Letanía de la Santísima Virgen María

Cantor:

1. Holy Mary, *Response 1*
   Mother of God, *Response 1*
   Mother of the Church, *Response 2*

Cantor:

1. Santa María, Response 1
   Madre de Dios, Response 1
   Madre de la Iglesia, Response 2

Response 1

O - ra pro no - bis.

Response 2

To refrain
O - ra pro no - bis.

Refrain

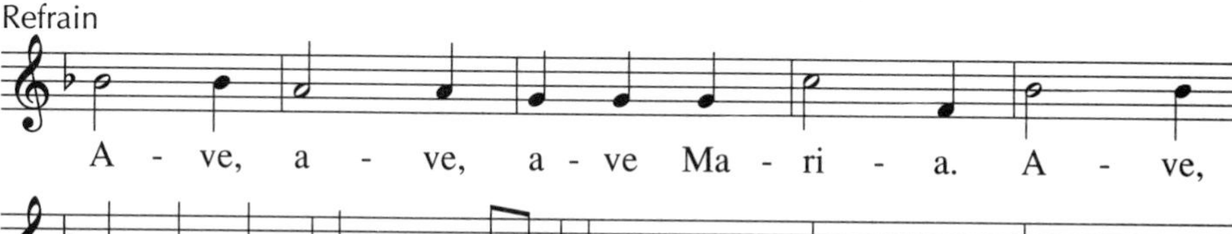
A - ve, a - ve, a - ve Ma - ri - a. A - ve,

a - ve Ma - ri - a.

Cantor:

2. Mother of good counsel, *Response 1*
   Mother most pure, *Response 1*
   Mirror of justice, *Response 2*

3. Refuge of sinners, *Response 1*
   Morning star, *Response 1*
   Mary, Queen of peace, *Response 2*

4. Gate of heaven, *Response 1*
   Queen of angels, *Response 1*
   Health of the sick, *Response 2*

Cantor:

2. Madre del buen consejo, Response 1
   Madre purísima, Response 1
   Espejo de justicia, Response 2

3. Refugio de los pecadores, Response 1
   Estrella de la mañana, Response 1
   Reina de la paz, Response 2

4. Puerta del cielo, Response 1
   Reina de los ángeles, Response 1
   Salud de los enfermos, Response 2

Text: Based on the Litany of Loretto; Tony E. Alonso, b.1980
Tune: Refrain based on LOURDES HYMN; Tony E. Alonso, b.1980

210 What You Have Done for Me

Verse 1
1. I am the hun - gry, I am the poor,
I am the stran - ger out - side your door. So
when you feed the hun - gry, when you clothe the poor
I will no long - er be just a stran - ger at your door.
Refrain
What you have done for the least of my chil - dren
you have done for me. What you have giv - en, with
noth - ing left to give, you have giv - en me.
To verses
4
Last time
3
me.
Verse 2
2. Come all you bless - ed, come and re - joice. In -

her - it the king - dom pre - pared for you. For
you are my chil - dren, called to serve as keep - ers of the
vi - sion and speak - ers of the word.
D.S.
Verse 3
3. I will look to you when life on earth has end - ed.
Those who give will re - ceive, those who seek will find; so
seek my face in ev-'ry face and see the eyes of God!
D.S.

Text: Based on Matthew 25:24–41; Tony E. Alonso, b.1980
Tune: Tony E. Alonso, b.1980

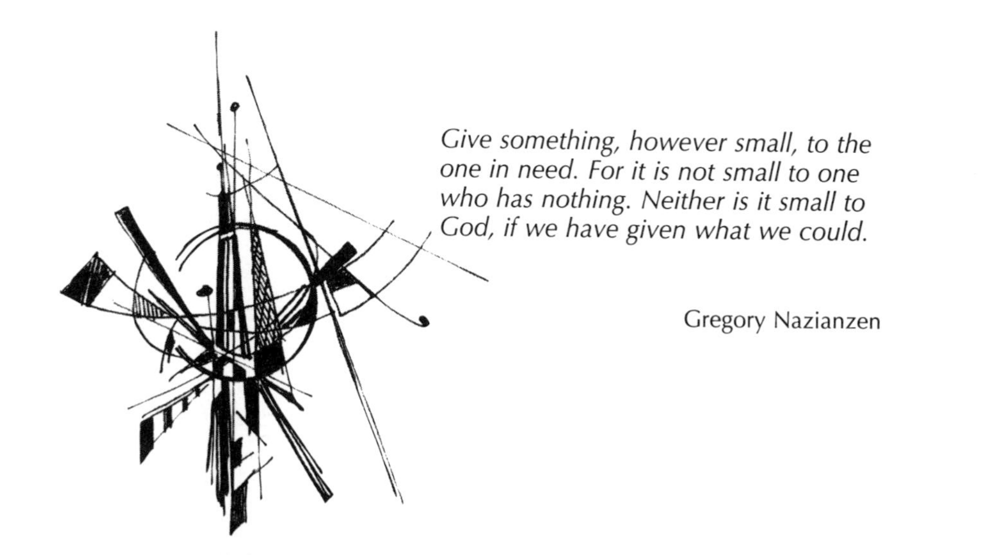

Give something, however small, to the one in need. For it is not small to one who has nothing. Neither is it small to God, if we have given what we could.

Gregory Nazianzen

211 A Place at the Table

Verses
1. For ev - 'ry - one born, a place at the ta - ble, for
2. For wom - an and man, a place at the ta - ble, re -
3. For young and for old, a place at the ta - ble, a
4. For just and un - just, a place at the ta - ble, a -
5. For ev - 'ry - one born, a place at the ta - ble, to
ev - 'ry - one born, clean wa - ter and bread, a
vis - ing the roles, de - cid - ing the share, with
voice to be heard, a part in the song, the
bus - er, a - bused, with need to for - give, in
live with - out fear, and sim - ply to be, to
shel - ter, a space, a safe place for grow - ing, for
wis - dom and grace, di - vid - ing the pow - er, for
hands of a child in hands that are wrin - kled, for
an - ger, in hurt, a mind - set of mer - cy, for
work, to speak out, to wit - ness and wor - ship, for
ev - 'ry - one born, a star o - ver - head.
wom - an and man, a sys - tem that's fair.
young and for old, the right to be - long. And
just and un - just, a new way to live.
ev - 'ry - one born, the right to be free.
Refrain
God will de - light when we are cre - a - tors of
jus - tice and joy, yes, God will de - light
when we are cre - a - tors of jus - tice,

jus - tice and joy!

Text: Shirley Erena Murray, b.1931, © 1998, Hope Publishing Co.
Tune: Lori True, b.1961, © 2001, GIA Publications, Inc.

WILL THE CIRCLE BE UNBROKEN? 212

1. Will the cir - cle be un - bro - ken? Will the
2. Will the words our God has spo - ken be re -
3. Here the bod - y, blessed and bro - ken, and the
pow'r of death pre - vail? Will the voic - es seek - ing
vised or be ig - nored? Will the love that made and
blood of Christ out - poured is the on - ly food of
jus - tice be re - ject - ed and grow frail?
formed us be re - ject - ed for the sword?
free - dom for the ser-vants of the Lord.
Will re - venge re - place for - give - ness? Will our
Will the God who cries, "For - give - ness is the
Here the sto - ries shared at ta - ble call us
pride re - place God's peace? Will the in - no-cents be
on - ly way to peace," be blocked out by cries of
all to peace - ful ways: show us Christ in all cre -
vic - tims and the vi - o - lence in-crease?
an - ger? Will the fight - ing ev - er cease?
a - tion, show us love's the on - ly way.

Text: Tony E. Alonso, b.1980
Tune: Tony E. Alonso, b.1980

213 Seek Truth, Make Peace, Reverence Life

Refrain
Seek truth, make peace, rev-'rence
life, rev-'rence life; seek truth, make peace,
rev-'rence life, rev-'rence life.
Verse 1
1. Com-pelled by the Gos-pel, out-raged by in-jus-tice,
stirred by the wis-dom of God: seek truth,
D.S.
Verses 2–4
2. Give us the cour-age to name and re-sist the forc-es of
3. When e-vil with-in or with-out us di-vides by gen-der, by
4. Let this be the vi-sion we claim for the earth, a day when all
ha-tred and greed; may we walk as one with the poor and op-
class, or by race, we will work for a cir-cle of love o-pen
war-fare shall cease. May the seeds that we nur-ture of jus-tice and
pressed 'gainst the pow-ers that keep them in need.
wide where all may be wel-comed and graced. Seek truth,
love yield a life-giv-ing har-vest of peace.
D.S.

Text: Refrain and verse 1 inspired by Adrian Dominican Sisters' Vision Statement, 2004, adapt. by Marty Haugen, b.1950,

Tune: Marty Haugen, b.1950; adapt. by Gary Daigle, b.1957,

GIVE US YOUR PEACE 214

Refrain
Je - sus, give us your peace. Bring us to - geth - er. Let all the fight - ing cease.
Shat - ter all our hearts of stone. Give us a heart for love a - lone. Oh woh
Repeat each time
To verses
Last time
Verses
1. Some days the road I walk is lone - ly, and it's so hard to find a friend.
2. Some days the walk - ing makes me wea - ry and my soul yearns to be re - lieved.
3. Some days the strength I need is fail - ing, and then, O Lord, I turn to you.
E - ven then I know, some-where in my soul, your love is far too great to com-pre-hend. Oh woh
You, my Lord, are strong. You pull me a - long. Your love is far too great to be be-lieved. Oh woh
I need nev - er fear, you are al - ways near. What-ev - er hap-pens, you will pull me through. Oh woh
D.S.

Text: Michael Mahler, b.1981
Tune: Michael Mahler, b.1981

215 Salaam Aleikum / May Peace Be in Your Hearts

Solo:
Sa-laam a - lei - kum,
sa-laam a - lei - kum,
All:
Ho - yah!
Ho -

sa - laam a - lei - kum!
yah!
Ho - yah, ho - yah, ho - yah, ho - yah, ho -

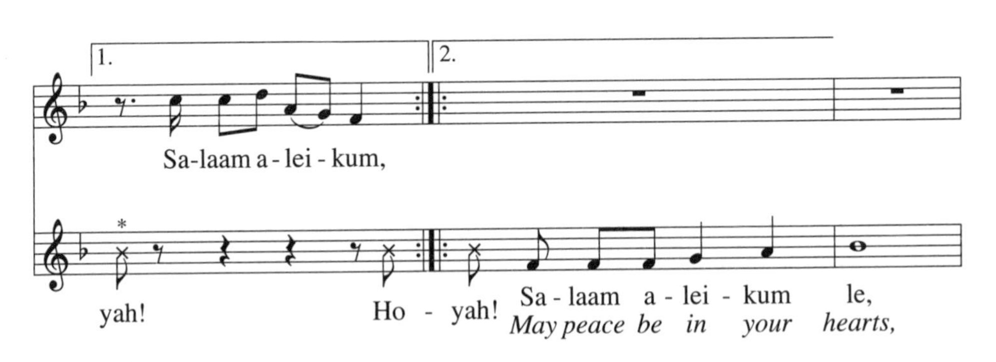
1.
2.
Sa-laam a - lei - kum,
*
yah!
Ho - yah!
Sa - laam a - lei - kum le,
May peace be in your hearts,

sa - laam a - lei - kum le,
may peace be in your homes,
sa - laam a - lei - kum le,
may peace be in your land,

*Last time, end here.

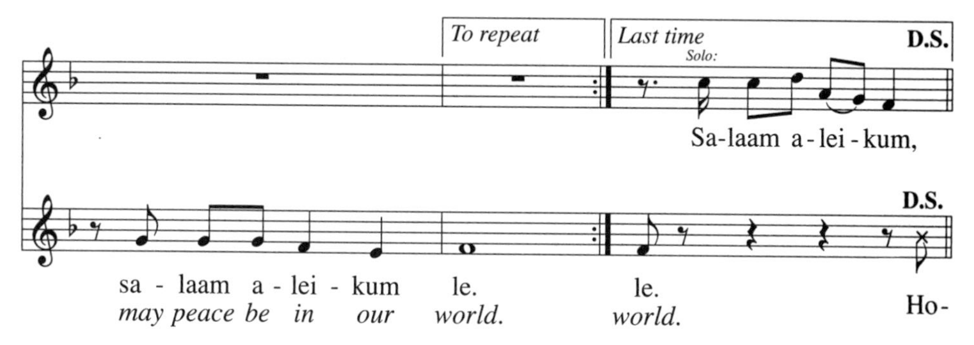
To repeat
Last time
Solo:
D.S.
Sa-laam a-lei-kum,
sa - laam a - lei - kum le.
may peace be in our world.
le.
world.
Ho-

Text: Traditional Ghanaian
Tune: Traditional Ghanaian; arr. by Marc Anderson and Marty Haugen, b.1950, © 2007, GIA Publications, Inc.

The Peace of the Earth / 216
La Paz de la Tierra

The peace of the earth be with you, the
La paz de la tie-rra es - té con ti - go, la
peace of the heav - ens, too. The peace of the riv - ers
paz de los cie-los tam - bién. La paz de los rí - os es -
be with you, the peace of the o - ceans, too:
té con ti - go, la paz de los ma-res tam - bién. La
deep peace fall - ing o - ver you,
paz pro - fun - da ca - yen - do so - bre ti. La
God's peace grow - ing in you.
paz pro - fun - da cre - cien - do en ti.

Text: Traditional Guatemalan; trans. by Christine Carson
Tune: Traditional Guatemalan; arr. by John L. Bell, b.1949

217 our heritage of song

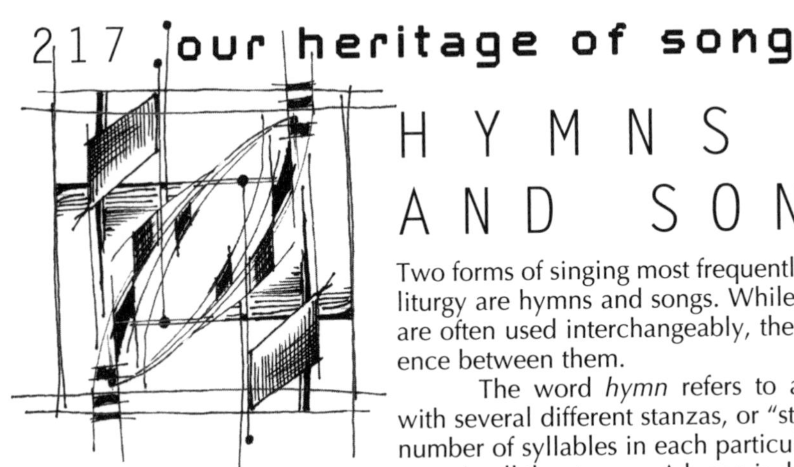

HYMNS AND SONGS

Two forms of singing most frequently used in the liturgy are hymns and songs. While these words are often used interchangeably, there is a difference between them.

The word *hymn* refers to a poetic text with several different stanzas, or "strophes." The number of syllables in each particular line is the same in all the stanzas. A hymn is designed to be sung to a tune, which is called a "hymn tune." As an example: "As a Fire Is Meant for Burning" *(no. 218)* is the hymn (the words) and BEACH SPRING is the tune (the name of the tune can be found beneath the song in capital letters).

The form of a *song* is less formal and much more varied than that of a hymn. Most commonly, it refers to a piece of music with verses that vary in length and a refrain.

Both hymns and songs are a key part of the way we give voice to our praise and thanksgiving during liturgy. There are times when one of these forms works better than the other. For instance, singing a hymn as the gathering song is a great way to begin because everyone can join in on all of the verses. But during Communion when people can't carry books in procession, it is better to sing a song in which a cantor might sing the verses and all can join in on an easily memorized refrain. *TA*

218 As a Fire Is Meant for Burning / Como un Fuego Brilla y Quema

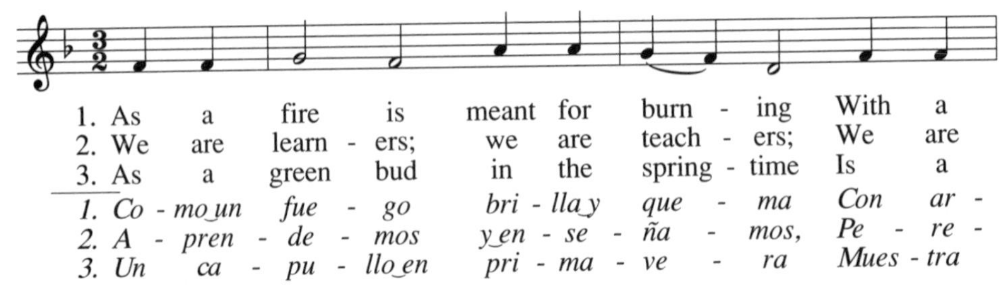
1. As a fire is meant for burn - ing With a
2. We are learn - ers; we are teach - ers; We are
3. As a green bud in the spring - time Is a
1. Co - mo_un fue - go bri - lla_y que - ma Con ar -
2. A - pren - de - mos y_en - se - ña - mos, Pe - re -
3. Un ca - pu - llo_en pri - ma - ve - ra Mues - tra

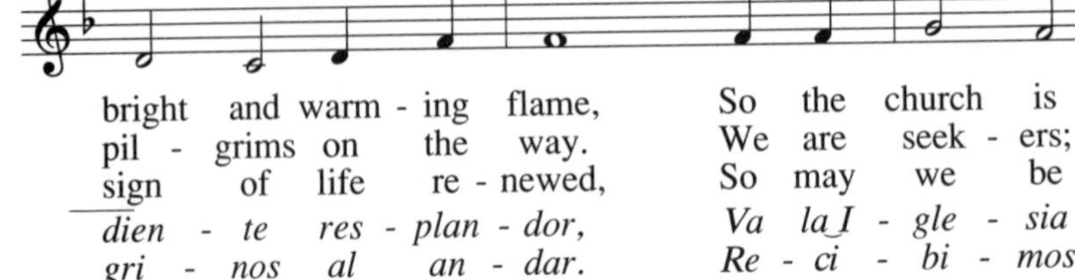
bright and warm - ing flame, So the church is meant for
pil - grims on the way. We are seek - ers; we are
sign of life re - newed, So may we be signs of
dien - te res - plan - dor, Va la_I - gle - sia mi - sio -
gri - nos al an - dar. Re - ci - bi - mos mien - tras
nue - va cre - a - ción. Un cris - tia - no que_u - ni -

mis - sion, Giv - ing glo - ry to God's name. As we
giv - ers; We are ves - sels made of clay. By our
one - ness 'Mid earth's peo - ples, man - y hued. As a
ne - ra Dan - do glo - ria a su Se - ñor. Con fer -
da - mos, So - mos ba - rro por que - brar. Al vi -
fi - ca Vi - ve la re - su - rrec - ción. Co - mo
wit - ness to the Gos - pel, We would
gen - tle, lov - ing ac - tions, We would
rain - bow lights the heav - ens When a
vor del e - van - ge - lio, Lis - tos
vir con gen - ti - le - za Re - fle -
bri - lla el ar - co i - ris Si la
build a bridge of care, Join - ing hands a - cross the
show that Christ is light. In a hum - ble, lis - t'ning
storm is past and gone, May our lives re - flect the
pa - ra cons - tru - ir Puen - tes de her - man - dad y
ja - mos luz y a - mor. Un es - pí - ri - tu hu -
tem - pes - tad se fue, Que tu vi - da sea ra -
na - tions, Find - ing neigh - bors ev - 'ry - where.
Spir - it, We would live to God's de - light.
ra - diance Of God's new and glor - ious dawn.
cui - do, Nues - tras ma - nos hay que u - nir.
mil - de Es la di - cha del Se - ñor.
dian - te Y que glo - ria a Dios le dé.

219 Sing a New World

Verses
1. Sum-moned by the God who made us Rich in
2. Trust the good - ness of cre - a - tion; Trust the
3. Bring the hopes of ev - 'ry na - tion; Bring the
4. Draw to - geth - er at one ta - ble All the
our di - ver - si - ty, Gath - ered now in cel - e -
wis - dom deep with - in. Dare to dream the vi - sion
art of ev - 'ry race. Weave a song of peace and
hu - man fam - i - ly; Shape a cir - cle ev - er
bra - tion, Rich - er still in u - ni - ty:
prom - ised Sprung from seed of what has been.
jus - tice: Let it sound through time and space.
wid - er And a peo - ple ev - er free.
Refrain
Let us bring the gifts that dif - fer And, in
splen - did, var - ied ways, Sing a new world in - to
be - ing, One in love and one in praise.

God Is Here / Está Aquí 220

Verse 1

1. Why do you stare at the skies up above
while your hearts are broken and looking for love?
Don't get lost in the things of the past,
but believe in the promise of a truth that will last.

Refrain

God is here, God is here. One thing I know:
Es-tá a-quí, es-tá a-quí. ¡Yo sé que Dios
God is here! God is here, God is here.
es-tá a-quí! Es-tá a-quí, es-tá a-quí.
One thing I know: God is here!
¡Yo sé que Dios es-tá a-quí!

Verses 2–6

2. Why do you dwell on what's happened before?
Release all that burdens you; open the door.
The future we reach toward is not found in the sky,
for the reign of God's glory will never die!

3. Here in this place, with the gifts that we bring,
the Body of Christ is found— our reason to sing!
In our coming and going, in ev'ry day,
God's presence is stirring here proclaiming the way!

4. With our strengths and our talents, in our weakness and fear;
in joy and in sorrow, God's healing is near.
In growth and in faith, in the darkness of sin,
a new hope is present here where love can begin!

5. The church that we ache for can be found in this place,
in our working for justice; in the presence of grace.
For we are God's people, all holy and strong;
to serve is our mission, with Christ as our song!

6. Why do you seek the living among the dead?
Jesus is risen, friends, just as he said.
All things are made new, true to God's Word;
it's beginning right here, right now, haven't you heard?

Text: David Haas, b.1957
Tune: David Haas, b.1957

221 How Can We Be Silent

Verses

1. How can we be si - lent when we know our God is near, bring - ing
2. How can we be si - lent when our God has con - quered death, stretch - ing
3. How can we be si - lent as we turn our eyes a - way and ig -
4. How can we be si - lent, not give praise with all our hearts, for Christ
5. How can we be si - lent when our souls are filled with awe at the

light to those in dark - ness, to the worth - less, end - less worth?
out his arms to suf - fer so that we might have new life?
nore the poor and bro - ken who lie bleed - ing in the street?
Je - sus is our Sav - ior and com - pas - sion is our king?
beau - ty of cre - a - tion and the mer - cy of our Lord?

How can we be si - lent when we are the voice of Christ, speak-ing
How can we be si - lent when we know that Je - sus rose, and will
How can we be si - lent when we're called to heal and serve in the
How can we be si - lent when God gave us life to be vi - brant
How can we be si - lent when we yearn to sing new songs? In our

jus - tice to the na - tions, breath-ing love to all the earth?
come a - gain in glo - ry, end - ing suf - fer - ing and strife?
im - age of Lord Je - sus, who has stooped to wash our feet?
in - stru - ments of wor - ship, made to laugh and dance and sing?
hearts a fire is burn - ing and it will not be ig - nored!

Refrain *May be sung as a canon.*

1.
None can stop the Spir - it
2.
burn - ing now in - side us.
3.
We will shape the fu - ture.
4.
We will not be si - lent!
D.C.

Coda
Cantor:
We will not be si - lent.
All:
We will not be si - lent.

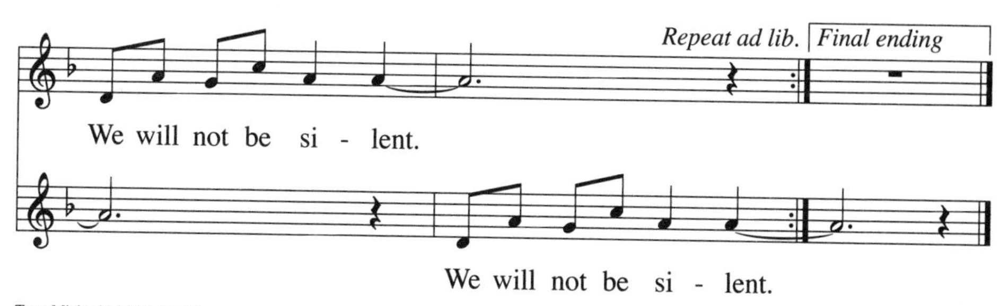
Repeat ad lib.
Final ending
We will not be si - lent.
We will not be si - lent.

Text: Michael Mahler, b.1981
Tune: Michael Mahler, b.1981

We Will Go, Lord 222

Ostinato Refrains*
We will go, Lord, where you would have us go, and we will do what you would have us do. We will
Last time
Lord Je - sus, we will fol - low you.
Last time
We will be strong. We will be strong.
Last time

*Refrains may be sung consecutively or simultaneously.

Text: Shannon Cerneka, b.1975 and Orin Johnson, b.1973
Tune: Shannon Cerneka, b.1975 and Orin Johnson, b.1973

223 Journeying Prayer

freely
God a - head and God be - hind, God be on the
path I wind. God a - bove and God be - low,
God be ev - 'ry - where I go.
♩ = 82
God a - head and God be-hind, God be on the path I wind.
God a - bove and God be-low, God be ev - 'ry - where I go.
God in the steep, God in the shade, God me safe keep, come
to my aid. This day, O Lord, with me go,
if life ebb or if it flow. This day, O Lord,
be with me, on firm ground or while at sea.

On o - cean deep keep me, Sav - ior, keep. As
I go o - ver land give me your hand.
When trou - bles come near, pro - tect with your eye. From
all that I dread may I be led.
D.S.

Text: *Prayer of the Breton Fisherman*, David Adam, © 1985, alt. Published by Morehouse Publishing.
Tune: Paul Melley, b.1973, © 2008, GIA Publications, Inc.

Christ be with me, Christ within me,
Christ behind me, Christ before me,
Christ beside me, Christ to win me,
Christ to comfort me and restore me,
Christ beneath me, Christ above me,
Christ in quiet, Christ in danger,
Christ in hearts of all that love me,
Christ in mouth of friend and stranger.

The Breastplate of St. Patrick

224 You Will Know

Verse 1

1. Take off your shoes; this is ho - ly ground you walk on.
O - pen your eyes; this is ho - ly fire you see.
Show me your face, a re - flec - tion of my glo - ry,
and you will know who I am.

Verses 2–4

2. Take off in flight; this is ho - ly ground that lifts you.
3. Take in the sight; you're on my ho - ly moun - tain.
4. Take up his cross; this is ho - ly wood you car - ry.

O - pen your arms; this is ho - ly wind you feel.
O - pen your ears; these are ho - ly words you hear.
O - pen your hands; this is ho - ly work you do.

Show me your tears, flow-ing down your face in riv - ers, and you will
Be - hold Christ's face, a re - flec - tion of my glo - ry, and you will
Share in his love, poured out for you for-ev - er, and you will

know who I am. You will know that I have healed you. You will
know who I am. You will know that I have loved him. You will
know who I am. You will know that he has loved you. You will

Last time to Coda *Repeat first time only*

know who I am: I am your God.
know who I am: I am your God.
know who I am: I am your

MISSION
5
D.S.
Coda
God. You will know who I am, I am your God.
4
Text: Robert VerEecke, S.J.
Tune: Paul Melley, b.1973
© 2008, GIA Publications, Inc.
BUILD US A TABLE 225
Verses
Solo:
1. Walls mark our bound-'ries and keep us a - part;
2. Walls make us sure who is in and who's out;
3. Once we were stran - gers, di - vid - ed, a - lone.
walls keep the world from our eyes and our heart.
walls keep us safe from all ques - tion and doubt,
Hate and dis - trust built a wall stone by stone.
Ta - bles are round, mak - ing room for one more,
but at a ta - ble in o - pen ex - change
Now at a ta - ble the bread that we share
wel - com - ing friends we had not known be - fore.
new ties are formed as our lives re - ar - range.
joins us to Christ in a cir - cle of care.
All:
So
So
So
Refrain
build us a ta-ble and tear down the wall! Christ is our host. There is
room for us all! Build us a ta-ble and tear down the wall!
Christ is our host. There is room for us all!
Last time
3
Text: Ruth Duck, b.1947, © 1994, The Pilgrim Press, alt.
Tune: Lori True, b.1961; acc. by Paul Tate, © 2007, GIA Publications, Inc.

226 Look to Christ

Refrain
Look to Christ to be your light; fol - low,
Leave be - hind your for - mer self and live.
Don't look back, don't be a - fraid; fol - low,
1.–4.
To verses
5.
Come to Christ, walk with Christ, and live.
live.
Verses
1. Who is the one who calls us to live our life to the full?
2. Who is the one who sees ev - 'ry - thing we say and do?
3. Who is the one who gives new sight to those who are blind?
4. Who is the one who weeps for us? Who can this be?
Who is the one who calls us to bear the
Who is the one who knows us and still for -
Who is the one who wash - es and makes us
Who is the one who rolls the stone a -
cross?
gives?
new?
way?
Who is the one who calls us all to
Who is the source and foun - tain of grace that
Who is the one who o - pens our eyes that
Who is the one who cries to us all to

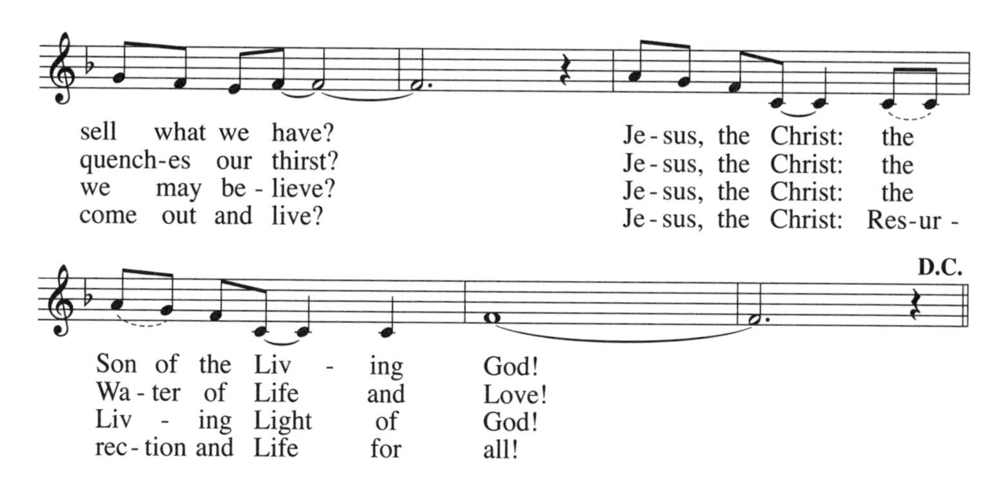
sell what we have?
quench-es our thirst?
we may be - lieve?
come out and live?
Je - sus, the Christ: the
Je - sus, the Christ: the
Je - sus, the Christ: the
Je - sus, the Christ: Res-ur -
D.C.
Son of the Liv - ing God!
Wa - ter of Life and Love!
Liv - ing Light of God!
rec - tion and Life for all!

Text: David Haas, b.1957
Tune: David Haas, b.1957

our sacraments and rites 227

HOLY ORDERS

All who are baptized make up "a chosen race, a royal priesthood, a holy nation" (1 Peter 2:9), a people set apart to offer the eternal sacrifice of Jesus Christ. Still, since the time of the apostles, God has called some members of the Church to minister to the others through the deaconate and the priesthood. In the sacrament of holy orders a man accepts this call from God, which is expressed through the Church's representative, the bishop.

Ordained deacons, priests, and bishops have a unique role within the Catholic community and exercise this service by teaching, leading worship, and offering pastoral guidance.

The sacrament of holy orders has distinct rites for the ordination of bishops, priests, and deacons. A bishop is always the minister of the sacrament. Each rite includes an imposition of hands by the bishop on the head of the one being ordained, signifying the outpouring of the gifts of the Holy Spirit for ministry. *RK*

228 To Follow You

Verse 1
1. Who are you, God? And who am I?
What are you call - ing me to be?
When I lis - ten to my heart, I can hear you whis-per,
ask - ing me, lov - ing - ly, to come and fol - low you.
Refrain
Here I am, did I hear you call my name?
Here I am, as you will. Speak, my God, I am
read - y to be - gin. Here I am, I come to fol - low
To verses and bridge
you.
Last time
you. Here I am, I come to fol - low
you, to fol - low you.

MISSION
Verse 2
2. I've trav - eled long and far to fol-low you. A
stran - ger and a pil - grim in this world.
Some - times I won-der what this jour-ney will bring. And you
guide me, faith - ful - ly to find a home in you.
D.S.
Verse 3
3. My heart sings of the love that I've found in you, a
love that dwells in all of your cre - a - tion.
Some-times I won - der what to-mor-row brings. Give me the
grace to love and to be faith-ful, to be more like you.
D.S.
Bridge
This is what I want, this is what I seek, this is
what I de-sire with all my heart.
D.S.

Text: Chris de Silva, b.1967, and Lovina Francis Pammit, OSF
Tune: Chris de Silva, b.1967

229 My Savior, Your Son

Verses

Solo:

1. I was born and bap-tized to live as yours and yours a-lone, but that was so long a-go. I've changed as I have grown. And now, when world-ly pres-sures, grief and an-ger, guilt and shame keep push-ing me fur-ther from your flame, you call me by name.

2. The path you've pre-pared for me will not be free from strife, but if I can see it through, I know I'll see new life. So here I stand, pre-pared to bear the cross of faith I claim, and know-ing I'll nev-er be the same. You called me by name.

Refrain

All:

I fol-lowed your voice. You set me a-part. You saved me a place in the space of your heart. You gave me a choice. My choos-ing is done. I've cho-sen to fol-low my Sav-ior, your Son. My Sav-ior, your Son.

1. | 2. And

Bridge
I will be your hands, giv-ing help where I'm a - ble. And
I will be your voice, call-ing all to the ta - ble. If
I see with your eyes, turn-ing foe in-to friend, then you will
be my peace at jour-ney's end. You called me by name.
Refrain
I fol - lowed your voice. You set me a - part. You
saved me a place in the space of your heart. You gave me a choice.
My choos-ing is done. I've cho-sen to fol - low you.
I fol-lowed your voice. You set me a - part. You saved me a place
in the space of your heart. You gave me a choice. My choos-ing is done.
I've cho-sen to fol - low my Sav - ior, your Son.
My Sav - ior, your Son.
4
My Sav - ior, your Son.
Text: Michael Mahler, b.1981
Tune: Michael Mahler, b.1981
© 2008, GIA Publications, Inc.

230 Go Out to the World

Verses
1. With hands of justice and faith, we go to serve the world, to bring good news to the poor and oppressed.
(2. With lives of) courage and strength, we spread the message of love to all the weak, the lonely, the hurt.
(3. With gentle) spirits, we go to share the message of peace with all the troubled, lost, and distressed.
With hearts of love and of hope, we go to live the word that empowers us to new life.
With lives that answer the call, we spread the word of God that empowers us to new life.
With humble spirits, we go to share the love of God that empowers us to new life.
Refrain
Go out to the world and tell all the good news,
tell all the good news of God's endless love.
Go out to the world and tell all the good news,

To verses
tell all the good news of God's end-less love.
To bridge and Last time
Last time Solo:
2. With lives of God's end-less love. With
3. With gen-tle
Bridge
warmth in our hearts, we of-fer peace and con-so-la-tion. We reach
out to the world, reach out to the world!
D.S.

Text: Chris de Silva, b.1967
Tune: Chris de Silva, b.1967

our greatest gift, the Eucharist 231

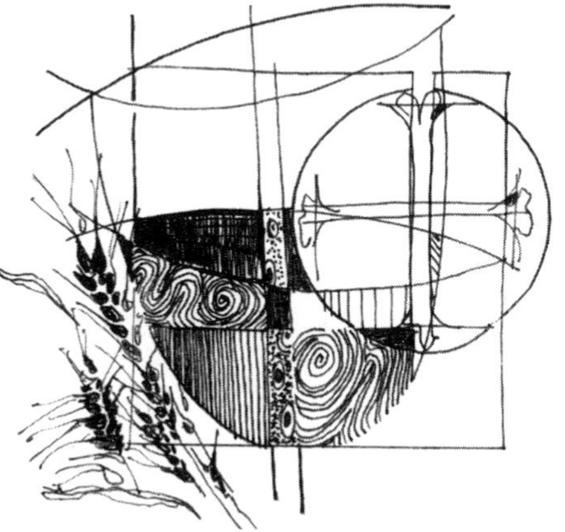

SENDING

After we have gathered, heard the word of God, given thanks, and been nourished at the table of the Lord, we are strengthened to return to our daily lives. In the concluding rite, we receive a blessing and then are sent out "to love and serve the Lord." This dismissal reminds us that all we have done in our celebration leads us out into the world to (in the words of St. Augustine) become what we have received: the body and blood of Christ. We are sent out to the world to live the word we have heard proclaimed in our midst, to nourish others as we have been nourished until it is time to regather and once again share in the greatest gift of the Church, the Eucharist. *TA*

232 Faith, Hope, and Love

Verses
1. Faith will o - pen the eyes of the blind,
2. The burn - ing sand, hope will make like a pool,
and the ears of the deaf be clear.
and the thirst - y ground, bub - bling springs.
Then the lame will leap like a deer
Then the des - ert will bloom like a flow'r,
and the voice-less will sing for joy,
and all sigh - ing will flee a - way,
and the voice-less shall sing for joy.
and all sigh - ing will flee a - way.
We got-ta have
Refrain
faith. We got-ta have hope. We got-ta have love. We got-ta have love! And the great-est of these gifts from a - bove, the great - est of these is love!
1., 3.
Last time to Coda
To verse 2
3

2.
Bridge
great-est of these is love.
Love will o-pen our eyes
to the poor in spir - it.
Love will o - pen our arms
to those who mourn.
Love will o - pen our hearts
to the ones who hun - ger and thirst, for they shall
have their fill!
D.S.
We got - ta have
Coda
Faith, hope, and love now.
Faith, hope, and love now.
Faith, hope, got - ta have love!
Repeat as desired

Text: Paul Melley, b.1973
Tune: Paul Melley, b.1973

233 God Is Love

Verse 1
1. Let us love one an-oth - er for love is God's way.
In each deed that we do, with each word that we say.
If we treat ev - 'ry per - son
with com-pas-sion and care,
we come clos - er to God,
for it's some - thing we share.
Refrain
God is love. God is love, and all who live in
love live in God, and God lives in them.
God is love. God is love, and all who live in
love live in God, and God lives in them.

LOVE
Third time to bridge
To verse 2
Last time
Verse 2
2. Love means more than af-fec - tion or the ab-sence of strife.
Love is watch-ing your on - ly son lay down his life.
When we love with-out rea - son,
and be-yond all con-trol,
then the love of our Lord
is made per - fect - ly whole.
D.S.
Bridge
Don't be a-fraid, and nev-er dis-may. God's love has the pow-
er to take fear a - way. But lov - ing the Lord
is not where it ends. You must love your neigh -
bors as your friends.
D.S.

Text: 1 John 4:7–21: adapt. by Michael Mahler, b.1981
Tune: Michael Mahler, b.1981

234 Love beyond All Telling

Verses
1. God's cho - sen ones, we are ho - ly and be-lov- ed, made as light, the light we long to see.
2. Peace of Christ tak-ing hold with-in our be - ing brings us love, the love to live as one.
3. God's fam - i - ly, we are learn-ing to be ho- ly, blessed with peace, the peace we learn to live.
God's gen - tle ones, we are pa - tient and for - giv - ing, shared as hope, the hope we yearn to be.
Word of Christ is a - live with each heart beat - ing, gives us joy, the joy to sing as one. Your
This fam - i - ly, we are try - ing to live whol- ly, blessed with grace, the grace when we for-give.
Refrain
love be-yond all tell - ing finds a ho - ly dwell-ing in our hearts.
Love be-yond all tell - ing makes a ho - ly dwell-ing here with us.
To verses
Love be-yond all tell-ing, God with us. God with us.
Love be-yond all tell - ing, here with us.
Love be-yond all tell - ing, here with us.

Text: Chris de Silva, b.1967
Tune: Chris de Silva, b.1967

The Lord Is My Light 235

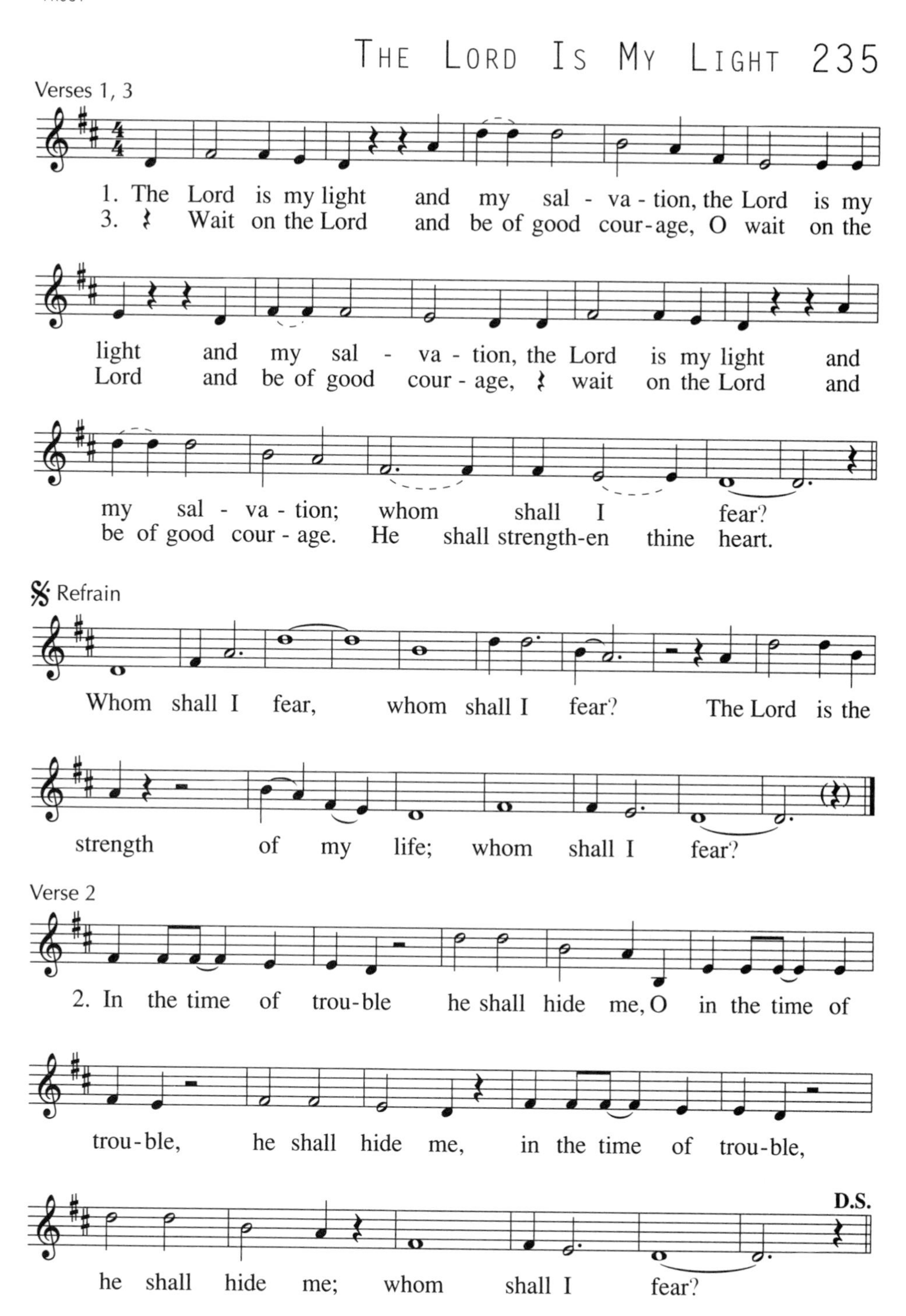
Verses 1, 3
1. The Lord is my light and my sal - va - tion, the Lord is my
3. Wait on the Lord and be of good cour - age, O wait on the
light and my sal - va - tion, the Lord is my light and
Lord and be of good cour - age, wait on the Lord and
my sal - va - tion; whom shall I fear?
be of good cour - age. He shall strength-en thine heart.
Refrain
Whom shall I fear, whom shall I fear? The Lord is the
strength of my life; whom shall I fear?
Verse 2
2. In the time of trou - ble he shall hide me, O in the time of
trou - ble, he shall hide me, in the time of trou - ble,
he shall hide me; whom shall I fear?
D.S.

Text: Lillian Bouknight
Tune: Lillian Bouknight; arr. by Paul Gainer

236 Be Still and Know

Verses

1. Be still and know that he is God.
2. Be still and know that he is God.
3. Be still and know that he is God.

Be still and know that he is ho - ly.
Be still and know that he is faith - ful.
Be still and know he is our Fa - ther.

Be still, oh, rest - less soul of mine.
Con - sid - er all that he has done:
Come rest your head up - on his breast;

Bow be - fore the Prince of Peace. let the
stand in awe and be a - mazed and know that
lis - ten to the rhy - thm of his un -

Last time to Coda 1.

noise and clam - or cease.
he will nev - er change.
fail - ing heart of love.

2.

Be still. Be

Refrain

still and know that he is God. Be

still and know that he is God.

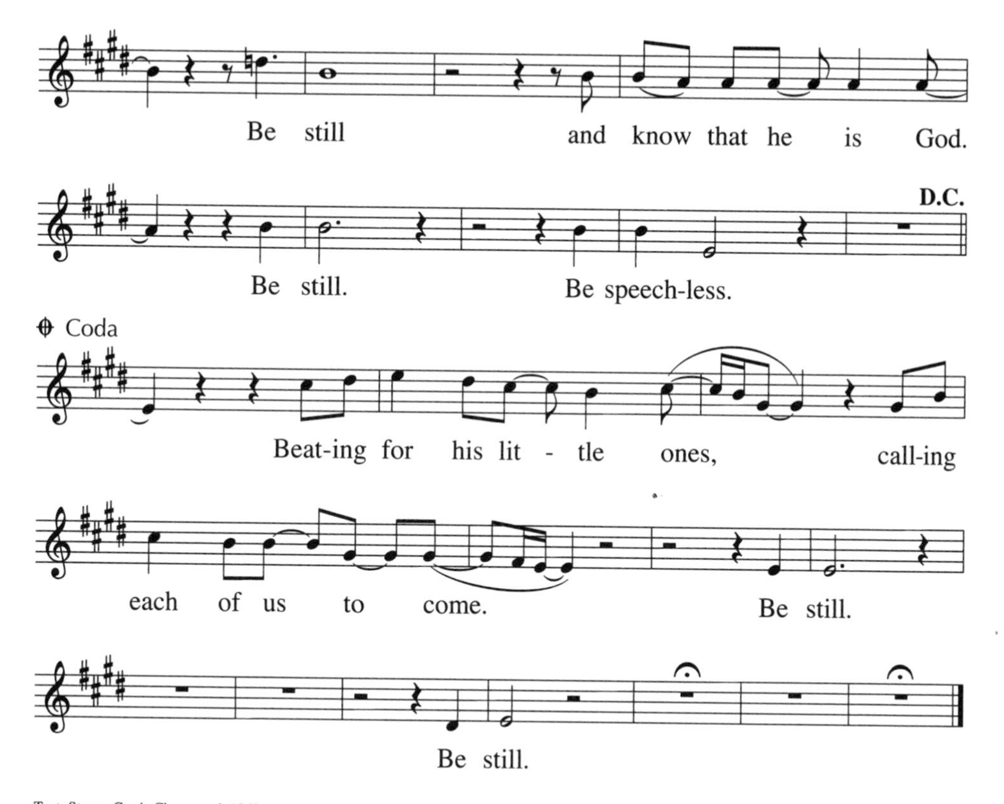

Be still and know that he is God.
D.C.
Be still. Be speech-less.
Coda
Beat-ing for his lit - tle ones, call-ing
each of us to come. Be still.
Be still.

Text: Steven Curtis Chapman, b.1962
Tune: Steven Curtis Chapman, b.1962

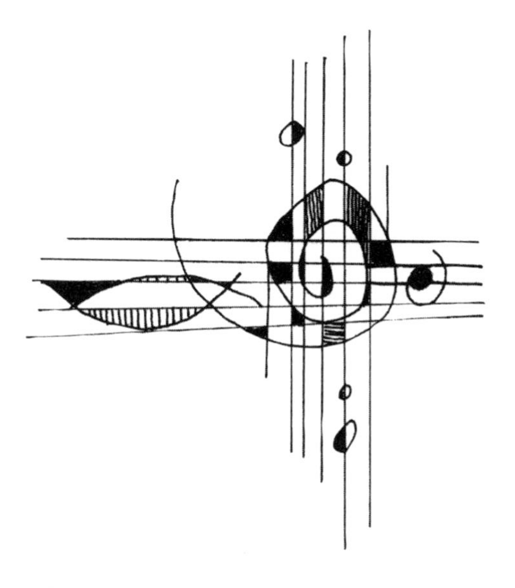

237 Take, Lord, Receive

Verse 1
1. Take, Lord, and re-ceive my lib - er-ty; take, Lord, and re - ceive my mem - o-ry; take, Lord, and re-ceive my un-der-stand - ing, my en - tire will, my en - tire will.
Refrain
Give me on-ly your love and your grace and I am rich; I need noth - ing else.
Give me on-ly your love and your grace and I am rich e-nough.
1., 3.
Take, Lord, re - ceive.
To verse 2
2.
Take, Lord, re - ceive.
To bridge

Verse 2
2. Take, Lord, and re - ceive all I have, re -
ceive all I have and call my own. Take, Lord, and re-ceive all I
have or hold, you have giv - en me, you have giv-en me.
D.S.
Bridge
Take and re - ceive now: I re - store it all to you and sur -
ren - der it whol - ly to be gov - erned by your will,
gov - erned by your will.
D.S.

Text: St. Ignatius of Loyola
Tune: Paul Melley, b.1973

We can do no great things;
only small things with great love.

Teresa of Calcutta

238 You Are Strong, You Are Holy

Verses
1. Lord, you lead through sea and des - ert, You lead to prom - ised lands. We are your own ho - ly peo - ple, In your cov - e - nant we stand!
2. Lord, you lead to cool - ing wa - ters, You lead to green - ing fields. Lord, you lead to deep - 'ning val - leys Where your com - fort is re - vealed!
3. So we fol - low where you lead us, Where you walk a - long the shore, Where you suf - fer in the gar - den, When you rise to die no more!
Refrain
You are strong, you are ho - ly, you are mer - cy and peace. You are love, you are jus - tice. Your grace and fa - vor nev - er cease!
3

GUIDE MY FEET 239

Verses
1. Guide my feet while I run this race. Guide my feet
2. Hold my hand while I run this race. Hold my hand
3. Be my friend while I run this race. Be my friend
4. Stand by me while I run this race. Stand by me
while I run this race. Guide my feet while I run this race, 'cause I
while I run this race. Hold my hand while I run this race, 'cause I
while I run this race. Be my friend while I run this race, 'cause I
while I run this race. Stand by me while I run this race, 'cause I
1.
2.–4.
don't want to run this race in vain.
don't want to run this race in vain. Lord, guide my
don't want to run this race in vain. Lord, guide my
don't want to run this race in vain. Lord, guide my
Refrain
feet and keep my way. Can't make a step with-out you, I
1.
2.
D.C.
don't want to run this race in vain, Lord, guide my vain.

240 River of Hope

Refrain
There's a riv - er of hope, there's a moun-tain of peace,
there's an o - cean of joy wait-ing some-where for me.
If I trust in my God, not what I see but what I know,
To verses
To bridge
I will al-ways find a riv-er of hope. hope.
Verses
1. I jour-ney to the heart of life, to the riv - er of hope, the face of Christ,
2. The voice with-in guides me home, as - sur-ing me I'm nev-er a -
lone.
where all of life bless-es me and all of love
Where I go I car - ry love. Where I am,
sets me free.
I'm in love.
Some-where deep in - side of me
D.S.
there's a place that gives me all I need.
Bridge
I know there's a riv - er, and I know there's a riv - er, and
D.S.
I know there's a riv - er of hope.

Text: Susan J. Paul, b.1962
Tune: Susan J. Paul, b.1962

IN YOUR PRESENCE 241

Refrain
In your pres-ence I will dwell all my days. Just like a
spar-row, I will find a home in you, and in your
pres-ence I will live for all e-ter-ni - ty. Now and al-
Last time to Coda
ways, I long to be with you.
Verses
1. O God, you are the God whom I seek; my soul
2. In your ho - ly place I see you in glo-ry; your lov-ing
3. I will bless you all my life; with lift-ed
4. O God, you are my strength and my help, and in the
thirsts for you like dry earth longs for wa-ter.
kind - ness is great - er than life.
hands, I will call up - on your name.
shad - ow of your wings I shout for joy.
D.C.
You are my God whom I seek.
You are the God whom I seek.
I will sing your praise.
My soul clings to you.
Coda
Last time
you. I long to be with you. I long to be with

Text: Based on Psalm 63 and 84; Chris de Silva, b.1967
Tune: Chris de Silva, b.1967

242 our liturgical books

LECTIONARY

From the earliest times, when the Church gathered for worship they read from the Old Testament, the various writings of the Apostles (as they became available in a particular community), recited the Psalms, and used portions of Scripture to praise and worship God. At Mass, we do the same! The Scripture readings we hear proclaimed at Mass during the Liturgy of the Word are taken from the Lectionary, a liturgical book that helps guide the Church through each of the seasons of the church year. The Lectionary is not the Bible but rather includes selections from it: Scripture from the Old Testament, the Psalms, the New Testament epistles, and the four gospels. During the major seasons of the year the weekly readings are chosen because of their relation to a particular mystery of our faith. During the Sundays in Ordinary Time various books of the New Testament are read in a semi-continuous fashion.

The Lectionary is organized into a three-year cycle of readings for Sundays. Year A focuses on the gospel of Matthew, Year B focuses on the gospel of Mark, and Year C on the gospel of Luke. John's gospel is used during Lenten Sundays for the scrutiny readings important to the Rite of Christian Initiation of Adults, at Easter time, and during some Sundays in Year B. The weekday readings are divided into a two-year cycle and generally only one reading is proclaimed before the gospel.

The Lectionary reminds us that the Scriptures are an essential part of all liturgical celebrations.

SACRAMENTARY

The Sacramentary is the book used for the celebration of Mass by the presiding priest. It contains all the necessary prayers for the various Masses the Church celebrates over the year as well as specific directions (known as rubrics) on how the Mass is to be celebrated. The book includes opening prayers, prayers over the gifts, prayers after Communion, and solemn blessings, as well as eucharistic prayers and prefaces for Sunday liturgies and other eucharistic celebrations. Entrance and Communion antiphons are also included. The Scripture readings are found in a separate book called the Lectionary.

BREVIARY

St. Paul tells us to "pray without ceasing" (1 Thessalonians 5:17), "singing psalms, hymns, and spiritual songs with gratitude in your hearts to God" (Colossians 3:16). From earliest times, the Church has done exactly that by praying the Liturgy of the Hours (also called the Divine Office), a liturgical form of prayer that is prayed at various hours of the day. The Liturgy of the Hours is one way we as Catholics can pray always.

The "hours" refer to the time of the day, rather than the amount of time it takes to pray. The prayer usually lasts between ten and twenty minutes, depending upon how it is prayed. Each hour includes a selection of psalms (or canticles), and one or two readings from Scripture, the writings of saints, or other documents.

The breviary is the book that contains the Liturgy of the Hours. Breviaries were originally created for clergy and religious who were not able to pray the Liturgy of the Hours in community. The compact book makes it possible for anyone to carry the prayers of the hours at any time.

PRINTED WORSHIP AIDS

To promote the full, conscious, and active participation of the assembly, most parishes provide printed worship aids for Sunday Masses and other special liturgical events. These aids often contain the complete outline of the liturgical celebration, including Scripture readings, responses and acclamations, and other music. Worship aids are often used during major feast days or celebrations such as funerals, where members of the assembly may not be familiar with the rites, or when multiple languages are spoken at the liturgies. Both permanent and disposable books as well as handouts intended for one-time use can be found in various churches. *LD*

243 I Cry before You

Refrain

I cry be-fore you, and plead with you!

If on - ly you would hear me.

If on - ly you would hear me.

Last time

Verse 1

Cantor:

1. Each day I reach for you in dis - tress,

each night I raise my hands in prayer, my

spir-it finds no com-fort. I groan when I think of

you; I re-mem-ber and I grow faint.

D.C.

Verse 2

Cantor:

2. You keep me from sleep. Trou-bled, my voice can-not

speak. I re-mem-ber days of old, and years gone by; each

night, mem-'ries fill my heart. I ache and ques-tion.

D.C.

Verse 3
Cantor:
3. Will you al - ways re - ject me? Nev-er a-gain be con-
tent? Have you stopped lov-ing me and cut me off for ev-er? Will
you for-get to pit-y? Will an-ger block your mer-cy?
D.C.
Text: Psalm 77; adapt. by Lori True, b.1961
Tune: Lori True, b.1961
© 2000, GIA Publications, Inc.
GOD REMEMBERS 244
1. God re-mem-bers pain: Nail by nail, thorn by thorn,
2. God re-mem-bers joy: Touch of love, taste of food,
3. God re-mem-bers us: All we were, all we are,
Hun - ger, thirst, and mus - cles torn. Time may dull our griefs And
All our sens - es know is good. Love and life flow by And
Lives with - in our Lov - er's care. Time may dull our minds And
heal our less - er wounds, But in e-ter-nal Love Yes-ter-day is
pre - cious days are gone, But in e-ter-nal Love Ev - 'ry day is
death will take us all, But in e-ter-nal Love Ev - 'ry life is
now, And pain is in the heart of God.
now, And joy is in the heart of God.
now: Our life is hid with Christ in God.

Text: Colossians 3:3–4; Brian Wren, b.1936, © 1993, Hope Publishing Company
Tune: GOD REMEMBERS, 5 6 7 5 6 6 5 8; Marty Haugen, b.1950, © 2003, GIA Publications, Inc.

245 O God, Why Are You Silent?

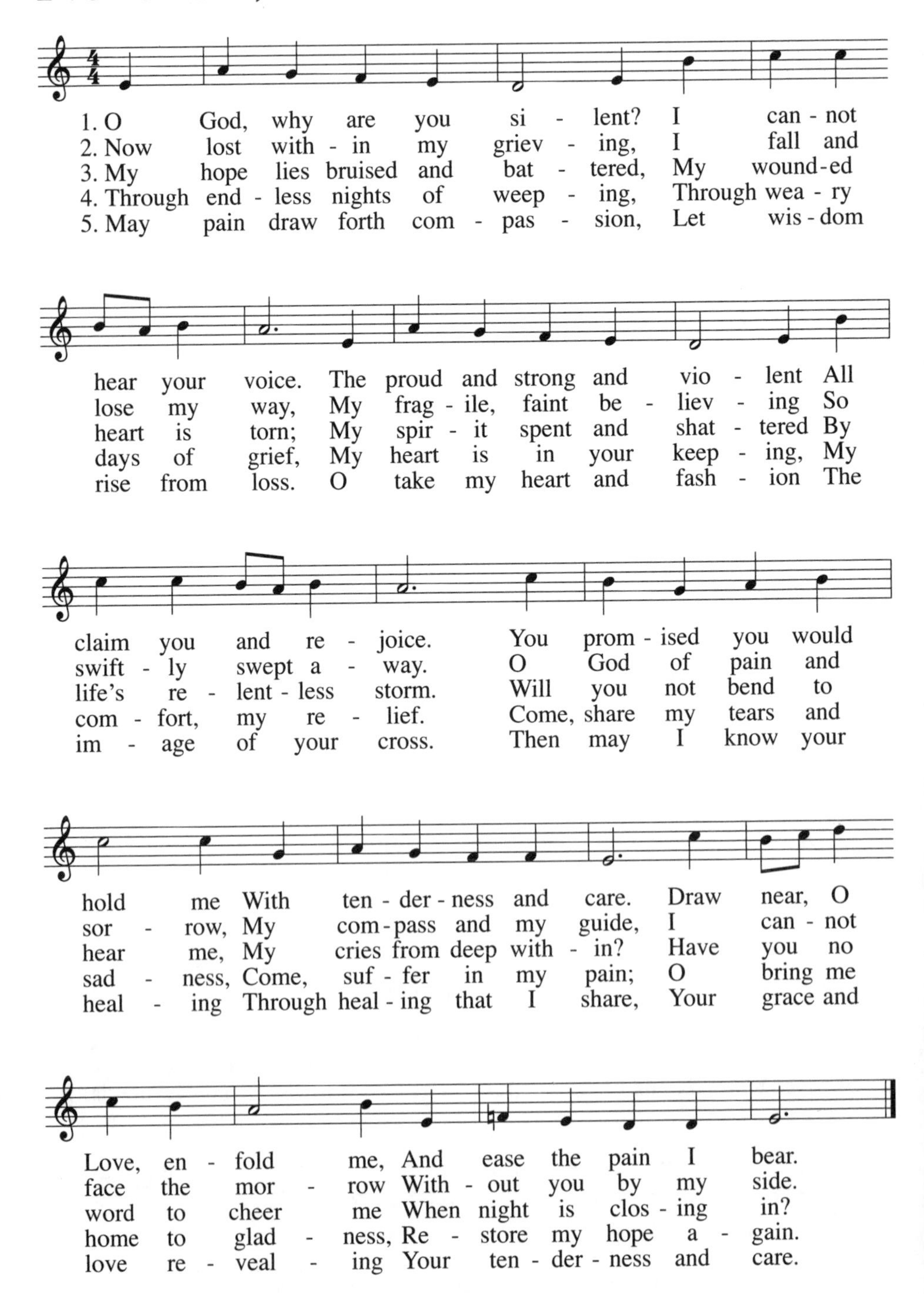
1. O God, why are you si - lent? I can - not
2. Now lost with - in my griev - ing, I fall and
3. My hope lies bruised and bat - tered, My wound-ed
4. Through end - less nights of weep - ing, Through wea - ry
5. May pain draw forth com - pas - sion, Let wis - dom
hear your voice. The proud and strong and vio - lent All
lose my way, My frag - ile, faint be - liev - ing So
heart is torn; My spir - it spent and shat - tered By
days of grief, My heart is in your keep - ing, My
rise from loss. O take my heart and fash - ion The
claim you and re - joice. You prom - ised you would
swift - ly swept a - way. O God of pain and
life's re - lent - less storm. Will you not bend to
com - fort, my re - lief. Come, share my tears and
im - age of your cross. Then may I know your
hold me With ten - der - ness and care. Draw near, O
sor - row, My com - pass and my guide, I can - not
hear me, My cries from deep with - in? Have you no
sad - ness, Come, suf - fer in my pain; O bring me
heal - ing Through heal - ing that I share, Your grace and
Love, en - fold me, And ease the pain I bear.
face the mor - row With - out you by my side.
word to cheer me When night is clos - ing in?
home to glad - ness, Re - store my hope a - gain.
love re - veal - ing Your ten - der - ness and care.

Text: Marty Haugen, b.1950, © 2003, GIA Publications, Inc.
Tune: PASSION CHORALE, 7 6 7 6 D; Hans Leo Hassler, 1564–1612; harm. by Marty Haugen, b.1950, © 2003, GIA Publications, Inc.

Our God Reigns 246

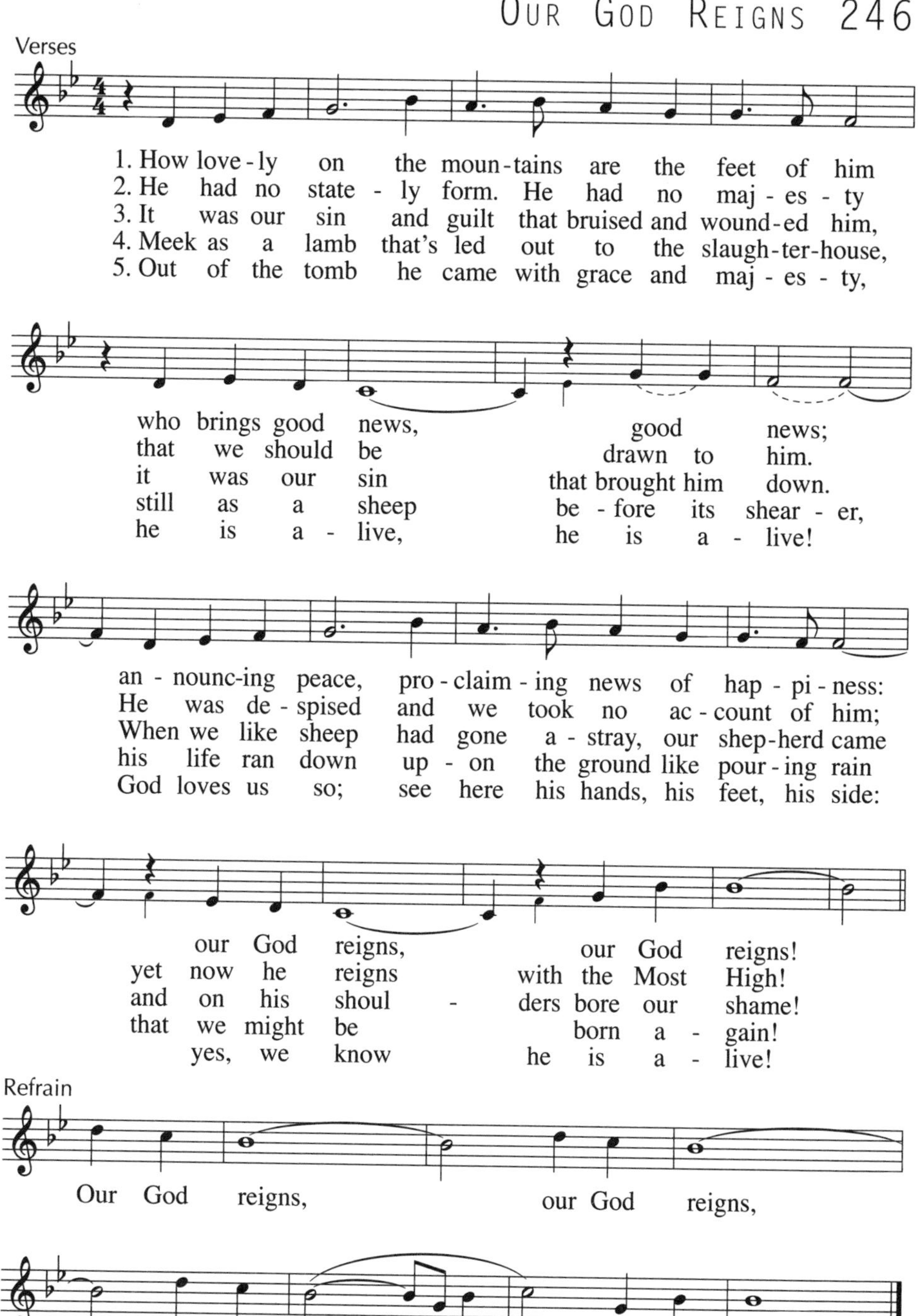
Verses
1. How love-ly on the moun-tains are the feet of him
2. He had no state - ly form. He had no maj - es - ty
3. It was our sin and guilt that bruised and wound-ed him,
4. Meek as a lamb that's led out to the slaugh-ter-house,
5. Out of the tomb he came with grace and maj - es - ty,
who brings good news, good news;
that we should be drawn to him.
it was our sin that brought him down.
still as a sheep be - fore its shear - er,
he is a - live, he is a - live!
an - nounc-ing peace, pro - claim - ing news of hap - pi - ness:
He was de - spised and we took no ac - count of him;
When we like sheep had gone a - stray, our shep-herd came
his life ran down up - on the ground like pour - ing rain
God loves us so; see here his hands, his feet, his side:
our God reigns, our God reigns!
yet now he reigns with the Most High!
and on his shoul - ders bore our shame!
that we might be born a - gain!
yes, we know he is a - live!
Refrain
Our God reigns, our God reigns,
our God reigns, our God reigns!

Text: Leonard E. Smith, Jr., b.1942
Tune: Leonard E. Smith, Jr., b.1942; arr. by Stephen A. Beddia

247 I Am

Refrain
I am the Gate: who-ev-er en-ters by me will be saved. I am the Vine: those who a-bide in me bear much fruit.
I am the Light of the world. I am the Good Shep-herd. I am the Way, the Truth, and the Life.
Verses 1, 4
Cantor:
1. A-bide in me as I in you, you that I call my friends.
4. I go be-fore you now; lift up your hearts with joy.

What - ev - er you ask in my name,
I am with you al - ways,
it will be done for you.
till the end of time.
D.C.
Verses 2, 3
Cantor(s):
2. I came that you might have life
3. Walk no more in dark - ness;
and have it a - bun - dant - ly.
I give you the light of life.
I know my own, and they know me.
The One who sent me lives in me.
Fol - low me, and know my voice.
Hear the truth and be set free.
D.C.

Text: John 10:9–11, 14:6, 14, 15:4, 5; Paul Melley, b.1973
Tune: Paul Melley, b.1973

248 HUMBLED

Verses
1. Let us be poured out, gift for oth - ers, emp - tied till all that's left is you.
2. Let us give all our priv - 'lege o - ver, spill - ing it out for those in need.
And live the song of serv - ice out loud, so that all things will be made new.
Give us the man - ner of Christ Je - sus, and we will fol - low where you lead.
Be - cause the Word be - came flesh, there is a love for the love - less.
Though in the form of God, he nev - er clutched for great - ness.
So ev - 'ry tongue should con - fess the name of Je - sus.
So ev - 'ry tongue should con - fess the name of Je - sus.

Refrain
He emp-tied him-self, took the form of a slave,
com-ing in hu-man like-ness to show
the way. He hum-bled him-self to death on a cross,
re-ceiv-ing a name a-bove ev-'ry oth-er name.
4
To verse 2
Coda
Ev-'ry tongue con-fess-ing, all in heav-en and on earth.
Ev-'ry tongue con-fess-ing, all in heav-en and on earth.
D.S.

Text: Based on Philippians 2:5–11; Paul Melley
Tune: Paul Melley

249 For God So Loved the World

Refrain
For God so loved the world, God gave the on - ly Son,
so that ev-'ry-one who be-lieves in him may not die, but have life.
Last time to Coda
So much God loved, the world, so much God loves the world.
Verses 1, 2
1. The Word be-came flesh and dwelt a - mong us; full of
2. As Mo - ses lift - ed up the ser - pent so that
grace, full of truth he made his home. He came to his own who would
all who looked to it might live, the Son of Man must be
know him not, though all who be - hold him,
lift - ed up so that all who be - lieve,
D.C.
all who re-ceive him are called the chil - dren of God.
all who look to him may have e - ter - nal life.
Verse 3
3. God's Son came not to con - demn the world, but that the
world may be saved through him, and all who be-lieve in the

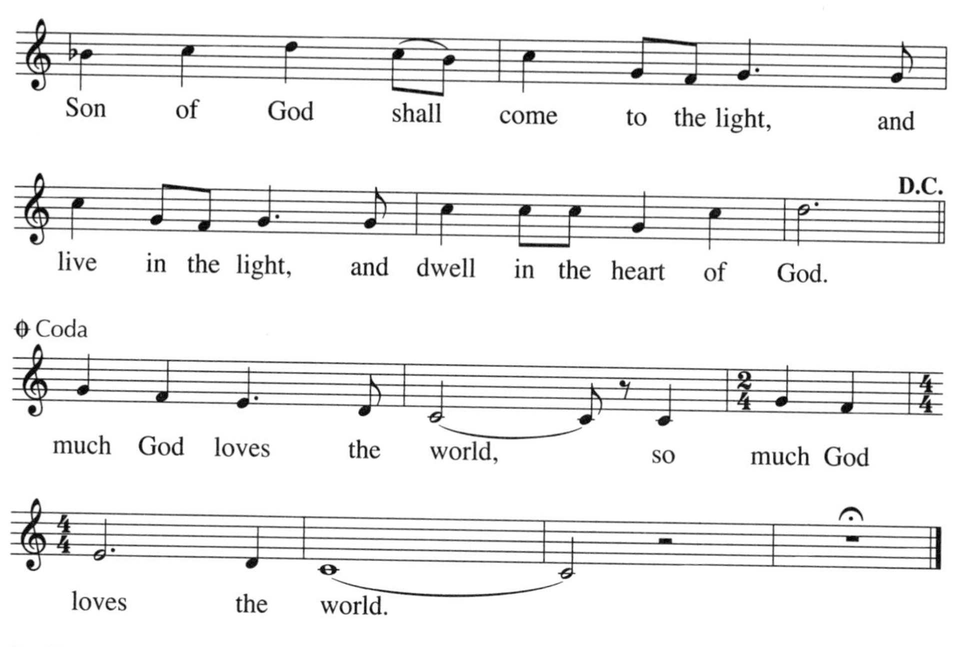
Son of God shall come to the light, and
live in the light, and dwell in the heart of God.
D.C.
Coda
much God loves the world, so much God
loves the world.

Text: John 1:11–12, 14, 3:14–17, 21; Marty Haugen, b.1950, and Susan Briehl, b.1952
Tune: Marty Haugen, b.1950

Jesus, Your Spirit / Kristus, Din Ande 250

Ostinato Refrain

Je - sus, your Spir - it in us is a well-spring of life ev - er - last - ing.
Kris - tus, din An - de i oss är en käl - la med por - lan - de va - ten.

Text: Psalm 63:2–5, 8–9; Taizé Community
Tune: Taizé Community

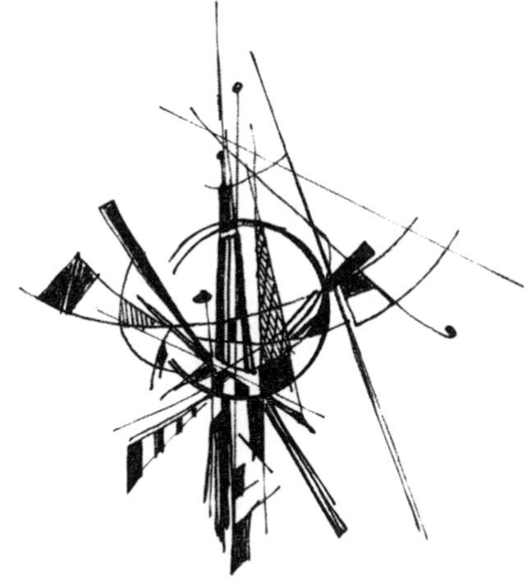

251 Jesus, You Brought Me All the Way

Refrain
Je - sus, you brought me all the way. You
car - ry my bur - dens ev - er - y day. You are
such a won - der - ful Sav - ior, I've nev - er known you to
fail me yet, 'cause you brought me, 'cause you brought
me, 'cause you brought me, 'cause you brought
me. Je - sus, you brought me all of the way.
Last time
Verses
Solo (very freely):
3
1. Trou - bles and tri - als, they seem to block my way.
2. Went to the val - ley one day to pray.
Some - times I find it so dif - fi - cult to pray.
My soul got hap - py and I stayed there all day.

Oh, but there's one thing I can tru-ly say: that you've brought me, thank God, all the way.
D.C.
Text: Kenneth W. Louis, b.1956
Tune: Kenneth W. Louis, b.1956
© 2001, GIA Publications, Inc.
NOTHING CAN EVER 252
Refrain A
Noth-ing can ev-er come be-tween us and the love of God, the love of God re-vealed to us in Christ Je - sus.
Last time
Verses B
O
O

Text: The Taizé Community
Tune: The Taizé Community

253 Were I the Perfect Child of God

1. Were I the per - fect child of God whose
2. Yet God, who knows me first and last, who's
3. Then sprin - kle wa - ter on my brow as,
faith was deep and love was broad,
seen my best, my worst, my past,
in this place, I make my vow
not doubt - ful, guilt - y, worn or flawed, I'd
has shown his love in - tense and vast by
to own and love my Sav - ior now and
glad - ly fol-low Je - sus. But I'm the child of
meet - ing me in Je - sus. For Christ, though killed at
give my-self to Je - sus. God grant me what I
what I've been, es-tranged by much I've done and seen,
Cal - va - ry by sins like mine and folk like me,
still re - quire that I, in oth - ers, might in - spire
a - fraid to show the love I mean, un -
has ris'n, for - giv'n and set me free, made
the hid - den hope, the deep de - sire to
fit to fol-low Je - sus.
fit to fol-low Je - sus.
love and fol-low Je - sus.
3
D.C.
Final ending

So Longs My Soul 254

Verses
1. As pants the hart for run - ning streams when heat - ed in the chase, so longs my soul, for you, my God and your re - fresh - ing grace.
2. God of my strength, how long should I, like one for - got - ten, mourn? With bro - ken heart I lie ex - posed to my op - press - ors' scorn.
3. So why cast down, my rest - less soul? hope still and you shall sing the praise of One who is my God, and love's e - ter - nal spring.
Refrain
So longs my soul, O God, it longs for you, so longs my soul. So longs my soul, O God, it longs for you and your re - fresh - ing grace.
D.C.
Final ending

Text: Based on Psalm 42; Liam Lawton, b.1959
Tune: Liam Lawton, b.1959; arr. by John Drummond

255 BELONG

Verses
1. You are my light and my sal - va - tion;
2. I gaze on the beau - ty of my Sav - ior.
3. The good-ness, the glo - ry of God's king - dom:
whom should I fear? And why should I be
One thing I ask, one thing of my Lord
this I will see, this place of e - ter -
a - fraid? My shel - ter, my ref -
I seek: to live in the house
nal peace. I wait for my God,
uge, my pro - tec - tion,
of my Re - deem - er,
my hope, my free - dom,
1., 2.
God's ho - ly light.
God's safe em - brace.
To refrain
3.
God's sav - ing grace.
Interlude
6
Refrain
I be-long to you, I be - long to you, my God.
I be-long to you, I be - long
to you, my God.
3

Text: Based on Psalm 27 and 1 Corinthians 1:10; Chris de Silva, b.1967
Tune: Chris de Silva, b.1967

OVER MY HEAD 256
Refrain
O-ver my head, I hear mu-sic in the air; o-ver my head,
I hear mu-sic in the air; o-ver my head, I hear
Last time to Coda
mu-sic in the air; there must be a God some-where.
Solo:
1. Oh,
2. And
3. Now
Verses
when the world is si-lent,
when I'm feel-ing lone-ly, I hear mu-sic in the air;
when I think on Je-sus,
All:
Solo:
oh,
and
now
when the world is si-lent,
when I'm feel-ing lone-ly, I hear mu-sic in the air;
when I think on Je-sus,
oh,
and
now
when the world is si-lent,
when I'm feel-ing lone-ly, I hear mu-sic in the air;
when I think on Je-sus,
there must be a God some-where. O-ver my head,
Coda
mu-sic in the air; there must be a God some-where.

Text: African American Spiritual
Tune: African American Spiritual; adapt. by John L. Bell, b.1979, arr. by Gary Daigle, b.1957,

257 O God, You Search Me

1. O God, you search me and you know me. All my
2. You know my rest - ing and my ris - ing. You dis -
3. Be - fore a word is on my tongue, Lord, You have
4. Al - though your Spir - it is up - on me, Still I
5. For you cre - at - ed me and shaped me, Gave me

thoughts lie o - pen to your gaze. When I
cern my pur - pose from a - far, And with
known its mean - ing through and through. You are
search for shel - ter from your light. There is
life with - in my moth - er's womb. For the

walk or lie down you are be - fore me: Ev - er the
love ev - er - last - ing you be - siege me: In ev - 'ry
with me be - yond my un - der - stand - ing: God of my
no - where on earth I can es - cape you: E - ven the
won - der of who I am I praise you: Safe in your

mak - er and keep - er of my days.
mo - ment of life or death, you are.
pres - ent, my past and fu - ture, too.
dark - ness is ra - diant in your sight.
hands, all cre - a - tion is made new.

Text: Based on Psalm 139; Bernadette Farrell, b.1957
Tune: Bernadette Farrell, b.1957; arr. by Gary Daigle, b.1957

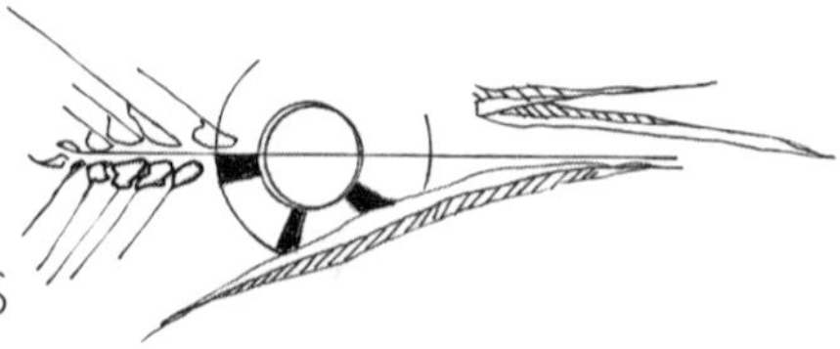

258 I Will Give Thanks

Verse 1

Solo:

1. Great are your works, O Lord, to be treas-ured for  all time. Good are your works, O Lord; your

+ Assembly:
wis-dom lives for - ev - er. And with all
Refrain
my heart, I will give thanks to you,
To bridge after Vs. 3
and with all my heart, I will give thanks to you.
Verses 2, 3
2. Gra - cious are you, O Lord; you have shown
3. Great are your works, O God; you re - deemed
your love to us. Glo - ri-ous are
us as you said. Ho - ly and
+ Assembly:
you, O Lord; you feed us as you prom-ised. And with all
awe-some God, your wis-dom lives for - ev - er.
Bridge
You show your pow - er to your peo - ple, giv-ing us lands
of all the na - tions. You show your gen - tle - ness and mercy; the works of your hands are right and true, and
+ Assembly:
D.S.
I will praise you for-ev-er and ev - er. And with all

Text: Based on Psalm 111; Chris de Silva, b.1967
Tune: Chris de Silva, b.1967

259 Malo! Malo! Thanks Be to God

Refrain
Cantor:
Ma - lo! Ma - lo! Thanks be to God!
All:
Ma - lo! Ma - lo! Thanks be to God!
Cantor:
O - bri - ga - do! Al - le - lu - ia!
All:
O - bri - ga - do! Al - le - lu - ia!
Cantor:
¡Gra - ci - as! Kam sa ham ni da!
All:
¡Gra - ci - as! Kam sa ham ni da!
Cantor:
Ma - lo! Ma - lo! Thanks be to God!
All:
Ma - lo! Ma - lo! Thanks be to God!
To verses
1. Si
Cantor:
Last time
Cantor:
Ma - lo! Ma - lo! Thanks be to God!
All:
Ma - lo! Ma - lo! Thanks be to God!
Repeat ad lib.
Verse 1
Cantor: 1. Yu - 'us ma - a' - se!
All: 1. Si Yu - 'us ma - a' - se!
Teri - ma ka - sih! Ma -
Teri - ma ka - sih!

ra - ming sa - la - mat!
Ma - ra - ming sa - la - mat!
Dan - ke schön! Dzię - ku - ję!
Dan - ke schön! Dzie - ku - je!
We thank you, Lord!
D.C.
We thank you, Lord!
Verse 2
2. Mè - si bo - kou!
2. Mè - si bo - kou!
Xie xie! A - ri - ga - tō!
Xie xie! A - ri -
Gra - zie!
ga - tō! Gra - zie!
Cám ơn! We thank you, Lord!
Cám ơn!
D.C.
We thank you, Lord!

Text: Jesse Manibusan, b.1958
Tune: Jesse Manibusan, b.1958; acc. by Ken Canedo, b.1953

260 our sacraments and rites

CONFIRMATION

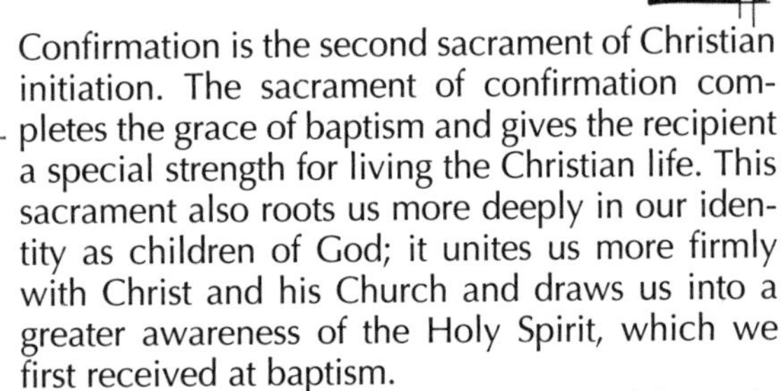

Confirmation is the second sacrament of Christian initiation. The sacrament of confirmation completes the grace of baptism and gives the recipient a special strength for living the Christian life. This sacrament also roots us more deeply in our identity as children of God; it unites us more firmly with Christ and his Church and draws us into a greater awareness of the Holy Spirit, which we first received at baptism.

Through the inexpressible gift of the Holy Spirit himself, which is received in the sacrament of confirmation, we are more strictly obliged to spread and defend the faith both by word and by deed as true witnesses of Christ.

Confirmation is usually administered by the bishop, who anoints the candidate on the forehead with the holy oil of chrism and prays using the ancient ritual of the laying on of hands while saying, "Be sealed with the Gift of the Holy Spirit." *LD/RK*

261 We Are Called / Dios Nos Llama

Verses
1. Come! Live in the light!
2. Come! O - pen your heart!
3. Sing! Sing a new song!
Shine with the joy and the love of the Lord! We are
Show your mer - cy to all those in fear! We are
Sing of that great day when all will be one! God will
called to be light for the king - dom, to
called to be hope for the hope - less so all
reign, and we'll walk with each oth - er as
live in the free - dom of the cit - y of God!
ha - tred and blind - ness will be no more!
sis - ters and broth - ers u - nit - ed in love!

Refrain / Estribillo
We are called to act with jus - tice,
¡Dios nos lla - ma a o - brar con jus - ti - cia,
we are called to love ten - der - ly, we are
Dios nos lla - ma a a - mar tier - na - men - te y a ser -
called to serve one an - oth - er, to
vir - nos u - nos a o - tros, ca - mi -
walk hum - bly with God!
nan - do jun - to con él!
3
Estrofas 1, 2
1. ¡Ven - gan y vi - van a la luz!
2. ¡A - bran sus co - ra - zo - nes!
¡Bri - llen con el go - zo y a - mor del Se - ñor, Quien nos
¡Mues - tren com - pa - sión al que vi - ve en te - mor! Dios nos
lla - ma a ser la luz en su rei - no y a vi -
lla - ma a o - fre - cer su es - pe - ran - za que
Al estribillo
vir li - bre - men - te en la ciu - dad de Dios!
no ha - ya más o - dio, ce - gue - ra, y mal - dad!

Estrofa 3
3. ¡Can - ten un cán - ti-co nue - vo! ¡A - nun-cien el
dí - a de la sal-va - ción! Rei-na - rá el Se - ñor, y su
Al estribilllo
pue-blo es-ta - rá ca-mi - nan-do en fra - ter-na u - nión!

Text: Micah 6:8; David Haas, b.1957; tr. by Ronald F. Krisman, b.1946
Tune: David Haas, b.1957

262 our greatest gift, the Eucharist

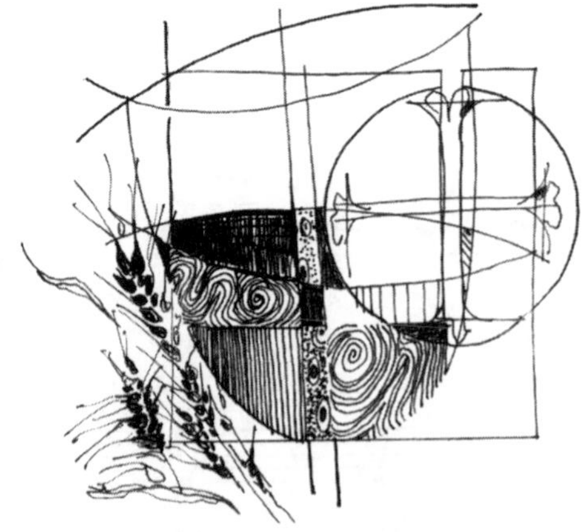

MEAL

The word *Eucharist* means "thanksgiving." This is exactly what we do during the Liturgy of the Eucharist: we give God thanks and praise. After the table has been prepared with bread and wine and a collection taken up for the needs of the community, we are ready to join in a great prayer of thanksgiving, the eucharistic prayer. This is the central prayer of the Mass. In it we celebrate the greatness of God, the mystery of Christ's life, death, and resurrection and the transformation of simple gifts of bread and wine into the body and blood of Christ. The priest speaks the words of the prayer as we affirm them through the acclamations throughout the prayer (Holy, memorial acclamation, and Amen).

Following the eucharistic prayer, we pray the Lord's Prayer, share a sign of peace, and sing the Lamb of God as the Eucharistic bread is broken. During Communion, we join in song and are nourished by Christ's body and blood. After Communion, we share a moment of silence, giving thanks for what we have received. The Liturgy of the Eucharist concludes with the prayer after Communion. *TA*

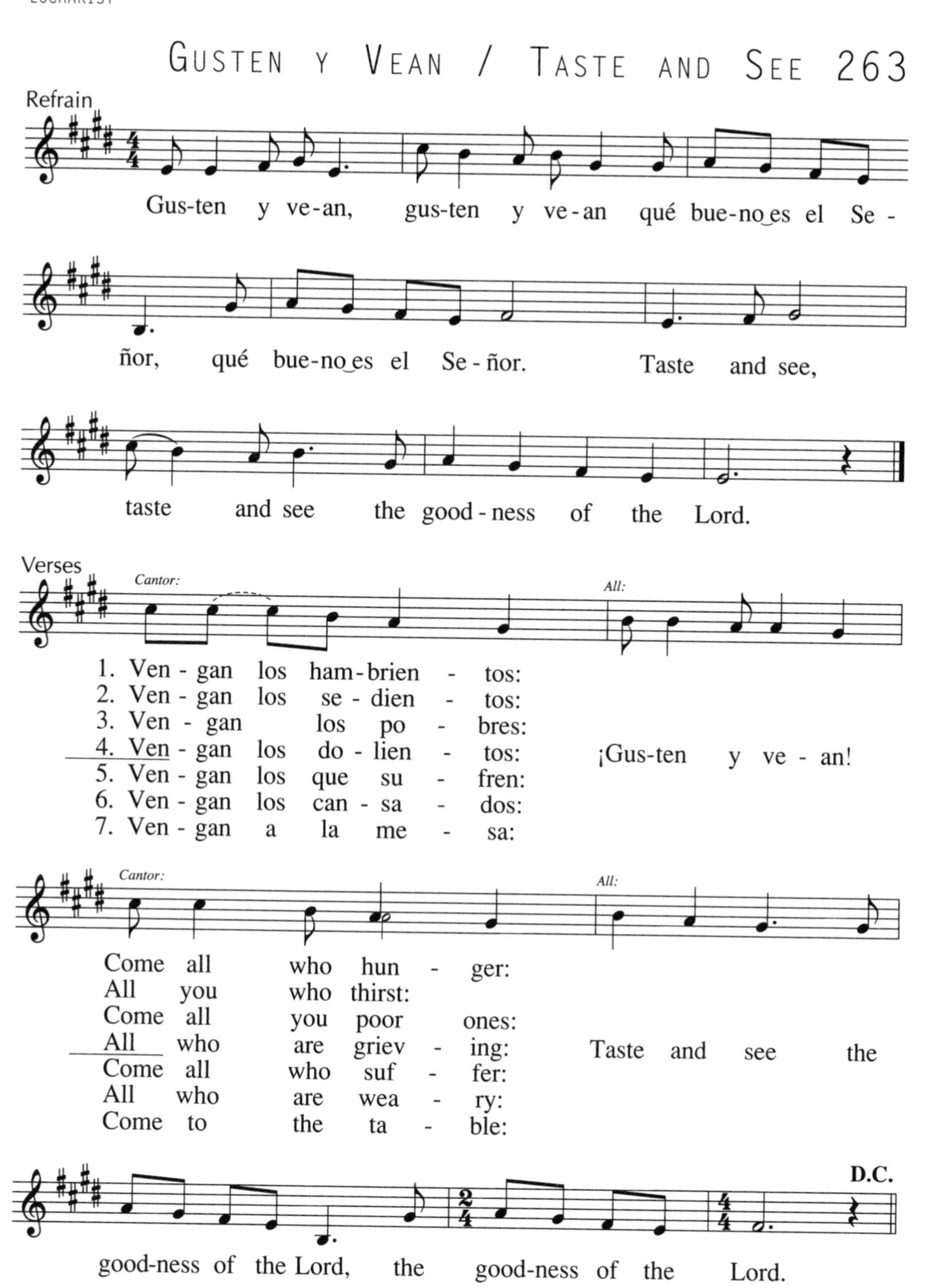
GUSTEN Y VEAN / TASTE AND SEE 263
Refrain
Gus-ten y ve-an, gus-ten y ve-an qué bue-no es el Se - ñor, qué bue-no es el Se - ñor. Taste and see, taste and see the good - ness of the Lord.
Verses
Cantor:
1. Ven - gan los ham-brien - tos:
2. Ven - gan los se - dien - tos:
3. Ven - gan los po - bres:
4. Ven - gan los do - lien - tos:
5. Ven - gan los que su - fren:
6. Ven - gan los can - sa - dos:
7. Ven - gan a la me - sa:
All:
¡Gus-ten y ve - an!
Cantor:
Come all who hun - ger:
All you who thirst:
Come all you poor ones:
All who are griev - ing:
Come all who suf - fer:
All who are wea - ry:
Come to the ta - ble:
All:
Taste and see the good-ness of the Lord, the good-ness of the Lord.
D.C.

Text: Based on Psalm 34; Tony E. Alonso, b.1980
Tune: Tony E. Alonso, b.1980

264 O Taste and See

Refrain

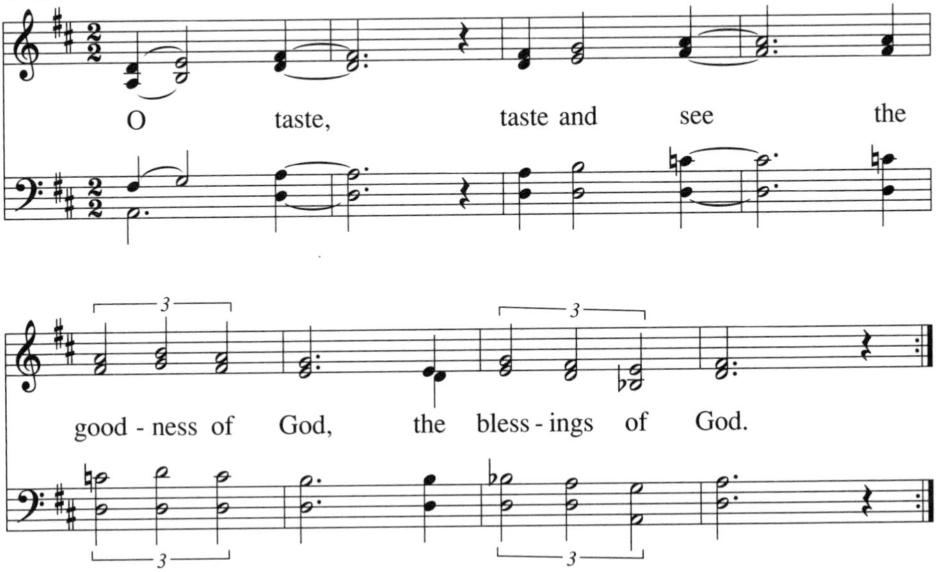

O taste, taste and see the good - ness of God, the bless - ings of God.

Verses

1. I will sing God's praises all the days that I shall live.
   My soul will glory in my God, the lowly will hear and be glad.
   O glorify God's name with me, together let us rejoice.

2. For God has heard my anguished cries, and delivered me from all my foes.
   O look to God that you might shine, your faces be radiant with joy.

3. When the poor cry out, God hears and saves them,
   rescues them from their distress.
   God's angel watches near to those who look to their God to save them.

4. O taste and see that God is good, how happy the ones who find refuge.
   The mighty shall grow weak and hungry, those who seek God lack nothing.

5. Come, my children, hear me, I will teach you the fear of God.
   Come, all of you who thirst for life and seek joy in all of your days.

6. For God is close to the brokenhearted, near to those crushed in spirit.
   The hand of God redeems your life, a refuge for all those who seek.

Text: Psalm 34:2–4, 5–6, 7–8, 9, 11, 12–13, 19; Marty Haugen, b.1950
Tune: Marty Haugen, b.1950

COME, TASTE AND SEE 265

Refrain
Come, taste and see God's kind-ness and mer-cy and nev-er-end-ing love. Come, taste and see the good-ness of the Lord, the good-ness of the Lord.
To verses
Final ending

Verses

1. I will bless the Lord with each breath I take
   and praise God's name now and always.
   Let my soul glory in the Lord, my God;
   the lowly hear, they hear the Lord and are glad.

2. Glorify the Lord, all you people, with me.
   Sing praise to God's name, all you nations, with one voice.
   I called God and he answered my plea
   and rescued me, saved me from all my fears.

3. Only in the Lord I am radiant with joy, and I look to God;
   in the Lord I am not ashamed.
   For God listens to all the poor, he listens to the poor.
   From all my trials, God saves and lets me go free.

Text: Based on Psalm 34:2–7; Chris de Silva
Tune: Chris de Silva

266 We Are One Body

Refrain
We are one bod - y, one bod-y in Christ; and we do not stand a-
lone. We are one bod - y, one bod - y in Christ;
To verses
and he came that we might have life.
Last time
He came that we might have life.
Verses 1–2, 4–5
1. When you eat my bod - y and you drink my
2. Can you hear them cry - ing, can you feel their
4. I have come, your Sav - ior, that you might have
5. At the name of Je - sus ev - 'ry knee shall
blood, I will live in you and you will live in my
pain? Will you feed my hun - gry, will you help my
life, through the tears and sor - row, through the toils and
bend; Je - sus is the Lord and he will come a -
love. When you eat my bod - y and you drink my
lame? See the un - born ba - by, the for - got - ten
strife. Lis - ten when I call you, for I know your
gain. At the name of Je - sus ev - 'ry knee shall

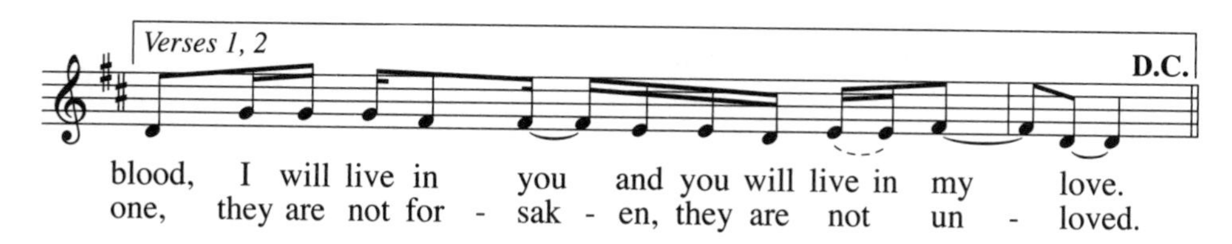
Verses 1, 2
D.C.
blood, I will live in you and you will live in my love.
one, they are not for - sak - en, they are not un - loved.

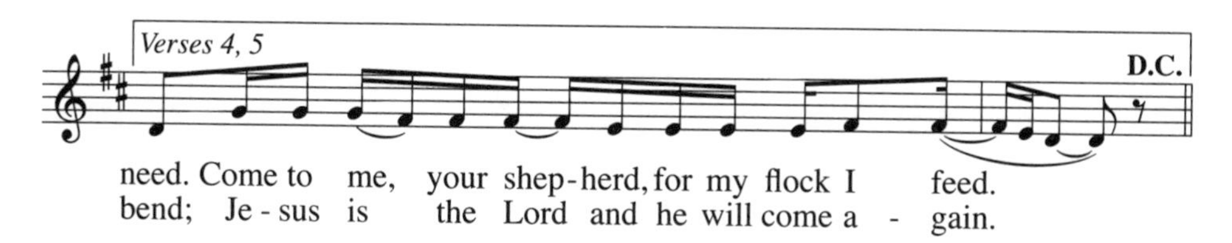
Verses 4, 5
D.C.
need. Come to me, your shep-herd, for my flock I feed.
bend; Je - sus is the Lord and he will come a - gain.

Verses 3, 6

3. I am the Way, the Truth, the Life,
   I am the Final Sacrifice.
   I am the Way, the Truth, the Life;
   he who believes in me will have eternal life.

6. On the rock of Peter, see my Church I build.
   Come receive my spirit, with my gifts be filled.
   For you are my body, you're my hands and feet.
   Speak my word of life to ev'ryone you meet.

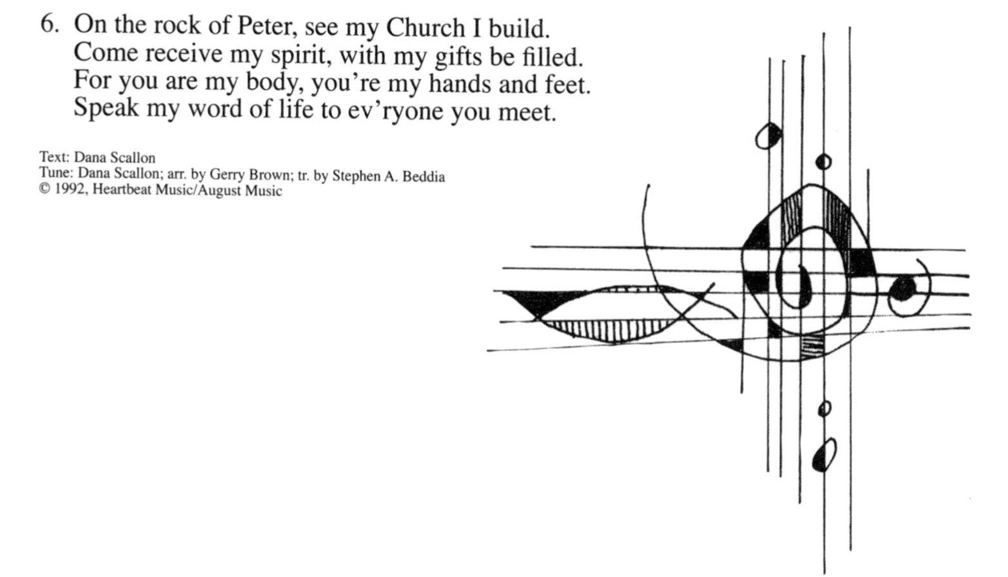

Text: Dana Scallon
Tune: Dana Scallon; arr. by Gerry Brown; tr. by Stephen A. Beddia

267 With This Bread

Refrain
With this bread we will walk with each oth - er,
with this cup we will fol-low the Lord. Com - pas - sion,
love o - ver - flow - ing, God's love ev - er know-ing, we
share it in our song.
Verses 1, 2
1. To of - fer as - sis - tance when oth - ers are blind to the need,
2. Wash-ing the wounds of di - vi - sion, we seek to ease pain.
to give lov - ing care to each oth -
Shar - ing the bur - den of oth -
er is plant - ing God's seed.
ers, like God's gen - tle rain.
Be -
Walk - ing the prom - ise and fall - ing on mer - cy, be -
friend-ing the one who is lone - ly and lost, be -
D.C.
liev - ing we'll walk with you.
liev - ing we'll walk with you.

Verse 3
3. We hold the key to our fu - ture as we share our souls,
nur-tur-ing love in a time when com-pas-sion un-folds.
Danc-ing in joy,
shar-ing in won - der the prayer that we sing to you.
D.C.

Text: Kate Cuddy, b.1953
Tune: Kate Cuddy, b.1953

O Jesus in the Blessed Sacrament,
I would like to be filled with love for you;
keep me closely united with you,
may my heart be near to yours.

John XXIII

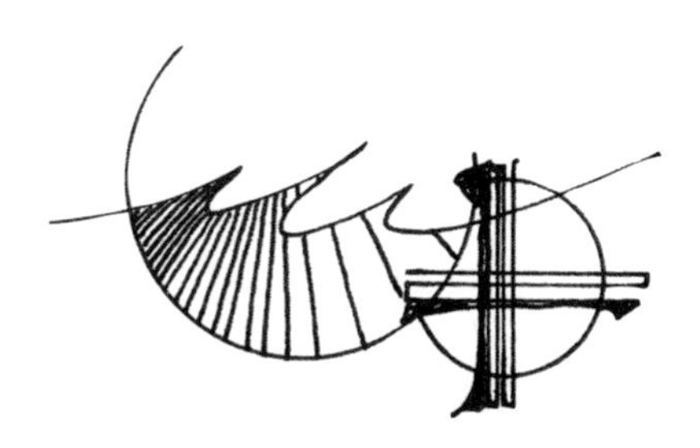

268 We Give You Thanks

Verses
1. For the bread and wine we share here, for the
2. For the move-ment deep with - in us, for the
3. For the wa - ter bring-ing new life, for the
friends that we em - brace, for the peace we find in heal-ing,
sto - ries that we bring, for the signs of God's com-pas-sion,
fra - grance of re - lease, for the fire that blaz - es for-ward,
for all who gath - er in this place, for the
for the jour-ney that we sing, for the
for the call to bring forth peace, for the
faith of those a - round us, for the dead and all those
Word that holds our prom - ise, for the gifts that we can
blind-ness now en - light-ened, for the bound that are now
here, for the hope we find in mem - 'ry, for the
claim, for the won - ders that sur-round us, for the
free, for the bright-ness of your new day, for the
love that draws us near:
song that sings our name:
king-dom we will be:
We give you thanks, we
give you thanks for the grace to re-ceive, in you we be -
3
3

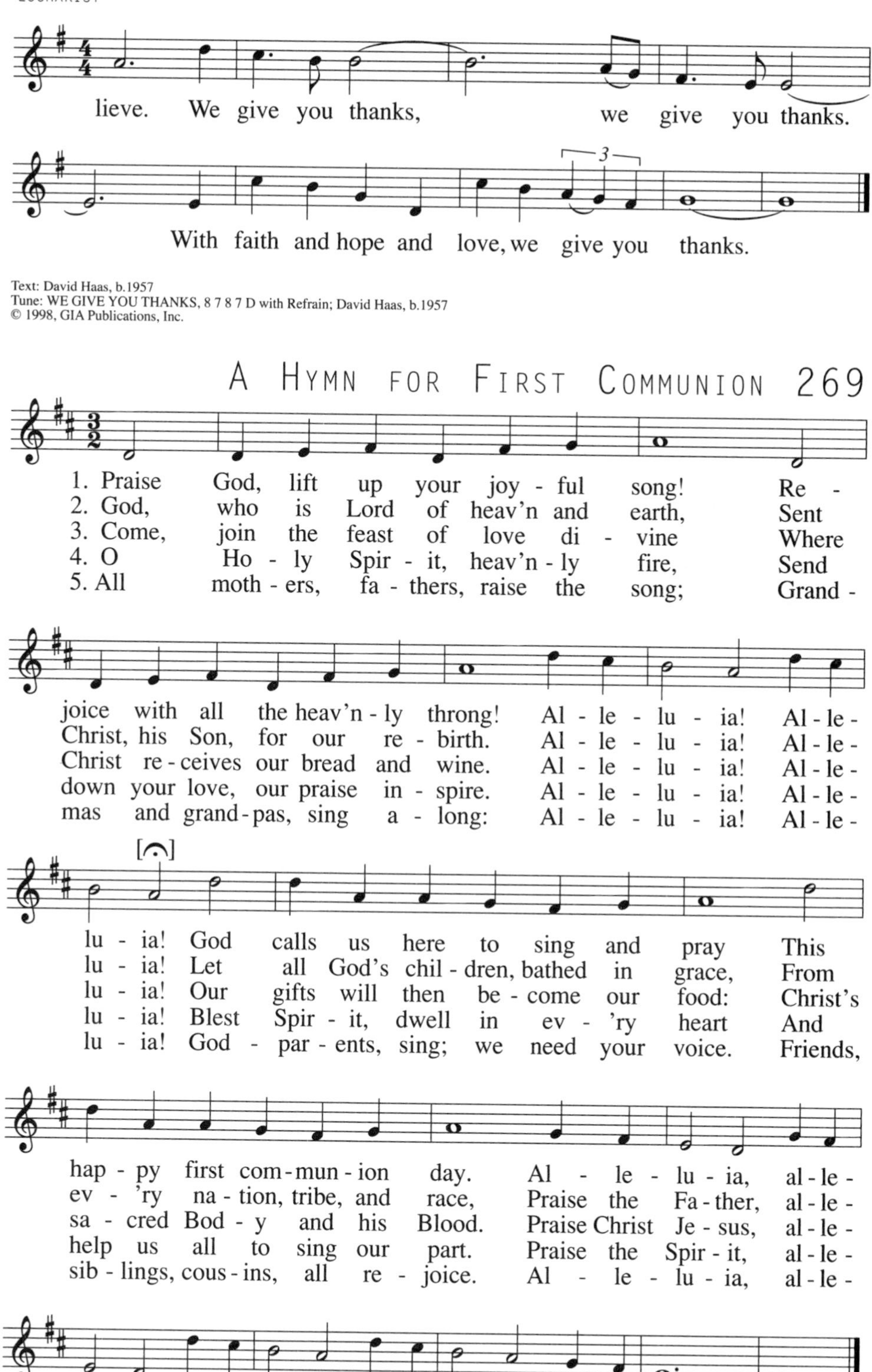
lieve. We give you thanks, we give you thanks.
With faith and hope and love, we give you thanks.
Text: David Haas, b.1957
Tune: WE GIVE YOU THANKS, 8 7 8 7 D with Refrain; David Haas, b.1957
© 1998, GIA Publications, Inc.
A HYMN FOR FIRST COMMUNION 269
1. Praise God, lift up your joy - ful song! Re - joice with all the heav'n - ly throng! Al - le - lu - ia! Al - le - lu - ia! God calls us here to sing and pray This hap - py first com - mun - ion day. Al - le - lu - ia, al - le - lu - ia! Al - le - lu - ia! Al - le - lu - ia! Al - le - lu - ia!
2. God, who is Lord of heav'n and earth, Sent Christ, his Son, for our re - birth. Al - le - lu - ia! Al - le - lu - ia! Let all God's chil - dren, bathed in grace, From ev - 'ry na - tion, tribe, and race, Praise the Fa - ther, al - le - lu - ia!
3. Come, join the feast of love di - vine Where Christ re - ceives our bread and wine. Al - le - lu - ia! Al - le - lu - ia! Our gifts will then be - come our food: Christ's sa - cred Bod - y and his Blood. Praise Christ Je - sus, al - le - lu - ia!
4. O Ho - ly Spir - it, heav'n - ly fire, Send down your love, our praise in - spire. Al - le - lu - ia! Al - le - lu - ia! Blest Spir - it, dwell in ev - 'ry heart And help us all to sing our part. Praise the Spir - it, al - le - lu - ia!
5. All moth - ers, fa - thers, raise the song; Grand - mas and grand - pas, sing a - long: Al - le - lu - ia! Al - le - lu - ia! God - par - ents, sing; we need your voice. Friends, sib - lings, cous - ins, all re - joice. Al - le - lu - ia, al - le - lu - ia!

Text: Michael A. Cymbala, b.1948, and Ronald F. Krisman, b.1946, © 2008, GIA Publications, Inc.
Tune: LASST UNS ERFREUEN, LM with alleluias; *Geistliche Kirchengasange*, Cologne, 1623; harm. by Ralph Vaughan Williams, 1872-1958

270 I Will Take the Cup of Salvation

Refrain

I will take the cup of sal - va - tion, and call on the name of the Lord. I will take the cup of sal-va-tion, and call on the name of the Lord.

Verse 1

Cantor:

1. How shall I make a re - turn to the LORD for all the good he has done for me? The cup of sal-va-tion I will take up, and I will call up-on the name of the LORD.

D.C.

Verse 2

Cantor:

2. O pre - cious in the eyes of the LORD is the death of his faith-ful ones. I am your ser-vant, the son of your hand-maid; you have loos-ened my bonds.

D.C.

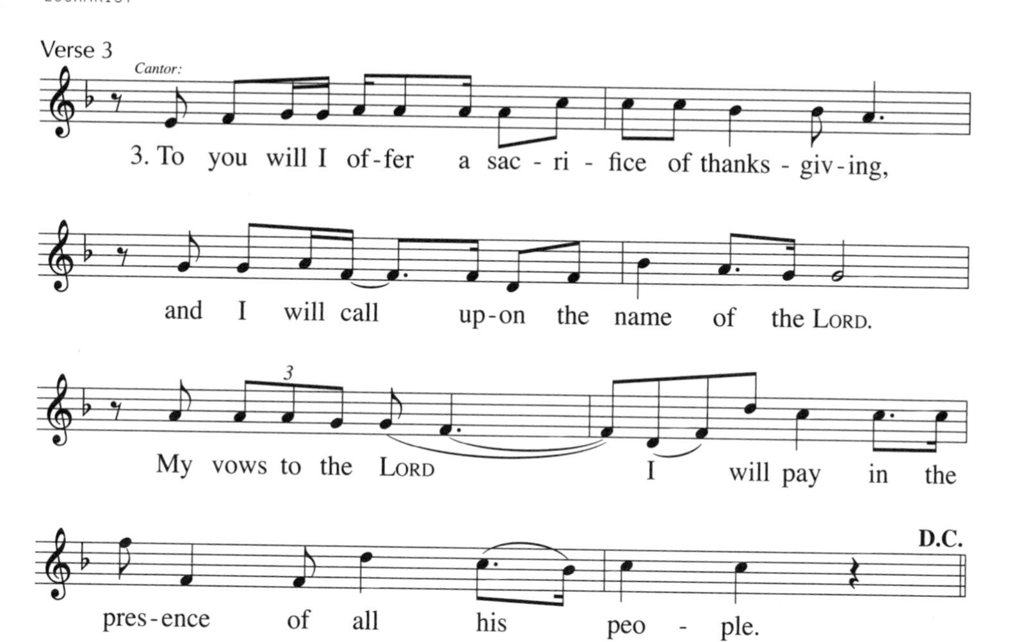
Verse 3
Cantor:
3. To you will I of-fer a sac - ri - fice of thanks - giv - ing,
and I will call up-on the name of the LORD.
3
My vows to the LORD I will pay in the
D.C.
pres-ence of all his peo - ple.

271 EMMAUS

Verse 1
1. As we jour-neyed on our way and re-mem-bered Christ our friend,
our eyes were slow to rec-og-nize, our
hearts to com-pre-hend. Now a stran-ger at our side,
we talked with him on the way of all the things
that hap-pened that led us to this day.
Refrain
In the break-ing of the bread we have
known you, O Lord. By your word have we been led
to the break-ing of the bread.
1., 3. To verse 2
Last time
2. To bridge
Verse 2
2. Then he o-pened up the Word of the

proph-ets who had said, "Your Sav-ior first must suf - fer, then
rise from the dead." As our jour - ney found its end
and the dark of night drew near, we told the stran-
ger, "Stay with us till morn-ing's light ap - pears."
D.S.
Bridge
It was at ta - ble then we knew why our hearts were set a - blaze:
This stran-ger was our broth-er a - ris - en from the grave!
Interlude
4
D.S.

Text: Based on Luke 24:13–35; Tony E. Alonso, b.1980
Tune: Tony E. Alonso, b.1980

EUCHARIST

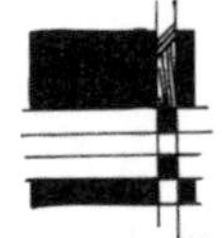

The sacraments of baptism, confirmation, and the holy Eucharist are the three sacraments of Christian initiation. In all sacraments, God gives us the gift of grace, the divine life of the Holy Trinity; but in the Eucharist, God gives us the gift of himself as our spiritual food. Eucharist is at the heart of the Church's life. Our regular participation in the Eucharist is the most important sign of our commitment to what we believe.

The sacrament of the Eucharist has its origin at the Last Supper when, on the night before he died, Jesus took bread, "blessed and broke it, and gave it to his disciples and said, 'Take, eat, this is my body'" (Matthew 26:26). He also took a cup of wine, "gave thanks and passed it to his disciples, saying, 'This cup which is poured out for you is the new covenant in my blood'" (Luke 22:20).

Catholics believe that Christ is truly present when gifts of bread and wine are transformed into the body and blood of Christ during the eucharistic prayer. When we receive this sacrament we are strengthened in our relationship with Christ and the whole Church. We are nourished by the Eucharist to go forth to continue to witness and serve in Christ's name. *LD*

SPIRIT AND GRACE 273

Verses
1. Spir - it of grace, here in this meal;
2. Spir - it and grace, here in this meal;
3. Spir - it and grace, here in this place;
4. Spir - it of God, send - ing us forth;
you are the wind that breathes through the field.
you are the life that flows through the vine.
you are the light that shines in this space.
we spread your wis-dom through-out all the earth.
Gath - er the wheat and form us in Christ.
Gath - er this drink and form us in Christ.
Gath - er your peo - ple and form us in Christ.
Gath - er the na - tions and form us in Christ.
Come, be our source and breath of life.
Come, be our source and blood of life.
Come, be the heart - beat of our lives.
Come, be the pres - ence in our lives.
Refrain
In the bread, blessed, bro - ken and shared,
Christ is our life, whose pres-ence we bear. Come, O
Spir - it, make your grace re - vealed in this
ho - ly meal.
3
D.C.
Final ending

Text: Ricky Manalo, CSP, b.1965
Tune: Ricky Manalo, CSP, b.1965; vocals arr. by Craig S. Kingsbury, b.1952

274 Unless a Grain

Verse 1
1. Un - less a grain falls to the earth and dies, it can
nev - er be - come man-y, on - ly one. And all the
rain - fall and the sun - ny skies can-not bring
to life the sow - ing not be - gun.
Refrain
I would die a lit-tle, I would die a lit-tle to my - self, to
bring to you a gift you can - not buy. Will you die
a lit - tle? Will you die a lit-tle bit for
Last time to Coda
me? And in dy - ing will we rise a - gain to
life?

Verse 2
2. And so our love goes it will live or die, we will
seek our own or seek each oth - er's good. But when the tears
fall and the well runs dry, will the
sac - ri - fice of love be un - der - stood?
D.S.
Coda
life?
And in dy-ing will we rise a-gain to life?

Text: Tom Franzak, b.1954
Tune: Tom Franzak, b.1954

I am a nobody; I am a small rope,
a tiny ladder, the tail end, a leaf.

Juan Diego

275 We Are One

Refrain
We are one, one in the bod - y, one in the Spirit of the Lord. Here, we be - come food for the hungry, drink for the thirst - y. At this ta - ble of love, by faith,
we are all made one.
Verses
1. Be - yond the bread we break, we live the prom-
2. As we re - ceive your love, we look to give
3. Sum-moned as food for all, we take the gos -
ise of new life. Be - yond the cup we take,
love in re - turn, and we be - lieve your love
pel to the world. When we do good for all,
we share our lives with one an - oth -
will change our hearts to end di - vi -
we hear the call to choose com - pas -
er:
sion: Then we'll know the pres - ence of God.
sion:
D.C.

Text: Based on Ephesians 4:4–6; Chris de Silva, b.1967
Tune: Chris de Silva, b.1967

I HAVE BEEN ANOINTED 276

Refrain
I have been a - noint - ed with the song of the Lord! A song of
love and com-pas - sion, a song to set me free! God is my
rock of sal-va - tion! A bea - con for my soul! Hal - le -
lu - jah! A - men! Hal - le - lu - jah! A - men! Praise to the
1. Last time
2. To verse
rock and the well - spring, cre - a - tor of my soul! Oh, soul!
Verse
My heart knew dark-ness, My soul was filled with de - spair,
Life-less and si - lent, no mu - sic an - y -
where, and then my Lord and com-pan - ion, He filled my wait - ing
D.C.
soul: Hal-le - lu - jah! Hal-le - lu - jah! For God has made me whole!

Text: Steven C. Warner, b.1954
Tune: Steven C. Warner, b.1954; arr. by Peter M. Kolar, b.1973

277 Make Me Holy

Verses
1. Pre - pare my mind, pre - pare my soul, pre -
2. Con - sume my mind, con - sume my soul, con -
3. Re - store my mind, re - store my soul, re -
pare my heart and make me whole: pre - pare me for the awe-
sume my heart and make me whole: con - sume me with the awe-
store my heart and make me whole: re - store me with the awe-
some - ness of you. Re - new in me a
some - ness of you. De - stroy my pride, de -
some - ness of you. Re - dec - o - rate me
spir - it strong, re - mind me that it's sin that's wrong, cre -
stroy my hate, de - stroy the things that sep - a - rate, and
from with - in, re - fur - nish me with sa - cred - ness, re -
ate in me com - plete de - sire for you!
keep me from re - turn - ing back to you!
build me with a yearn - ing love for you!
Refrain
Make me ho - ly, Lord,
make me ho - ly, Lord.

Make me ho - ly, Lord,

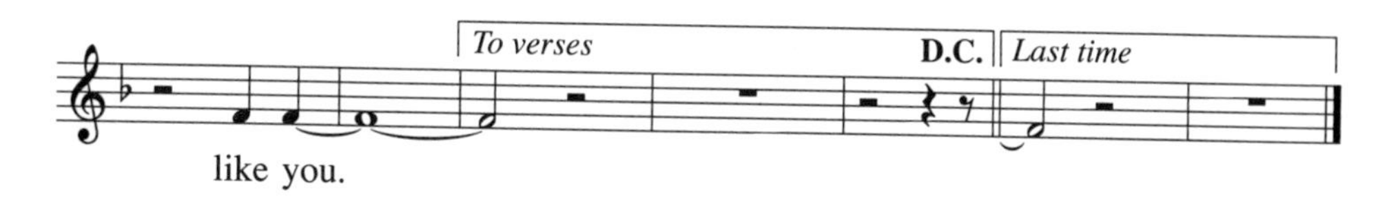
To verses
D.C.
Last time
like you.

Text: Aaron Thompson
Tune: Aaron Thompson; arr. by Joshua Evanovich, b.1984

GOD IS FORGIVENESS / BÓG JEST MIŁOŚCIĄ 278

Ostinato Refrain

God is for - give-ness. Dare to for-give and God will be with you.
Bóg jest mi - łoś - cią miej-cie od - wa - gę żyć dla mi - łoś - ci.
God is for - give - ness. Love, and do not fear.
Bóg jest mi - łos - cią. Nie lę - kaj - cie się.

Text: The Taizé Community
Tune: The Taizé Community

MARRIAGE

The mutual and lifelong commitment of a man and a woman in marriage has always been understood by people of faith as a sacred covenant, since marriage is viewed as a gift from God for the human race. In that light, all marriages are holy.

But Jesus Christ raised the marriage of two Christians to an even greater dignity when he made it a sacrament of the Church, that is, an effective sign of his divine presence in the world. As he himself lived and died for his beloved spouse, the Church, so Christian spouses live for each other in the grace-filled bond of love.

Marriage requires unselfishness, perseverance, and hard work. The sacrament of matrimony offers special graces to the bride and groom to live out "in mutual and lasting fidelity" the vows they make to each other and to God in the presence of the Christian community.

At their wedding the spouses themselves are the ministers of the sacrament of matrimony to each other; the priest or deacon who presides over the wedding serves as the authorized witness of the Church and prays the nuptial blessing of the Church over the spouses. *RK*

LOVE ENDURES 280

Verses 1, 2
1. Love is pa-tient, love is kind. Love is gen-tle, love's not blind.
(2. Love is) gra-cious, love is sure. Love is car-ing, love en-dures.
1.
2.
Love is all you have, all you need. Love is all you are. 2. Love is are.
Refrain
For love en-dures, love en-dures all things. For
Last time to Coda
love en-dures, love will nev - er end.
Verse 3
3
3. Love is heal-ing and for - giv - ing. Love is hop-ing and
trust-ing. Love is cre-at-ing and liv - ing.

D.S.

Love is peace, love is joy, love is more. For

Coda

Love will nev - er end.

Text: Based on 1 Corinthians; James E. Moore, Jr., b.1951
Tune: James E. Moore, Jr., b.1951

281 I Know That My Redeemer Lives

Refrain
I know that my re - deem - er lives: on the last day
I shall rise a - gain, and in my flesh I shall see
God. On the last day I shall rise a - gain!
Verses
Cantor:
1. I shall see my Sav - ior's face; and my own
2. With - in my heart this hope I hold; that in my
eyes shall be - hold my God.
flesh I shall see my God.
All:
On the last day
On the last day
D.C.
I shall rise a - gain!
I shall rise a - gain!

Text: Job 19:25–27; David Haas, b.1957
Tune: David Haas, b.1957

282 our sacraments and rites

FUNERAL RITES

Catholics believe that like Jesus Christ, who was raised from the dead, Christians will experience a similar resurrection from the dead on the last day. Our belief in life after death brings joy and comfort to us when we are faced with the loss of a loved one.

When we gather for a funeral, we celebrate various rites that provide hope and consolation to the living and remind us of God's unending and infinite love during times of great loss and sadness. Funerals also remind us of the spiritual bond that exists between the living and the dead (also known as the communion of saints).

The principal funeral rites are the vigil for the deceased, the funeral liturgy, and the rite of committal, which is held at the actual burial place—grave, tomb, or crematorium.

In the funeral rites we offer praise and thanksgiving for the gift of the life of the deceased and we also offer prayers entrusting the one who has died to God's mercy and care. *LD*

I Know That My Redeemer Lives 283

Verses
1. I know that my Re-deem-er lives, the One who calls me home. I long to see God face-to-face, to see with my own eyes.
2. I know that I shall one day see the good-ness of the Lord, when God will wipe a-way our tears, and death will be no more.
3. The last day I shall rise a-gain, shall be re-made like God. My home shall be by God's own side, the dy-ing, ris-ing Lord.
Refrain
I know that my Re-deem-er lives, that I shall rise a-gain. I know that my Re-deem-er lives, that I shall rise a-gain.
Last time

Text: Based on Job 19, Psalm 27, Isaiah 25; Scott Soper, b.1961
Tune: Scott Soper, b.1961

2 © 2003, GIA Publications, Inc.
3 © 2007, GIA Publications, Inc.
4 © 2003, World Library Publications, 3708 River Rd. Franklin Park, IL 60131-2158. www.wlpmusic.com 800-566-6150. All rights reserved.
5 © 1993, Tom Booth. Published by OCP. P.O. Box 13248, Portland, OR 97213-0248. All rights reserved. Used with permission.
8 Text: Verse tr. © 1985, The Church Pension Fund. Used by permission of Church Publishing Incorporated, New York. Refrain: © 2004, GIA Publications, Inc.
10 Arr.: © 2000, GIA Publications, Inc.
12 Verses text: © 1998, Hope Publishing Co., Carol Stream, IL 60188. All rights reserved. Used by permission. Verses tune: © 2005, GIA Publications, Inc.
15 © 1984, 2008, GIA Publications, Inc.
16 © 1991, GIA Publications, Inc.
17 Text: © 1970, Confraternity of Christian Doctrine; alt. verses, © 1999, Aaron Thompson. Tune: © 1999, Aaron Thompson. Published by World Library Publications, 3708 River Rd. Franklin Park, IL 60131-2158. www.wlpmusic.com 800-566-6150. All rights reserved.
18 Verses text: © 2003, GIA Publications, Inc. Verse tr. © 2008, GIA Publications, Inc.; Refrain text: © 1973, ICEL. Tune: © 2003, GIA Publications, Inc.
20 © 2000, 2002, Tom Booth. Published by spiritandsong.com®. P.O. Box 13248, Portland, OR 97213-0248. All rights reserved. Used with permission.
21 Arr.: © 2000, GIA Publications, Inc.
22 Text: © 1969, ICEL. Music: © 2008, GIA Publications, Inc.
23 Arr.: © 2003, GIA Publications, Inc.
24 © 2001, GIA Publications, Inc.
25 © 2005, GIA Publications, Inc.
27 © 1981, Les Presses de Taizé, GIA Publications, Inc., agent
29 © 2008, GIA Publications, Inc.
31 Text tr.: © 1975, 1986, GIA Publications, Inc. Acc.: © 1986, GIA Publications, Inc.
33 © 1997, GIA Publications, Inc.
34 © 2002, World Library Publications, 3708 River Rd. Franklin Park, IL 60131-2158. www.wlpmusic.com 800-566-6150. All rights reserved.
35 © 2008, GIA Publications, Inc.
36 © 2008, GIA Publications, Inc.
38 © 1986, GIA Publications, Inc.
39 © 2003, GIA Publications, Inc.
40 Acc.: © 1975, GIA Publications, Inc.
43 © 2000, GIA Publications, Inc.
44 © 2008, GIA Publications, Inc.
45 © 1995, Mercy/Vineyard Publishing (ASCAP) Admin. in North America by Music Services o/b/o Vineyard Music USA
46 © 1989, GIA Publications, Inc.
48 Text tr.: © 2008, GIA Publications, Inc.
49 Text: © 2005, GIA Publications, Inc. Tune: © 2007, GIA Publications, Inc.
51 Tune: © 2004, World Library Publications, 3708 River Rd. Franklin Park, IL 60131-2158. www.wlpmusic.com 800-566-6150. All rights reserved.
52 © 2004, World Library Publications, 3708 River Rd. Franklin Park, IL 60131-2158. www.wlpmusic.com 800-566-6150. All rights reserved.
53 © 2007, GIA Publications, Inc.
54 © 2002, GIA Publications, Inc.
55 © 2000, GIA Publications, Inc.
56 © 2008, GIA Publications, Inc.
57 © 2008, GIA Publications, Inc.
58 © 1991, Ken Canedo and Bob Hurd. Published by OCP. P.O. Box 13248, Portland, OR 97213-0248. All rights reserved. Used with permission.
59 Text: © 1968, 1981, 1997, ICEL. Music: © 2002, GIA Publications, Inc.
60 © 2007, GIA Publications, Inc.
62 Verse text: © 1970, Confraternity of Christian Doctrine. Refrain trans. © 1969, ICEL. Music: © 2008, GIA Publications, Inc.
64 Verse text: © 1970, 1997, 1998, Confraternity of Christian Doctrine. Refrain trans. © 1969, ICEL. Music: © 2008, GIA Publications, Inc.
65 © 2003, GIA Publications, Inc.
66 Verse text: © 1970, Confraternity of Christian Doctrine. Refrain trans. © 1969, 1981, ICEL. Music: © 1997, GIA Publications, Inc.
67 © 1991, 1992, Bob Hurd. Published by OCP. P.O. Box 13248, Portland, OR 97213-0248. All rights reserved. Used with permission.
68 Verse text: © 1970, 1997, 1998, Confraternity of Christian Doctrine. Refrain trans. © 1969, ICEL. Music: © 2008, GIA Publications, Inc.
69 Verse text: © 1970, 1997, 1998, Confraternity of Christian Doctrine. Refrain trans. © 1969, ICEL. Music: © 2008, GIA Publications, Inc.
70 © 2004, GIA Publications, Inc.
71 Verse text: © 1970, 1997, 1998, Confraternity of Christian Doctrine. Refrain trans. © 1969, ICEL. Music: © 2000, 2004, Curtis Stephan. Published by OCP. P.O. Box 13248, Portland, OR 97213-0248. All rights reserved. Used with permission.
72 Verse text: © 1970, 1997, 1998, Confraternity of Christian Doctrine. Refrain trans. © 1974, ICEL. Music: © 1997, 1998, Steve Angrisano. Published by OCP. P.O. Box 13248, Portland, OR 97213-0248. All rights reserved. Used with permission.
73 © 2003, GIA Publications, Inc.
74 Verse text: © 2004, Janèt Sullivan Whitaker. Refrain trans. © 1969, 1981, 1997, ICEL. Music: © 2004, Janèt Sullivan Whitaker. Published by OCP. P.O. Box 13248, Portland, OR 97213-0248. All rights reserved. Used with permission.
75 Verses text: © 1970, 1997, 1998, Confraternity of Christian Doctrine. Refrain trans. © 1969, ICEL. Music: © 2007, GIA Publications, Inc.
76 © 1998, GIA Publications, Inc.
77 © 2001, GIA Publications, Inc.
79 © 2008, GIA Publications, Inc.
80 Verses text: © 1970, 1997, 1998, Confraternity of Christian Doctrine. Refrain trans. © 1969, ICEL. Music: © 2008, GIA Publications, Inc.
81 Verses text: © 1970, Confraternity of Christian Doctrine. Refrain trans. © 1969, ICEL. Music: © 2008, GIA Publications, Inc.
82 Verses text and music: © 2008, GIA Publications, Inc. Refrain tr. © 1969, ICEL
83 Verses text: © 1970, 1997, 1998, Confraternity of Christian Doctrine. Refrain trans. © 1969, ICEL. Music: © 2008, GIA Publications, Inc.
84 © 2008, GIA Publications, Inc.
85 Verses text: © 1970, Confraternity of Christian Doctrine. Refrain text and music: © 2008, GIA Publications, Inc.

86 © 2000, GIA Publications, Inc.
87 © 2004, GIA Publications, Inc.
88 © 2003, GIA Publications, Inc.
89 Text: © David Higham Assoc. Ltd. Arr.: © 2008, GIA Publications, Inc.
90 Text: © 1996, Hope Publishing Co., Carol Stream, IL 60188. All rights reserved. Used by permission. Tune: © 2001, GIA Publications, Inc.
91 © 2004, GIA Publications, Inc.
92 © 2004, GIA Publications, Inc.
93 Music: © 1993, 1999, Jesse Manibusan. Published by OCP. P.O. Box 13248, Portland, OR 97213-0248. All rights reserved. Used with permission.
94 © 1997, 1998, Steve Angrisano and Thomas N. Tomaszek. Published by OCP. P.O. Box 13248, Portland, OR 97213-0248. All rights reserved. Used with permission.
95 © 1990, GIA Publications, Inc.
96 © 1989, 1999, MARANATHA PRAISE, INC. Admin. in North America by Music Services o/b/o Maranatha.
97 © 1995, Curious? Music UK (PRS) (Admin. EMI Christian Music Publishing) International Copyright Secured. All Rights Reserved. Used by Permission.
98 © 2005, GIA Publications, Inc.
99 © 1997, 2003, GIA Publications, Inc.
100 © 1998, Tom Booth. Published by OCP. P.O. Box 13248, Portland, OR 97213-0248. All rights reserved. Used with permission.
101 © 2007, GIA Publications, Inc.
102 © 2005, Iona Community, GIA Publications, Inc., agent
103 © 2004, World Library Publications, 3708 River Rd. Franklin Park, IL 60131-2158. www.wlpmusic.com 800-566-6150. All rights reserved.
104 © 2008, GIA Publications, Inc.
105 © 2002, 2004, Thankyou Music. (Admin. EMI Christian Music Publishing) International Copyright Secured. All Rights Reserved. Used by Permission.
106 Text adapt.: © 2005, GIA Publications, Inc. Arr.: © 1990, Iona Community, GIA Publications, Inc., agent. Sprinkling rite verses and adapt.: © 2005, GIA Publications, Inc.
107 © 2001, GIA Publications, Inc.
108 © 2001, 2004, Worshiptogether.com songs (ASCAP)/Six Steps Music (ASCAP). All rights reserved. (Admin. EMI Christian Music Publishing) International Copyright Secured. All Rights Reserved. Used by Permission.
109 © 1993, 2004, Darlene Zschech/Hillsong Publishing. Administered in the U.S. and Canada by Integrity's Hosanna! Music (Hal Leonard Publishing Corp.)
110 © 2002, GIA Publications, Inc.
111 © 2000, 2004, Meaux Mercy and Storm Boy Music (Admin. EMI Christian Music Publishing) International Copyright Secured. All Rights Reserved. Used by Permission, and New Spring, a division of Zomba Enterprises, Inc. (ASCAP).
114 © 2003, 2004, Steve Angrisano. Published by spiritandsong.com®. P.O. Box 13248, Portland, OR 97213-0248. All rights reserved. Used with permission.
115 © 1998, GIA Publications, Inc.
116 Harm.: © 1988, GIA Publications, Inc.
117 © 1991, 1992, Jaime Cortez. Published by OCP. P.O. Box 13248, Portland, OR 97213-0248. All rights reserved. Used with permission.
118 © 1993, Tom Booth. Published by OCP. P.O. Box 13248, Portland, OR 97213-0248. All rights reserved. Used with permission.
119 © 2003, GIA Publications, Inc.
120 © 1995, Mercy/Vineyard Publising (ASCAP) Admin. in North America by Music Services o/b/o Vineyard Music USA
122 © 1998, 2000, Janèt Sullivan Whitaker. Published by OCP. P.O. Box 13248, Portland, OR 97213-0248. All rights reserved. Used with permission.
123 © 1997, 1998, Steve Angrisano and Thomas N. Tomaszek. Published by OCP. P.O. Box 13248, Portland, OR 97213-0248. All rights reserved. Used with permission.
124 Arr.: © 2008, GIA Publications, Inc.
125 © 1996, Tom Booth. Published by OCP. P.O. Box 13248, Portland, OR 97213-0248. All rights reserved. Used with permission.
126 © 2002, Aaron Thompson, published by World Library Publications, 3708 River Rd. Franklin Park, IL 60131-2158. www.wlpmusic.com 800-566-6150. All rights reserved.
127 © 1999, Worshiptogether.com Songs (ASCAP) (Admin. EMI Christian Music Publishing) International Copyright Secured. All Rights Reserved. Used by Permission.
128 © 1991, 2005, GIA Publications, Inc.
129 Text: English text © 2008, GIA Publications, Inc.
130 © 2000, GIA Publications, Inc.
131 © 1997, GIA Publications, Inc.
132 © 2002, GIA Publications, Inc.
133 © 2008, GIA Publications, Inc.
134 © 2006, 2008, GIA Publications, Inc.
135 2007, GIA Publications, Inc.
136 © 1993, 2000, Bernadette Farrell. Published by OCP. P.O. Box 13248, Portland, OR 97213-0248. All rights reserved. Used with permission.
137 © 1993, BMG Songs, Inc. (ASCAP)
138 © 1984, Utryck, Walton Music Corporation, agent
139 © 1989, 1999, Make Way Music. Administered in North, South and Central America by Integrity's Hosanna! Music (Hal Leonard Publishing Corp.)
140 © 1997, 2003, GIA Publications, Inc.
141 © 1998, Vineyard Songs (UK/EIRE) (PRS). Admin. in North America by Music Services.
142 Text: © 1967, Gooi en Sticht, bv., Baarn, The Netherlands. Exclusive English language agent: OCP. P.O. Box 13248, Portland, OR 97213-0248. All rights reserved. Used with permission. Tune: © 2008, GIA Publications, Inc.
143 © 2001, Thankyou Music. (Admin. EMI Christian Music Publishing) International Copyright Secured. All Rights Reserved. Used by Permission.
144 © 1991, Bob Hurd. Published by OCP. P.O. Box 13248, Portland, OR 97213-0248. All rights reserved. Used with permission.
145 © 1994, GIA Publications, Inc.
147 Additional text and tune adapt.: © 2008, GIA Publications, Inc.
148 © 1998, Tom Kendzia. Published by OCP. P.O. Box 13248, Portland, OR 97213-0248. All rights reserved. Used with permission.
149 Text: 1987, Iona Community, GIA Publications, Inc., agent. Tr. and arr.: © 2008, GIA Publications, Inc.
150 © 1997, 1998, Steve Agrisano and Thomas N. Tomaszek. Published by OCP. P.O. Box 13248, Portland, OR 97213-0248. All rights reserved. Used with permission.

Acknowledgments/*continued*

151 © 1992, BMG Songs, Inc. and Kid Brothers of St. Frank Publishing. All rights on behalf of Kid Brothers of St. Frank Publishing administered by BMG Songs, Inc. All rights reserved. Used with Permission.
152 © 2008, GIA Publications, Inc.
153 © 1991, Tom Booth. Published by OCP. P.O. Box 13248, Portland, OR 97213-0248. All rights reserved. Used with permission.
154 © 2003, Danielle Rose Skorich, published by World Library Publications, 3708 River Rd. Franklin Park, IL 60131-2158. www.wlpmusic.com 800-566-6150. All rights reserved.
155 © 1998, Ricky Manalo, CSP. Published by OCP. P.O. Box 13248, Portland, OR 97213-0248. All rights reserved. Used with permission.
156 © 2003, World Library Publications, 3708 River Rd. Franklin Park, IL 60131-2158. www.wlpmusic.com 800-566-6150. All rights reserved.
158 © 2000, World Library Publications, 3708 River Rd. Franklin Park, IL 60131-2158. www.wlpmusic.com 800-566-6150. All rights reserved.
159 © 2003, GIA Publications, Inc.
160 © 1993, GIA Publications, Inc.
162 © 1995, The Iona Community, GIA Publications, Inc., agent
163 © 1997, 2008, GIA Publications, Inc.
164 © 1994, 1999, Curious? Music U.K. (PRS) (Admin. EMI Christian Music Publishing) International Copyright Secured. All Rights Reserved. Used by Permission.
165 Text: © 1999, Steve Angrisano, Thomas N. Tomaszek, and Christi Smith. Tune: © 1999, Steve Angrisano and Patrick Smith. Published by OCP. P.O. Box 13248, Portland, OR 97213-0248. All rights reserved. Used with permission.
166 © 1990, Ariose and Mountain Spring Music (ASCAP) (Admin. EMI Christian Music Publishing) International Copyright Secured. All Rights Reserved. Used by Permission.
167 © 1998, 1999, World Library Publications, 3708 River Rd. Franklin Park, IL 60131-2158. www.wlpmusic.com 800-566-6150. All rights reserved.
168 © 1996, Mercy/Vineyard Publishing (ASCAP) and Vineyard Songs (Canada) (SOCAN and Ion Publishing (SOCAN) Admin. in North America by Music Services o/b/o Vineyard Music USA
169 © 1998, Integrity's Hosanna! Music (admin. Hal Leonard Publishing Corp.)
170 © 2003, 2004, Matt Maher. Published by spiritandsong.com®. P.O. Box 13248, Portland, OR 97213-0248. All rights reserved. Used with permission.
171 © 2008, GIA Publications, Inc.
172 © 2007, Jesse Manibusan and OCP. P.O. Box 13248, Portland, OR 97213-0248. All rights reserved. Used with permission.
174 © 1988, 1998, 1999, Jesse Manibusan. Published by OCP. P.O. Box 13248, Portland, OR 97213-0248. All rights reserved. Used with permission.
175 © 2007, GIA Publications, Inc.
176 © 2003, 2004, Jesse Manibusan. Published by OCP. P.O. Box 13248, Portland, OR 97213-0248. All rights reserved. Used with permission.
177 © 1997, 2004, Integrity's Hosanna! Music (admin. Hal Leonard Publishing Corp.)
180 © 2003, GIA Publications, Inc.
181 © 2001, GIA Publications, Inc.
182 Music: © 1978, F.E.L. Publications, Ltd., assigned 1991 to The Lorenz Corp. Arr.: © 2008, GIA Publications, Inc.
183 © 2008, GIA Publications, Inc.
184 © 2005, GIA Publications, Inc.
185 © 2001, GIA Publications, Inc.
186 © 1993, 2000, GIA Publications, Inc.
187 Text and tune: © 1988, 2003, Michael John Poirier, published by Prayersongs Publishing Co., www.Prayersongs.com. Exclusive licensing agent, World Library Publications, 3708 River Rd. Franklin Park, IL 60131-2158. www.wlpmusic.com 800-566-6150. All rights reserved.
188 © 2001, Danielle Rose Skorich, published by World Library Publications, 3708 River Rd. Franklin Park, IL 60131-2158. www.wlpmusic.com 800-566-6150. All rights reserved.
189 © 2001, 2003, 2004, Joshua Blakesley. Published by spiritandsong.com®. P.O. Box 13248, Portland, OR 97213-0248. All rights reserved. Used with permission.
190 © 1990, Vineyard Songs (Canada) and Ion Publishing (SOCAN) Admin. in North America by Music Services o/b/o Vineyard Music USA
191 © 2003, GIA Publications, Inc.
193 © 1999, GIA Publications, Inc.
194 © 2002, GIA Publications, Inc.
195 © 1990, World Library Publications, 3708 River Rd. Franklin Park, IL 60131-2158. www.wlpmusic.com 800-566-6150. All rights reserved.
196 © 1995, 2001, 2003, Thankyou Music. (Admin. EMI Christian Music Publishing) International Copyright Secured. All Rights Reserved. Used by Permission.
197 © 2003, 2004, Matt Maher. Published by spiritandsong.com®. P.O. Box 13248, Portland, OR 97213-0248. All rights reserved. Used with permission.
198 © 2000, 2001, GIA Publications, Inc.
199 © 2007, Les Presses de Taizé, GIA Publications, Inc., agent
200 © 1979, GIA Publications, Inc.
201 © 2003, GIA Publications, Inc.
204 © 1993 GIA Pubications, Inc.
206 © 2007, GIA Publications, Inc.
208 © 1989, GIA Publications, Inc.
209 © 2008, GIA Publications, Inc.
210 © 2001, GIA Publications, Inc.
211 Text: © 1998, Hope Publishing Co., Carol Stream, IL 60188. All rights reserved. Used by permission. Tune: © 2001, GIA Publications, Inc.
212 © 2007, GIA Publications, Inc.
213 Text: Refrain and verse 1, © 2004, Adrian Dominican Sisters; verses 2–4, © 2007, GIA Publications, Inc. Tune: © 2007, 2008, GIA Publications, Inc.
214 © 2001, GIA Publications, Inc.
215 Arr.: © 2007, GIA Publications, Inc.
216 © 1998, Christine Carson and The Iona Community, GIA Publications, Inc., agent
218 Text: © 1992, 2008, GIA Publications, Inc. Harm.: © 1985, GIA Publications, Inc.
219 Text: © 1991, Sisters of St. Benedict. Published by OCP. P.O. Box 13248, Portland, OR 97213-0248. All rights reserved. Used with permission. Arr.: © 2008, GIA Publications, Inc.
220 © 2004, GIA Publications, Inc.
221 © 2003, GIA Publications, Inc.
222 © 2008, GIA Publications, Inc.

223 Text: © 1985, David Adam. Published by Morehouse Publishing. Tune: © 2008, GIA Publications, Inc.

224 © 2008, GIA Publications, Inc.

225 Text: © 1994, The Pilgrim Press. Tune: © 2007, GIA Publications, Inc.

226 © 2007, GIA Publications, Inc.

228 © 2008, GIA Publications, Inc.

229 © 2008, GIA Publications, Inc.

230 © 2007, GIA Publications, Inc.

232 © 2008, GIA Publications, Inc.

233 © 2008, GIA Publications, Inc.

234 © 2008, GIA Publications, Inc.

235 Copyright © 1980, 1981 by Savgos Music, Inc. and PEERMUSIC III, LTD. International Copyright Secured. All Rights Reserved. Used by permission.

236 © 1999, Sparrow Song (BMI). (Admin. EMI Christian Music Publishing) International Copyright Secured. All Rights Reserved. Used by Permission.

237 © 2008, GIA Publications, Inc.

238 Text: © 1991, GIA Publications, Inc. Tune: © 2003, GIA Publications, Inc.

239 Arr.: © 2002, GIA Publications, Inc.

240 © 2003, GIA Publications, Inc.

241 © 2007, GIA Publications, Inc.

243 © 2000, GIA Publications, Inc.

244 Text: © 1993, Hope Publishing Co., Carol Stream, IL 60188. All rights reserved. Used by permission. Tune: © 2003, GIA Publications, Inc.

245 Text and harm.: © 2003, GIA Publications, Inc.

246 © 1974, 1978, New Jerusalem Music

247 © 2007, GIA Publications, Inc.

248 © 2008, GIA Publications, Inc.

249 © 2005, GIA Publications, Inc.

250 © 2003, Les Presses de Taizé, GIA Publications, Inc., agent

251 © 2001, GIA Publications, Inc.

252 © 2007, Les Presses de Taizé, GIA Publications, Inc., agent

253 Text: © 2004, Iona Community, GIA Publications, Inc., agent. Arr.: © 2007, GIA Publications, Inc.

254 © 2002, GIA Publications, Inc.

255 © 2008, GIA Publications, Inc.

256 Tune adapt.: © 1979, Iona Community, GIA Publications, Inc., agent; arr. © 2008, GIA Publications, Inc.

257 © 1992, Bernadette Farrell. Published by OCP. P.O. Box 13248, Portland, OR 97213-0248. All rights reserved. Used with permission.

258 © 2008, GIA Publications, Inc.

259 © 1993, 1999, Jesse Manibusan. Published by OCP. P.O. Box 13248, Portland, OR 97213-0248. All rights reserved. Used with permission.

261 © 1988, 2008, GIA Publications, Inc.

263 © 2008, GIA Publications, Inc.

264 © 1993, GIA Publications, Inc.

265 © 2007, GIA Publications, Inc.

266 © 1992, Heartbeat Music/August Music

267 © 2001, GIA Publications, Inc.

268 © 1998, GIA Publications, Inc.

269 Text: © 2008, GIA Publications, Inc.

270 Verses text: © 1970, 1997, 1998, Confraternity of Christian Doctine; refrain trans. © 1969, 1981, 1997, ICEL. Tune: © 1997, 2000, 2003, Cynthia Cummins. Published by OCP. P.O. Box 13248, Portland, OR 97213-0248. All rights reserved. Used with permission.

271 © 2007, GIA Publications, Inc.

273 © 2006, Ricky Manalo, CSP. Published by OCP. P.O. Box 13248, Portland, OR 97213-0248. All rights reserved. Used with permission.

274 © 2008, GIA Publications, Inc.

275 © 2007, GIA Publications, Inc.

276 © 1996, 1999, World Library Publications, 3708 River Rd. Franklin Park, IL 60131-2158. www.wlpmusic.com 800-566-6150. All rights reserved.

277 © 2008, GIA Publications, Inc.

278 © 2007, Les Presses de Taizé, GIA Publications, Inc., agent

280 © 2002, GIA Publications, Inc.

281 © 1990, GIA Publications, Inc.

283 © 1990, Scott Soper. Published by OCP. P.O. Box 13248, Portland, OR 97213-0248. All rights reserved. Used with permission.

285 Scripture Passages Related to Hymns

GENESIS
1:3 Let There Be Light 57
1:3–5 Morning Has Broken 89
3:19 Remember You Are Dust / Del Polvo Eres Tú 18
9:13 As a Fire Is Meant for Burning / Como un Fuego Brilla y Quema 218
15:1 Amazing Grace 124
15:13 Sometimes by Step 151
22:1 Psalm 40: Here I Am 70
22:17 Let Us Worship the Lord 98
26:4 Let Us Worship the Lord 98
28:12 We Are Climbing Jacob's Ladder 23
33:14 You Are Strong, You Are Holy 238
35:3 Be with Me, Lord 118
46:2 Psalm 40: Here I Am 70
50:21 Be with Me 133

EXODUS
3:4 I Will Choose Christ 153
3:4 Psalm 40: Here I Am 70
3:5–6 You Will Know 224
3:6 To Follow You 228
3:11 To Follow You 228
3:15 To Follow You 228
8:10 Shout to the Lord 109
13:21 Come, Holy Spirit 52
14:13 Now 186
15:2 Shout to the Lord 109
20: O Come, O Come, Emmanuel 10
31:13 Let Us Worship the Lord 98
32:13 Let Us Worship the Lord 98
33:13 You Will Know 224

LEVITICUS
19:18 Get It Together 152
20:26 Purify My Heart 190
21:8 My Savior, Your Son 229
25:38 To Follow You 228
26:6 Lord, Hear My Prayer / Óyenos, Señor 185
26:12 Now Is the Time 148
26:13 Come and See 39

NUMBERS
15:41 To Follow You 228

DEUTERONOMY
6:5 Get It Together 152
10:12 Get It Together 152
10:17 To Follow You 228
21:8 Mercy, O God 24
28:6 God Is Here / Está Aquí 217
31:6 Now Is the Time 148
32:4 Be Still and Know 236
32:4 Let Us Worship the Lord 98

JOSHUA
5:15 You Will Know 224
22:5 Get It Together 152

1 SAMUEL
2:2 You Are Strong, You Are Holy 238
3:1–9 I Will Choose Christ 153
3:4–8 Psalm 40: Here I Am 70
3:4–10 To Follow You 228
3:8 The Summons / El Llamado 149
6:6 Gather Your People 144
12:4–9 Strength for the Journey 187
12:20 Find Us Ready 5
12:24 Be Still and Know 236
18:18 To Follow You 228
22:47 I Have Been Anointed 276
25:6 Salaam Aleikum / May Peace Be in Your Hearts 215

2 SAMUEL
7:22 Shout to the Lord 109
7:28 Amazing Grace 124
9:8 To Follow You 228
22:3 Shout to the Lord 109
22:3, 47 Mighty King 114
22:32 To Follow You 228
22:33 Shout to the Lord 109
22:37 Guide My Feet 239

1 KINGS
8:23 To Follow You 228
8:56 Amazing Grace 124
19:12 God Is Good 172
19:12–13 To Follow You 228
19:12–13 You Are Mine / Contigo Estoy 128

2 KINGS
6:17 Spirit of God 54

1 CHRONICLES
16:29 Lord, I Lift Your Name on High 96
17:16 To Follow You 228
17:20 Shout to the Lord 109
17:26 Amazing Grace 124
23:13 Purify My Heart 190
29:11 Shout to the Lord 109
29:14 To Follow You 228

2 CHRONICLES
2:6 To Follow You 228
6:29–30 Spirit of God 54
7:3 Rain Down 117
7:3 Send Down the Fire 46
14:6 Lord, Hear My Prayer / Óyenos, Señor 185
21:7 Trading My Sorrows 169

NEHEMIAH
9:12 Come, Holy Spirit 52
9:27 Mercy, O God 24

JOB
1:20–22 Blessed Be Your Name 105
4:4 Make Us Worthy 180
5:23 The Peace of the Earth / La Paz de la Tierra 213
19:25–26 I Know That My Redeemer Lives 283
19:25–27 I Know That My Redeemer Lives 281
24:17 Come, Holy Spirit 52
28:24 Look to Christ 226
33:6 Belong 255

PSALMS
3:3 Amazing Grace 124
4:1 Mercy, O God 24
4:3 Purify My Heart 190
4:6 Shine on Us 140
5:4 Psalm 63: My Soul Is Thirsting 72
5:8 For All Time 183
5:11 Easter Alleluia 38
7:7 Gather Your People 144
8:1 How Excellent Is Thy Name 99
8:9 How Excellent Is Thy Name 99
9:10 To Know Darkness 56
11:6 Send Down the Fire 46

Scripture Passages Related to Hymns/*cont.*

14:2 To Know Darkness 56
16:7 Let Evening Fall 92
16:8 The Clouds' Veil 131
16:18 With You by My Side 115
17:9 No More Fear 126
18:2 Mighty King 114
18:2–4 Psalm 18: I Love You, Lord, My Strength 62
18:3 How Excellent Is Thy Name 99
18:18 Be with Me, Lord 118
18:47 Psalm 18: I Love You, Lord, My Strength 62
18:51 Psalm 18: I Love You, Lord, My Strength 62
19:1 Awake to the Day 4
19:7 Go Out in the World 156
19:8–11 Psalm 19: Lord, You Have the Words 64
22:2 O God, Why Are You Silent? 245
22:2 Quietly, Peacefully 135
22:11 Be with Me 133
22:11 Be with Me, Lord 118
22:16 Holiness Is Faithfulness 154
22:26 To Know Darkness 56
23:2 You Are Strong, You Are Holy 238
23:2 Your Grace Is Enough 170
23:4 Bring Us Home 25
23:6 In Your Presence 241
25:1 Psalm 25: I Lift My Soul to You 65
25:1 Psalm 25: To You, O God, I Lift Up My Soul 67
25:1 Psalm 25: To You, O Lord, I Lift My Soul 66
25:4–5 Psalm 25: I Lift My Soul to You 65
25:4–5 Psalm 25: To You, O God, I Lift Up My Soul 67
25:4–5 Psalm 25: To You, O Lord, I Lift My Soul 66
25:8–10 Psalm 25: To You, O God, I Lift Up My Soul 67
25:8–10 Psalm 25: To You, O Lord, I Lift My Soul 66
25:8–11 Psalm 25: I Lift My Soul to You 65
25:14 Psalm 25: To You, O God, I Lift Up My Soul 67
25:14 Psalm 25: To You, O Lord, I Lift My Soul 66
26:3 Mercy, O God 24
27:1 Belong 255
27:1 Let Us Worship the Lord 98
27:1 The Lord Is My Light 235
27:1 The Lord Is My Light and My Salvation 176
27:1 With You by My Side 115
27:4 Belong 255
27:5 The Lord Is My Light 235
27:6 No More Fear 126
27:7–9 The Lord Is My Light and My Salvation 176
27:8 To Know Darkness 56
27:8 What You Have Done for Me 210
27:13 I Know That My Redeemer Lives 283
27:13 The Face of God 167
27:13–14 Belong 255
27:13–14 I Am Sure I Shall See 199
27:13–14 The Lord Is My Light and My Salvation 176
27:14 The Lord Is My Light 235
28:7 Shout to the Lord 109
30:5 Trading My Sorrows 169
31:1–2 I Give My Spirit 35
31:12–13 I Give My Spirit 35
31:14 With You by My Side 115
31:15–16 I Give My Spirit 35
31:17 I Give My Spirit 35
31:25 I Give My Spirit 35
32:7 Be with Me, Lord 118
32:10 Let Evening Fall 92
33: Rain Down 117
33:12 Psalm 33: The Earth Is Full of the Goodness 68
33:18 Psalm 33: The Earth Is Full of the Goodness 68
33:20–22 Psalm 33: The Earth Is Full of the Goodness 68
34:2–7 Come, Taste and See 265
34:2–7 Psalm 34: I Will Bless the Lord at All Times 69
34:2–9 O Taste and See 264
34:9 Gusten y Vean / Taste and See 263
34:10 To Know Darkness 56
34:11 Gusten y Vean / Taste and See 263
34:11–13 O Taste and See 264
34:19 Gusten y Vean / Taste and See 263
34:19 O Taste and See 264
36:9 To Know Darkness 56
37:40 Journeying Prayer 223
38:10 Give Us Your Peace 214
40:2 Psalm 40: Here I Am 70
40:4 Psalm 40: Here I Am 70
40:7 Psalm 40: Here I Am 70
40:8 Cry the Gospel 100
40:8 Quietly, Peacefully 135
40:10 Psalm 40: Here I Am 70
40:16 To Know Darkness 56
42:2 So Longs My Soul 254
42:10–12 So Longs My Soul 254
42:11 I Have Been Anointed 276
43:1 Journeying Prayer 223
43:3 Shine, Jesus, Shine 139
43:5 I Have Been Anointed 276
44:4 You Are My King (Amazing Love) 127
46:2–4 Be Still 132
46:6 Be Still 132
46:8 Be Still 132
46:10 Be Still and Know 236
46:10 I Will Choose Christ 153
46:11 You Are Mine / Contigo Estoy 128
46:11–12 Be Still 132
47:1 Make a Joyful Noise 104
47:2–3 Psalm 47: God Mounts His Throne 71
47:6–9 Psalm 47: God Mounts His Throne 71
47:8 Our God Reigns 246
49:5 Be with Me, Lord 118
50:5 Gather Your People 144
50:15 Be with Me, Lord 118
51:2 Gather Your People 144
51:2 Make Us Worthy 180
51:2 River of Life 189
51:2 The Face of God 167
51:2 Turn My Heart, O God 194
51:7 Gather Your People 144
51:7 Make Us Worthy 180
51:7 River of Life 189
51:7 The Face of God 167
51:7 Turn My Heart, O God 194
51:10 Breath of Life 55
51:10 Make Me Holy 277
51:12 Turn My Heart, O God 194
56:4–5 Nothing Can Ever 252
56:10–14 Nothing Can Ever 252
61:4–5 In Your Presence 241
62:5 Let Evening Fall 92

Scripture Passages Related to Hymns/*cont.*

62:7 Mighty King 114
63:1 With You by My Side 115
63:1–6 In Your Presence 241
63:2–5 Jesus, Your Spirit / Kristus, Din Ande 250
63:2–9 Psalm 63: My Soul Is Thirsting 72
63:4 I Will Lift Up Your Name 94
63:4 Lord, I Lift Your Name on High 96
63:8–9 In Your Presence 241
63:8–9 Jesus, Your Spirit / Kristus, Din Ande 250
64:9 Be Still and Know 236
66:1 Make a Joyful Noise 104
66:2 Sing to the Glory of God 107
66:5 Come and See 39
66:10 Shout to the North 97
66:20 Malo! Malo! Thanks Be to God 259
67:1 Shine on Us 140
67:17 Be with Me, Lord 118
68:34 Shout to the Lord 109
68:35 Malo! Malo! Thanks Be to God 259
72:1–7 Psalm 72: Every Nation on Earth 73
72:7 On That Holy Mountain 195
72:12–14 Psalm 72: Every Nation on Earth 73
72:17 Awake to the Day 4
72:18–19 Psalm 72: Every Nation on Earth 73
72:19 Blessed Be Your Name 105
73:21 River of Hope 240
73:26 Let Us Worship the Lord 98
76:16 Thanks and Praise 103
77:1–10 Quietly, Peacefully 135
77:2–11 I Cry before You 243
81:1 Make a Joyful Noise 104
81:7 Be with Me, Lord 118
82:4 Journeying Prayer 223
84:2–4 Better Is One Day 196
84:4 In Your Presence 241
84:5 Make a Joyful Noise 104
84:7 Better Is One Day 196
84:11 Better Is One Day 196
85:8–14 Psalm 85: Let Us See Your Kindness 75
85:8–14 Psalm 85: Lord, Show Us Your Mercy and Love 74
85:10 Prepare! Prepare! 3
86:2 With You by My Side 115
86:8 Shout to the Lord 109
86:10 Easter Alleluia 38
86:15 Fresh as the Morning 90
89:1 I Could Sing of Your Love Forever 164
89:9 How Can I Keep From Singing? 116
89:9 River of Life 189
89:9 The God of Second Chances 184
90:1–4 In Every Age 122
90:12 In Every Age 122
90:14 We Praise You 110
91:2 Shout to the Lord 109
92:2 We Praise You 110
92:10 I Have Been Anointed 276
94:16 Guide My Feet 239
94:16–17 The Clouds' Veil 131
94:16–17 With You by My Side 115
94:22 Shout to the Lord 109
95:2 Make a Joyful Noise 104
95:6 Come All You People / Uyai Mose 147
95:8 Gather Your People 144
96:1–2 Psalm 96: Sing a Song to the Lord 76
96:1–3 Psalm 96: Proclaim God's Marvelous Deeds 77
96:4 How Excellent Is Thy Name 99
96:7–8 Psalm 96: Sing a Song to the Lord 76
96:10 Psalm 96: Proclaim God's Marvelous Deeds 77
96:10 Psalm 96: Sing a Song to the Lord 76
96:13 Psalm 96: Sing a Song to the Lord 76
96:36 Easter Alleluia 38
98:4 Make a Joyful Noise 104
98:4 Shout to the Lord 109
98:6 Make a Joyful Noise 104
99:9 Be Still and Know 236
100:1 Make a Joyful Noise 104
100:1 Shout to the Lord 109
102:2 Be with Me, Lord 118
103:1–6 Psalm 103: Bless the Lord, My Soul 79
103:8 Psalm 103: Bless the Lord, My Soul 79
103:14 Psalm 103: Bless the Lord, My Soul 79
103:17 Psalm 103: Bless the Lord, My Soul 79
103:21–22 Psalm 103: Bless the Lord, My Soul 79
104:14 Come and See 39
104:25 We Praise You 110
104:30 Come, Holy Spirit 52
104:30 Send Down the Fire 46
104:30 Way, Truth, and Life 193
105:3–4 To Know Darkness 56
105:4 What You Have Done for Me 210
105:8 Trading My Sorrows 169
106:1 Thanks and Praise 103
107:8 Thanks and Praise 103
107:9 I Have Been Anointed 276
107:14 O Come, O Come, Emmanuel 10
107:21 Thanks and Praise 103
107:29 How Can I Keep From Singing? 116
107:29 The God of Second Chances 184
107:29–30 River of Life 189
107:30 The God of Second Chances 184
109:9 River of Life 189
111: I Will Give Thanks 258
112:4 Make Us Worthy 180
113:2 Blessed Be Your Name 105
113:3 We Praise You 110
115:5 Your Grace Is Enough 170
115:18 Shout to the Lord 109
116:12–13 I Will Take the Cup of Salvation 270
116:15–18 I Will Take the Cup of Salvation 270
116:16 Come and See 39
117:1 Let Us Worship the Lord 98
118:1 Forever 108
118:1–2 Psalm 118: This Is the Day 80
118:16–17 Forever 108
118:16–17 Psalm 118: This Is the Day 80
118:22–24 Psalm 118: This Is the Day 80
118:22–24 This Is the Day 44
118:28 Sometimes by Step 151
118:28 With You by My Side 115
118:29 Forever 108
119:8 Open the Eyes of My Heart 177
119:9 To Follow You 228
119:18 Open My Eyes 174
119:18 Spirit of God 54
119:18 The God of Second Chances 184
119:24 Guide My Feet 239
119:28 Turn My Heart, O God 194
119:36 Quietly, Peacefully 135
119:55 God of Wonders 111
119:76 Quietly, Peacefully 135
119:105 Guide My Feet 239
119:105 Hold Us, Jesus 175
119:146 Be with Me, Lord 118
119:153 Be with Me, Lord 118
119:170 Be with Me, Lord 118
119:173 My Savior, Your Son 229
121:1–2 Psalm 121: Our Help Is from the Lord 81
121:3–6 Psalm 121: Our Help Is from the Lord 81

122:1–9 Psalm 122: Let Us Go Rejoicing 82
126:2 We Praise You 110
130:1–7 Psalm 130: Out of the Depths 84
130:1–7 Psalm 130: With the Lord There Is Mercy 83
134:1 Let Evening Fall 92
134:2 Thanks and Praise 103
139:1–8 O God, You Search Me 257
139:1–10 Psalm 139: Before I Was Born 86
139:7–9 Journeying Prayer 223
139:10 For All Time 183
139:10 Guide My Feet 239
139:11–14 O God, You Search Me 257
139:13 Psalm 139: Before I Was Born 86
139:16 O God, You Search Me 257
139:16b–17 Psalm 139: Before I Was Born 86
140:1 Journeying Prayer 223
143:10 Cry the Gospel 100
143:11 Be with Me, Lord 118
145:1–2 I Will Lift Up Your Name 94
145:1–5 All Generations Will Praise Your Name 101
145:8–11 I Will Lift Up Your Name 94
145:15–19 All Generations Will Praise Your Name 101
145:18 Rise Up in Splendor 17
146:8 Look to Christ 226
148: Come All You People / Uyai Mose 147
148:3 We Praise You 110
148:10 We Praise You 110
150:6 How Excellent Is Thy Name 99

PROVERBS
2:7 Amazing Grace 124
8:17 Sometimes by Step 151
8:20 Sometimes by Step 151
8:22 O Come, O Come, Emmanuel 10
10:25 How Can I Keep From Singing? 116
14:26 Lord, Hear My Prayer / Óyenos, Señor 185
17:3 Purify My Heart 190
28:5 To Know Darkness 56
30:5 Amazing Grace 124
30:8 Breathe 120
30:8–9 Lord's Prayer 182

ECCLESIASTES
3:2–8 May the Road Rise to Meet You 119
7:13 Be Still and Know 236
8:15 We Praise You 110

SONG OF SONGS
8:6 Take, O Take Me As I Am 162

SIRACH
28:2 Lord's Prayer 182

WISDOM
18:14–15 Creator of the Stars of Night 8

ISAIAH
2:3 Sometimes by Step 151
2:4 Gather Your People 144
2:4 Make Us Worthy 180
6:2–3 Holy God, We Praise Thy Name 113
6:3 Open the Eyes of My Heart 177
6:8 Psalm 40: Here I Am 70
6:12 Dream a Dream 12
7:14 God Is Here / Está Aquí 217
7:14 O Come, O Come, Emmanuel 10
7:14 Prepare! Prepare! 3
9:1 Child of Mercy 16
9:2 Make Us Worthy 180
9:2 O Come, O Come, Emmanuel 10
9:5 Child of Mercy 16
11:4 On That Holy Mountain 195
11:6 On That Holy Mountain 195
11:9 On That Holy Mountain 195
11:11 O Come, O Come, Emmanuel 10
11:19 Gather Your People 144
12:2 Shout to the Lord 109
22:22 O Come, O Come, Emmanuel 10
25:1 Sometimes by Step 151
25:1 With You by My Side 115
25:8 I Know That My Redeemer Lives 283
26:9 Sometimes by Step 151
33:2 Psalm 63: My Soul Is Thirsting 72
35:5 Let Us Worship the Lord 98
35:5–6 Faith, Hope, and Love 232
40:3–4 Awake to the Day 4
40:3–5 Prepare! Prepare! 3
40:11 We Are One Body 266
40:26 My Savior, Your Son 229
40:29 Holiness Is Faithfulness 154
40:29 Make Us Worthy 180
40:29 Rise Up in Splendor 17
41:1 Let Evening Fall 92
41:4 Let Us Worship the Lord 98
41:10 Find Us Ready 5
41:10 You Will Know 224
41:13 Guide My Feet 239
42:6 Guide My Feet 239
42:7 Look to Christ 226
42:7 The God of Second Chances 184
42:16 Mercy, O God 24
43:1 My Savior, Your Son 229
43:5 God Is Love 233
43:5 Look to Christ 226
43:5 Now Is the Time 148
43:18 God Is Here / Está Aquí 217
43:18 Let Us Worship the Lord 98
43:20 Let Us Worship the Lord 98
44:21 Now Is the Time 148
45:3 I Will Choose Christ 153
45:3 My Savior, Your Son 229
45:3 The Summons / El Llamado 149
45:3 To Know Darkness 56
45:4 Among All 206
45:4–7 You Will Know 224
45:6 I Will Choose Christ 153
45:7 To Know Darkness 56
45:8 Rain Down 117
45:8 Send Down the Fire 46
46:9 Shout to the Lord 109
49:7 Go Out in the World 156
49:15 Now Is the Time 148
51:12 Be with Me 133
52:3 How Beautiful 166
52:7 How Beautiful 166
52:7 Our God Reigns 246
53:2–7 Our God Reigns 246
53:6 Quietly, Peacefully 135
55:1 Rise Up in Splendor 17
55:6 To Know Darkness 56
58:9 Here I Am 125
58:9 To Follow You 228
58:10 Lord, Hear My Prayer / Óyenos, Señor 185
59:17 Awake to the Day 4
60:1 We Arise 91
60:1–8 Rise Up in Splendor 17
61:1 Come and See 39

61:1 Go Out to the World 230
61:1 We Give You Thanks 268
61:1 With This Bread 267
64:8 Be Still and Know 236
64:8 Dream a Dream 12
64:8 Easter Alleluia 38
65:25 Gather Your People 144
65:25 On That Holy Mountain 195

JEREMIAH
1:5 My Savior, Your Son 229
5:21 For All Time 183
5:21 Let There Be Light 57
10:6–7 Shout to the Lord 109
14:21 Your Grace Is Enough 170
15:21 Journeying Prayer 223
16:9 Shout to the Lord 109
23:23 To Follow You 228
31:25 I Have Been Anointed 276
32:42 Amazing Grace 124
33:11 Thanks and Praise 103
33:22 Let Us Worship the Lord 98
47:6 A Place at the Table 211
50:4 To Know Darkness 56

LAMENTATIONS
3:23 Your Grace Is Enough 170

EZEKIEL
16:60 Your Grace Is Enough 170
34:12 Go Light Your World 137
34:26 Send Down the Fire 46
34:31 You Will Know 224
36:26 Give Us Your Peace 214
37:5 Send Down the Fire 46
44:5 Faith, Hope, and Love 232
44:5 Let Us Worship the Lord 98

DANIEL
2:20 Blessed Be Your Name 105

HOSEA
8:14 Send Down the Fire 46

JOEL
2:1 Hallelujah, Hallelu! 2
2:12–13 Turn My Heart, O God 194
2:12–15 Remember You Are Dust / Del Polvo Eres Tú 18
2:16 Bring Us Home 25
2:16 Mercy, O God 24
2:21 Look to Christ 226
3:10 Gather Your People 144
3:10 Make Us Worthy 180

AMOS
2:2–5 Send Down the Fire 46
5:14 Unless a Grain 274
5:24 Let the River Flow 45
5:24 Send Down the Fire 46

MICAH
4:2 Sometimes by Step 151
4:3 Gather Your People 144
4:3 Lord, Hear My Prayer / Óyenos, Señor 185
4:3 Make Us Worthy 180
6:8 We Are Called / Dios Nos Llama 261

NAHUM
1:2 To Follow You 228

HABAKKUK
3:17–18 Blessed Be Your Name 105

ZEPHANIAH
2:3 To Know Darkness 56
3:15 No More Fear 126

HAGGAI
2:7 O Come, O Come, Emmanuel 10

ZECHARIAH
12:10 Send Down the Fire 46

MALACHI
3:1–3 Purify My Heart 190
3:10 Send Down the Fire 46

MATTHEW
1:23 Child of Mercy 16
1:23 God Is Here / Está Aquí 217
2: Night of Silence / Noche de Silencio 15
3:3 Awake to the Day 4
3:3 Find Us Ready 5
3:11–12 Living Spirit, Holy Fire 49
4:14–16 As a Fire Is Meant for Burning / Como un Fuego Brilla y Quema 218
4:16 Child of Mercy 16
4:16 How Can We Be Silent 221
4:16 Make Us Worthy 180
4:19 Come and Follow Me / Ven y Sígueme 163
4:19 The Summons / El Llamado 149
5:3–12 Make a Joyful Noise 104
5:3–12 Yours Is the Kingdom 201
5:6 Faith, Hope, and Love 232
5:8 Quietly, Peacefully 135
5:11–16 Cry the Gospel 100
5:12 Deny Yourself 171
5:13–15 Go Make a Difference 150
5:15 Get It Together 152
5:15 Go Light Your World 137
5:15 Go Out in the World 156
5:15 Let There Be Light 57
5:15 With One Voice 155
5:46–47 God Is Love 233
6:9–13 Lord's Prayer 182
6:11 Breathe 120
6:13 Journeying Prayer 223
6:22–23 Go Light Your World 137
6:31–34 To Follow You 228
7:7 Come and Follow Me / Ven y Sígueme 163
7:7 What You Have Done for Me 210
7:7 You Are the Way 165
7:13–14 Come and Follow Me / Ven y Sígueme 163
7:14 You Are the Way 165
8:2–3 Be Forgiven 20
8:19 We Will Go, Lord 222
8:22 Come and Follow Me / Ven y Sígueme 163
8:22 The Summons / El Llamado 149
8:26 How Can I Keep From Singing? 116
8:31 The God of Second Chances 184
9:9 The Summons / El Llamado 149
9:9–13 Make a Joyful Noise 104
9:21 I Am for You 160
9:21 Stop By, Lord 181
9:21–22 You Are the Way 165
9:22 Come and See 39
9:22 I Have Been Anointed 276

Scripture Passages Related to Hymns/*cont.*

9:22 Make Me Holy 277
9:22 The God of Second Chances 184
9:27–30 Be Forgiven 20
9:28–30 Spirit of God 54
9:29 Faith, Hope, and Love 232
9:30 Here I Am to Worship 143
9:30 The God of Second Chances 184
9:33 The God of Second Chances 184
10:8 Lord, Hear My Prayer / Óyenos, Señor 185
10:11 Make Us Worthy 180
10:12 Salaam Aleikum / May Peace Be in Your Hearts 215
10:27 Get It Together 152
10:38 Come and Gather 34
10:38 Holiness Is Faithfulness 154
10:38 Strength for the Journey 187
10:38 The Summons / El Llamado 149
10:38 You Will Know 224
10:39 Deny Yourself 171
10:39 Lead Me Home 197
11:5 Go Out to the World 230
11:5 Look to Christ 226
11:15 Come and Follow Me / Ven y Sígueme 163
11:15 Faith, Hope, and Love 232
11:25 God of Wonders 111
11:28 You Are Mine / Contigo Estoy 128
12:21 Sing a New World 219
12:43 The God of Second Chances 184
13:9 Come and Follow Me / Ven y Sígueme 163
13:13 Let There Be Light 57
13:15 Turn My Heart, O God 194
13:16 Let Us Worship the Lord 98
13:16 Open My Eyes 174
14:22–23 You Are Good to Me 134
14:24–25 I Am for You 160
14:24–32 Journeying Prayer 223
14:26 Come and See 39
14:27 God Is Love 233
14:36 I Am for You 160
14:36 I Have Been Anointed 276
14:36 Make Me Holy 277
14:36 Stop By, Lord 181
14:36 The God of Second Chances 184
14:36 You Are the Way 165
15:31 You Are the Way 165
16:18 We Are One Body 266
16:24 Come and Gather 34
16:24 Holiness Is Faithfulness 154
16:24 My Savior, Your Son 229
16:24 You Will Know 224
16:24–26 Deny Yourself 171
16:25 Lead Me Home 197
16:34 Strength for the Journey 187
17:18 The God of Second Chances 184
18:3 Turn My Heart, O God 194
18:11 Lord, I Lift Your Name on High 96
18:19 Be Still and Know 236
18:20 Alleluia! Give the Glory 58
18:20 Sing to the Glory of God 107
18:21–22 Lord's Prayer 182
19:8 Gather Your People 144
19:19 Get It Together 152
19:21–23 Give the Lord Your Heart 159
19:21 The Summons / El Llamado 149
19:27 We Will Go, Lord 222
19:27–29 Deny Yourself 171
19:28 God Is Here / Está Aquí 217
19:28 The Summons / El Llamado 149
19:30 Fresh as the Morning 90
19:30 Open My Eyes 174
20:16 Fresh as the Morning 90
20:16 Open My Eyes 174
20:28 How Beautiful 166
20:28 We Are One Body 266
20:33–34 Here I Am to Worship 143
21:14 Rise Up in Splendor 17
22:23 To Follow You 228
22:37–39 Get It Together 152
23:8 I Will Choose Christ 153
23:37 Bring Us Home 25
24:14 As a Fire Is Meant for Burning / Como un Fuego Brilla y Quema 218
24:14 Go Out to the World 230
24:42 Hallelujah, Hallelu! 2
24:44 Sign Me Up 200
24:45–51 Find Us Ready 5
25:13 Awake to the Day 4
25:13 Sign Me Up 200
25:31–40 What You Have Done for Me 210
25:34–36 Give the Lord Your Heart 159
25:34–40 Lord, Hear My Prayer / Óyenos, Señor 185
25:34–40 Shine on Us 140
25:35–36 With This Bread 267
25:44–45 We Are One Body 266
26:13 Go Out to the World 230
26:26–28 A Place at the Table 211
26:32 He Is Not Here 43
26:36–46 You Are Strong, You Are Holy 238
26:42 Lord's Prayer 182
27:31 Holiness Is Faithfulness 154
27:32 Holiness Is Faithfulness 154
27:33–35 How Beautiful 166
27:33–51 My Savior, My Friend 36
27:38 Holiness Is Faithfulness 154
27:44 Holiness Is Faithfulness 154
28:1–8 Come and See 39
28:1–8 O Sons and Daughters 40
28:2 Look to Christ 226
28:2 Shine on Us 140
28:5–10 He Is Not Here 43
28:6 God Is Here / Está Aquí 217
28:6–9 Jesus Christ Is Risen Today / El Señor Resucitó 42
28:10 God Is Love 233
28:10 Look to Christ 226
28:18–20 Come and See 39
28:19 Go Out in the World 156
28:19 Go Out to the World 230
28:19 Rise Up in Splendor 17
28:19 Spirit and Grace 273
28:19 We Are One 275
28:19 With One Voice 155
28:19–20 I Send You Out 158
28:20 I Am 247
28:20 I Am for You 160
28:20 River of Hope 240

MARK

1:2–4 Hallelujah, Hallelu! 2
1:3 Awake to the Day 4
1:7 The Summons / El Llamado 149
1:7–8 Hallelujah, Hallelu! 2
1:17 Come and Follow Me / Ven y Sígueme 163
1:26 The God of Second Chances 184
1:40–41 Be Forgiven 20
2:14 The Summons / El Llamado 149
2:14–17 Make a Joyful Noise 104

Scripture Passages Related to Hymns/*cont.*

4:21 Get It Together 152
4:21 Go Light Your World 137
4:21 Go Make a Difference 150
4:21 Let There Be Light 57
4:21 With One Voice 155
4:23 Come and Follow Me / Ven y Sígueme 163
4:37–41 Journeying Prayer 223
4:39 How Can I Keep From Singing? 116
5:1–20 Come and See 39
5:12 The God of Second Chances 184
5:28 Come and See 39
5:28 I Am for You 160
5:28 I Have Been Anointed 276
5:28 Make Me Holy 277
5:28 Stop By, Lord 181
5:28 The God of Second Chances 184
5:28–34 You Are the Way 165
5:36 God Is Love 233
5:36 Look to Christ 226
6:13 The God of Second Chances 184
6:45–52 You Are Good to Me 134
6:47–49 I Am for You 160
6:50 God Is Love 233
6:56 Come and See 39
6:56 I Am for You 160
6:56 I Have Been Anointed 276
6:56 Make Me Holy 277
6:56 Stop By, Lord 181
6:56 The God of Second Chances 184
6:56 You Are the Way 165
7:16 Come and Follow Me / Ven y Sígueme 163
7:29 The God of Second Chances 184
8:18 Let There Be Light 57
8:22–25 Open My Eyes 174
8:23–25 Here I Am to Worship 143
8:23–25 Let the River Flow 45
8:34 Come and Follow Me / Ven y Sígueme 163
8:34 Come and Gather 34
8:34 Holiness Is Faithfulness 154
8:34 My Savior, Your Son 229
8:34 Strength for the Journey 187
8:34 The Summons / El Llamado 149
8:34 You Will Know 224
8:34–36 Deny Yourself 171
8:35 Lead Me Home 197
9:24 Thanks and Praise 103
9:25–26 The God of Second Chances 184
9:35 Fresh as the Morning 90
9:35 Open My Eyes 174
10:5 Gather Your People 144
10:21 Come and Gather 34
10:21 Holiness Is Faithfulness 154
10:21 The Summons / El Llamado 149
10:21 You Will Know 224
10:28 We Will Go, Lord 222
10:29 Deny Yourself 171
10:31 Fresh as the Morning 90
10:31 Open My Eyes 174
10:38 Come and Follow Me / Ven y Sígueme 163
10:45 Bring Us Home 25
10:45 How Beautiful 166
10:46–52 Be Forgiven 20
10:51–52 Let the River Flow 45
10:51–52 Look to Christ 226
12:27 To Follow You 228
12:29–33 Get It Together 152
13:10 Go Out to the World 230
13:35 Hallelujah, Hallelu! 2
14:9 Go Out to the World 230
14:32–41 You Are Strong, You Are Holy 238
15:21 Holiness Is Faithfulness 154
15:21 Strength for the Journey 187
15:22 How Beautiful 166
15:22–47 My Savior, My Friend 36
15:27 Holiness Is Faithfulness 154
15:34 My Savior, My Friend 36
16:1–8 Come and See 39
16:1–8 O Sons and Daughters 40
16:3 Shine on Us 140
16:3–4 Look to Christ 226
16:6 He Is Not Here 43
16:14 Gather Your People 144
16:15 Come and See 39
16:15 Cry the Gospel 100
16:15 Go Out to the World 230
16:17 Open My Eyes 174

LUKE
1:9 You Are Strong, You Are Holy 238
1:23 Awake to the Day 4
1:26–38 I Am for You 160
1:28–30 Among All 206
1:28–33 Ave Maria 203
1:28–33 Ave Maria 204
1:30 God Is Love 233
1:30 Hallelujah, Hallelu! 2
1:30 Look to Christ 226
1:38 Among All 206
1:38 Strength for the Journey 187
1:46–58 Canticle of the Turning 95
1:52 Fresh as the Morning 90
1:55 Trading My Sorrows 169
1:78–79 O Come, O Come, Emmanuel 10
1:79 Child of Mercy 16
1:79 Guide My Feet 239
1:79 Hold Us, Jesus 175
1:79 How Can We Be Silent 221
1:79 Way, Truth, and Life 193
2: Night of Silence / Noche de Silencio
2:6–20 Silent Night / Noche de Paz 14
2:11 Child of Mercy 16
2:14 Glory to God Most High 93
2:14 Halle, Halle, Halle 106
3:4 Awake to the Day 4
3:4 Hallelujah, Hallelu! 2
3:4–5 Prepare! Prepare! 3
3:8 Sign Me Up 200
3:16 Hallelujah, Hallelu! 2
4:18 Come and See 39
4:18 Go Out to the World 230
4:18 Look to Christ 226
4:18 We Give You Thanks 268
4:18 With This Bread 267
4:41 The God of Second Chances 184
5:12–13 Be Forgiven 20
5:27 The Summons / El Llamado 149
5:27–32 Make a Joyful Noise 104
6:19 I Am for You 160
6:19 Stop By, Lord 181
6:23 Deny Yourself 171
6:23 With This Bread 267
6:27 Unless a Grain 274
6:32–36 God Is Love 233
7:12–15 Be Forgiven 20
7:15 Let the River Flow 45
7:21 Look to Christ 226
7:22 Go Out to the World 230
7:22 Rise Up in Splendor 17

8:8 Come and Follow Me / Ven y Sígueme 163
8:24 How Can I Keep From Singing? 116
8:24 River of Life 189
8:24 The God of Second Chances 184
8:26–39 Come and See 39
8:33 The God of Second Chances 184
8:36 Come and See 39
8:36 I Have Been Anointed 276
8:36 Make Me Holy 277
8:36 The God of Second Chances 184
8:36 You Are the Way 165
8:46 Stop By, Lord 181
8:50 Come and See 39
8:50 I Have Been Anointed 276
8:50 Make Me Holy 277
8:50 The God of Second Chances 184
8:50 You Are the Way 165
9:23 Come and Follow Me / Ven y Sígueme 163
9:23 Come and Gather 34
9:23 Holiness Is Faithfulness 154
9:23 My Savior, Your Son 229
9:23 You Will Know 224
9:23–25 Deny Yourself 171
9:23, 59 The Summons / El Llamado 149
9:24 Lead Me Home 197
9:24 Strength for the Journey 187
9:42 The God of Second Chances 184
9:57 We Will Go, Lord 222
9:59–62 Come and Follow Me / Ven y Sígueme 163
9:61 We Will Go, Lord 222
10:21 God of Wonders 111
10:27 Get It Together 152
10:29–37 How Can We Be Silent 221
11:2–4 Lord's Prayer 182
11:3 Breathe 120
11:9 Come and Follow Me / Ven y Sígueme 163
11:9 What You Have Done for Me 210
11:14 The God of Second Chances 184
11:19 You Are the Way 165
11:33 Get It Together 152
11:33 Go Light Your World 137
11:33 Go Make a Difference 150
11:33 Let There Be Light 57
11:33 With One Voice 155
11:34 Go Light Your World 137
12:16–21 Give the Lord Your Heart 159
12:29–34 Give the Lord Your Heart 159
12:32 God Is Love 233
12:32 Look to Christ 226
12:35–48 Find Us Ready 5
12:37–39 Awake to the Day 4
12:40 Sign Me Up 200
12:43 Hallelujah, Hallelu! 2
13:24 Come and Follow Me / Ven y Sígueme 163
13:30 Fresh as the Morning 90
13:30 Open My Eyes 174
13:34 Bring Us Home 25
14:23 Sing a New World 219
14:27 Come and Gather 34
14:27 Holiness Is Faithfulness 154
14:27 Strength for the Journey 187
14:27 The Summons / El Llamado 149
14:27 You Will Know 224
14:33 Deny Yourself 171
14:35 Come and Follow Me / Ven y Sígueme 163
15:4–6 Make Us Worthy 180
15:8 Come and Follow Me / Ven y Sígueme 163
15:8 What You Have Done for Me 210
15:31 River of Hope 240
15:35–42 Be Forgiven 20
16:22 Let the River Flow 45
17:33 Deny Yourself 171
17:33 Lead Me Home 197
18:22 The Summons / El Llamado 149
18:29 Deny Yourself 171
19:9 Now 186
19:10 Lord, I Lift Your Name on High 96
19:43 No More Fear 126
20:36 A Place at the Table 211
20:38 To Follow You 228
21:25 Awake to the Day 4
22:17 Shine on Us 140
22:39–46 You Are Strong, You Are Holy 238
22:42 How Can We Be Silent 221
23:26 Holiness Is Faithfulness 154
23:28 Holiness Is Faithfulness 154
23:32–46 My Savior, My Friend 36
23:33 How Beautiful 166
23:42 Jesus, Remember Me / Jesús, Recuérdame 27
24:1–10 Come and See 39
24:1–12 O Sons and Daughters 40
24:2 Look to Christ 226
24:2 Shine on Us 140
24:5 God Is Here / Está Aquí 217
24:6 He Is Not Here 43
24:13–35 Emmaus 271
24:24 Come and See 39
24:31 Here I Am to Worship 143
24:31 The God of Second Chances 184
24:36 He Is Not Here 43
24:47 Come and See 39
24:47 Go Out to the World 230
24:49 Shout to the Lord 109

JOHN
1:5 Make Us Worthy 180
1:11–12 For God So Loved the World 249
1:14 For God So Loved the World 249
1:14 Humbled 248
1:23 Hallelujah, Hallelu! 2
1:29 Glory to God Most High 93
1:42 We Are One Body 266
1:43 The Summons / El Llamado 149
2:22 God Is Here / Está Aquí 217
3:5 I Am for You 160
3:14–17 For God So Loved the World 249
3:18 Seek Truth, Make Peace, Reverence Life 213
3:21 For God So Loved the World 249
4:13–15 Christ, Be Our Light 136
4:14 Jesus, Your Spirit / Kristus, Din Ande 250
4:14–15 This Is the Day 44
4:29 Come and See 39
4:39 Be Forgiven 20
5:4 I Have Been Anointed 276
5:4 Make Me Holy 277
5:4–6 The God of Second Chances 184
5:6 I Have Been Anointed 276
5:6 Make Me Holy 277
5:6 You Are the Way 165
5:6–9 Come and See 39
5:24 Faith, Hope, and Love 232
5:24 Open My Eyes 174

Scripture Passages Related to Hymns/*cont.*

6:15 This Is the Day 44
6:16–21 You Are Good to Me 134
6:18–19 I Am for You 160
6:18–21 Journeying Prayer 223
6:20 God Is Love 233
6:20 Look to Christ 226
6:56 We Are One Body 266
7:37–39 Jesus, Your Spirit / Kristus, Din Ande 250
8:12 Here I Am to Worship 143
8:12 Live in the Light 130
8:12 This Is the Day 44
8:31 All Are Welcome 145
9: Rise Up in Splendor 17
9:5 Here I Am to Worship 143
9:5 I Am 247
9:5 This Is the Day 44
9:6 Dream a Dream 12
9:10 Easter Alleluia 38
9:38 Thanks and Praise 103
9:39–41 Let There Be Light 57
10:3 My Savior, Your Son 229
10:3 The Summons / El Llamado 149
10:7 I Am 247
10:7–18 Easter Alleluia 38
10:9–11 I Am 247
10:10 We Are One Body 266
10:14 I Am 247
10:14 We Are Climbing Jacob's Ladder 23
10:15–17 God Is Love 233
10:27 I Am 247
10:27 My Savior, Your Son 229
11:24 Unless a Grain 274
11:25–26 This Is the Day 44
11:26 Breath of Life 55
11:27 Thanks and Praise 103
11:39–41 Shine on Us 140
11:40–44 This Is the Day 44
11:44 Let the River Flow 45
12:24 Unless a Grain 274
12:25 Lead Me Home 197
12:26 Come and Follow Me / Ven y Sígueme 163
12:46 I Am 247
12:47 Lord, I Lift Your Name on High 96
13:5 Come and Follow Me / Ven y Sígueme 163
13:5 How Can We Be Silent 221
13:25 Be Still and Know 236
13:34 Sing to the Glory of God 107
14:6 Every Move I Make 168
14:6 For All Time 183
14:6 Way, Truth, and Life 193
14:6 We Are One Body 266
14:6 You Are the Way 165
14:13 I Am 247
14:16 I Am 247
14:17 River of Hope 240
14:17 The Clouds' Veil 131
14:27 Look to Christ 226
14:27 Salaam Aleikum / May Peace Be in Your Hearts 215
14:27 You Are Mine / Contigo Estoy 128
15:4–5 I Am 247
15:4–5 Spirit and Grace 273
15:5 Alleluia! Give the Glory 58
15:12 Sing to the Glory of God 107
15:13 God Is Love 233
15:13 Holiness Is Faithfulness 154
15:15 I Am 247
15:15 To Follow You 228
16:22 On That Day 198
16:36 In the Light
17:15 Lord's Prayer 182
18:1–11 You Are Strong, You Are Holy 238
19:17 How Beautiful 166
19:17–30 My Savior, My Friend 36
19:18 Holiness Is Faithfulness 154
19:25 Come and Gather 34
19:34 Gather Your People 144
19:34 My Savior, My Friend 36
20: O Sons and Daughters 40
20:1 Shine on Us 140
20:3–10 Come and See 39
20:21 Come and See 39
20:21 Go Out to the World 230
20:21 He Is Not Here 43
20:22 Veni, Creator Spiritus 51
20:22 We Are One Body 266
20:25–27 My Savior, My Friend 36
20:27 Our God Reigns 246
21:19 The Summons / El Llamado 149
21:20 Be Still and Know 236

ACTS

1:8 Come, Holy Ghost / En Nuestro Ser Mora, Creador 48
1:8 Go Out in the World 156
1:8 Spirit and Grace 273
1:8 We Are One 275
1:8 We Are One Body 266
1:8 With One Voice 155
1:11 God Is Here / Está Aquí 217
2:1–4 Living Spirit, Holy Fire 49
2:2–4 Come, Holy Spirit 52
2:2–4 Send Down the Fire 46
2:24 A Place at the Table 211
3:1–10 Rise Up in Splendor 17
4:24 Mighty King 114
7:32 To Follow You 228
7:33 You Will Know 224
8:7–8 Rise Up in Splendor 17
8:22 Rise Up in Splendor 17
8:25 Cry the Gospel 100
9:10 Psalm 40: Here I Am 70
9:31 Go Out to the World 230
10:45 Humbled 248
13:2 Purify My Heart 190
13:25 Hallelujah, Hallelu! 2
13:47 Christ, Be Our Light 136
13:47 Go Make a Difference 150
13:47 Look to Christ 226
17:24–25 God of Wonders 111
18:9–10 Here I Am 125
22:16 No More Fear 126
26:20 Christ, Be Our Light 136
26:20 Turn My Heart, O God 194
28:27 Turn My Heart, O God 194

ROMANS

1:16 Christ, Be Our Light 136
2:19 How Can We Be Silent 221
2:19 Make Us Worthy 180
3:24 How Beautiful 166
3:29 To Follow You 228
6:4 Shine on Us 140
6:4 We Are One Body 266
6:9 You Are Strong, You Are Holy 238
6:13 Shine on Us 140
6:17 Malo! Malo! Thanks Be to God 259
7:25 Malo! Malo! Thanks Be to God 259
8:2 Spirit of God 54

Scripture Passages Related to Hymns/*cont.*

8:2 Were I the Perfect Child of God 253
8:14–15 All Who Are Led by the Spirit 53
8:17 Shout to the Lord 109
8:22–23 All Who Are Led by the Spirit 53
8:26–27 All Who Are Led by the Spirit 53
8:29 All Are Welcome 145
8:31–39 Nothing Can Ever 252
8:38 Your Grace Is Enough 170
9:20–21 Easter Alleluia 38
9:24 You Are Mine / Contigo Estoy 128
10:15 How Beautiful 166
10:15 Our God Reigns 246
12:5 Gather Your People 144
12:5 Shine on Us 140
12:5 We Are One Body 266
12:20 Lord, Hear My Prayer / Óyenos, Señor 185
13:8 Sing to the Glory of God 107
13:9 Get It Together 152
13:11 Awake to the Day 4
13:11 Now 186
13:13 Live in the Light 130
14:11 Come, Now Is the Time to Worship 141
14:11 Rise Up in Splendor 17
15:5 How Can We Be Silent 221
15:11 Let Us Worship the Lord 98
15:12 Sing a New World 219

1 CORINTHIANS
1:2–3 Rise Up in Splendor 17
1:9 Be Still and Know 236
1:9 Fresh as the Morning 90
3:9 To Follow You 228
3:23 Belong 255
7:23 Here I Am to Worship 143
9:14 Cry the Gospel 100
10:13 Be Still and Know 236
10:16 Shine on Us 140
10:24 Unless a Grain 274
12: Sing a New World 219
12:4–11 Come, Holy Ghost / En Nuestro Ser Mora, Creador 48
12:4–11 Living Spirit, Holy Fire 49
12:12 Gather Your People 144
12:12 Shine on Us 140
12:12 We Are One Body 266
12:20 Shine on Us 140
12:27 Gather Your People 144
13:2–8 Where True Love and Charity Are Found / Ubi Caritas 31
13:4 Love Endures 280
13:7 Love Endures 280
13:13 Faith, Hope, and Love 232
15:20 Shine on Us 140
15:55 A Place at the Table 211
15:55–56 Come and See 39
15:57 Malo! Malo! Thanks Be to God 259

2 CORINTHIANS
1:24 Lord, Hear My Prayer / Óyenos, Señor 185
2:14 Malo! Malo! Thanks Be to God 259
3:3 Spirit of God 54
3:18 Shine, Jesus, Shine 139
4:6 Shine, Jesus, Shine 139
4:7 As a Fire Is Meant for Burning / Como un Fuego Brilla y Quema 218
4:8 Trading My Sorrows 169
5:15 The Face of God 167
5:17 God Is Here / Está Aquí 217
5:17 Living Spirit, Holy Fire 49
5:17 Sing a New World 219
5:18 Dream a Dream 12
5:20–6:2 Remember You Are Dust / Del Polvo Eres Tú 18
6:2 Mercy, O God 24
6:16 Now Is the Time 148
6:18 All Who Are Led by the Spirit 53
8:9 Here I Am to Worship 143
9:8 River of Hope 240
9:12 God Is Here / Está Aquí 217
9:15 Malo! Malo! Thanks Be to God 259
12:9 Make Us Worthy 180
12:9 Take, Lord, Receive 237
12:9 Your Grace Is Enough 170
12:10 Holiness Is Faithfulness 154

GALATIANS
1:3–4 Be Still and Know 236
1:4 Journeying Prayer 223
1:15 My Savior, Your Son 229
2:2 Guide My Feet 239
3:14 How Beautiful 166
3:26–29 Sing a New World 219
4:28—5:1 Sing a New World 219
5:13 God Is Here / Está Aquí 217
5:13 To Follow You 228
5:14 Get It Together 152
5:22 Seek Truth, Make Peace, Reverence Life 213
6:14 Glory in the Cross 33

EPHESIANS
1:5 Rise Up in Splendor 17
1:19–23 Holy God, We Praise Thy Name 113
2:19–22 Sing a New World 219
3:18–19 I Will Sing a Song of Love 102
3:19 Love beyond All Telling 234
4:1–24 One Lord 191
4:4–6 We Are One 275
4:4, 18 Gather Your People 144
4:5 Come, Holy Spirit 52
4:11–16 Sing a New World 219
4:22 Look to Christ 226
4:30 Spirit of God 54
5:8 I Am 247
5:8 Make Us Worthy 180
5:8 Mercy, O God 24
5:13 To Know Darkness 56
5:14 Look to Christ 226
5:14 We Arise 91

PHILIPPIANS
1:11 Shine, Jesus, Shine 139
1:20 Be Still and Know 236
2:5–11 Humbled 248
2:6–11 At Your Name 29
2:10 We Are One Body 266
2:10–11 Creator of the Stars of Night 8
2:10–11 Here I Am to Worship 143
2:11 Come, Now Is the Time to Worship 141
2:11 Rise Up in Splendor 17
2:15 In the Light
2:22 Lord, Hear My Prayer / Óyenos, Señor 185
3:8 Halle, Halle, Halle 106
3:13 Look to Christ 226
4:7 Bring Us Home 25
4:20 Be Still and Know 236

Scripture Passages Related to Hymns/*cont.*

COLOSSIANS
1:6 Go Out to the World 230
1:14 Here I Am to Worship 143
1:14 How Beautiful 166
3:3–4 God Remembers 244
3:15 How Can I Keep From Singing? 116
3:15 Salaam Aleikum / May Peace Be in Your Hearts 215
3:15–16 Love beyond All Telling 234
3:16 Turn My Heart, O God 194
3:17 Cry the Gospel 100

1 THESSALONIANS
4:7 To Follow You 228
5:6 Awake to the Day 4
5:15 Unless a Grain 274
5:19 Spirit and Grace 273
5:24 Be Still and Know 236

1 TIMOTHY
1:12–15 To Follow You 228
1:15 Lord, I Lift Your Name on High 96
2:6 Here I Am to Worship 143
6:17 How Can I Keep From Singing? 116

2 TIMOTHY
1:9 To Follow You 228
1:9 You Are Mine / Contigo Estoy 128
4:8 On That Day 198
4:10 Journeying Prayer 223

HEBREWS
3:8 Gather Your People 144
4:7 Gather Your People 144
6:19 Cry the Gospel 100
7:19 God Is Here / Está Aquí 217
9:15 How Beautiful 166
10:7 Cry the Gospel 100
10:9 Cry the Gospel 100
10:37 Prepare! Prepare! 3
11:9 Sometimes by Step 151
11:34 Holiness Is Faithfulness 154
12:1–3 Guide My Feet 239
12:2 Jesus Christ Is Risen Today / El Señor Resucitó 42
12:11 Seek Truth, Make Peace, Reverence Life 213

JAMES
2:1–13 All Are Welcome 145
2:8 Get It Together 152
4:15 We Will Go, Lord 222
5:8 Hallelujah, Hallelu! 2
5:8 Prepare! Prepare! 3
5:15 Be Forgiven 20

1 PETER
1:3 Fresh as the Morning 90
1:14–15 God Is Here / Está Aquí 217
1:15 To Follow You 228
1:20 The Face of God 167
1:22 Sing to the Glory of God 107
2:1–10 Sing a New World 219
2:4–5 Christ, Be Our Light 136
2:4–5 What Is This Place 142
2:9 Make Us Worthy 180
2:9 We Are Marching 138
2:20–21 To Follow You 228
2:21 All Who Are Led by the Spirit 53
2:21 We Will Go, Lord 222
3:8 I Have Been Anointed 276
4:8 Sing to the Glory of God 107
4:10–11 God Is Here / Está Aquí 217
5:5 God Is Here / Está Aquí 217
5:10 To Follow You 228

1 JOHN
1:7 Live in the Light 130
1:7 Look to Christ 226
1:7 River of Life 189
1:9 Be Still and Know 236
2:10 Live in the Light 130
2:20 I Am for You 160
2:27 Come, Holy Ghost / En Nuestro Ser Mora, Creador 48
3:1 Be Still and Know 236
3:1 To Follow You 228
3:10 Were I the Perfect Child of God 253
3:16 How Beautiful 166
3:18 Cry the Gospel 100
3:20 Look to Christ 226
4:4 Belong 255
4:7 God Is Love 233
4:7 Sing to the Glory of God 107
4:10 I Will Sing a Song of Love 102
4:10–16 Where True Love and Charity Are Found / Ubi Caritas 31
4:16 Easter Alleluia 38
4:16 God Is Love 233
4:19 I Will Sing a Song of Love 102
4:20–21 God Is Love 233
5:1 Were I the Perfect Child of God 253

3 JOHN
1:8 Lord, Hear My Prayer / Óyenos, Señor 185

JUDE
1:2 Easter Alleluia 38
1:25 Shout to the Lord 109

REVELATION
1:17 Look to Christ 226
3:3 Awake to the Day 4
3:15–16 I Will Sing a Song of Love 102
3:17 Fresh as the Morning 90
4:8 God of Wonders 111
4:8 Open the Eyes of My Heart 177
4:9–11 Alleluia! Give the Glory 58
5: Holy God, We Praise Thy Name 113
7:16 Dream a Dream 12
7:17 Gather Your People 144
11:17 We Give You Thanks 268
13:8 Halle, Halle, Halle 106
14:4 We Will Go, Lord 222
15:3 Thanks and Praise 103
16:15 Awake to the Day 4
20:6 A Place at the Table 211
20:15 Sign Me Up 200
21:2 On That Day 198
21:4 On That Day 198
21:5 Let Us Worship the Lord 98
21:5 Living Spirit, Holy Fire 49
21:12 On That Day 198
21:23 On That Day 198
21:26 On That Day 198
22:7 Prepare! Prepare! 3
22:20 Come, Lord Jesus 123

SEASONS AND FEASTS

ADVENT

58 Alleluia! Give the Glory
4 Awake to the Day
136 Christ, Be Our Light
123 Come, Lord Jesus
7 Creator Alme Siderum
8 Creator of the Stars of Night
5 Find Us Ready
2 Hallelujah, Hallelu!
208 Holy Is Your Name
10 O Come, O Come, Emmanuel
195 On That Holy Mountain
3 Prepare! Prepare!
65 Psalm 25: I Lift My Soul to You
67 Psalm 25: To You, O God, I Lift Up My Soul
66 Psalm 25: To You, O Lord, I Lift My Soul
75 Psalm 85: Let Us See Your Kindness
74 Psalm 85: Lord, Show Us Your Mercy and Love
82 Psalm 122: Let Us Go Rejoicing
200 Sign Me Up
(also Topical Index: Second Coming, Messianic)

CHRISTMAS SEASON

16 Child of Mercy
12 Dream a Dream
249 For God So Loved the World
59 Gospel Acclamation
143 Here I Am to Worship
15 Night of Silence / Noche de Silencio
77 Psalm 96: Proclaim God's Marvelous Deeds
76 Psalm 96: Sing a Song to the Lord
14 Silent Night / Noche de Paz

MARY, MOTHER OF GOD

206 Among All
203 Ave Maria
204 Ave Maria
209 Litany of Mary / Letanía de la Santísima Virgen María
(also Blessed Virgin Mary)

EPIPHANY

73 Psalm 72: Every Nation on Earth
17 Rise Up in Splendor

ASH WEDNESDAY

24 Mercy, O God
73 Psalm 72: Every Nation on Earth
18 Remember You Are Dust / Del Polvo Eres Tú

LENT

124 Amazing Grace
20 Be Forgiven
132 Be Still
133 Be with Me
118 Be with Me, Lord
255 Belong
105 Blessed Be Your Name
25 Bring Us Home
141 Come, Now Is the Time to Worship
171 Deny Yourself
183 For All Time
249 For God So Loved the World
21 Give Me Jesus
278 God Is Forgiveness / Bóg Jest Miłością
143 Here I Am to Worship
175 Hold Us, Jesus
122 In Every Age
27 Jesus, Remember Me / Jesús, Recuérdame
251 Jesus, You Brought Me All the Way
22 Lenten Gospel Acclamation
277 Make Me Holy
24 Mercy, O God
245 O God, Why Are You Silent?
174 Open My Eyes
177 Open the Eyes of My Heart
246 Our God Reigns
64 Psalm 19: Lord, You Have the Words
65 Psalm 25: I Lift My Soul to You
67 Psalm 25: To You, O God, I Lift Up My Soul
66 Psalm 25: To You, O Lord, I Lift My Soul
79 Psalm 103: Bless the Lord, My Soul
84 Psalm 130: Out of the Depths
83 Psalm 130: With the Lord There Is Mercy
135 Quietly, Peacefully
18 Remember You Are Dust / Del Polvo Eres Tú
17 Rise Up in Splendor
189 River of Life
188 Shelter Your Name
254 So Longs My Soul
187 Strength for the Journey
237 Take, Lord, Receive
235 The Lord Is My Light
194 Turn My Heart, O God
261 We Are Called / Dios Nos Llama
23 We Are Climbing Jacob's Ladder
253 Were I the Perfect Child of God
115 With You by My Side
(also Penance; Topical Index: Cross, Mercy, Social Concern)

PALM SUNDAY

29 At Your Name
34 Come and Gather
33 Glory in the Cross
248 Humbled
35 I Give My Spirit
27 Jesus, Remember Me / Jesús, Recuérdame
36 My Savior, My Friend
252 Nothing Can Ever
246 Our God Reigns
(also Christ the King)

HOLY THURSDAY

278 God Is Forgiveness / Bóg Jest Miłością
270 I Will Take the Cup of Salvation
252 Nothing Can Ever
246 Our God Reigns
31 Where True Love and Charity Are Found / Ubi Caritas
(also Good Friday, Eucharist)

GOOD FRIDAY

29 At Your Name
34 Come and Gather
33 Glory in the Cross
154 Holiness Is Faithfulness
248 Humbled
35 I Give My Spirit
27 Jesus, Remember Me / Jesús, Recuérdame
36 My Savior, My Friend
252 Nothing Can Ever
246 Our God Reigns

EASTER VIGIL

88 Exodus 15: Let Us Sing to the Lord
108 Forever
178 Litany of the Saints
40 O Sons and Daughters
64 Psalm 19: Lord, You Have the Words
68 Psalm 33: The Earth Is Full of the Goodness
(also Easter Season)

EASTER SEASON

60 Alleluia: Song of the Spirit
58 Alleluia! Give the Glory
39 Come and See
38 Easter Alleluia
271 Emmaus
108 Forever
220 God Is Here / Está Aquí
59 Gospel Acclamation
106 Halle, Halle, Halle
43 He Is Not Here
247 I Am
42 Jesus Christ Is Risen Today / El Señor Resucitó
226 Look to Christ
40 O Sons and Daughters
246 Our God Reigns
80 Psalm 118: This Is the Day
140 Shine on Us
44 This Is the Day
127 You Are My King (Amazing Love)

ASCENSION

101 All Generations Will Praise Your Name
39 Come and See
100 Cry the Gospel
156 Go Out in the World
220 God Is Here / Está Aquí
59 Gospel Acclamation
247 I Am
160 I Am for You
96 Lord, I Lift Your Name on High
71 Psalm 47: God Mounts His Throne
17 Rise Up in Splendor
155 With One Voice
(also Easter Season)

PENTECOST

53 All Who Are Led by the Spirit
60 Alleluia: Song of the Spirit
58 Alleluia! Give the Glory
55 Breath of Life

Liturgical Index/*continued*

48 Come, Holy Ghost / En Nuestro Ser Mora, Creador
52 Come, Holy Spirit
137 Go Light Your World
59 Gospel Acclamation
45 Let the River Flow
49 Living Spirit, Holy Fire
148 Now Is the Time
46 Send Down the Fire
273 Spirit and Grace
54 Spirit of God
51 Veni, Creator Spiritus
266 We Are One Body

SOLEMNITITES AND FEASTS

TRINITY SUNDAY

113 Holy God, We Praise Thy Name
57 Let There Be Light
129 May the Peace of Christ Be with You / Ki Ri Su To No
17 Rise Up in Splendor
56 To Know Darkness

CHRIST THE KING

116 How Can I Keep From Singing?
114 Mighty King
71 Psalm 47: God Mounts His Throne
73 Psalm 72: Every Nation on Earth
77 Psalm 96: Proclaim God's Marvelous Deeds
76 Psalm 96: Sing a Song to the Lord
139 Shine, Jesus, Shine
109 Shout to the Lord
31 Where True Love and Charity Are Found / Ubi Caritas
127 You Are My King (Amazing Love)

TRIUMPH OF THE CROSS

33 Glory in the Cross
80 Psalm 118: This Is the Day

ALL SAINTS

201 Yours Is the Kingdom
131 The Clouds' Veil

DEDICATION OF A CHURCH

145 All Are Welcome
64 Psalm 19: Lord, You Have the Words
80 Psalm 118: This Is the Day
82 Psalm 122: Let Us Go Rejoicing
142 What Is This Place

BLESSED VIRGIN MARY

206 Among All
203 Ave Maria
204 Ave Maria
95 Canticle of the Turning
59 Gospel Acclamation
208 Holy Is Your Name
160 I Am for You
209 Litany of Mary / Letanía de la Santísima Virgen María
70 Psalm 40: Here I Am

RITES OF THE CHURCH

BAPTISM / CHRISTIAN INITIATION

124 Amazing Grace
38 Easter Alleluia
102 I Will Sing a Song of Love
178 Litany of the Saints
64 Psalm 19: Lord, You Have the Words
69 Psalm 34: I Will Bless the Lord at All Times
70 Psalm 40: Here I Am
72 Psalm 63: My Soul Is Thirsting
79 Psalm 103: Bless the Lord, My Soul
81 Psalm 121: Our Help Is from the Lord
235 The Lord Is My Light
261 We Are Called / Dios Nos Llama
134 You Are Good to Me

EUCHARIST

269 A Hymn for First Communion
211 A Place at the Table
145 All Are Welcome
124 Amazing Grace
225 Build Us a Table
16 Child of Mercy
265 Come, Taste and See
38 Easter Alleluia
271 Emmaus
144 Gather Your People
263 Gusten y Vean / Taste and See
166 How Beautiful
270 I Will Take the Cup of Salvation
259 Malo! Malo! Thanks Be to God
40 O Sons and Daughters
264 O Taste and See
70 Psalm 40: Here I Am
72 Psalm 63: My Soul Is Thirsting
140 Shine on Us
273 Spirit and Grace
235 The Lord Is My Light
274 Unless a Grain
138 We Are Marching
275 We Are One
266 We Are One Body
268 We Give You Thanks
110 We Praise You
142 What Is This Place
31 Where True Love and Charity Are Found / Ubi Caritas
212 Will the Circle Be Unbroken?
267 With This Bread
(also Topical Index: Praise, Thanksgiving)

FUNERAL

124 Amazing Grace
255 Belong
38 Easter Alleluia
199 I Am Sure I Shall See
283 I Know That My Redeemer Lives
281 I Know That My Redeemer Lives
42 Jesus Christ Is Risen Today / El Señor Resucitó
27 Jesus, Remember Me / Jesús, Recuérdame
252 Nothing Can Ever
65 Psalm 25: I Lift My Soul to You
67 Psalm 25: To You, O God, I Lift Up My Soul
66 Psalm 25: To You, O Lord, I Lift My Soul
72 Psalm 63: My Soul Is Thirsting
79 Psalm 103: Bless the Lord, My Soul
82 Psalm 122: Let Us Go Rejoicing
84 Psalm 130: Out of the Depths
83 Psalm 130: With the Lord There Is Mercy
235 The Lord Is My Light
176 The Lord Is My Light and My Salvation
128 You Are Mine / Contigo Estoy
(also Easter; Topical Index: Death, Eternal Life)

MARRIAGE

265 Come, Taste and See
94 I Will Lift Up Your Name
280 Love Endures
119 May the Road Rise to Meet You
264 O Taste and See
68 Psalm 33: The Earth Is Full of the Goodness
69 Psalm 34: I Will Bless the Lord at All Times
81 Psalm 121: Our Help Is from the Lord
274 Unless a Grain
275 We Are One
31 Where True Love and Charity Are Found / Ubi Caritas
(also Topical Index: Love of God for Us, Love for Others, Praise, Thanksgiving, Vocation)

PASTORAL CARE OF THE SICK

124 Amazing Grace
132 Be Still
133 Be with Me
118 Be with Me, Lord
55 Breath of Life
120 Breathe
123 Come, Lord Jesus
141 Come, Now Is the Time to Worship
265 Come, Taste and See
244 God Remembers
263 Gusten y Vean / Taste and See
125 Here I Am
175 Hold Us, Jesus
243 I Cry before You
276 I Have Been Anointed
251 Jesus, You Brought Me All the Way
45 Let the River Flow
130 Live in the Light
185 Lord, Hear My Prayer / Óyenos, Señor
129 May the Peace of Christ Be with You / Ki Ri Su To No
126 No More Fear
245 O God, Why Are You Silent?
264 O Taste and See
65 Psalm 25: I Lift My Soul to You
67 Psalm 25: To You, O God, I Lift Up My Soul
66 Psalm 25: To You, O Lord, I Lift My Soul

68 Psalm 33: The Earth Is Full of the Goodness
69 Psalm 34: I Will Bless the Lord at All Times
72 Psalm 63: My Soul Is Thirsting
79 Psalm 103: Bless the Lord, My Soul
81 Psalm 121: Our Help Is from the Lord
189 River of Life
54 Spirit of God
181 Stop By, Lord
131 The Clouds' Veil
184 The God of Second Chances
235 The Lord Is My Light
169 Trading My Sorrows
115 With You by My Side
134 You Are Good to Me
128 You Are Mine / Contigo Estoy
(also Topical Index: Healing, Comfort)

PENANCE

124 Amazing Grace
20 Be Forgiven
120 Breathe
25 Bring Us Home
141 Come, Now Is the Time to Worship
183 For All Time
278 God Is Forgiveness / Bóg Jest Miłością
125 Here I Am
185 Lord, Hear My Prayer / Óyenos, Señor
277 Make Me Holy
180 Make Us Worthy
24 Mercy, O God
252 Nothing Can Ever
65 Psalm 25: I Lift My Soul to You
67 Psalm 25: To You, O God, I Lift Up My Soul
66 Psalm 25: To You, O Lord, I Lift My Soul
79 Psalm 103: Bless the Lord, My Soul
84 Psalm 130: Out of the Depths
83 Psalm 130: With the Lord There Is Mercy
87 Psalm 141: Like Burning Incense, O Lord
189 River of Life
188 Shelter Your Name
103 Thanks and Praise
167 The Face of God
184 The God of Second Chances
235 The Lord Is My Light
169 Trading My Sorrows
194 Turn My Heart, O God
23 We Are Climbing Jacob's Ladder
253 Were I the Perfect Child of God
127 You Are My King (Amazing Love)
170 Your Grace Is Enough
(also Topical Index: Love of God for Us, Mercy, Praise, Trust)

BENEDICTION

113 Holy God, We Praise Thy Name

ORDINATION

163 Come and Follow Me / Ven y Sígueme
156 Go Out in the World
166 How Beautiful
178 Litany of the Saints
104 Make a Joyful Noise
77 Psalm 96: Proclaim God's Marvelous Deeds
76 Psalm 96: Sing a Song to the Lord
190 Purify My Heart
162 Take, O Take Me As I Am
51 Veni, Creator Spiritus

287 Topical Index

ALIENATION

115 Be with Me
95 Build Us a Table
90 Canticle of the Turning
243 Fresh as the Morning
245 I Cry before You
35 I Give My Spirit
133 I Will Sing a Song of Love
135 O God, Why Are You Silent?
194 Quietly, Peacefully
102 Turn My Heart, O God
225 With You by My Side

ANGELS

113 Holy God, We Praise Thy Name
209 Litany of Mary / Letanía de la Santísima Virgen María
40 O Sons and Daughters
264 O Taste and See
85 Psalm 138: Lord, I Thank You
155 With One Voice

ART

219 Sing a New World

BEAUTY

255 Belong
196 Better Is One Day
143 Here I Am to Worship
166 How Beautiful
221 How Can We Be Silent

BLESSING

105 Blessed Be Your Name
106 Halle, Halle, Halle
102 I Will Sing a Song of Love
72 Psalm 63: My Soul Is Thirsting
79 Psalm 103: Bless the Lord, My Soul
91 We Arise
110 We Praise You
253 Were I the Perfect Child of God

BROTHERHOOD & SISTERHOOD

225 Build Us a Table
144 Gather Your People
137 Go Light Your World
98 Let Us Worship the Lord
261 We Are Called / Dios Nos Llama
31 Where True Love and Charity Are Found / Ubi Caritas

CAPTIVITY

53 All Who Are Led by the Spirit
95 Canticle of the Turning
183 For All Time
90 Fresh as the Morning
126 No More Fear
10 O Come, O Come, Emmanuel
73 Psalm 72: Every Nation on Earth
46 Send Down the Fire

CELEBRATION

219 Sing a New World
169 Trading My Sorrows

CHALLENGE OF THE GOSPEL

218 As a Fire Is Meant for Burning / Como un Fuego Brilla y Quema
34 Come and Gather
39 Come and See
49 Living Spirit, Holy Fire
229 My Savior, Your Son
149 The Summons / El Llamado
210 What You Have Done for Me
201 Yours Is the Kingdom

CHRISTIAN LIFE

211 A Place at the Table
145 All Are Welcome
218 As a Fire Is Meant for Burning / Como un Fuego Brilla y Quema
34 Come and Gather
100 Cry the Gospel
171 Deny Yourself
5 Find Us Ready
152 Get It Together
230 Go Out to the World
166 How Beautiful
248 Humbled
153 I Will Choose Christ
226 Look to Christ
185 Lord, Hear My Prayer / Óyenos, Señor
104 Make a Joyful Noise
180 Make Us Worthy
191 One Lord
189 River of Life
139 Shine, Jesus, Shine
151 Sometimes by Step
167 The Face of God
149 The Summons / El Llamado
155 With One Voice
267 With This Bread
115 With You by My Side
201 Yours Is the Kingdom

CHURCH

211 A Place at the Table
145 All Are Welcome
218 As a Fire Is Meant for Burning / Como un Fuego Brilla y Quema
225 Build Us a Table
141 Come, Now Is the Time to Worship
100 Cry the Gospel
144 Gather Your People
220 God Is Here / Está Aquí
166 How Beautiful
209 Litany of Mary / Letanía de la Santísima Virgen María
40 O Sons and Daughters
140 Shine on Us
97 Shout to the North
219 Sing a New World
193 Way, Truth, and Life
266 We Are One Body
142 What Is This Place

CITY OF GOD

198 On That Day
82 Psalm 122: Let Us Go Rejoicing
261 We Are Called / Dios Nos Llama

COMFORT

132 Be Still
236 Be Still and Know
133 Be with Me
118 Be with Me, Lord
120 Breathe
34 Come and Gather
48 Come, Holy Ghost / En Nuestro Ser Mora, Creador
123 Come, Lord Jesus
111 God of Wonders
125 Here I Am
175 Hold Us, Jesus
283 I Know That My Redeemer Lives
122 In Every Age
27 Jesus, Remember Me / Jesús, Recuérdame
130 Live in the Light
180 Make Us Worthy
129 May the Peace of Christ Be with You / Ki Ri Su To No
119 May the Road Rise to Meet You
15 Night of Silence / Noche de Silencio
126 No More Fear
245 O God, Why Are You Silent?
73 Psalm 72: Every Nation on Earth
84 Psalm 130: Out of the Depths
83 Psalm 130: With the Lord There Is Mercy
86 Psalm 139: Before I Was Born
135 Quietly, Peacefully
117 Rain Down
109 Shout to the Lord
97 Shout to the North
131 The Clouds' Veil
235 The Lord Is My Light
155 With One Voice
115 With You by My Side
134 You Are Good to Me
128 You Are Mine / Contigo Estoy
127 You Are My King (Amazing Love)
238 You Are Strong, You Are Holy
201 Yours Is the Kingdom

COMMANDMENTS

64 Psalm 19: Lord, You Have the Words
66 Psalm 25: To You, O Lord, I Lift My Soul

COMMISSIONING

136 Christ, Be Our Light
150 Go Make a Difference
160 I Am for You
104 Make a Joyful Noise
149 The Summons / El Llamado
128 You Are Mine / Contigo Estoy

COMMITMENT

166 How Beautiful
153 I Will Choose Christ
122 In Every Age
70 Psalm 40: Here I Am
149 The Summons / El Llamado
115 With You by My Side

COMMUNION *(see Liturgical Index: Eucharist)*

COMMUNION OF SAINTS

102 I Will Sing a Song of Love
178 Litany of the Saints

200 Sign Me Up
268 We Give You Thanks

COMMUNITY
211 A Place at the Table
145 All Are Welcome
218 As a Fire Is Meant for Burning / Como un Fuego Brilla y Quema
225 Build Us a Table
136 Christ, Be Our Light
144 Gather Your People
214 Give Us Your Peace
220 God Is Here / Está Aquí
234 Love beyond All Telling
140 Shine on Us
138 We Are Marching
275 We Are One
266 We Are One Body
268 We Give You Thanks
142 What Is This Place

COMPASSION
101 All Generations Will Praise Your Name
20 Be Forgiven
55 Breath of Life
233 God Is Love
221 How Can We Be Silent
276 I Have Been Anointed
98 Let Us Worship the Lord
130 Live in the Light
245 O God, Why Are You Silent?
65 Psalm 25: I Lift My Soul to You
67 Psalm 25: To You, O God, I Lift Up My Soul
66 Psalm 25: To You, O Lord, I Lift My Soul
79 Psalm 103: Bless the Lord, My Soul
46 Send Down the Fire
167 The Face of God
184 The God of Second Chances
193 Way, Truth, and Life
275 We Are One
268 We Give You Thanks
267 With This Bread

COMPLACENCY
159 Give the Lord Your Heart

CONFIDENCE
132 Be Still
236 Be Still and Know
255 Belong
265 Come, Taste and See
214 Give Us Your Peace
220 God Is Here / Está Aquí
233 God Is Love
239 Guide My Feet
208 Holy Is Your Name
116 How Can I Keep From Singing?
199 I Am Sure I Shall See
281 I Know That My Redeemer Lives
122 In Every Age
27 Jesus, Remember Me / Jesús, Recuérdame
223 Journeying Prayer
119 May the Road Rise to Meet You
15 Night of Silence / Noche de Silencio
65 Psalm 25: I Lift My Soul to You
67 Psalm 25: To You, O God, I Lift Up My Soul
66 Psalm 25: To You, O Lord, I Lift My Soul
68 Psalm 33: The Earth Is Full of the Goodness
72 Psalm 63: My Soul Is Thirsting
81 Psalm 121: Our Help Is from the Lord
84 Psalm 130: Out of the Depths
83 Psalm 130: With the Lord There Is Mercy
86 Psalm 139: Before I Was Born
87 Psalm 141: Like Burning Incense, O Lord
240 River of Hope
54 Spirit of God
169 Trading My Sorrows
165 You Are the Way
170 Your Grace Is Enough

CONVERSION
124 Amazing Grace
180 Make Us Worthy
186 Now
191 One Lord
190 Purify My Heart
189 River of Life
188 Shelter Your Name
200 Sign Me Up
187 Strength for the Journey
184 The God of Second Chances
149 The Summons / El Llamado
194 Turn My Heart, O God
193 Way, Truth, and Life
261 We Are Called / Dios Nos Llama

COURAGE
206 Among All
20 Be Forgiven
100 Cry the Gospel
230 Go Out to the World
125 Here I Am
35 I Give My Spirit
27 Jesus, Remember Me / Jesús, Recuérdame
114 Mighty King
126 No More Fear
148 Now Is the Time
235 The Lord Is My Light
56 To Know Darkness
193 Way, Truth, and Life
261 We Are Called / Dios Nos Llama
115 With You by My Side

COVENANT
171 Deny Yourself
160 I Am for You
65 Psalm 25: I Lift My Soul to You
67 Psalm 25: To You, O God, I Lift Up My Soul
66 Psalm 25: To You, O Lord, I Lift My Soul
238 You Are Strong, You Are Holy

CREATION
147 Come All You People / Uyai Mose
38 Easter Alleluia
172 God Is Good
111 God of Wonders
221 How Can We Be Silent
99 How Excellent Is Thy Name
258 I Will Give Thanks
94 I Will Lift Up Your Name
102 I Will Sing a Song of Love
280 Love Endures
89 Morning Has Broken
257 O God, You Search Me
68 Psalm 33: The Earth Is Full of the Goodness
79 Psalm 103: Bless the Lord, My Soul
86 Psalm 139: Before I Was Born
109 Shout to the Lord
219 Sing a New World
216 The Peace of the Earth / La Paz de la Tierra
228 To Follow You
268 We Give You Thanks
110 We Praise You
212 Will the Circle Be Unbroken?

CROSS
145 All Are Welcome
29 At Your Name
34 Come and Gather
90 Fresh as the Morning
33 Glory in the Cross
154 Holiness Is Faithfulness
248 Humbled
153 I Will Choose Christ
42 Jesus Christ Is Risen Today / El Señor Resucitó
197 Lead Me Home
226 Look to Christ
96 Lord, I Lift Your Name on High
36 My Savior, My Friend
229 My Savior, Your Son
245 O God, Why Are You Silent?
187 Strength for the Journey
23 We Are Climbing Jacob's Ladder
224 You Will Know

DANCE
221 How Can We Be Silent
164 I Could Sing of Your Love Forever
148 Now Is the Time
65 Psalm 25: I Lift My Soul to You
67 Psalm 25: To You, O God, I Lift Up My Soul
66 Psalm 25: To You, O Lord, I Lift My Soul
138 We Are Marching
267 With This Bread
165 You Are the Way

DEATH
203 Ave Maria
204 Ave Maria
20 Be Forgiven
21 Give Me Jesus
159 Give the Lord Your Heart
244 God Remembers
154 Holiness Is Faithfulness
283 I Know That My Redeemer Lives
153 I Will Choose Christ
270 I Will Take the Cup of Salvation
122 In Every Age

Topical Index/*continued*

42 Jesus Christ Is Risen Today / El Señor Resucitó
45 Let the River Flow
119 May the Road Rise to Meet You
126 No More Fear
252 Nothing Can Ever
148 Now Is the Time
257 O God, You Search Me
198 On That Day
73 Psalm 72: Every Nation on Earth
131 The Clouds' Veil
274 Unless a Grain
110 We Praise You
212 Will the Circle Be Unbroken?

DISCIPLESHIP
53 All Who Are Led by the Spirit
58 Alleluia! Give the Glory
206 Among All
20 Be Forgiven
118 Be with Me, Lord
55 Breath of Life
163 Come and Follow Me / Ven y Sígueme
39 Come and See
100 Cry the Gospel
171 Deny Yourself
38 Easter Alleluia
183 For All Time
152 Get It Together
159 Give the Lord Your Heart
150 Go Make a Difference
156 Go Out in the World
230 Go Out to the World
154 Holiness Is Faithfulness
221 How Can We Be Silent
247 I Am
160 I Am for You
158 I Send You Out
153 I Will Choose Christ
226 Look to Christ
104 Make a Joyful Noise
229 My Savior, Your Son
191 One Lord
70 Psalm 40: Here I Am
190 Purify My Heart
46 Send Down the Fire
151 Sometimes by Step
162 Take, O Take Me As I Am
167 The Face of God
149 The Summons / El Llamado
228 To Follow You
261 We Are Called / Dios Nos Llama
222 We Will Go, Lord
253 Were I the Perfect Child of God
210 What You Have Done for Me
31 Where True Love and Charity Are Found / Ubi Caritas
155 With One Voice
267 With This Bread

ECOLOGY
12 Dream a Dream

ECUMENISM
124 Amazing Grace
10 O Come, O Come, Emmanuel
31 Where True Love and Charity Are Found / Ubi Caritas

ENCOURAGEMENT
124 Amazing Grace
90 Fresh as the Morning
261 We Are Called / Dios Nos Llama

ETERNAL LIFE
58 Alleluia! Give the Glory
255 Belong
196 Better Is One Day
55 Breath of Life
39 Come and See
171 Deny Yourself
249 For God So Loved the World
199 I Am Sure I Shall See
241 In Your Presence
250 Jesus, Your Spirit / Kristus, Din Ande
197 Lead Me Home
45 Let the River Flow
40 O Sons and Daughters
198 On That Day
195 On That Holy Mountain
64 Psalm 19: Lord, You Have the Words
200 Sign Me Up
131 The Clouds' Veil
176 The Lord Is My Light and My Salvation
44 This Is the Day
266 We Are One Body
201 Yours Is the Kingdom

EVANGELIZATION
206 Among All
218 As a Fire Is Meant for Burning / Como un Fuego Brilla y Quema
152 Get It Together
156 Go Out in the World
230 Go Out to the World
220 God Is Here / Está Aquí
43 He Is Not Here
166 How Beautiful
160 I Am for You
158 I Send You Out
76 Psalm 96: Sing a Song to the Lord
261 We Are Called / Dios Nos Llama
275 We Are One
266 We Are One Body
155 With One Voice

EVENING
95 Canticle of the Turning
8 Creator of the Stars of Night
271 Emmaus
208 Holy Is Your Name
122 In Every Age
92 Let Evening Fall
130 Live in the Light
245 O God, Why Are You Silent?
79 Psalm 103: Bless the Lord, My Soul
81 Psalm 121: Our Help Is from the Lord
87 Psalm 141: Like Burning Incense, O Lord
110 We Praise You
142 What Is This Place

EXILE
25 Bring Us Home
10 O Come, O Come, Emmanuel

FAITH
145 All Are Welcome
124 Amazing Grace
34 Come and Gather
39 Come and See
48 Come, Holy Ghost / En Nuestro Ser Mora, Creador
52 Come, Holy Spirit
123 Come, Lord Jesus
100 Cry the Gospel
171 Deny Yourself
168 Every Move I Make
232 Faith, Hope, and Love
249 For God So Loved the World
152 Get It Together
230 Go Out to the World
172 God Is Good
220 God Is Here / Está Aquí
154 Holiness Is Faithfulness
166 How Beautiful
164 I Could Sing of Your Love Forever
281 I Know That My Redeemer Lives
114 Mighty King
229 My Savior, Your Son
148 Now Is the Time
40 O Sons and Daughters
191 One Lord
256 Over My Head
64 Psalm 19: Lord, You Have the Words
67 Psalm 25: To You, O God, I Lift Up My Soul
66 Psalm 25: To You, O Lord, I Lift My Soul
68 Psalm 33: The Earth Is Full of the Goodness
69 Psalm 34: I Will Bless the Lord at All Times
71 Psalm 47: God Mounts His Throne
72 Psalm 63: My Soul Is Thirsting
73 Psalm 72: Every Nation on Earth
103 Thanks and Praise
167 The Face of God
149 The Summons / El Llamado
169 Trading My Sorrows
275 We Are One
266 We Are One Body
268 We Give You Thanks
267 With This Bread
134 You Are Good to Me
165 You Are the Way
170 Your Grace Is Enough
201 Yours Is the Kingdom

FAITHFULNESS OF GOD
101 All Generations Will Praise Your Name
132 Be Still
236 Be Still and Know
108 Forever
90 Fresh as the Morning
214 Give Us Your Peace
156 Go Out in the World
220 God Is Here / Está Aquí
244 God Remembers
125 Here I Am

208 Holy Is Your Name
94 I Will Lift Up Your Name
122 In Every Age
251 Jesus, You Brought Me All the Way
250 Jesus, Your Spirit / Kristus, Din Ande
223 Journeying Prayer
98 Let Us Worship the Lord
180 Make Us Worthy
119 May the Road Rise to Meet You
252 Nothing Can Ever
257 O God, You Search Me
65 Psalm 25: I Lift My Soul to You
67 Psalm 25: To You, O God, I Lift Up My Soul
66 Psalm 25: To You, O Lord, I Lift My Soul
68 Psalm 33: The Earth Is Full of the Goodness
79 Psalm 103: Bless the Lord, My Soul
80 Psalm 118: This Is the Day
85 Psalm 138: Lord, I Thank You
86 Psalm 139: Before I Was Born
117 Rain Down
131 The Clouds' Veil
228 To Follow You
110 We Praise You
115 With You by My Side
238 You Are Strong, You Are Holy

FAMILY LIFE
269 A Hymn for First Communion
82 Psalm 122: Let Us Go Rejoicing

FEAR
53 All Who Are Led by the Spirit
124 Amazing Grace
133 Be with Me
34 Come and Gather
39 Come and See
52 Come, Holy Spirit
123 Come, Lord Jesus
214 Give Us Your Peace
278 God Is Forgiveness / Bóg Jest Miłością
233 God Is Love
43 He Is Not Here
125 Here I Am
154 Holiness Is Faithfulness
130 Live in the Light
49 Living Spirit, Holy Fire
24 Mercy, O God
126 No More Fear
252 Nothing Can Ever
264 O Taste and See
64 Psalm 19: Lord, You Have the Words
68 Psalm 33: The Earth Is Full of the Goodness
72 Psalm 63: My Soul Is Thirsting
184 The God of Second Chances
235 The Lord Is My Light
176 The Lord Is My Light and My Salvation
149 The Summons / El Llamado
44 This Is the Day
194 Turn My Heart, O God
261 We Are Called / Dios Nos Llama
253 Were I the Perfect Child of God
115 With You by My Side
128 You Are Mine / Contigo Estoy

FOOD
269 A Hymn for First Communion
211 A Place at the Table
145 All Are Welcome
120 Breathe
136 Christ, Be Our Light
244 God Remembers
263 Gusten y Vean / Taste and See
208 Holy Is Your Name
247 I Am
182 Lord's Prayer
75 Psalm 85: Let Us See Your Kindness
74 Psalm 85: Lord, Show Us Your Mercy and Love
140 Shine on Us
273 Spirit and Grace
275 We Are One
266 We Are One Body
212 Will the Circle Be Unbroken?

FORGIVENESS
211 A Place at the Table
206 Among All
20 Be Forgiven
25 Bring Us Home
278 God Is Forgiveness / Bóg Jest Miłością
125 Here I Am
158 I Send You Out
226 Look to Christ
182 Lord's Prayer
234 Love beyond All Telling
280 Love Endures
180 Make Us Worthy
24 Mercy, O God
67 Psalm 25: To You, O God, I Lift Up My Soul
66 Psalm 25: To You, O Lord, I Lift My Soul
68 Psalm 33: The Earth Is Full of the Goodness
79 Psalm 103: Bless the Lord, My Soul
84 Psalm 130: Out of the Depths
83 Psalm 130: With the Lord There Is Mercy
18 Remember You Are Dust / Del Polvo Eres Tú
188 Shelter Your Name
167 The Face of God
184 The God of Second Chances
194 Turn My Heart, O God
253 Were I the Perfect Child of God
212 Will the Circle Be Unbroken?
127 You Are My King (Amazing Love)

FREEDOM
211 A Place at the Table
53 All Who Are Led by the Spirit
255 Belong
55 Breath of Life
95 Canticle of the Turning
163 Come and Follow Me / Ven y Sígueme
265 Come, Taste and See
8 Creator of the Stars of Night
171 Deny Yourself
88 Exodus 15: Let Us Sing to the Lord
90 Fresh as the Morning
144 Gather Your People
106 Halle, Halle, Halle
154 Holiness Is Faithfulness
247 I Am
160 I Am for You
164 I Could Sing of Your Love Forever
102 I Will Sing a Song of Love
130 Live in the Light
24 Mercy, O God
114 Mighty King
126 No More Fear
70 Psalm 40: Here I Am
135 Quietly, Peacefully
240 River of Hope
139 Shine, Jesus, Shine
219 Sing a New World
107 Sing to the Glory of God
54 Spirit of God
184 The God of Second Chances
44 This Is the Day
193 Way, Truth, and Life
261 We Are Called / Dios Nos Llama
253 Were I the Perfect Child of God
212 Will the Circle Be Unbroken?
134 You Are Good to Me
128 You Are Mine / Contigo Estoy

FRIENDSHIP
225 Build Us a Table
12 Dream a Dream
239 Guide My Feet
247 I Am
65 Psalm 25: I Lift My Soul to You
67 Psalm 25: To You, O God, I Lift Up My Soul
66 Psalm 25: To You, O Lord, I Lift My Soul
72 Psalm 63: My Soul Is Thirsting
267 With This Bread

GATHERING
145 All Are Welcome
58 Alleluia! Give the Glory
25 Bring Us Home
136 Christ, Be Our Light
147 Come All You People / Uyai Mose
34 Come and Gather
48 Come, Holy Ghost / En Nuestro Ser Mora, Creador
141 Come, Now Is the Time to Worship
100 Cry the Gospel
5 Find Us Ready
144 Gather Your People
143 Here I Am to Worship
113 Holy God, We Praise Thy Name
24 Mercy, O God
148 Now Is the Time
82 Psalm 122: Let Us Go Rejoicing
91 We Arise
268 We Give You Thanks
142 What Is This Place
165 You Are the Way

Topical Index/*continued*

GENTLENESS
15 Night of Silence / Noche de Silencio

GIVING
218 As a Fire Is Meant for Burning / Como un Fuego Brilla y Quema
163 Come and Follow Me / Ven y Sígueme
183 For All Time
90 Fresh as the Morning
159 Give the Lord Your Heart
166 How Beautiful
153 I Will Choose Christ
65 Psalm 25: I Lift My Soul to You
79 Psalm 103: Bless the Lord, My Soul
46 Send Down the Fire
274 Unless a Grain
193 Way, Truth, and Life
268 We Give You Thanks
210 What You Have Done for Me

GOD THE FATHER (CREATOR)
269 A Hymn for First Communion
236 Be Still and Know
147 Come All You People / Uyai Mose
100 Cry the Gospel
90 Fresh as the Morning
93 Glory to God Most High
137 Go Light Your World
111 God of Wonders
106 Halle, Halle, Halle
99 How Excellent Is Thy Name
160 I Am for You
35 I Give My Spirit
276 I Have Been Anointed
57 Let There Be Light
182 Lord's Prayer
114 Mighty King
89 Morning Has Broken
229 My Savior, Your Son
257 O God, You Search Me
139 Shine, Jesus, Shine
56 To Know Darkness

GOING FORTH
206 Among All
39 Come and See
48 Come, Holy Ghost / En Nuestro Ser Mora, Creador
100 Cry the Gospel
137 Go Light Your World
150 Go Make a Difference
156 Go Out in the World
113 Holy God, We Praise Thy Name
160 I Am for You
158 I Send You Out
119 May the Road Rise to Meet You
77 Psalm 96: Proclaim God's Marvelous Deeds
76 Psalm 96: Sing a Song to the Lord
273 Spirit and Grace
138 We Are Marching
222 We Will Go, Lord
155 With One Voice

GOSPEL *(see Word of God)*

GRACE
269 A Hymn for First Communion
211 A Place at the Table
145 All Are Welcome
124 Amazing Grace
206 Among All
203 Ave Maria
204 Ave Maria
255 Belong
48 Come, Holy Ghost / En Nuestro Ser Mora, Creador
171 Deny Yourself
168 Every Move I Make
249 For God So Loved the World
172 God Is Good
45 Let the River Flow
57 Let There Be Light
98 Let Us Worship the Lord
226 Look to Christ
234 Love beyond All Telling
180 Make Us Worthy
245 O God, Why Are You Silent?
246 Our God Reigns
135 Quietly, Peacefully
117 Rain Down
139 Shine, Jesus, Shine
97 Shout to the North
14 Silent Night / Noche de Paz
254 So Longs My Soul
273 Spirit and Grace
237 Take, Lord, Receive
103 Thanks and Praise
44 This Is the Day
228 To Follow You
194 Turn My Heart, O God
91 We Arise
268 We Give You Thanks
238 You Are Strong, You Are Holy
170 Your Grace Is Enough

GRIEVING
232 Faith, Hope, and Love
244 God Remembers
245 O God, Why Are You Silent?
194 Turn My Heart, O God

GROWTH
211 A Place at the Table
218 As a Fire Is Meant for Burning / Como un Fuego Brilla y Quema
220 God Is Here / Está Aquí
49 Living Spirit, Holy Fire
216 The Peace of the Earth / La Paz de la Tierra
149 The Summons / El Llamado

GUIDANCE
206 Among All
132 Be Still
118 Be with Me, Lord
120 Breathe
100 Cry the Gospel
168 Every Move I Make
88 Exodus 15: Let Us Sing to the Lord
183 For All Time
152 Get It Together
239 Guide My Feet
250 Jesus, Your Spirit / Kristus, Din Ande
223 Journeying Prayer
98 Let Us Worship the Lord
130 Live in the Light
180 Make Us Worthy
119 May the Road Rise to Meet You
245 O God, Why Are You Silent?
174 Open My Eyes
65 Psalm 25: I Lift My Soul to You
67 Psalm 25: To You, O God, I Lift Up My Soul
66 Psalm 25: To You, O Lord, I Lift My Soul
73 Psalm 72: Every Nation on Earth
81 Psalm 121: Our Help Is from the Lord
86 Psalm 139: Before I Was Born
87 Psalm 141: Like Burning Incense, O Lord
135 Quietly, Peacefully
140 Shine on Us
151 Sometimes by Step
187 Strength for the Journey
103 Thanks and Praise
167 The Face of God
228 To Follow You
193 Way, Truth, and Life
23 We Are Climbing Jacob's Ladder
134 You Are Good to Me
238 You Are Strong, You Are Holy
165 You Are the Way

HARVEST
12 Dream a Dream

HEALING
145 All Are Welcome
20 Be Forgiven
132 Be Still
118 Be with Me, Lord
55 Breath of Life
120 Breathe
34 Come and Gather
123 Come, Lord Jesus
33 Glory in the Cross
220 God Is Here / Está Aquí
125 Here I Am
175 Hold Us, Jesus
221 How Can We Be Silent
160 I Am for You
164 I Could Sing of Your Love Forever
45 Let the River Flow
185 Lord, Hear My Prayer / Óyenos, Señor
280 Love Endures
180 Make Us Worthy
119 May the Road Rise to Meet You
126 No More Fear
245 O God, Why Are You Silent?
195 On That Holy Mountain
117 Rain Down
17 Rise Up in Splendor
189 River of Life
46 Send Down the Fire
97 Shout to the North
181 Stop By, Lord
184 The God of Second Chances
169 Trading My Sorrows
194 Turn My Heart, O God
268 We Give You Thanks

110 We Praise You
115 With You by My Side
128 You Are Mine / Contigo Estoy
127 You Are My King (Amazing Love)

HEAVEN
255 Belong
196 Better Is One Day
171 Deny Yourself
88 Exodus 15: Let Us Sing to the Lord
111 God of Wonders
113 Holy God, We Praise Thy Name
283 I Know That My Redeemer Lives
102 I Will Sing a Song of Love
197 Lead Me Home
209 Litany of Mary / Letanía de la Santísima Virgen María
40 O Sons and Daughters
182 Lord's Prayer
104 Make a Joyful Noise
75 Psalm 85: Let Us See Your Kindness
74 Psalm 85: Lord, Show Us Your Mercy and Love
128 You Are Mine / Contigo Estoy

HOLINESS
206 Among All
204 Ave Maria
203 Ave Maria
236 Be Still and Know
100 Cry the Gospel
220 God Is Here / Está Aquí
111 God of Wonders
154 Holiness Is Faithfulness
178 Litany of the Saints
234 Love beyond All Telling
104 Make a Joyful Noise
277 Make Me Holy
177 Open the Eyes of My Heart
64 Psalm 19: Lord, You Have the Words
194 Turn My Heart, O God
238 You Are Strong, You Are Holy
224 You Will Know

HOLY NAME
29 At Your Name
105 Blessed Be Your Name
95 Canticle of the Turning
265 Come, Taste and See
8 Creator of the Stars of Night
88 Exodus 15: Let Us Sing to the Lord
113 Holy God, We Praise Thy Name
208 Holy Is Your Name
99 How Excellent Is Thy Name
248 Humbled
94 I Will Lift Up Your Name
270 I Will Take the Cup of Salvation
250 Jesus, Your Spirit / Kristus, Din Ande
96 Lord, I Lift Your Name on High
182 Lord's Prayer
264 O Taste and See
68 Psalm 33: The Earth Is Full of the Goodness
73 Psalm 72: Every Nation on Earth
77 Psalm 96: Proclaim God's Marvelous Deeds
76 Psalm 96: Sing a Song to the Lord
79 Psalm 103: Bless the Lord, My Soul
109 Shout to the Lord
97 Shout to the North
103 Thanks and Praise

HOLY SPIRIT
53 All Who Are Led by the Spirit
55 Breath of Life
48 Come, Holy Ghost / En Nuestro Ser Mora, Creador
52 Come, Holy Spirit
100 Cry the Gospel
93 Glory to God Most High
137 Go Light Your World
106 Halle, Halle, Halle
160 I Am for You
45 Let the River Flow
57 Let There Be Light
49 Living Spirit, Holy Fire
129 May the Peace of Christ Be with You / Ki Ri Su To No
148 Now Is the Time
191 One Lord
46 Send Down the Fire
139 Shine, Jesus, Shine
273 Spirit and Grace
54 Spirit of God
56 To Know Darkness
51 Veni, Creator Spiritus

HOMECOMING
124 Amazing Grace
25 Bring Us Home
283 I Know That My Redeemer Lives
197 Lead Me Home
180 Make Us Worthy
119 May the Road Rise to Meet You
245 O God, Why Are You Silent?
135 Quietly, Peacefully
228 To Follow You
194 Turn My Heart, O God
134 You Are Good to Me
128 You Are Mine / Contigo Estoy

HOMELESS
136 Christ, Be Our Light
140 Shine on Us
210 What You Have Done for Me

HOPE
101 All Generations Will Praise Your Name
206 Among All
255 Belong
163 Come and Follow Me / Ven y Sígueme
52 Come, Holy Spirit
123 Come, Lord Jesus
232 Faith, Hope, and Love
5 Find Us Ready
90 Fresh as the Morning
144 Gather Your People
230 Go Out to the World
220 God Is Here / Está Aquí
143 Here I Am to Worship
175 Hold Us, Jesus
208 Holy Is Your Name
116 How Can I Keep From Singing?
199 I Am Sure I Shall See
35 I Give My Spirit
281 I Know That My Redeemer Lives
122 In Every Age
27 Jesus, Remember Me / Jesús, Recuérdame
185 Lord, Hear My Prayer / Óyenos, Señor
234 Love beyond All Telling
280 Love Endures
180 Make Us Worthy
24 Mercy, O God
15 Night of Silence / Noche de Silencio
148 Now Is the Time
245 O God, Why Are You Silent?
191 One Lord
65 Psalm 25: I Lift My Soul to You
67 Psalm 25: To You, O God, I Lift Up My Soul
66 Psalm 25: To You, O Lord, I Lift My Soul
68 Psalm 33: The Earth Is Full of the Goodness
69 Psalm 34: I Will Bless the Lord at All Times
70 Psalm 40: Here I Am
72 Psalm 63: My Soul Is Thirsting
77 Psalm 96: Proclaim God's Marvelous Deeds
76 Psalm 96: Sing a Song to the Lord
81 Psalm 121: Our Help Is from the Lord
84 Psalm 130: Out of the Depths
83 Psalm 130: With the Lord There Is Mercy
86 Psalm 139: Before I Was Born
87 Psalm 141: Like Burning Incense, O Lord
135 Quietly, Peacefully
117 Rain Down
140 Shine on Us
219 Sing a New World
254 So Longs My Soul
44 This Is the Day
194 Turn My Heart, O God
261 We Are Called / Dios Nos Llama
91 We Arise
268 We Give You Thanks
253 Were I the Perfect Child of God
128 You Are Mine / Contigo Estoy

HORROR OF WAR
185 Lord, Hear My Prayer / Óyenos, Señor
186 Now
212 Will the Circle Be Unbroken?

HUMILITY
218 As a Fire Is Meant for Burning / Como un Fuego Brilla y Quema
29 At Your Name
141 Come, Now Is the Time to Worship
230 Go Out to the World
208 Holy Is Your Name
248 Humbled
104 Make a Joyful Noise

Topical Index/*continued*

65 Psalm 25: I Lift My Soul to You
67 Psalm 25: To You, O God, I Lift Up My Soul
66 Psalm 25: To You, O Lord, I Lift My Soul
188 Shelter Your Name
187 Strength for the Journey
162 Take, O Take Me As I Am
261 We Are Called / Dios Nos Llama
201 Yours Is the Kingdom

HUNGER
101 All Generations Will Praise Your Name
95 Canticle of the Turning
136 Christ, Be Our Light
12 Dream a Dream
90 Fresh as the Morning
244 God Remembers
263 Gusten y Vean / Taste and See
208 Holy Is Your Name
197 Lead Me Home
185 Lord, Hear My Prayer / Óyenos, Señor
186 Now
264 O Taste and See
140 Shine on Us
44 This Is the Day
275 We Are One
266 We Are One Body
201 Yours Is the Kingdom

IMMORTALITY *(see Death, Eternal Life)*

INCARNATION
29 At Your Name
203 Ave Maria
204 Ave Maria
16 Child of Mercy
249 For God So Loved the World
143 Here I Am to Worship
248 Humbled
114 Mighty King
14 Silent Night / Noche de Paz

INTERFAITH
281 I Know That My Redeemer Lives
64 Psalm 19: Lord, You Have the Words
65 Psalm 25: I Lift My Soul to You
67 Psalm 25: To You, O God, I Lift Up My Soul
66 Psalm 25: To You, O Lord, I Lift My Soul
68 Psalm 33: The Earth Is Full of the Goodness
69 Psalm 34: I Will Bless the Lord at All Times
71 Psalm 47: God Mounts His Throne
72 Psalm 63: My Soul Is Thirsting
73 Psalm 72: Every Nation on Earth
75 Psalm 85: Let Us See Your Kindness
235 The Lord Is My Light
138 We Are Marching
91 We Arise

JESUS CHRIST
269 A Hymn for First Communion
145 All Are Welcome
58 Alleluia! Give the Glory
218 As a Fire Is Meant for Burning / Como un Fuego Brilla y Quema
29 At Your Name
204 Ave Maria
225 Build Us a Table
16 Child of Mercy
34 Come and Gather
39 Come and See
123 Come, Lord Jesus
100 Cry the Gospel
38 Easter Alleluia
249 For God So Loved the World
90 Fresh as the Morning
152 Get It Together
21 Give Me Jesus
214 Give Us Your Peace
93 Glory to God Most High
137 Go Light Your World
220 God Is Here / Está Aquí
106 Halle, Halle, Halle
2 Hallelujah, Hallelu!
43 He Is Not Here
166 How Beautiful
116 How Can I Keep From Singing?
248 Humbled
247 I Am
160 I Am for You
283 I Know That My Redeemer Lives
153 I Will Choose Christ
42 Jesus Christ Is Risen Today / El Señor Resucitó
27 Jesus, Remember Me / Jesús, Recuérdame
251 Jesus, You Brought Me All the Way
250 Jesus, Your Spirit / Kristus, Din Ande
57 Let There Be Light
226 Look to Christ
129 May the Peace of Christ Be with You / Ki Ri Su To No
89 Morning Has Broken
229 My Savior, Your Son
252 Nothing Can Ever
246 Our God Reigns
256 Over My Head
17 Rise Up in Splendor
188 Shelter Your Name
139 Shine, Jesus, Shine
140 Shine on Us
109 Shout to the Lord
97 Shout to the North
273 Spirit and Grace
181 Stop By, Lord
167 The Face of God
149 The Summons / El Llamado
56 To Know Darkness
253 Were I the Perfect Child of God
127 You Are My King (Amazing Love)

JOURNEY
218 As a Fire Is Meant for Burning / Como un Fuego Brilla y Quema
25 Bring Us Home
39 Come and See
100 Cry the Gospel
271 Emmaus
33 Glory in the Cross
153 I Will Choose Christ
223 Journeying Prayer
197 Lead Me Home
24 Mercy, O God
229 My Savior, Your Son
72 Psalm 63: My Soul Is Thirsting
240 River of Hope
46 Send Down the Fire
151 Sometimes by Step
187 Strength for the Journey
167 The Face of God
184 The God of Second Chances
228 To Follow You
193 Way, Truth, and Life
138 We Are Marching
268 We Give You Thanks
267 With This Bread
115 With You by My Side

JOY
211 A Place at the Table
206 Among All
95 Canticle of the Turning
123 Come, Lord Jesus
265 Come, Taste and See
38 Easter Alleluia
232 Faith, Hope, and Love
244 God Remembers
154 Holiness Is Faithfulness
208 Holy Is Your Name
116 How Can I Keep From Singing?
164 I Could Sing of Your Love Forever
102 I Will Sing a Song of Love
122 In Every Age
241 In Your Presence
251 Jesus, You Brought Me All the Way
250 Jesus, Your Spirit / Kristus, Din Ande
197 Lead Me Home
234 Love beyond All Telling
280 Love Endures
104 Make a Joyful Noise
114 Mighty King
89 Morning Has Broken
148 Now Is the Time
264 O Taste and See
198 On That Day
64 Psalm 19: Lord, You Have the Words
68 Psalm 33: The Earth Is Full of the Goodness
69 Psalm 34: I Will Bless the Lord at All Times
71 Psalm 47: God Mounts His Throne
77 Psalm 96: Proclaim God's Marvelous Deeds
76 Psalm 96: Sing a Song to the Lord
80 Psalm 118: This Is the Day
82 Psalm 122: Let Us Go Rejoicing
135 Quietly, Peacefully
140 Shine on Us
109 Shout to the Lord
44 This Is the Day
169 Trading My Sorrows

110 We Praise You
127 You Are My King (Amazing Love)

JUDGMENT
102 I Will Sing a Song of Love
77 Psalm 96: Proclaim God's Marvelous Deeds
76 Psalm 96: Sing a Song to the Lord
210 What You Have Done for Me

JUSTICE
211 A Place at the Table
145 All Are Welcome
101 All Generations Will Praise Your Name
4 Awake to the Day
95 Canticle of the Turning
136 Christ, Be Our Light
90 Fresh as the Morning
152 Get It Together
33 Glory in the Cross
150 Go Make a Difference
230 Go Out to the World
172 God Is Good
220 God Is Here / Está Aquí
208 Holy Is Your Name
116 How Can I Keep From Singing?
35 I Give My Spirit
102 I Will Sing a Song of Love
209 Litany of Mary / Letanía de la Santísima Virgen María
40 O Sons and Daughters
180 Make Us Worthy
252 Nothing Can Ever
10 O Come, O Come, Emmanuel
195 On That Holy Mountain
3 Prepare! Prepare!
64 Psalm 19: Lord, You Have the Words
65 Psalm 25: I Lift My Soul to You
67 Psalm 25: To You, O God, I Lift Up My Soul
66 Psalm 25: To You, O Lord, I Lift My Soul
73 Psalm 72: Every Nation on Earth
75 Psalm 85: Let Us See Your Kindness
74 Psalm 85: Lord, Show Us Your Mercy and Love
77 Psalm 96: Proclaim God's Marvelous Deeds
76 Psalm 96: Sing a Song to the Lord
79 Psalm 103: Bless the Lord, My Soul
135 Quietly, Peacefully
117 Rain Down
213 Seek Truth, Make Peace, Reverence Life
46 Send Down the Fire
219 Sing a New World
193 Way, Truth, and Life
261 We Are Called / Dios Nos Llama
142 What Is This Place
212 Will the Circle Be Unbroken?
155 With One Voice
238 You Are Strong, You Are Holy
170 Your Grace Is Enough
201 Yours Is the Kingdom

KINGDOM
5 Find Us Ready
27 Jesus, Remember Me / Jesús, Recuérdame
186 Now
198 On That Day
71 Psalm 47: God Mounts His Throne
18 Remember You Are Dust / Del Polvo Eres Tú
261 We Are Called / Dios Nos Llama
268 We Give You Thanks
210 What You Have Done for Me

KINGDOM / REIGN OF GOD
145 All Are Welcome
4 Awake to the Day
255 Belong
159 Give the Lord Your Heart
113 Holy God, We Praise Thy Name
182 Lord's Prayer
246 Our God Reigns
77 Psalm 96: Proclaim God's Marvelous Deeds
76 Psalm 96: Sing a Song to the Lord
46 Send Down the Fire
140 Shine on Us
149 The Summons / El Llamado
134 You Are Good to Me
201 Yours Is the Kingdom

LABOR
211 A Place at the Table
92 Let Evening Fall

LAMB
106 Halle, Halle, Halle
246 Our God Reigns
167 The Face of God

LAMENT
118 Be with Me, Lord
123 Come, Lord Jesus
244 God Remembers
116 How Can I Keep From Singing?
243 I Cry before You
245 O God, Why Are You Silent?

LAW
64 Psalm 19: Lord, You Have the Words
135 Quietly, Peacefully

LIBERATION
53 All Who Are Led by the Spirit
25 Bring Us Home
95 Canticle of the Turning
39 Come and See
8 Creator of the Stars of Night
144 Gather Your People
106 Halle, Halle, Halle
160 I Am for You
276 I Have Been Anointed
102 I Will Sing a Song of Love
270 I Will Take the Cup of Salvation
49 Living Spirit, Holy Fire
24 Mercy, O God
10 O Come, O Come, Emmanuel
70 Psalm 40: Here I Am
54 Spirit of God
44 This Is the Day

LIFE
39 Come and See
48 Come, Holy Ghost / En Nuestro Ser Mora, Creador
12 Dream a Dream
159 Give the Lord Your Heart
244 God Remembers
221 How Can We Be Silent
247 I Am
153 I Will Choose Christ
102 I Will Sing a Song of Love
226 Look to Christ
96 Lord, I Lift Your Name on High
280 Love Endures
119 May the Road Rise to Meet You
114 Mighty King
252 Nothing Can Ever
148 Now Is the Time
257 O God, You Search Me
264 O Taste and See
64 Psalm 19: Lord, You Have the Words
65 Psalm 25: I Lift My Soul to You
86 Psalm 139: Before I Was Born
135 Quietly, Peacefully
240 River of Hope
189 River of Life
213 Seek Truth, Make Peace, Reverence Life
46 Send Down the Fire
151 Sometimes by Step
273 Spirit and Grace
176 The Lord Is My Light and My Salvation
194 Turn My Heart, O God
274 Unless a Grain
275 We Are One
266 We Are One Body
268 We Give You Thanks
110 We Praise You
134 You Are Good to Me
128 You Are Mine / Contigo Estoy

LIGHT
58 Alleluia! Give the Glory
124 Amazing Grace
218 As a Fire Is Meant for Burning / Como un Fuego Brilla y Quema
255 Belong
55 Breath of Life
25 Bring Us Home
136 Christ, Be Our Light
163 Come and Follow Me / Ven y Sígueme
52 Come, Holy Spirit
8 Creator of the Stars of Night
100 Cry the Gospel
249 For God So Loved the World
90 Fresh as the Morning
144 Gather Your People
152 Get It Together
137 Go Light Your World
150 Go Make a Difference
111 God of Wonders
247 I Am
122 In Every Age

Topical Index/*continued*

57 Let There Be Light
98 Let Us Worship the Lord
130 Live in the Light
226 Look to Christ
234 Love beyond All Telling
180 Make Us Worthy
24 Mercy, O God
114 Mighty King
252 Nothing Can Ever
148 Now Is the Time
257 O God, You Search Me
198 On That Day
135 Quietly, Peacefully
46 Send Down the Fire
139 Shine, Jesus, Shine
140 Shine on Us
107 Sing to the Glory of God
273 Spirit and Grace
235 The Lord Is My Light
176 The Lord Is My Light and My Salvation
56 To Know Darkness
261 We Are Called / Dios Nos Llama
138 We Are Marching
91 We Arise
110 We Praise You
155 With One Voice
115 With You by My Side
128 You Are Mine / Contigo Estoy

LONELINESS
133 Be with Me
225 Build Us a Table
163 Come and Follow Me / Ven y Sígueme
230 Go Out to the World
154 Holiness Is Faithfulness
102 I Will Sing a Song of Love
130 Live in the Light
240 River of Hope
140 Shine on Us
44 This Is the Day
194 Turn My Heart, O God
267 With This Bread
115 With You by My Side

LOSS
90 Fresh as the Morning
244 God Remembers
130 Live in the Light
245 O God, Why Are You Silent?
194 Turn My Heart, O God
267 With This Bread

LOVE FOR GOD
101 All Generations Will Praise Your Name
38 Easter Alleluia
232 Faith, Hope, and Love
152 Get It Together
159 Give the Lord Your Heart
233 God Is Love
102 I Will Sing a Song of Love
49 Living Spirit, Holy Fire
62 Psalm 18: I Love You, Lord, My Strength
82 Psalm 122: Let Us Go Rejoicing
188 Shelter Your Name
109 Shout to the Lord
97 Shout to the North
23 We Are Climbing Jacob's Ladder
275 We Are One
253 Were I the Perfect Child of God

LOVE FOR OTHERS
145 All Are Welcome
206 Among All
218 As a Fire Is Meant for Burning / Como un Fuego Brilla y Quema
136 Christ, Be Our Light
163 Come and Follow Me / Ven y Sígueme
232 Faith, Hope, and Love
152 Get It Together
214 Give Us Your Peace
150 Go Make a Difference
230 Go Out to the World
278 God Is Forgiveness / Bóg Jest Miłością
220 God Is Here / Está Aquí
233 God Is Love
221 How Can We Be Silent
49 Living Spirit, Holy Fire
280 Love Endures
119 May the Road Rise to Meet You
186 Now
191 One Lord
174 Open My Eyes
240 River of Hope
213 Seek Truth, Make Peace, Reverence Life
46 Send Down the Fire
219 Sing a New World
107 Sing to the Glory of God
184 The God of Second Chances
228 To Follow You
194 Turn My Heart, O God
274 Unless a Grain
261 We Are Called / Dios Nos Llama
275 We Are One
268 We Give You Thanks
31 Where True Love and Charity Are Found / Ubi Caritas
212 Will the Circle Be Unbroken?
267 With This Bread

LOVE OF GOD FOR US
145 All Are Welcome
58 Alleluia! Give the Glory
20 Be Forgiven
236 Be Still and Know
55 Breath of Life
265 Come, Taste and See
171 Deny Yourself
168 Every Move I Make
88 Exodus 15: Let Us Sing to the Lord
5 Find Us Ready
249 For God So Loved the World
90 Fresh as the Morning
214 Give Us Your Peace
156 Go Out in the World
230 Go Out to the World
172 God Is Good
233 God Is Love
244 God Remembers
154 Holiness Is Faithfulness
208 Holy Is Your Name
166 How Beautiful
116 How Can I Keep From Singing?
248 Humbled
164 I Could Sing of Your Love Forever
243 I Cry before You
276 I Have Been Anointed
258 I Will Give Thanks
94 I Will Lift Up Your Name
102 I Will Sing a Song of Love
241 In Your Presence
250 Jesus, Your Spirit / Kristus, Din Ande
197 Lead Me Home
92 Let Evening Fall
98 Let Us Worship the Lord
130 Live in the Light
234 Love beyond All Telling
180 Make Us Worthy
129 May the Peace of Christ Be with You / Ki Ri Su To No
119 May the Road Rise to Meet You
24 Mercy, O God
126 No More Fear
252 Nothing Can Ever
245 O God, Why Are You Silent?
257 O God, You Search Me
198 On That Day
191 One Lord
174 Open My Eyes
177 Open the Eyes of My Heart
246 Our God Reigns
65 Psalm 25: I Lift My Soul to You
67 Psalm 25: To You, O God, I Lift Up My Soul
66 Psalm 25: To You, O Lord, I Lift My Soul
69 Psalm 34: I Will Bless the Lord at All Times
72 Psalm 63: My Soul Is Thirsting
75 Psalm 85: Let Us See Your Kindness
74 Psalm 85: Lord, Show Us Your Mercy and Love
79 Psalm 103: Bless the Lord, My Soul
85 Psalm 138: Lord, I Thank You
86 Psalm 139: Before I Was Born
135 Quietly, Peacefully
117 Rain Down
189 River of Life
46 Send Down the Fire
139 Shine, Jesus, Shine
109 Shout to the Lord
97 Shout to the North
254 So Longs My Soul
187 Strength for the Journey
237 Take, Lord, Receive
167 The Face of God
149 The Summons / El Llamado
228 To Follow You
275 We Are One
266 We Are One Body
91 We Arise
268 We Give You Thanks
110 We Praise You
253 Were I the Perfect Child of God
31 Where True Love and Charity Are Found / Ubi Caritas
212 Will the Circle Be Unbroken?
267 With This Bread
134 You Are Good to Me

127 You Are My King (Amazing Love)
238 You Are Strong, You Are Holy
224 You Will Know
170 Your Grace Is Enough

MAJESTY AND POWER
101 All Generations Will Praise Your Name
29 At Your Name
95 Canticle of the Turning
88 Exodus 15: Let Us Sing to the Lord
111 God of Wonders
258 I Will Give Thanks
42 Jesus Christ Is Risen Today / El Señor Resucitó
250 Jesus, Your Spirit / Kristus, Din Ande
182 Lord's Prayer
246 Our God Reigns
71 Psalm 47: God Mounts His Throne
76 Psalm 96: Sing a Song to the Lord
80 Psalm 118: This Is the Day
109 Shout to the Lord
155 With One Voice

MERCY
211 A Place at the Table
95 Canticle of the Turning
52 Come, Holy Spirit
265 Come, Taste and See
168 Every Move I Make
88 Exodus 15: Let Us Sing to the Lord
5 Find Us Ready
144 Gather Your People
125 Here I Am
175 Hold Us, Jesus
208 Holy Is Your Name
221 How Can We Be Silent
243 I Cry before You
258 I Will Give Thanks
197 Lead Me Home
98 Let Us Worship the Lord
130 Live in the Light
104 Make a Joyful Noise
24 Mercy, O God
65 Psalm 25: I Lift My Soul to You
67 Psalm 25: To You, O God, I Lift Up My Soul
66 Psalm 25: To You, O Lord, I Lift My Soul
68 Psalm 33: The Earth Is Full of the Goodness
73 Psalm 72: Every Nation on Earth
75 Psalm 85: Let Us See Your Kindness
74 Psalm 85: Lord, Show Us Your Mercy and Love
79 Psalm 103: Bless the Lord, My Soul
80 Psalm 118: This Is the Day
84 Psalm 130: Out of the Depths
83 Psalm 130: With the Lord There Is Mercy
117 Rain Down
18 Remember You Are Dust / Del Polvo Eres Tú
17 Rise Up in Splendor
46 Send Down the Fire
139 Shine, Jesus, Shine
103 Thanks and Praise
167 The Face of God
261 We Are Called / Dios Nos Llama
91 We Arise
267 With This Bread
238 You Are Strong, You Are Holy
170 Your Grace Is Enough
201 Yours Is the Kingdom

MESSIANIC
16 Child of Mercy
73 Psalm 72: Every Nation on Earth
76 Psalm 96: Sing a Song to the Lord

MINISTRY
132 Be Still
136 Christ, Be Our Light
183 For All Time
137 Go Light Your World
221 How Can We Be Silent
153 I Will Choose Christ
104 Make a Joyful Noise
186 Now
191 One Lord
70 Psalm 40: Here I Am
190 Purify My Heart
140 Shine on Us
228 To Follow You
261 We Are Called / Dios Nos Llama
23 We Are Climbing Jacob's Ladder
266 We Are One Body
110 We Praise You
222 We Will Go, Lord
210 What You Have Done for Me
31 Where True Love and Charity Are Found / Ubi Caritas
155 With One Voice

MISSION
101 All Generations Will Praise Your Name
218 As a Fire Is Meant for Burning / Como un Fuego Brilla y Quema
225 Build Us a Table
100 Cry the Gospel
88 Exodus 15: Let Us Sing to the Lord
33 Glory in the Cross
230 Go Out to the World
220 God Is Here / Está Aquí
43 He Is Not Here
221 How Can We Be Silent
160 I Am for You
158 I Send You Out
94 I Will Lift Up Your Name
223 Journeying Prayer
226 Look to Christ
229 My Savior, Your Son
77 Psalm 96: Proclaim God's Marvelous Deeds
76 Psalm 96: Sing a Song to the Lord
80 Psalm 118: This Is the Day
46 Send Down the Fire
103 Thanks and Praise
149 The Summons / El Llamado
228 To Follow You
261 We Are Called / Dios Nos Llama
138 We Are Marching
222 We Will Go, Lord
210 What You Have Done for Me
31 Where True Love and Charity Are Found / Ubi Caritas
155 With One Voice
128 You Are Mine / Contigo Estoy
224 You Will Know

MORNING
88 Exodus 15: Let Us Sing to the Lord
111 God of Wonders
223 Journeying Prayer
209 Litany of Mary / Letanía de la Santísima Virgen María
40 O Sons and Daughters
89 Morning Has Broken
186 Now
64 Psalm 19: Lord, You Have the Words
68 Psalm 33: The Earth Is Full of the Goodness
71 Psalm 47: God Mounts His Throne
72 Psalm 63: My Soul Is Thirsting
75 Psalm 85: Let Us See Your Kindness
74 Psalm 85: Lord, Show Us Your Mercy and Love
77 Psalm 96: Proclaim God's Marvelous Deeds
76 Psalm 96: Sing a Song to the Lord
80 Psalm 118: This Is the Day
151 Sometimes by Step
169 Trading My Sorrows
91 We Arise
110 We Praise You

MUSIC MINISTRY
101 All Generations Will Praise Your Name
108 Forever
172 God Is Good
220 God Is Here / Está Aquí
221 How Can We Be Silent
99 How Excellent Is Thy Name
164 I Could Sing of Your Love Forever
102 I Will Sing a Song of Love
104 Make a Joyful Noise
264 O Taste and See
256 Over My Head
70 Psalm 40: Here I Am
77 Psalm 96: Proclaim God's Marvelous Deeds
76 Psalm 96: Sing a Song to the Lord
107 Sing to the Glory of God
103 Thanks and Praise
155 With One Voice
267 With This Bread

MYSTERY OF GOD
12 Dream a Dream
113 Holy God, We Praise Thy Name
86 Psalm 139: Before I Was Born
31 Where True Love and Charity Are Found / Ubi Caritas

Topical Index/*continued*

NATION
269 A Hymn for First Communion
198 On That Day
68 Psalm 33: The Earth Is Full of the Goodness
215 Salaam Aleikum / May Peace Be in Your Hearts
261 We Are Called / Dios Nos Llama

NEW CREATION
52 Come, Holy Spirit
116 How Can I Keep From Singing?
160 I Am for You
283 I Know That My Redeemer Lives
45 Let the River Flow
49 Living Spirit, Holy Fire
36 My Savior, My Friend
70 Psalm 40: Here I Am
140 Shine on Us
219 Sing a New World
169 Trading My Sorrows

OBEDIENCE
206 Among All
70 Psalm 40: Here I Am

OFFERING
105 Blessed Be Your Name
270 I Will Take the Cup of Salvation
65 Psalm 25: I Lift My Soul to You
67 Psalm 25: To You, O God, I Lift Up My Soul
66 Psalm 25: To You, O Lord, I Lift My Soul
70 Psalm 40: Here I Am
87 Psalm 141: Like Burning Incense, O Lord
188 Shelter Your Name
237 Take, Lord, Receive
162 Take, O Take Me As I Am
115 With You by My Side

PASCHAL MYSTERY
20 Be Forgiven
34 Come and Gather
39 Come and See
33 Glory in the Cross
106 Halle, Halle, Halle
43 He Is Not Here
42 Jesus Christ Is Risen Today / El Señor Resucitó
140 Shine on Us

PATIENCE
95 Canticle of the Turning
122 In Every Age

PEACE
145 All Are Welcome
206 Among All
236 Be Still and Know
25 Bring Us Home
12 Dream a Dream
144 Gather Your People
152 Get It Together
214 Give Us Your Peace
150 Go Make a Difference
230 Go Out to the World
106 Halle, Halle, Halle
43 He Is Not Here
175 Hold Us, Jesus
116 How Can I Keep From Singing?
197 Lead Me Home
209 Litany of Mary / Letanía de la Santísima Virgen María
40 O Sons and Daughters
185 Lord, Hear My Prayer / Óyenos, Señor
234 Love beyond All Telling
280 Love Endures
104 Make a Joyful Noise
180 Make Us Worthy
129 May the Peace of Christ Be with You / Ki Ri Su To No
119 May the Road Rise to Meet You
229 My Savior, Your Son
148 Now Is the Time
10 O Come, O Come, Emmanuel
40 O Sons and Daughters
195 On That Holy Mountain
191 One Lord
246 Our God Reigns
3 Prepare! Prepare!
73 Psalm 72: Every Nation on Earth
75 Psalm 85: Let Us See Your Kindness
74 Psalm 85: Lord, Show Us Your Mercy and Love
82 Psalm 122: Let Us Go Rejoicing
215 Salaam Aleikum / May Peace Be in Your Hearts
213 Seek Truth, Make Peace, Reverence Life
46 Send Down the Fire
14 Silent Night / Noche de Paz
219 Sing a New World
184 The God of Second Chances
216 The Peace of the Earth / La Paz de la Tierra
193 Way, Truth, and Life
91 We Arise
268 We Give You Thanks
142 What Is This Place
212 Will the Circle Be Unbroken?
155 With One Voice
128 You Are Mine / Contigo Estoy
238 You Are Strong, You Are Holy
201 Yours Is the Kingdom

PEOPLE OF GOD
53 All Who Are Led by the Spirit
52 Come, Holy Spirit
249 For God So Loved the World
90 Fresh as the Morning
144 Gather Your People
156 Go Out in the World
220 God Is Here / Está Aquí
208 Holy Is Your Name
258 I Will Give Thanks
270 I Will Take the Cup of Salvation
178 Litany of the Saints
234 Love beyond All Telling
148 Now Is the Time
68 Psalm 33: The Earth Is Full of the Goodness
46 Send Down the Fire
167 The Face of God
142 What Is This Place
238 You Are Strong, You Are Holy
170 Your Grace Is Enough
201 Yours Is the Kingdom

PERSEVERANCE
171 Deny Yourself
90 Fresh as the Morning
137 Go Light Your World
69 Psalm 34: I Will Bless the Lord at All Times
70 Psalm 40: Here I Am
86 Psalm 139: Before I Was Born
97 Shout to the North
23 We Are Climbing Jacob's Ladder
115 With You by My Side

PETITION / PRAYER
145 All Are Welcome
101 All Generations Will Praise Your Name
53 All Who Are Led by the Spirit
206 Among All
204 Ave Maria
203 Ave Maria
133 Be with Me
255 Belong
136 Christ, Be Our Light
48 Come, Holy Ghost / En Nuestro Ser Mora, Creador
123 Come, Lord Jesus
265 Come, Taste and See
7 Creator Alme Siderum
8 Creator of the Stars of Night
5 Find Us Ready
183 For All Time
21 Give Me Jesus
106 Halle, Halle, Halle
175 Hold Us, Jesus
247 I Am
164 I Could Sing of Your Love Forever
243 I Cry before You
35 I Give My Spirit
27 Jesus, Remember Me / Jesús, Recuérdame
251 Jesus, You Brought Me All the Way
250 Jesus, Your Spirit / Kristus, Din Ande
92 Let Evening Fall
45 Let the River Flow
57 Let There Be Light
209 Litany of Mary / Letanía de la Santísima Virgen María
40 O Sons and Daughters
178 Litany of the Saints
185 Lord, Hear My Prayer / Óyenos, Señor
182 Lord's Prayer
104 Make a Joyful Noise
180 Make Us Worthy
126 No More Fear
10 O Come, O Come, Emmanuel
245 O God, Why Are You Silent?
264 O Taste and See
174 Open My Eyes
177 Open the Eyes of My Heart
69 Psalm 34: I Will Bless the Lord at All Times
72 Psalm 63: My Soul Is Thirsting
73 Psalm 72: Every Nation on Earth
75 Psalm 85: Let Us See Your Kindness

74 Psalm 85: Lord, Show Us Your Mercy and Love
84 Psalm 130: Out of the Depths
83 Psalm 130: With the Lord There Is Mercy
87 Psalm 141: Like Burning Incense, O Lord
117 Rain Down
215 Salaam Aleikum / May Peace Be in Your Hearts
46 Send Down the Fire
54 Spirit of God
181 Stop By, Lord
162 Take, O Take Me As I Am
184 The God of Second Chances
176 The Lord Is My Light and My Salvation
149 The Summons / El Llamado
56 To Know Darkness
194 Turn My Heart, O God
138 We Are Marching
266 We Are One Body
110 We Praise You
253 Were I the Perfect Child of God
267 With This Bread
115 With You by My Side
165 You Are the Way

PILGRIMAGE
218 As a Fire Is Meant for Burning / Como un Fuego Brilla y Quema
228 To Follow You
193 Way, Truth, and Life

POVERTY
95 Canticle of the Turning
52 Come, Holy Spirit
159 Give the Lord Your Heart
263 Gusten y Vean / Taste and See
197 Lead Me Home
79 Psalm 103: Bless the Lord, My Soul
69 Psalm 34: I Will Bless the Lord at All Times
73 Psalm 72: Every Nation on Earth
210 What You Have Done for Me

POVERTY OF SPIRIT
163 Come and Follow Me / Ven y Sígueme
232 Faith, Hope, and Love
159 Give the Lord Your Heart
104 Make a Joyful Noise
201 Yours Is the Kingdom

PRAISE
269 A Hymn for First Communion
211 A Place at the Table
101 All Generations Will Praise Your Name
58 Alleluia! Give the Glory
29 At Your Name
105 Blessed Be Your Name
95 Canticle of the Turning
16 Child of Mercy
147 Come All You People / Uyai Mose
34 Come and Gather
141 Come, Now Is the Time to Worship
265 Come, Taste and See
100 Cry the Gospel
38 Easter Alleluia
88 Exodus 15: Let Us Sing to the Lord
108 Forever
93 Glory to God Most High
172 God Is Good
111 God of Wonders
106 Halle, Halle, Halle
143 Here I Am to Worship
113 Holy God, We Praise Thy Name
208 Holy Is Your Name
221 How Can We Be Silent
99 How Excellent Is Thy Name
164 I Could Sing of Your Love Forever
258 I Will Give Thanks
94 I Will Lift Up Your Name
102 I Will Sing a Song of Love
241 In Your Presence
42 Jesus Christ Is Risen Today / El Señor Resucitó
250 Jesus, Your Spirit / Kristus, Din Ande
197 Lead Me Home
98 Let Us Worship the Lord
49 Living Spirit, Holy Fire
96 Lord, I Lift Your Name on High
259 Malo! Malo! Thanks Be to God
114 Mighty King
89 Morning Has Broken
257 O God, You Search Me
40 O Sons and Daughters
264 O Taste and See
198 On That Day
62 Psalm 18: I Love You, Lord, My Strength
68 Psalm 33: The Earth Is Full of the Goodness
69 Psalm 34: I Will Bless the Lord at All Times
70 Psalm 40: Here I Am
71 Psalm 47: God Mounts His Throne
72 Psalm 63: My Soul Is Thirsting
73 Psalm 72: Every Nation on Earth
75 Psalm 85: Let Us See Your Kindness
74 Psalm 85: Lord, Show Us Your Mercy and Love
77 Psalm 96: Proclaim God's Marvelous Deeds
76 Psalm 96: Sing a Song to the Lord
79 Psalm 103: Bless the Lord, My Soul
82 Psalm 122: Let Us Go Rejoicing
85 Psalm 138: Lord, I Thank You
140 Shine on Us
109 Shout to the Lord
97 Shout to the North
219 Sing a New World
107 Sing to the Glory of God
254 So Longs My Soul
151 Sometimes by Step
103 Thanks and Praise
194 Turn My Heart, O God
91 We Arise
110 We Praise You
155 With One Voice
134 You Are Good to Me
127 You Are My King (Amazing Love)
165 You Are the Way

PRESENCE OF GOD
269 A Hymn for First Communion
101 All Generations Will Praise Your Name
204 Ave Maria
203 Ave Maria
132 Be Still
133 Be with Me
118 Be with Me, Lord
196 Better Is One Day
120 Breathe
183 For All Time
249 For God So Loved the World
108 Forever
90 Fresh as the Morning
214 Give Us Your Peace
278 God Is Forgiveness / Bóg Jest Miłością
220 God Is Here / Está Aquí
239 Guide My Feet
2 Hallelujah, Hallelu!
125 Here I Am
175 Hold Us, Jesus
247 I Am
283 I Know That My Redeemer Lives
241 In Your Presence
223 Journeying Prayer
92 Let Evening Fall
96 Lord, I Lift Your Name on High
234 Love beyond All Telling
119 May the Road Rise to Meet You
148 Now Is the Time
245 O God, Why Are You Silent?
257 O God, You Search Me
264 O Taste and See
174 Open My Eyes
256 Over My Head
3 Prepare! Prepare!
75 Psalm 85: Let Us See Your Kindness
74 Psalm 85: Lord, Show Us Your Mercy and Love
77 Psalm 96: Proclaim God's Marvelous Deeds
76 Psalm 96: Sing a Song to the Lord
86 Psalm 139: Before I Was Born
135 Quietly, Peacefully
46 Send Down the Fire
188 Shelter Your Name
139 Shine, Jesus, Shine
140 Shine on Us
107 Sing to the Glory of God
273 Spirit and Grace
54 Spirit of God
181 Stop By, Lord
131 The Clouds' Veil
176 The Lord Is My Light and My Salvation
56 To Know Darkness
275 We Are One
110 We Praise You
142 What Is This Place
210 What You Have Done for Me
31 Where True Love and Charity Are Found / Ubi Caritas
267 With This Bread

Topical Index/*continued*

115 With You by My Side

PROMISE
53 All Who Are Led by the Spirit
124 Amazing Grace
95 Canticle of the Turning
171 Deny Yourself
33 Glory in the Cross
220 God Is Here / Está Aquí
43 He Is Not Here
208 Holy Is Your Name
258 I Will Give Thanks
245 O God, Why Are You Silent?
65 Psalm 25: I Lift My Soul to You
109 Shout to the Lord
219 Sing a New World
275 We Are One
268 We Give You Thanks
267 With This Bread
170 Your Grace Is Enough

PROVIDENCE
101 All Generations Will Praise Your Name
105 Blessed Be Your Name
95 Canticle of the Turning
38 Easter Alleluia
90 Fresh as the Morning
208 Holy Is Your Name
160 I Am for You
27 Jesus, Remember Me / Jesús, Recuérdame
98 Let Us Worship the Lord
89 Morning Has Broken
15 Night of Silence / Noche de Silencio
257 O God, You Search Me
256 Over My Head
68 Psalm 33: The Earth Is Full of the Goodness
69 Psalm 34: I Will Bless the Lord at All Times
72 Psalm 63: My Soul Is Thirsting
73 Psalm 72: Every Nation on Earth
75 Psalm 85: Let Us See Your Kindness
74 Psalm 85: Lord, Show Us Your Mercy and Love
79 Psalm 103: Bless the Lord, My Soul
80 Psalm 118: This Is the Day
81 Psalm 121: Our Help Is from the Lord
86 Psalm 139: Before I Was Born
87 Psalm 141: Like Burning Incense, O Lord
117 Rain Down
115 With You by My Side

RACIAL RECONCILIATION
269 A Hymn for First Communion
225 Build Us a Table
102 I Will Sing a Song of Love
213 Seek Truth, Make Peace, Reverence Life
31 Where True Love and Charity Are Found / Ubi Caritas

RECONCILIATION
145 All Are Welcome
55 Breath of Life
150 Go Make a Difference
278 God Is Forgiveness / Bóg Jest Miłością
125 Here I Am
277 Make Me Holy
10 O Come, O Come, Emmanuel
79 Psalm 103: Bless the Lord, My Soul
188 Shelter Your Name
194 Turn My Heart, O God
275 We Are One
91 We Arise
267 With This Bread

REDEMPTION
143 Here I Am to Worship
154 Holiness Is Faithfulness
166 How Beautiful
281 I Know That My Redeemer Lives
258 I Will Give Thanks
42 Jesus Christ Is Risen Today / El Señor Resucitó
96 Lord, I Lift Your Name on High
180 Make Us Worthy
264 O Taste and See
79 Psalm 103: Bless the Lord, My Soul
84 Psalm 130: Out of the Depths
83 Psalm 130: With the Lord There Is Mercy
87 Psalm 141: Like Burning Incense, O Lord

REFUGE
236 Be Still and Know
255 Belong
196 Better Is One Day
120 Breathe
90 Fresh as the Morning
116 How Can I Keep From Singing?
35 I Give My Spirit
122 In Every Age
250 Jesus, Your Spirit / Kristus, Din Ande
209 Litany of Mary / Letanía de la Santísima Virgen María
40 O Sons and Daughters
257 O God, You Search Me
264 O Taste and See
62 Psalm 18: I Love You, Lord, My Strength
68 Psalm 33: The Earth Is Full of the Goodness
72 Psalm 63: My Soul Is Thirsting
87 Psalm 141: Like Burning Incense, O Lord
117 Rain Down
109 Shout to the Lord
235 The Lord Is My Light
176 The Lord Is My Light and My Salvation
194 Turn My Heart, O God
115 With You by My Side
134 You Are Good to Me

REMEMBRANCE
27 Jesus, Remember Me / Jesús, Recuérdame
148 Now Is the Time
65 Psalm 25: I Lift My Soul to You
67 Psalm 25: To You, O God, I Lift Up My Soul
66 Psalm 25: To You, O Lord, I Lift My Soul
79 Psalm 103: Bless the Lord, My Soul
268 We Give You Thanks
142 What Is This Place

RENEWAL
269 A Hymn for First Communion
52 Come, Holy Spirit
49 Living Spirit, Holy Fire
89 Morning Has Broken
70 Psalm 40: Here I Am
189 River of Life
188 Shelter Your Name

REPENTANCE *(see Forgiveness, Liturgical Index: Penance)*

REST
132 Be Still
159 Give the Lord Your Heart
116 How Can I Keep From Singing?
122 In Every Age
197 Lead Me Home
257 O God, You Search Me
135 Quietly, Peacefully
194 Turn My Heart, O God

RESURRECTION *(see Liturgical Index: Easter)*

SACRAMENT
140 Shine on Us
142 What Is This Place

SACRIFICE
29 At Your Name
34 Come and Gather
171 Deny Yourself
154 Holiness Is Faithfulness
166 How Beautiful
221 How Can We Be Silent
270 I Will Take the Cup of Salvation
197 Lead Me Home
114 Mighty King
65 Psalm 25: I Lift My Soul to You
70 Psalm 40: Here I Am
140 Shine on Us
274 Unless a Grain

SAINTS
100 Cry the Gospel
178 Litany of the Saints
200 Sign Me Up
131 The Clouds' Veil

SALVATION
58 Alleluia! Give the Glory
124 Amazing Grace
29 At Your Name
255 Belong
55 Breath of Life
16 Child of Mercy
136 Christ, Be Our Light
265 Come, Taste and See
38 Easter Alleluia

88 Exodus 15: Let Us Sing to the Lord
249 For God So Loved the World
35 I Give My Spirit
276 I Have Been Anointed
281 I Know That My Redeemer Lives
270 I Will Take the Cup of Salvation
42 Jesus Christ Is Risen Today / El Señor Resucitó
98 Let Us Worship the Lord
96 Lord, I Lift Your Name on High
114 Mighty King
186 Now
264 O Taste and See
62 Psalm 18: I Love You, Lord, My Strength
65 Psalm 25: I Lift My Soul to You
67 Psalm 25: To You, O God, I Lift Up My Soul
66 Psalm 25: To You, O Lord, I Lift My Soul
72 Psalm 63: My Soul Is Thirsting
73 Psalm 72: Every Nation on Earth
75 Psalm 85: Let Us See Your Kindness
74 Psalm 85: Lord, Show Us Your Mercy and Love
77 Psalm 96: Proclaim God's Marvelous Deeds
79 Psalm 103: Bless the Lord, My Soul
87 Psalm 141: Like Burning Incense, O Lord
135 Quietly, Peacefully
18 Remember You Are Dust / Del Polvo Eres Tú
235 The Lord Is My Light
176 The Lord Is My Light and My Salvation
91 We Arise
165 You Are the Way

SALVATION HISTORY
142 What Is This Place

SEASONS
122 In Every Age
119 May the Road Rise to Meet You
15 Night of Silence / Noche de Silencio

SECOND COMING
4 Awake to the Day
52 Come, Holy Spirit
221 How Can We Be Silent
281 I Know That My Redeemer Lives
17 Rise Up in Splendor
140 Shine on Us
200 Sign Me Up
261 We Are Called / Dios Nos Llama
266 We Are One Body

SECURITY
211 A Place at the Table
255 Belong
196 Better Is One Day
123 Come, Lord Jesus
122 In Every Age
250 Jesus, Your Spirit / Kristus, Din Ande
223 Journeying Prayer
130 Live in the Light
180 Make Us Worthy
119 May the Road Rise to Meet You
245 O God, Why Are You Silent?
257 O God, You Search Me
62 Psalm 18: I Love You, Lord, My Strength
81 Psalm 121: Our Help Is from the Lord
135 Quietly, Peacefully
117 Rain Down
184 The God of Second Chances
235 The Lord Is My Light
115 With You by My Side
134 You Are Good to Me

SEEKING
218 As a Fire Is Meant for Burning / Como un Fuego Brilla y Quema
255 Belong
136 Christ, Be Our Light
265 Come, Taste and See
183 For All Time
220 God Is Here / Está Aquí
154 Holiness Is Faithfulness
247 I Am
241 In Your Presence
257 O God, You Search Me
264 O Taste and See
191 One Lord
174 Open My Eyes
177 Open the Eyes of My Heart
69 Psalm 34: I Will Bless the Lord at All Times
75 Psalm 85: Let Us See Your Kindness
74 Psalm 85: Lord, Show Us Your Mercy and Love
76 Psalm 96: Sing a Song to the Lord
135 Quietly, Peacefully
213 Seek Truth, Make Peace, Reverence Life
254 So Longs My Soul
151 Sometimes by Step
176 The Lord Is My Light and My Salvation
228 To Follow You
56 To Know Darkness
193 Way, Truth, and Life
253 Were I the Perfect Child of God
210 What You Have Done for Me
212 Will the Circle Be Unbroken?
267 With This Bread
165 You Are the Way

SERVICE
145 All Are Welcome
58 Alleluia! Give the Glory
206 Among All
163 Come and Follow Me / Ven y Sígueme
183 For All Time
159 Give the Lord Your Heart
137 Go Light Your World
150 Go Make a Difference
230 Go Out to the World
220 God Is Here / Está Aquí
166 How Beautiful
221 How Can We Be Silent
248 Humbled
160 I Am for You
153 I Will Choose Christ
270 I Will Take the Cup of Salvation
229 My Savior, Your Son
186 Now
191 One Lord
261 We Are Called / Dios Nos Llama
275 We Are One
110 We Praise You
210 What You Have Done for Me
267 With This Bread

SHARING
206 Among All
225 Build Us a Table
136 Christ, Be Our Light
230 Go Out to the World
233 God Is Love
49 Living Spirit, Holy Fire
245 O God, Why Are You Silent?
273 Spirit and Grace
275 We Are One
268 We Give You Thanks
210 What You Have Done for Me
212 Will the Circle Be Unbroken?
267 With This Bread
224 You Will Know

SHEPHERD
38 Easter Alleluia
247 I Am
246 Our God Reigns
23 We Are Climbing Jacob's Ladder
266 We Are One Body

SICKNESSS *(see Comfort, Healing, Suffering; Liturgical Index: Pastoral Care of the Sick)*

SIN
20 Be Forgiven
39 Come and See
183 For All Time
220 God Is Here / Está Aquí
106 Halle, Halle, Halle
125 Here I Am
143 Here I Am to Worship
175 Hold Us, Jesus
158 I Send You Out
197 Lead Me Home
182 Lord's Prayer
277 Make Me Holy
180 Make Us Worthy
246 Our God Reigns
65 Psalm 25: I Lift My Soul to You
66 Psalm 25: To You, O Lord, I Lift My Soul
72 Psalm 63: My Soul Is Thirsting
79 Psalm 103: Bless the Lord, My Soul
84 Psalm 130: Out of the Depths
83 Psalm 130: With the Lord There Is Mercy
18 Remember You Are Dust / Del Polvo Eres Tú
17 Rise Up in Splendor
189 River of Life
167 The Face of God
184 The God of Second Chances

Topical Index/*continued*

194 Turn My Heart, O God
23 We Are Climbing Jacob's Ladder
253 Were I the Perfect Child of God

SOCIAL CONCERN
95 Canticle of the Turning
136 Christ, Be Our Light
137 Go Light Your World
150 Go Make a Difference
116 How Can I Keep From Singing?
221 How Can We Be Silent
248 Humbled
186 Now
213 Seek Truth, Make Peace, Reverence Life
46 Send Down the Fire
149 The Summons / El Llamado
261 We Are Called / Dios Nos Llama
266 We Are One Body
210 What You Have Done for Me
31 Where True Love and Charity Are Found / Ubi Caritas
212 Will the Circle Be Unbroken?
155 With One Voice

SONG
269 A Hymn for First Communion
145 All Are Welcome
101 All Generations Will Praise Your Name
196 Better Is One Day
55 Breath of Life
95 Canticle of the Turning
265 Come, Taste and See
88 Exodus 15: Let Us Sing to the Lord
232 Faith, Hope, and Love
108 Forever
172 God Is Good
220 God Is Here / Está Aquí
113 Holy God, We Praise Thy Name
116 How Can I Keep From Singing?
221 How Can We Be Silent
99 How Excellent Is Thy Name
248 Humbled
164 I Could Sing of Your Love Forever
276 I Have Been Anointed
102 I Will Sing a Song of Love
241 In Your Presence
42 Jesus Christ Is Risen Today / El Señor Resucitó
250 Jesus, Your Spirit / Kristus, Din Ande
96 Lord, I Lift Your Name on High
234 Love beyond All Telling
104 Make a Joyful Noise
114 Mighty King
89 Morning Has Broken
40 O Sons and Daughters
264 O Taste and See
198 On That Day
256 Over My Head
65 Psalm 25: I Lift My Soul to You
70 Psalm 40: Here I Am
71 Psalm 47: God Mounts His Throne
72 Psalm 63: My Soul Is Thirsting
77 Psalm 96: Proclaim God's Marvelous Deeds
76 Psalm 96: Sing a Song to the Lord
84 Psalm 130: Out of the Depths
83 Psalm 130: With the Lord There Is Mercy
85 Psalm 138: Lord, I Thank You
87 Psalm 141: Like Burning Incense, O Lord
135 Quietly, Peacefully
46 Send Down the Fire
140 Shine on Us
97 Shout to the North
219 Sing a New World
107 Sing to the Glory of God
254 So Longs My Soul
103 Thanks and Praise
44 This Is the Day
194 Turn My Heart, O God
193 Way, Truth, and Life
261 We Are Called / Dios Nos Llama
138 We Are Marching
268 We Give You Thanks
110 We Praise You
155 With One Voice
267 With This Bread
115 With You by My Side
165 You Are the Way
170 Your Grace Is Enough

STORY
55 Breath of Life
271 Emmaus
70 Psalm 40: Here I Am
139 Shine, Jesus, Shine
268 We Give You Thanks

STRANGER
225 Build Us a Table
271 Emmaus
228 To Follow You
210 What You Have Done for Me

STRENGTH
145 All Are Welcome
133 Be with Me
100 Cry the Gospel
88 Exodus 15: Let Us Sing to the Lord
108 Forever
33 Glory in the Cross
230 Go Out to the World
220 God Is Here / Está Aquí
175 Hold Us, Jesus
154 Holiness Is Faithfulness
116 How Can I Keep From Singing?
199 I Am Sure I Shall See
35 I Give My Spirit
122 In Every Age
130 Live in the Light
180 Make Us Worthy
62 Psalm 18: I Love You, Lord, My Strength
72 Psalm 63: My Soul Is Thirsting
85 Psalm 138: Lord, I Thank You
109 Shout to the Lord
254 So Longs My Soul
187 Strength for the Journey
103 Thanks and Praise
235 The Lord Is My Light
176 The Lord Is My Light and My Salvation
169 Trading My Sorrows
222 We Will Go, Lord
115 With You by My Side
128 You Are Mine / Contigo Estoy
238 You Are Strong, You Are Holy
170 Your Grace Is Enough

STRUGGLE
90 Fresh as the Morning
180 Make Us Worthy
119 May the Road Rise to Meet You
189 River of Life
46 Send Down the Fire
188 Shelter Your Name
151 Sometimes by Step
181 Stop By, Lord
187 Strength for the Journey
103 Thanks and Praise
167 The Face of God
194 Turn My Heart, O God
266 We Are One Body
134 You Are Good to Me

SUFFERING
53 All Who Are Led by the Spirit
132 Be Still
105 Blessed Be Your Name
34 Come and Gather
265 Come, Taste and See
271 Emmaus
232 Faith, Hope, and Love
90 Fresh as the Morning
244 God Remembers
263 Gusten y Vean / Taste and See
125 Here I Am
175 Hold Us, Jesus
221 How Can We Be Silent
243 I Cry before You
35 I Give My Spirit
102 I Will Sing a Song of Love
122 In Every Age
42 Jesus Christ Is Risen Today / El Señor Resucitó
251 Jesus, You Brought Me All the Way
197 Lead Me Home
92 Let Evening Fall
104 Make a Joyful Noise
36 My Savior, My Friend
229 My Savior, Your Son
126 No More Fear
264 O Taste and See
69 Psalm 34: I Will Bless the Lord at All Times
140 Shine on Us
266 We Are One Body
110 We Praise You
128 You Are Mine / Contigo Estoy
224 You Will Know
201 Yours Is the Kingdom

SUNDAY
225 Build Us a Table
141 Come, Now Is the Time to Worship
281 I Know That My Redeemer Lives

TEACHING
145 All Are Welcome

218 As a Fire Is Meant for Burning / Como un Fuego Brilla y Quema
152 Get It Together
153 I Will Choose Christ
65 Psalm 25: I Lift My Soul to You
67 Psalm 25: To You, O God, I Lift Up My Soul
66 Psalm 25: To You, O Lord, I Lift My Soul
46 Send Down the Fire

TEMPTATION
125 Here I Am
56 To Know Darkness
194 Turn My Heart, O God

THANKSGIVING
108 Forever
159 Give the Lord Your Heart
172 God Is Good
106 Halle, Halle, Halle
258 I Will Give Thanks
270 I Will Take the Cup of Salvation
197 Lead Me Home
259 Malo! Malo! Thanks Be to God
70 Psalm 40: Here I Am
79 Psalm 103: Bless the Lord, My Soul
80 Psalm 118: This Is the Day
82 Psalm 122: Let Us Go Rejoicing
85 Psalm 138: Lord, I Thank You
103 Thanks and Praise
91 We Arise
268 We Give You Thanks
110 We Praise You

THIRST
136 Christ, Be Our Light
244 God Remembers
263 Gusten y Vean / Taste and See
175 Hold Us, Jesus
241 In Your Presence
226 Look to Christ
24 Mercy, O God
264 O Taste and See
72 Psalm 63: My Soul Is Thirsting
117 Rain Down
189 River of Life
140 Shine on Us
44 This Is the Day
275 We Are One
201 Yours Is the Kingdom

TIME
122 In Every Age
119 May the Road Rise to Meet You
186 Now
148 Now Is the Time
257 O God, You Search Me
219 Sing a New World
151 Sometimes by Step

TRANSITION
211 A Place at the Table
225 Build Us a Table
95 Canticle of the Turning
90 Fresh as the Morning
33 Glory in the Cross
277 Make Me Holy
180 Make Us Worthy
190 Purify My Heart
188 Shelter Your Name
139 Shine, Jesus, Shine
140 Shine on Us
200 Sign Me Up
184 The God of Second Chances
169 Trading My Sorrows
194 Turn My Heart, O God

TRINITY
93 Glory to God Most High
113 Holy God, We Praise Thy Name
158 I Send You Out
57 Let There Be Light
129 May the Peace of Christ Be with You / Ki Ri Su To No
17 Rise Up in Splendor
56 To Know Darkness

TRUST
124 Amazing Grace
206 Among All
132 Be Still
236 Be Still and Know
163 Come and Follow Me / Ven y Sígueme
239 Guide My Feet
116 How Can I Keep From Singing?
199 I Am Sure I Shall See
35 I Give My Spirit
241 In Your Presence
27 Jesus, Remember Me / Jesús, Recuérdame
92 Let Evening Fall
280 Love Endures
119 May the Road Rise to Meet You
15 Night of Silence / Noche de Silencio
252 Nothing Can Ever
257 O God, You Search Me
256 Over My Head
64 Psalm 19: Lord, You Have the Words
65 Psalm 25: I Lift My Soul to You
67 Psalm 25: To You, O God, I Lift Up My Soul
66 Psalm 25: To You, O Lord, I Lift My Soul
68 Psalm 33: The Earth Is Full of the Goodness
69 Psalm 34: I Will Bless the Lord at All Times
70 Psalm 40: Here I Am
72 Psalm 63: My Soul Is Thirsting
76 Psalm 96: Sing a Song to the Lord
81 Psalm 121: Our Help Is from the Lord
84 Psalm 130: Out of the Depths
83 Psalm 130: With the Lord There Is Mercy
85 Psalm 138: Lord, I Thank You
86 Psalm 139: Before I Was Born
87 Psalm 141: Like Burning Incense, O Lord
117 Rain Down
17 Rise Up in Splendor
240 River of Hope
219 Sing a New World
237 Take, Lord, Receive
103 Thanks and Praise
235 The Lord Is My Light
44 This Is the Day
169 Trading My Sorrows
238 You Are Strong, You Are Holy

TRUTH
145 All Are Welcome
132 Be Still
163 Come and Follow Me / Ven y Sígueme
249 For God So Loved the World
172 God Is Good
220 God Is Here / Está Aquí
247 I Am
164 I Could Sing of Your Love Forever
98 Let Us Worship the Lord
114 Mighty King
148 Now Is the Time
3 Prepare! Prepare!
65 Psalm 25: I Lift My Soul to You
67 Psalm 25: To You, O God, I Lift Up My Soul
66 Psalm 25: To You, O Lord, I Lift My Soul
75 Psalm 85: Let Us See Your Kindness
74 Psalm 85: Lord, Show Us Your Mercy and Love
85 Psalm 138: Lord, I Thank You
87 Psalm 141: Like Burning Incense, O Lord
213 Seek Truth, Make Peace, Reverence Life
46 Send Down the Fire
139 Shine, Jesus, Shine
97 Shout to the North
91 We Arise

UNDERSTANDING
271 Emmaus
175 Hold Us, Jesus
257 O God, You Search Me
174 Open My Eyes
177 Open the Eyes of My Heart
86 Psalm 139: Before I Was Born
237 Take, Lord, Receive

UNITY
211 A Place at the Table
145 All Are Welcome
218 As a Fire Is Meant for Burning / Como un Fuego Brilla y Quema
214 Give Us Your Peace
160 I Am for You
185 Lord, Hear My Prayer / Óyenos, Señor
234 Love beyond All Telling
10 O Come, O Come, Emmanuel
198 On That Day
191 One Lord
82 Psalm 122: Let Us Go Rejoicing
213 Seek Truth, Make Peace, Reverence Life
140 Shine on Us
219 Sing a New World
275 We Are One
266 We Are One Body
31 Where True Love and Charity Are Found / Ubi Caritas

Topical Index/*continued*

UNIVERSE
111 God of Wonders
113 Holy God, We Praise Thy Name
130 Live in the Light
219 Sing a New World

VOCATION
144 Gather Your People
226 Look to Christ
104 Make a Joyful Noise
191 One Lord
162 Take, O Take Me As I Am
228 To Follow You
110 We Praise You
128 You Are Mine / Contigo Estoy
(also Discipleship)

WATER
136 Christ, Be Our Light
144 Gather Your People
241 In Your Presence
226 Look to Christ
114 Mighty King
117 Rain Down
240 River of Hope
189 River of Life
44 This Is the Day
268 We Give You Thanks
253 Were I the Perfect Child of God
134 You Are Good to Me

WAY, TRUTH, & LIFE
136 Christ, Be Our Light
168 Every Move I Make
183 For All Time
154 Holiness Is Faithfulness
247 I Am
213 Seek Truth, Make Peace, Reverence Life
131 The Clouds' Veil
193 Way, Truth, and Life
266 We Are One Body
165 You Are the Way

WELCOME
211 A Place at the Table
145 All Are Welcome
225 Build Us a Table
141 Come, Now Is the Time to Worship
119 May the Road Rise to Meet You
213 Seek Truth, Make Peace, Reverence Life

WISDOM
211 A Place at the Table
258 I Will Give Thanks
57 Let There Be Light
245 O God, Why Are You Silent?
64 Psalm 19: Lord, You Have the Words
87 Psalm 141: Like Burning Incense, O Lord
135 Quietly, Peacefully
213 Seek Truth, Make Peace, Reverence Life
219 Sing a New World
273 Spirit and Grace
193 Way, Truth, and Life
110 We Praise You

WITNESS
211 A Place at the Table
101 All Generations Will Praise Your Name
53 All Who Are Led by the Spirit
206 Among All
218 As a Fire Is Meant for Burning / Como un Fuego Brilla y Quema
136 Christ, Be Our Light
163 Come and Follow Me / Ven y Sígueme
39 Come and See
123 Come, Lord Jesus
100 Cry the Gospel
88 Exodus 15: Let Us Sing to the Lord
152 Get It Together
156 Go Out in the World
230 Go Out to the World
172 God Is Good
208 Holy Is Your Name
116 How Can I Keep From Singing?
248 Humbled
94 I Will Lift Up Your Name
45 Let the River Flow
114 Mighty King
229 My Savior, Your Son
174 Open My Eyes
70 Psalm 40: Here I Am
77 Psalm 96: Proclaim God's Marvelous Deeds
76 Psalm 96: Sing a Song to the Lord
80 Psalm 118: This Is the Day
213 Seek Truth, Make Peace, Reverence Life
46 Send Down the Fire
139 Shine, Jesus, Shine
103 Thanks and Praise
275 We Are One
266 We Are One Body
155 With One Voice
201 Yours Is the Kingdom

WORD OF GOD
145 All Are Welcome
58 Alleluia! Give the Glory
124 Amazing Grace
4 Awake to the Day
118 Be with Me, Lord
120 Breathe
95 Canticle of the Turning
136 Christ, Be Our Light
271 Emmaus
90 Fresh as the Morning
230 Go Out to the World
220 God Is Here / Está Aquí
160 I Am for You
57 Let There Be Light
234 Love beyond All Telling
104 Make a Joyful Noise
180 Make Us Worthy
89 Morning Has Broken
64 Psalm 19: Lord, You Have the Words
117 Rain Down
139 Shine, Jesus, Shine
193 Way, Truth, and Life
268 We Give You Thanks
110 We Praise You
212 Will the Circle Be Unbroken?
155 With One Voice
128 You Are Mine / Contigo Estoy

WORK *(see Labor)*

WORLD
206 Among All
225 Build Us a Table
95 Canticle of the Turning
147 Come All You People / Uyai Mose
163 Come and Follow Me / Ven y Sígueme
100 Cry the Gospel
137 Go Light Your World
156 Go Out in the World
230 Go Out to the World
154 Holiness Is Faithfulness
221 How Can We Be Silent
99 How Excellent Is Thy Name
158 I Send You Out
102 I Will Sing a Song of Love
98 Let Us Worship the Lord
77 Psalm 96: Proclaim God's Marvelous Deeds
76 Psalm 96: Sing a Song to the Lord
215 Salaam Aleikum / May Peace Be in Your Hearts
139 Shine, Jesus, Shine
273 Spirit and Grace
31 Where True Love and Charity Are Found / Ubi Caritas
155 With One Voice

WORSHIP *(see Praise)*

Adam, David 223
Adrian Dominican Sisters' Vision Statement 213
African American Spiritual 21 23 239 256
Alonso, Tony E. 60 70 90 92 106 209 210 212 253 263 271
Anderson, Marc 215
Andrews, Jerome V. 182
Angotti, John 34 51 52 103 158
Angrisano, Steve 72 94 114 123 150 165
Archer, Ed 22 64 68 69 83
Baloche, Paul 177
Barker, John 4
Barnett, Marie 120
Batastini, Robert J. 116
Beaker 151
Beddia, Stephen A. 246 266
Bell, John L. 102 106 147 149 162 216 253
Berrell, Paul L. 98
Berthier, Jacques 27
Bettis, Doris Wesley 181
Blakesley, Joshua 189
Bolduc, Ed 4 5 20 45 51 52 71 96 97 100 103 105 108 109 118 125 126 127 141 153 156 164 167 168 170 174 177 187 196 197
Booth, Tom 5 20 100 118 125 153
Bouknight, Lillian 235
Boyer, Horace Clarence 23
Briehl, Susan 249
Brinker, David 189
Brown, Gerry 266
Browning, Carol 8 185
Byrd, Marc 111
Cabrera, Juan Bautista 42
Callanan, Ian 134
Campbell, Derek 43
Canedo, Ken 58 93 114 174 259
Carson, Christine 216
Caswall, Edward 48
Cerneka, Shannon 29 35 62 79 80 85 152 183 222
Chant 7 203
Chapman, Steven Curtis 236
Children's Bells, The 89
Chiusano, Gerard 163
Compleat Psalmodist, The 42
Cooney, Rory 95 160 186 193
Cortez, Jaime 117 185
Cuddy, Kate 115 198 267
Cummins, Cynthia 270
Cymbala, Michael A. 269
Daigle, Gary 10 134 142 147 149 152 186 193 198 213 219 256 257
Doerksen, Brian 141 190
Drummond, John 254
Duck, Ruth 49 218 225
Dufner, Delores 219
Dunstan, Sylvia G. 238
Dvorák, Antonin 135
Evanovich, Joshua 277
Evans, Darrell 45 169
Farjeon, Eleanor 89
Farrell, Bernadette 136 257
Fernández, Santiago 128
Fliedner, Federico 14
Foote, Billy James 127
Founds, Rick 96
Franz, Ignaz 113
Franzak, Tom 163 274
Gaelic 89
Gainer, Paul 235
Geistliche Kirchengasange 269
Gibson, Jim 185
Glover, Rob 140 204
Gondo, Alexander 147
Graves, Avis D. 239
Gruber, Franz X. 14
Haas, David 16 55 86 110 115 128 184 208 220 226 261 268 281
Hassler, Hans Leo 245
Haugen, Marty 38 46 145 194 213 215 218 244 245 249 264
Higdon, John W. 99
Hindalong, Steve 111
Houze, Daniel 182
Huck, Gabe 106
Hughes, Tim 143
Hurd, Bob 58 67 144
Ignatius of Loyola, St. 237
Irish traditional 95 208
Japanese folk melody 129
Johnson, Orin 35 56 62 79 80 82 152 183 222
Joncas, Michael 53
Joubert, Joseph 99
Judge, Jeffrey 15
Kantor, Dan 15 204
Katholisches Gesangbuch 113
Keating, Marshall 87
Kendrick, Graham 139
Kendzia, Tom 148
Kingsbury, Craig S. 58 117 144 273
Kolar, Peter M. 276

Krisman, Ronald F. 18 48 149 163 261 269
Lambillotte, Louis, SJ 48 60
Latin 7 8 10 31 51
Lawton, Liam 76 131 254
Lectionary for Mass 59 74 270
Light, Deanna 25
Litany of Loretto 209
Liturgy of the Hours, The 72
Louis, Kenneth W. 77 251
Lowry, Robert 116
Lyra Davidica 42
MacAller, Dominic 58 67 144
Maher, Matt 170 196 197
Mahler, Michael 2 39 73 88 91 130 159 180 201 214 221 229 233 253
Manalo, Ricky 155 273
Manibusan, Jesse 93 172 174 176 259
Marriott, John 57
Mattingly, Joe 195
Maurus, Rabanus 48
McCann, John 76 131
Melley, Paul 57 75 81 84 171 223 224 232 237 247 248
Metcalfe, Jerome 200
Modlin, Rick 72 94 111 120 123 139 150 165 270
Mohr, Joseph 14
Moore, James E., Jr. 54 107 132 280
Morris, Kenneth 200
Mullins, Rich 151
Murray, Shirley Erena 12 90 211
Neale, John M. 10 40
New American Bible 17 62 64 66 68 69 71 75 80 81 83 85
Newton, John 124
O'Brien, Francis Patrick 24
Oosterhuis, Huub 142
Pammit, Lovina Francis, OSF 228
Pando-Connolly, Georgina 218
Pappelis, Gus 176
Paris, Twila 166
Paul, Susan J. 240
Pishner, Stephen 3 59
Poirier, Michael John 187
Prayer of the Breton Fisherman 223
Proulx, Richard 31 40 48
Redman, Beth 105
Redman, Matt 105 196
Rees, John 124
Rice, Chris 137
Roberts, Leon C. 66
Roman Missal 178
Rose, Danielle 154 188
Ruis, David 168
Sacramentary 18
Sacred Harp, The 218
Scallon, Dana 266
Scottish traditional 149 253
Silva, Chris de 36 44 101 104 175 206 228 230 234 241 255 258 265 275
Sisters of St. Joseph Carondelet 129
Smith, Christi 165
Smith, David 142
Smith, Leonard E., Jr. 246
Smith, Martin 97 164
Smith, Pat 165
Soper, Scott 33 283
South African 138
Stephan, Curtis 71
Taize Community 27 199 250 252 278
Tate, Paul A. 18 25 34 65 89 98 124 158 225 238
Teresa, Frances, OSC 36
Thompson, Aaron 17 126 277
Tisserand, Jean 40
Tomaszek, Tom 94 123 150 165
Tomlin, Chris 108
Traditional 12 118
Traditional Caribbean 106
Traditional Ghanaian 215
Traditional Guatemalan 216
Traditional Irish blessing 119
True, Lori 12 49 65 87 119 129 135 191 211 225 243
Vaughan Williams, Ralph 269
VerEecke, Robert, S.J. 224
Virginia Harmony 124
Walker, Christopher 270
Walworth, Clarence 113
Warner, Steven C. 276
Wesley, Charles 42
Wessel, Matt 133
Whitaker, Janèt Sullivan 74 122
Williams, Nolan, Jr. 21
Wren, Brian 244
Wyeth's Repository of Sacred Music, Pt. II 219
Yancy, Kevin 200
Young, John F. 14
Zschech, Darlene 109

269 A Hymn for First Communion
211 A Place at the Table
145 All Are Welcome
101 All Generations Will Praise Your Name
53 All Who Are Led by the Spirit
58 Alleluia! Give the Glory
60 Alleluia: Song of the Spirit
124 Amazing Grace
127 Amazing Love (You Are My King)
206 Among All
218 As a Fire Is Meant for Burning / Como un Fuego Brilla y Quema
254 As pants the hart for running streams
271 As we journeyed on our way
29 At Your Name
203 Ave Maria
204 Ave Maria
4 Awake to the Day
20 Be Forgiven
132 Be Still
236 Be Still and Know
133 Be with Me
118 Be with Me, Lord
86 Before I Was Born - Psalm 139
255 Belong
196 Better Is One Day
79 Bless the Lord, My Soul - Psalm 103
201 Blessed are you, the humble in spirit
105 Blessed Be Your Name
278 Bóg Jest Miłością / God Is Forgiveness
55 Breath of Life
120 Breathe
55 Breathe on me, breath of life
25 Bring Us Home
225 Build Us a Table
95 Canticle of the Turning
16 Child of Mercy
136 Christ, Be Our Light
15 Cold are the people
147 Come All You People / Uyai Mose
163 Come and Follow Me / Ven y Sígueme
34 Come and Gather
39 Come and See
163 Come, be my light
48 Come, Holy Ghost / En Nuestro Ser Mora, Creador
52 Come, Holy Spirit
261 Come! Live in the light
123 Come, Lord Jesus
141 Come, Now Is the Time to Worship
184 Come now, O God of second chances
265 Come, Taste and See
148 Come to us, you who say, "I will not forget you."
104 Come with me and I will show you
218 Como un Fuego Brilla y Quema / As a Fire Is Meant for Burning
128 Contigo Estoy / You Are Mine
7 Creator Alme Siderum
8 Creator of the Stars of Night
100 Cry the Gospel
18 Del Polvo Eres Tú / Remember You Are Dust
171 Deny Yourself
261 Dios Nos Llama / We Are Called
12 Dream a Dream
38 Easter Alleluia
149 El Llamado / The Summons
42 El Señor Resucitó / Jesus Christ Is Risen Today
271 Emmaus
35 Empty, broken, lifeless
48 En Nuestro Ser Mora, Creador / Come, Holy Ghost
220 Está Aquí / God Is Here
131 Even though the rain hides the stars
168 Every Move I Make
73 Every Nation on Earth - Psalm 72
88 Exodus 15: Let Us Sing to the Lord
232 Faith will open the eyes of the blind
232 Faith, Hope, and Love
5 Find Us Ready
183 For All Time
211 For everyone born, a place at the table
249 For God So Loved the World
268 For the bread and wine we share here
110 For your sun that brightens the day
108 Forever
90 Fresh as the Morning
144 Gather Your People
152 Get It Together
21 Give Me Jesus
108 Give thanks to the Lord
159 Give the Lord Your Heart
214 Give Us Your Peace
93 Glory, Glory to God
33 Glory in the Cross
93 Glory to God Most High
33 Glory, we glory in the cross
137 Go Light Your World
150 Go Make a Difference
156 Go Out in the World
230 Go Out to the World
223 God ahead and God behind

278 God Is Forgiveness / Bóg Jest Miłością
172 God Is Good
220 God Is Here / Está Aquí
233 God Is Love
71 God Mounts His Throne - Psalm 47
90 God of the Bible
111 God of Wonders
244 God Remembers
234 God's chosen ones
56 God, our Father, we long to see you as you are
59 Gospel Acclamation
152 Gotta get it
258 Great are your works
170 Great is your faithfulness
239 Guide My Feet
263 Gusten y Vean / Taste and See
204 Hail Mary full of grace
106 Halle, Halle, Halle
2 Hallelujah, Hallelu!
43 He Is Not Here
125 Here I Am
70 Here I Am - Psalm 40
143 Here I Am to Worship
175 Hold Us, Jesus
154 Holiness Is Faithfulness
57 Holy and blessed three
113 Holy God, We Praise Thy Name
208 Holy Is Your Name
166 How Beautiful
116 How Can I Keep From Singing?
221 How Can We Be Silent
99 How Excellent Is Thy Name
196 How lovely is your dwelling place
246 How lovely on the mountains
248 Humbled
247 I Am
160 I Am for You
199 I Am Sure I Shall See
210 I am the hungry, I am the poor
158 I baptize you
167 I believe in my Lord Jesus
164 I Could Sing of Your Love Forever
243 I Cry before You
35 I Give My Spirit
276 I Have Been Anointed
21 I heard my mother say
281 I Know That My Redeemer Lives (Haas)
283 I Know That My Redeemer Lives (Soper)
62 I Love You Lord, My Strength - Psalm 18
158 I Send You Out
69 I Will Bless the Lord at All Times - Psalm 34
153 I Will Choose Christ
258 I Will Give Thanks
94 I Will Lift Up Your Name
102 I Will Sing a Song of Love
270 I Will Take the Cup of Salvation
229 I was born and baptized
187 I will be strength for the journey
128 I will come to you in the silence
101 I will proclaim your greatness
99 I will sing praises unto the Father
127 I'm forgiven because you were forsaken
169 I'm trading my sorrows
159 If you want to see the kingdom
122 In Every Age
241 In Your Presence
42 Jesus Christ Is Risen Today / El Señor Resucitó
214 Jesus, give us your peace
36 Jesus, hanging on the cross
27 Jesús, Recuérdame / Jesus, Remember Me
27 Jesus, Remember Me / Jesús, Recuérdame
251 Jesus, You Brought Me All the Way
250 Jesus, Your Spirit / Kristus, Din Ande
223 Journeying Prayer
129 Ki Ri Su To No / May the Peace of Christ Be with You
250 Kristus, Din Ande Jesus, Your Spirit
216 La Paz de la Tierra / The Peace of the Earth
197 Lead Me Home
22 Lenten Gospel Acclamation
92 Let Evening Fall
57 Let There Be Light
45 Let the poor man say, "I am rich in him"
45 Let the River Flow
82 Let Us Go Rejoicing - Psalm 122
75 Let Us See Your Kindness - Psalm 85
88 Let Us Sing to the Lord - Exodus 15
98 Let Us Worship the Lord
248 Let us be poured out gift for others
145 Let us build a house
233 Let us love one another
130 Let your love be a light
209 Letanía de la Santísima Virgen María / Litany of Mary

143 Light of the world
87 Like Burning Incense, O Lord - Psalm 141
209 Litany of Mary / Letanía de la Santísima Virgen María
178 Litany of the Saints
130 Live in the Light
49 Living Spirit, Holy Fire
122 Long before the mountains came to be
226 Look to Christ
136 Looking for light, we wait in darkness
185 Lord, Hear My Prayer / Óyenos, Señor
96 Lord, I Lift Your Name on High
85 Lord, I Thank You - Psalm 138
180 Lord, make us worthy
111 Lord of all creation
74 Lord, Show Us Your Mercy and Love - Psalm 85
139 Lord, the light of your love
64 Lord, You Have the Words - Psalm 19
238 Lord, you lead through sea and desert
182 Lord's Prayer
234 Love beyond All Telling
280 Love Endures
280 Love is patient
104 Make a Joyful Noise
277 Make Me Holy
180 Make Us Worthy
193 Make us a way worth walking
259 Malo! Malo! Thanks Be to God
215 May Peace Be in Your Hearts / Salaam Aleikum
129 May the Peace of Christ Be with You / Ki Ri Su To No
119 May the Road Rise to Meet You
97 Men of faith, rise up and sing
24 Mercy, O God
114 Mighty King
89 Morning Has Broken
109 My Jesus, my Savior
116 My life flows on in endless song
36 My Savior, My Friend
229 My Savior, Your Son
72 My Soul Is Thirsting - Psalm 63
95 My soul cries out with a joyful shout
15 Night of Silence / Noche de Silencio
126 No More Fear
14 Noche de Paz / Silent Night
15 Noche de Silencio / Night of Silence
252 Nothing Can Ever
186 Now
148 Now Is the Time
186 Now is the moment
10 O Come, O Come, Emmanuel
245 O God, Why Are You Silent?
257 O God, You Search Me
40 O Sons and Daughters
264 O Taste and See
198 On That Day
195 On That Holy Mountain
191 One Lord
174 Open My Eyes
177 Open the Eyes of My Heart
246 Our God Reigns
81 Our Help Is from the Lord - Psalm 121
84 Out of the Depths - Psalm 130
256 Over My Head
164 Over the mountains and the sea
185 Óyenos, Señor / Lord, Hear My Prayer
269 Praise God, lift up your joyful song!
103 Praise you, Lord, for your goodness
277 Prepare my mind
3 Prepare! Prepare!
77 Proclaim God's Marvelous Deeds - Psalm 96
62 Psalm 18: I Love You, Lord, My Strength
64 Psalm 19: Lord, You Have the Words
65 Psalm 25: I Lift My Soul to You
67 Psalm 25: To You, O God, I Lift Up My Soul
66 Psalm 25: To You, O Lord, I Lift My Soul
68 Psalm 33: The Earth Is Full of the Goodness
69 Psalm 34: I Will Bless the Lord at All Times
70 Psalm 40: Here I Am
71 Psalm 47: God Mounts His Throne
72 Psalm 63: My Soul Is Thirsting
73 Psalm 72: Every Nation on Earth
75 Psalm 85: Let Us See Your Kindness
74 Psalm 85: Lord, Show Us Your Mercy and Love
77 Psalm 96: Proclaim God's Marvelous Deeds
76 Psalm 96: Sing a Song to the Lord
79 Psalm 103: Bless the Lord, My Soul
80 Psalm 118: This Is the Day
81 Psalm 121: Our Help Is from the Lord
82 Psalm 122: Let Us Go Rejoicing
84 Psalm 130: Out of the Depths
83 Psalm 130: With the Lord There Is Mercy

Index of First Lines and Common Titles/*cont.*

85 Psalm 138: Lord, I Thank You
86 Psalm 139: Before I Was Born
87 Psalm 141: Like Burning Incense, O Lord
190 Purify My Heart
135 Quietly, Peacefully
117 Rain Down
18 Remember You Are Dust / Del Polvo Eres Tú
17 Rise Up in Splendor
240 River of Hope
189 River of Life
215 Salaam Aleikum / May Peace Be in Your Hearts
183 Searching for you, I get lost
213 Seek Truth, Make Peace, Reverence Life
46 Send Down the Fire
188 Shelter Your Name
140 Shine on Us
139 Shine, Jesus, Shine
109 Shout to the Lord
97 Shout to the North
200 Sign Me Up
14 Silent Night / Noche de Paz
219 Sing a New World
76 Sing a Song to the Lord - Psalm 96
107 Sing to the Glory of God
147 Sky and earth, moon and star
254 So Longs My Soul
151 Sometimes by Step
151 Sometimes the night is beautiful
273 Spirit and Grace
54 Spirit of God
273 Spirit of grace, here in this meal
181 Stop By, Lord
187 Strength for the Journey
219 Summoned by the God who made us
237 Take, Lord, Receive
162 Take, O Take Me As I Am
224 Take off your shoes
155 Take the Word and go out
263 Taste and See / Gusten y Vean
197 Thank you for the cross
103 Thanks and Praise
43 The angel spoke to the women
131 The Clouds' Veil
68 The Earth Is Full of the Goodness - Psalm 33
167 The Face of God
184 The God of Second Chances
235 The Lord Is My Light
176 The Lord Is My Light and My Salvation
216 The Peace of the Earth La Paz de la Tierra
149 The Summons / El Llamado
195 The wolf is the guest of the lamb
137 There is a candle in every soul
160 There is a mountain
240 There's a river of hope
44 This Is the Day
80 This Is the Day - Psalm 118
120 This is the air I breathe
228 To Follow You
56 To Know Darkness
169 Trading My Sorrows
18 Turn away from sin
194 Turn My Heart, O God
31 Ubi Caritas / Where True Love and Charity Are Found
274 Unless a Grain
147 Uyai Mose / Come All You People
163 Ven y Sígueme / Come and Follow Me
51 Veni, Creator Spiritus
193 Way, Truth, and Life
261 We Are Called / Dios Nos Llama
23 We Are Climbing Jacob's Ladder
138 We Are Marching
275 We Are One
266 We Are One Body
91 We Arise
39 We came there desperately
268 We Give You Thanks
110 We Praise You
140 We, though many, are one body
222 We Will Go, Lord
253 Were I the Perfect Child of God
142 What Is This Place
210 What You Have Done for Me
115 When I'm feeling all alone
31 Where True Love and Charity Are Found / Ubi Caritas
228 Who are you, God
220 Why do you stare at the skies above
212 Will the Circle Be Unbroken?
149 Will you come and follow me
230 With hands of justice and faith
155 With One Voice
267 With This Bread
83 With the Lord There Is Mercy - Psalm 130
115 With You by My Side
134 You Are Good to Me

Index of First Lines and Common Titles/*cont.*

128 You Are Mine / Contigo Estoy
127 You Are My King (Amazing Love)
238 You Are Strong, You Are Holy
165 You Are the Way
188 You are all I am not
255 You are my light and my salvation
100 You are the light of the world
114 You are the spirit bringing us light
224 You Will Know
170 Your Grace Is Enough
201 Yours Is the Kingdom